Ways of Knowing

An Introduction to Native Studies in Canada

Yale D. Belanger
University of Lethbridge

NELSON / E D U C A T I O N

1

NELSON / EDUCATION

Ways of Knowing: An Introduction to
Native Studies in Canada

by Yale D. Belanger

**Vice President,
Editorial Director:**
Evelyn Veitch

**Editor-in-Chief,
Higher Education:**
Anne Williams

Executive Editor:
Laura Macleod

Senior Marketing Manager:
David Tonen

**Director, Development, Higher
Education:**
Lenore Spence

Photo Researcher:
David Strand

Permissions Coordinator:
David Strand

Production Service:
Macmillan Publishing Solutions

Copy Editor:
Matthew Kudelka

Proofreader:
Susan Fitzgerald

Indexer:
Dave Luljak

Senior Production Coordinator:
Ferial Suleman

Design Director:
Ken Phipps

Managing Designer:
Franca Amore

Interior Design:
Peter Papayanakis

Cover Design:
Jennifer Leung

Cover and Part Opener Image:
"Two Hearts" by Roy Thomas,
silkscreen. © Roy Thomas
http://www.ahnisnabae-art.com

Compositor:
Macmillan Publishing Solutions

Printer:
RR Donnelley

**Library and Archives Canada
Cataloguing in Publication**

Belanger, Yale Deron, 1968-
   Ways of knowing : an
introduction to native studies in
Canada / Yale Belanger.

Includes bibliographical references
and index.
ISBN 978-0-17-644050-3

   1. Native peoples–Canada–
Textbooks. I. Title.

E78.C2B425 2009   971.004'97
C2009-900430-5

ISBN-13: 978-0-17-644050-3
ISBN-10: 0-17-644050-X

To

All of my teachers, past, present, future

&

Tammie-Jai.

About the Cover Artist

Roy Thomas (1949–2004), Woodland Ojibwa Artist

"Two Hearts" by Roy Thomas, silkscreen. © Roy Thomas. http://www.ahnisnabae-art.com.

Roy Thomas was an Ahnisnabae-born Ojibwa artist who devoted himself to learning the history and teachings of his people. Thomas' paintings have a quality that commands attention without overwhelming the viewer. His oeuvre reveals an illuminating simplicity—a conversation with Roy was comparable to the stroke of his paintbrush. Roy's work transcends the Ojibwa Woodland Style of his predecessors. His paintings incorporate elements of Ojibwa traditions, legends, and realistic depictions of Native life. Roy often worked with artistically gifted people of various backgrounds and his paintings reflect the ideas he drew from these experiences.

Roy devoted a great deal of time to learning about the ways of his people, their teachings, and the ways of nature. While he was basically a self-taught artist, Roy was guided by the memories of his grandparents who taught him what to paint. At an early age Roy could see the stories his grandparents told him. His grandparents recognized his talent and encouraged him to draw what he had seen through their stories.

The first time he drew, Roy used his pointing finger and drew on his grandmother's back as she told him stories. Eventually, Roy used a stick on the ground, on the beaches, on the snow banks, and in the dark with the end lit. Roy would tell his grandparents at the time that these drawings would disappear. His grandparents told him *"One day my grandson, these drawings will come back to you, what is yours is never gone away forever."* This was the beginning of Roy Thomas the Ahnisnabae artist.

Roy was a painter in the Ojibwa Woodland style. This style uses symbolisms and imagery inspired by the pictographs that Roy had also seen as a child. The presence of the pictographs and other artists also inspired Roy. The spirit of art and his elders also taught him what to paint. He painted the visions of the teachings of his people for his family, for the community, and for his nation.

During his 35-plus years of painting, Roy presented his art in numerous one-man shows in Canada and the United States. He participated in a number of group shows nationally and internationally. His work is found in many national and international collections including: The Art Gallery of Ontario, Toronto, Ontario; Esso Resources, Edmonton, Alberta; Foreign Affairs and International Trade (Canada); McMichael Canadian Collection, Kleinburg, Ontario; The Royal Ontario Museum, Toronto, Ontario; The National Museum of Man, Ottawa, Ontario; Thunder Bay Art Gallery, Thunder Bay, Ontario; Inuit Gallery, Mannheim, Germany; and the National Gallery of Ethnology, Osaka, Japan.

About the Author

Dr. Yale D. Belanger (Ph.D.) is an Assistant Professor of Native American Studies (NAS) at the University of Lethbridge (Alberta). Trained as a political historian, his doctoral work at Trent University focused on the emergence and evolution of Aboriginal political organizations in late nineteenth- and early twentieth-century Canada.

Currently the book review editor for the *Native Studies Review,* Dr. Belanger also sits (since 2002) on the editorial board of *Journal of Aboriginal Economic Development* (*JAED*). He is widely published in various edited compilations and in journals such as *Canadian Foreign Policy, Saskatchewan Institute on Public Policy, Alberta History, Canadian Journal of Native Studies, Native Studies Review,* and *American Indian Quarterly.*

In 2006 he produced *Gambling with the Future: The Evolution of Aboriginal Gaming in Canada* (Purich), the first book-length treatment of casino gaming as developed by Canada's First Nations. In 2008 he edited the third edition of *Aboriginal Self-Government in Canada: Current Trends and Issues.*

Dr. Belanger is a regular contributor to the Canadian and international media, having appeared on the Aboriginal Peoples Television Network (APTN), on *The National* with Peter Mansbridge, on CBC Radio International, in the *National Post,* and in other venues.

Dr. Belanger lives in Lethbridge with his wife Tammie-Jai and their two "girls" Jessie and Nicki.

Contents

Preface

This textbook emerges from my experience working in universities—specifically, from teaching Introduction to Native Studies and its many variations for the University of Lethbridge, the University of Manitoba, Brandon University, Trent University, and Keewatin Community College (now the University College of the North, Manitoba). When I was a neophyte instructor, students often spoke to me about the class—something I welcomed. They clearly felt comfortable engaging me in intense discussions about contemporary issues, which I also found stimulating. These discussions often led to questions about the class—why didn't I expand on the Aboriginal self-government debate? Was it possible to integrate more materials about Native health? Why did I gloss over Indigenous philosophies? This period was foundational to me as an instructor, for I took seriously my students' comments regarding what was lacking in terms of class content.

After teaching my first two classes at War Lake in northern Manitoba, I started journaling my thoughts and retained a notebook cataloguing the students' myriad questions and other concerns. By 2003 I had amassed a long list of issues that students wanted dealt with in class. Over time, various themes became evident. Once grouped into a dozen specific categories, I began teaching the class as a topics course, one that continues to evolve as new issues reach the headlines.

The one problem I encountered was finding appropriate textbooks—the texts I used tended to be historical narratives. I found that these histories—while comprehensive and well written—often left the students seeking more detail about specific issues confronting Native people generally, and many of my students directly. For example, when self-government was discussed in a textbook, it was usually too briefly, so I would have to expand on the issue in class; only then would the students have the detail they needed to fully understand why the issue was so important. My class notes grew increasingly detailed, and soon I had the makings of a Native Studies topics textbook, which I saw as a supplement to the available Native history texts. Realizing how important it was to keep textbook costs to a minimum, I knew I would also have to include enough historical information to draw out the key themes and issues. Over time, 12 chapters grew to 14. Each examined a specific theme reflecting the subject matter that students wanted to see integrated into my course, with the historical base included for context.

This textbook is designed to satisfy the needs identified by my past students and at the same time to present an academic interpretation of how Native people in Canada view the past four centuries of contact. It also highlights the sociopolitical and socioeconomic challenges affecting Native communities nationally. I have tried to avoid historicizing Native people in this book. Instead, I have contextualized the broader historical narrative in the hope of demonstrating how history continues to inform the evolution of self-government, urban-reserve development, literature, and health, to name a few areas of inquiry. Written in a style that largely avoids technical language, this book is unique in that it is meant for students who are being introduced for the first time to Native issues framed from an academic perspective.

Also important, this textbook is the first to be produced by a Native Studies student/graduate and represents the culmination of 15 years of ongoing teachings graciously offered by scholars, elders, and various community members. Students' questions have provided the framework. The elders' (academic and various Native communities) teachings have provided the foundation. The ideas and conclusions reflect my best attempt to reconcile these multiple philosophical outlooks and intricate thought processes into a textbook produced specifically for Native Studies students.

Acknowledgments

Many people have helped shape this work, and to those folks I owe a debt of gratitude. From my first classes at the University of Lethbridge to my graduate work at the University of Manitoba and doctoral studies at Trent University to my first full-time teaching assignment at the University of Saskatchewan, my academic teachers dot the physical landscape of Canada and continue to offer insights into the increasingly complex world of Native politics and social history. Over the years I have had the great privilege of working with elders in the various territories where I have lived—thank you for sharing your time and stories. I hope that the knowledge and context you have provided me has been accurately captured in the pages of this book.

I would like to thank all of those at Nelson Education for their support. I am grateful for the assistance I have received from Lenore Spence and Heather Parker and must thank Laura Macleod for recruiting me for this project. All of you have helped develop what we all feel is an innovative Native Studies textbook. The critical commentaries framed by endless optimism and scheduling flexibility (perhaps the most important aspect of this project) will not be forgotten. I hope the book in its published form meets all expectations.

This book could not have been completed without a study leave granted by the University of Lethbridge. I also owe gratitude to the reviewers for their insightful comments, which improved this book significantly. They include Rob Nestor (First Nations University of Canada), Jennifer Pettit (Mount Royal College), Susan Roy (University of British Columbia), Cynthia Wesley-Esquimaux (University of Toronto), and Greg Younging (University of British Columbia).

Finally, special thanks to Tammie-Jai, who has remained incredibly supportive of my work. Once again, I am grateful to have her in my life, something I never tire of saying.

Yale D. Belanger
September 2008
Lethbridge, Alberta

What Is Native Studies?

What is Native Studies? And why is it important for there to be a textbook specific to the discipline when volumes of history, sociology, and anthropology, for example, have always seemed to offer satisfactory instructional materials? I would answer that Native Studies is a relatively new field that embraces multiple theoretical frameworks from disciplines as diverse as history, sociology, psychology, and anthropology. These theories are generally applicable when pursuing an improved understanding of Native issues. But a Native Studies textbook can offer more:

- It can serve the need to recognize and rebuild Indigenous knowledge and to generate academic research that reflects Native perspectives.
- It can foster research approaches that more closely reflect Native experiences.

Instructors, researchers, and students of Native Studies must be able to integrate the theoretical perspectives of North American Native peoples into their analyses. To ignore those ideas is to risk forgetting to ask why certain Native groups responded to the colonialist onslaught in the ways that they did.

The first attempt at establishing a Native Studies program dates back to 1914, when Oklahoma senator Robert Owen introduced a resolution in the U.S. Congress calling for an Indian Studies program at the University of Oklahoma. The resolution failed. Then in 1937, university administrators attempted to establish such a program. Again, this failed. Then in 1949 the American Indian Institute opened its doors at the University of South Dakota. Not until 1964 did an American university found an independent Native Studies Department; this was at the University of Minnesota.[1] That program was a child of the Civil Rights Movement and of growing awareness of human rights among Americans. Native students had lobbied the University of Minnesota's administration for more classes that were specific to Indian issues. This approach worked at least as well on Canadian campuses, where a radical atmosphere combined with a desire to understand Native philosophies and to right past wrongs. The resulting curricula integrated new ideas and theories about Native people into the academy. These new programs attracted Native students to the universities; they also provided Native Studies students and instructors with an expansive context in which to investigate and present relevant issues.

Canada's first program in Native Studies was established at Trent University in 1969 under the auspices of the Indian–Eskimo Studies Department. Canadian scholar John Price has suggested that a combination of academic specialization, pressure from Native leaders, and a shift toward socially oriented research led to the rapid emergence of Native Studies as a field in its own right.[2] In 1971 and 1974 respectively, Brandon University and the University of Lethbridge established similar programs; soon after, so did the University of Manitoba, St. Thomas University, the University of Sudbury, and the University of Saskatchewan. Each of these institutions created departments in response to students' demands for improved educational opportunities for Native students. Most of these universities experienced increased enrollment as a result of these programs, which are still popular.[3]

Part of the popularity must have to do with the rising profile of Native issues nationally and indigenous issues internationally. Fears stirred up long before by the "salvage" anthropologists of the early twentieth century propelled the emergence of Native Studies. In particular, university administrators believed they were well situated to begin cataloguing and disseminating indigenous knowledge. They believed they would be able to preserve Native languages and cultures. Native representatives invited themselves to this party; in the case of the University of Lethbridge, for instance, they helped the institution forge a coherent vision statement and they influenced the development of the Native Studies curriculum. The difficult balance between maintaining an academic approach to Native Studies and ensuring community needs is reflected in the academic research being conducted today, which poses a challenge for most Native Studies professors and university administrators. Just two examples of this point are (1) the proliferation of innovative research methodologies and (2) the growing number of Native communities that have claimed responsibility for their own research.

Despite this early success, Native Studies still suffered from what University of Lethbridge Professor Emeritus and Native American Studies (NAS) department founder Leroy Little Bear (Kainai) referred to as an identity crisis. University of Minnesota Native Studies faculty member Russell Thornton articulated the tensions that led to this identity crisis:

> American Indian studies has developed along three basic lines since its inception. One, it has developed along the lines of Indian culture; that is, it has introduced Indian languages, music, art, literature, and ways of looking at the world into academia. Two, it has developed along social science lines; that is, it has attempted to consolidate existing bodies of knowledge pertaining to American Indians in social sciences, most notably anthropology and history, and also evaluate and reinterpret this knowledge. Three, Indian studies has developed along applied lines. It has examined Indian education, Indian social work, Indian health care and has attempted to make these areas more relevant to problems and conditions of Indian peoples.[4]

As quickly as many departments were established, they were confronted with complaints that most of the faculty employed were white males, who notwithstanding their ability to engage students were unlikely to be well versed in traditional aspects of Native societies. In response, various departments began debating the merits of not just involving elders, but hiring them as academic staff. Trent University led this charge and continues to employ elders as faculty. In recent years the elders' teachings have been combined with graduate programs (M.A. and Ph.D.); the result has been better informed students, which in turn has meant a deeper pool of potential faculty members to draw from. This, however, does not negate the need to include those elders who are willing to share their collected knowledge in the educational process.

Many of the issues just noted still influence Native Studies administrators. At the same time, much progress has been made as a result of this constant scrutiny and the correctives it has generated. Importantly, Native Studies departments have enabled academics to embrace an interdisciplinary approach to the study of Native issues while providing greater access to an increasingly multicultural student body that is willing to learn. The discipline had progressed to the point that six Native Studies departments were operating in Canada by the 1980s, along with various Native-focused programs housed in assorted anthropology and ethnic studies departments. Today, countless departments are offering diverse curricula. And, following in the footsteps of Trent University, several graduate programs in Native Studies have been founded. In 1999, Trent University established a doctoral program in Indigenous Studies, which made it only the second North American university to do so (the first was the University of Arizona in 1997).

Native Intellectual Tradition

University of California professor Jack Forbes (Powhatan-Delaware) was among a group of scholars who emerged during the 1960s to argue that there was in fact a Native intellectual tradition. They lobbied for recognition of Native Studies as a separate discipline. Forbes has recently suggested that in the years since his early work aimed at carving out this niche, Native Studies programs have become colonial captives within a university system that ignores disciplines that embrace issues considered peripheral by contemporary society.[5] All the same, he continues to believe that the intellectual traditions indigenous to North America might still bridge this gap. All optimism aside, this is a disconcerting trend, considering that he envisioned Native Studies evolving into a discipline that embraced Native life, thought, and history. The late Vine Deloria, Jr. (Standing Rock Sioux) emerged as an important spokesperson for American Indian issues, and in turn Native Studies. The son of an Episcopal missionary and born on the Lakota reservation in South Dakota, Deloria challenged the then-popular notion that Indians were little more than historical relics occupying derelict reservations best decommissioned and transferred to non-Native society.[6] Possessed of an acerbic wit, Deloria was no intellectual slouch: he held degrees in law and theology and was able to assess Native American philosophy and Western traditions at a sophisticated level. He later came to support Native Studies as "encompassing all the relevant knowledge and information concerning the relationship between American Indians and the rest of the world, be it the federal government, other religions, the world of art and music, or international and domestic economies."[7]

Not all were as enraptured with Native Studies, however. Russell Thornton contended in 1978 that Native Studies was ineffectual because it lacked disciplinary traditions—a concern that resonates to this day. At the time, his peers did not challenge him. Native Studies is still in its foundational stages and has faced its share of growing pains—not unlike anthropology, which emerged in the mid-nineteenth century as an academic discipline but did not gain widespread acceptance or academic credibility until the early twentieth century.[8] Native Studies is at a similar crossroads. For example, we in Native Studies do not embrace en masse Western theory to aid in our research. Rather, we try to examine Native issues from a Native perspective. This invariably distances those working in the discipline from Western theories when research agendas are being developed and pursued. Also a problem is the amount of time it takes to understand issues from a Native perspective instead of simply interpreting data through a Western lens.

Currently, I would argue that Native Studies as a discipline is stuck somewhere in the middle. Not quite an academic discipline in the Western sense, it is still not entirely account-able to Native ways of knowing. Various scholars concur with me, and many of them also argue that efforts to define Native Studies may be futile. Defining Native Studies is difficult because the individual departments are so widely dispersed, which influences curriculum develop-ment and instructional philosophies. It is no accident that the first Native Studies departments were founded in fairly close proximity to significant Native populations. This strongly influ-enced the operations of these departments. By forcing a definition, we may only be co-opting the discipline to meet accepted academic norms and further distancing ourselves from the community-based ideas that increasingly drive university research agendas in Canada. If that is so, we may find ourselves forced to ignore what makes Native Studies unique.

An example of geographic proximity: the Chippewa are the dominant Native popula-tion at the University of Minnesota (U of M). As a result, the Native Studies department there developed a curriculum that emphasizes Chippewa regional history, ways of knowing, and social, political, and economic issues. This focus has meant that the U of M's philosoph-ical orientation and approach to teaching Native Studies is markedly different from, say, what you will find at the Native American Studies (NAS) department at the University of Lethbridge, where most Native students are Blackfoot (Niitsítapi) and course offerings have been developed to reflect the needs of that southern Alberta population. Accepting this cul-tural uniqueness has enabled administrators to respond to local Native students' concerns. At the same time, it could be argued that establishing regionally specific curricula has made it more difficult to define Native Studies as a whole. I would argue that it is not a weakness or a shortcoming that regionally specific curricula have been developed to serve the inter-ests of local communities.

Native Studies was early on almost exclusively the domain of non-Native academics trained in a variety of disciplines ranging from law to sociology, anthropology, and history. Each discipline has its own unique approaches to research and teaching, so when it came time to begin writing about Native issues, these academics turned to the theoretical and conceptual frameworks they best understood: ideas rooted in the European intellectual tradition. The proliferation of work produced in the 1970s and early 1980s led to debate among scholars regarding "the best approach" to researching and writing about Native issues. Add in community-based concerns about these issues, and it soon was apparent that this "shotgun" approach to research was not always the best one for Native Studies. The material produced over the past four decades suggests how influential the academy has been in producing knowledge about the Native experience. Too often, researchers and writers have lacked cultural awareness, especially with regard to how local populations interpret these issues.

In the late 1990s, academics such as Sakej Youngblood Henderson (Chickasaw), Marie Battiste (Mi'kmaq), Linda T. Smith (Maori), and Lester-Irabinna Rigney (Narungga), to name a few, launched a dialogue about the need for researchers and instructors to embrace alternative ways of knowing that were more compatible with community-based aspirations.[9] Robert Allen Warrior (Osage) in his book *Tribal Secrets* spoke in detailed terms about various Native intellectual traditions that were separate and unique from Canadian and American intellectual traditions. He argued persuasively that embracing the Native perspective was vital to better understand and best ensure the survival of the Western intellectual tradition.[10]

Warrior's arguments were well timed: they led to greater academic acceptance of his and his predecessors' theories. Approaches to research specific to academic and community needs change often and will keep doing so. This change is aimed at decolonizing existing methodologies in Native research—at finding unique approaches that reflect both Indigenous and Western perspectives. Such approaches are necessary if we hope to decolonize our work with and among Native communities. Much depends on researchers' willingness to acknowledge Native intellectual authority and to accept this expertise as relevant, indeed inescapable. This will require academics to distance themselves from tried-and-true qualitative and quantitative research methods and instead trust the elders whose task it is to maintain their communities' knowledge and history. This does not mean abandoning academic rigour; but it does necessitate developing innovative techniques to integrate this knowledge. This radical departure has had to overcome certain obstacles. Academics must embrace the Native intellectual tradition so as not to freeze Native people in historic stasis; many have not. And it must be accepted that Native people can speak intelligently about the issues confronting their communities. Stating the latter point may seem somewhat ludicrous, yet academics and researchers who study Indians from a distance continue to have trouble with it; so do those who view community-based participation as a corrupting influence.

Native Studies is at a crossroads, as demonstrated by the shift from conducting research based in Western knowledge systems toward research that adapts philosophical issues such as epistemology into its structure. This is an important time in Native Studies, for the decolonization discussion is generating discipline-specific research methods that are producing innovative community-based research. More Native scholars and individuals trained in these unique knowledge systems are taking their place within these programs and the academy. Ph.D. programs are beginning to emerge to prepare the next generation of Native Studies scholars. That discipline must be able to convey its knowledge to both Native and non-Native students, most of whom will be working with Native people in the public and private spheres or in the academy.

A Word about Terminology

There are currently 614 First Nations communities in Canada. This does not include the various Métis and Inuit communities. Each of these communities presents itself on its website and in printed literature as a nation, or as a component of a larger Indigenous nation. Each of these communities is in the traditional sense not a "First Nation" or an "Aboriginal" community, for each claims its own name derived from the language of the people. The language we employ when discussing the First Peoples in Canada reflects legal classifications found in the *Indian Act* and various policies and laws relating to Indians. We tend to overlook how the people speak of their relations and their communities. Though most anthropologists and policymakers describe them as tribes and bands, Indigenous peoples in Canada tend to use "nation" and "confederacy" to describe their political models. English names such as MicMac, Maliseet, Iroquoian, Ojibwa, Cree, Montagnais, and Blackfoot are slowly being replaced by cultural names such as Mi'kmaq, Wendat, Haudenosaunee, Anishinaabe, Nehiyaw, Innu, and Niitsítapi. Still others have come to embrace the terms First Nations, First Peoples, and/or Indigenous; while others prefer the term "Indians," which is the terminology of treaties and the *Indian Act* (1876).[11]

Many of the legal and historical classifiers are now entrenched in our national consciousness. For the sake of clarity, I have adopted several descriptors to help the reader separate historical time periods, and to identify the language commonly utilized in political and academic discussions, while also using traditional Indigenous names. The term "Indigenous," for example, is utilized to describe the people and communities of Canada prior to Canadian Confederation in 1867. Indigenous does not represent a legal category, however. It is used in this text book to describe (1) the descendants of groups of people living in the territory at the time when other groups of different cultures or ethnic origin arrived there; (2) groups that have preserved almost intact the customs and traditions of their ancestors, which are similar to those characterized as Indigenous; and (3) those who have been placed under a state structure that incorporates national, social, and cultural characteristics distinct from their own.

Post-1867, the term "Native" will be used as a blanket descriptor when discussing several communities or when discussing Aboriginal people, a constitutionally entrenched term describing Canada's Indian, Inuit, and Métis peoples. Like the word Native, this term tends to gloss over cultural differences by failing to describe in specific terms Nehiyaw, Niitsítapi, Nisga'a, Innu, and Inuit, to name a few. This approach has the potential to obscure the legislative and administrative complexities unique to Native people in Canada. Because of the historic time period framing this analysis, the term "Indian" reflects its use in legislation or policy; it also appears in discussions concerning such legislation or policy, or in reference to issues related to Indian populations in the United States. Additional terms will be used; these include but are not limited to the following: Status Indian, Non-Status Indian, Registered Indian, Bill C–31, First Nation, and Eskimo, which in turn lead to descriptors that have legal status such as band, settlement, and tribal council. These multiple definitions described above make it difficult to accept one or even a handful of descriptors when writing.

Of final note, I almost always use the word Native owing to the recent backlash against the word Aboriginal. In Ontario in June 2008, for example, 42 Chiefs of the Anishinabek Nation launched a campaign to see the term Aboriginal eliminated. Noting that the term Aboriginal is "another means of assimilation through the displacement of our First Nation-specific inherent and treaty rights," the resolution also noted that "there are no aboriginal bands, aboriginal reserves, or aboriginal chiefs" and that the reference to "aboriginal rights" in Section 35 of the *Constitution Act* "was never meant to assimilate First Nations, Métis and Inuit into a homogeneous group."[12] Where possible I use the name of a specific community. I also employ the descriptors that the various people quoted in this book use. If someone for example self-identifies as being from the Blood Reserve, that is how he or she is represented in this text, although I regularly employ Kainai to describe the community. In an effort to remain consistent with history and politics textbooks and other academic materials examining Native issues, and so as not to confuse students who are new to Native Studies, I will use the academically maintained names such as Cree and Blackfoot, for example, with the names the peoples use themselves (Nehiyaw and Niitsítapi) in parentheses on first occasion. My hope is to provide a clearer context while demonstrating a degree of cultural sensitivity toward Canada's First Peoples.

NOTES

1. Donald K. Fixico, *The American Indian Mind in a Linear World: American Indian Studies and Traditional Knowledge* (New York: Routledge, 2003).

2. John A. Price, *Native Studies: American and Canadian Contexts* (Toronto: McGraw-Hill Ryerson, 1978), p. viii.

3. For a good overview of the Native Studies discipline's evolution, see Shona Taner, "The Development of Native Studies at Canadian Universities: Four Programs, Four Provinces, Four Decades" (M.A. thesis, University of Northern British Columbia, 1997).

4. Russell Thornton, "American Indian Studies as an Academic Discipline," *American Indian Culture and Research Journal* 2, nos. 3 and 4 (1978): 8.

5. Jack D. Forbes, "Intellectual Self-Determination and Sovereignty: Implications for Native Studies and for Native Intellectuals," *Wicazo Sa Review* 13, no. 1 (1998): 11–23.

6. Vine Deloria, Jr., *Custer Died for Your Sins: An Indian Manifesto* (London: Collier-MacMillan, 1969).

7. Vine Deloria, Jr., "Indian Studies—The Orphan of Academia," *Wicazo Sa Review* 2, no. 2 (1986): 1–7.

8. Thomas Biolsi and Larry Zimmerman, eds., *Indians and Anthropologists: Vine Deloria, Jr., and the Critique of Anthropology* (Tucson: University of Arizona Press, 1997).

9. Marie Battiste, ed., *Reclaiming Indigenous Voice and Vision* (Vancouver: UBC Press, 2000).

10. Robert A. Warrior, *Tribal Secrets: Recovering American Indian Intellectual Traditions* (Minneapolis: University of Minnesota Press, 1995).

11. David R. Newhouse and Yale D. Belanger, "Beyond the 'Indian Problem': Aboriginal Peoples and the Transformation of Canada (Chapter 19)," in *The Oxford Handbook of Canadian Politics*, ed. John C. Courtney and David E. Smith (Toronto: Oxford University Press, forthcoming 2009).

12. Anishinabek Nation, "Anishinabek Outlaw Term 'Aboriginal.'" [online] http://www.anishinabek .ca/index.php?option=com_content&task=view&id=304&Itemid=47. Last accessed September 21, 2008.

PHILOSOPHY AND WAYS OF KNOWING

1

Ways of Knowing

Why is it that Europeans have thought and we have worldviews? I don't hear much talk of the European worldview or Canadian worldview. Somehow, in my own mind, the use of the term "worldview" in this context tends to diminish the idea that it is the mind that has a key role in human life. There is little recognition of an aboriginal mind that thinks and imagines.

—David Newhouse, Onondaga (Onönda'gega')[1]

The academic recognition of Indigenous ways of knowing rooted in complex philosophical systems native to North America is a relatively recent development. This is not to suggest that the academy has consciously avoided or outright ignored these systems of thought. During the past three decades countless teachers and writers have, with varied success, attempted to integrate Indigenous philosophical tenets into university courses. Many would contend that the academy has shown unwillingness to engage such systems of thought; others would declare this ongoing experiment slightly successful. In general, though, a positive message may be taken from this experience: world views, rites, and traditions that academics once largely characterized as "Indian" have in the last two decades evolved into the study of Native philosophy—a study housed mainly but not exclusively in Native Studies programs.

In a broad sense, philosophy is the study people engage in as they attempt to understand the fundamental truths about themselves, the world in which they live, and their relationships with the world and one another. And not unlike Western ways of knowing, Indigenous ways of knowing are based on the notion that individuals are trained to comprehend their environment according to teachings found in stories developed specifically to describe collective lived experiences dating back thousands of years. It is within this lived experience that codes of conduct have been developed to assist folks in countless communities to maintain peaceful internal and external relations—or, for our purposes, balance. The ethics that have come to guide an individual's actions also materialized from this lived experience. Western philosophy nevertheless continues to dominate university classrooms by claiming to provide the exclusive window for examining how we as people know what we know. As a consequence, Native philosophy has been relegated to the academic periphery—in other words, ideas with enough substance to justify their own discipline have yet to generate sufficient academic legitimacy to free themselves from other disciplines. Thus, Native Studies has not yet obtained universal acceptance as an academic field of study, and neither have the foundational principles discussed in this chapter.

Unlike Western ways of knowing, which are indigenous to Europe, North American Indigenous philosophies developed in response to ecologically specific rhythms, patterns, and events. The introduction of Western ways of knowing to North America led to a clash between two distinctive thought systems. In many ways this incompatibility and the resultant four centuries of what could be described as no less than lethal interaction—the brunt of which was experienced by Indigenous peoples—guide how and what we investigate in Native Studies. Yet Native philosophy, as it has come to be known in recent years, is more than simply the study of the evolution of ethics and codes of conduct. It is an inclusive concept that embraces the worlds of science and spirituality, that embodies complex ideas even while paying homage to the origins and nature of the knowledge that emerged from within specific environments (see Chapter 2). It seeks to understand how these diverse forces informed and continue to inform the evolution of ethics and codes of conduct in Native communities.

It is difficult to pinpoint precisely when the discussion shifted from one of world view to one of philosophy. It is safe to say, however, that this took some time to occur. Dating back to first contact, non-Native peoples identified in their writings differences in how Indigenous peoples and Europeans perceived an array of concerns ranging from economic development to engagement with foreign peoples in political councils to the cultural importance of religious and social activities. Though these differences came to be acknowledged, they were not fully understood. In an attempt to counter this phenomenon and to present a Native perspective on events affecting Indigenous communities, a handful of Indigenous intellectuals beginning in the late eighteenth century began producing written works probing this diversity. When these words were downplayed or ignored, oftentimes a Native perspective of events could be found in official government correspondence. For example, the minutes and summaries of treaty negotiations in the 1870s highlighted Indigenous leaderships' adherence to the belief in their peoples' self-government and nationhood status. Rarely did such events stir up academic scrutiny, however. Even so, these differences did not go unnoticed, and by the mid-twentieth century, government officials and academics generally acknowledged that Native peoples experienced the world in unique and culturally specific ways.

Two events in the 1960s shook academics from their intellectual slumber. Both led to a renewed interest in Indigenous peoples, generally, and in Indigenous ways of knowing, specifically. The first was in 1964, when the University of Minnesota founded a Native Studies department. By this step, Native Studies was finally granted recognition in the academy, Native students were finally provided with culturally relevant course offerings, and scholars were finally extended academic legitimacy to explore Native issues. The second was the emergence of the late Lakota scholar Vine Deloria, Jr., the first Native intellectual of the postwar era to critically explore Native philosophy. In 1969 Deloria burst onto the literary scene with *Custer Died for Your Sins,* a scathing indictment of the Americans' treatment of Indigenous peoples. In 1973 he followed this book with *God Is Red: A Native View of Religion.* In it he aggressively challenged the widespread notion that Native traditions were historically frozen and no longer relevant to modern Native American populations.[2] Indigenous ways of knowing represented a viable alternative to Christian beliefs, he asserted, adding that the various and still-vibrant tribal religions were, for those still living on their traditional territories, "actual complexes of attitudes, beliefs, and practices fine-tuned to harmonize with the lands on which the people live."[3]

Deloria followed in 1977 with *The Metaphysics of Modern Existence,* which he opened with the suggestion that the "fundamental factor that keeps Indians and non-Indians from communicating is that they are speaking about two entirely different perceptions of the world."[4] Deloria's metaphysics was embraced by Native academics, though largely ignored by his non-Native critics, many of whom went so far as to describe the book as naive. However mixed its reception was, Deloria succeeded in highlighting the tensions associated with living according to a Native perspective—tensions that in many ways continue to confront those in the Native Studies discipline: "No matter how well educated an Indian may become," he wrote, "he or she always suspects that Western culture is not an adequate representation of reality. Life therefore becomes a schizophrenic balancing act wherein one holds that the creation, migration and ceremonial stories of the tribe are true and that the Western European view of the world is also true."[5]

Deloria's *Metaphysics,* and in particular his *God Is Red,* are still regarded as seminal works in Native philosophy.

During this period similar events were unfolding in Canada. In Alberta, the Blood (Kainai) philosopher Leroy Little Bear of the University of Lethbridge helped enrich the emergent dialogue pertaining to Native philosophy, forcing it to expand beyond the language of world view and religion to embrace new ideas that were becoming influential. Working alongside the late David Bohm, a past colleague of Albert Einstein, Little Bear initiated a number of conferences sponsored by the Fetzer Institute of Kalamazoo, Michigan. Those conferences brought together community members, trained linguists, scientists versed in quantum mechanics, and Native American scholars, who gathered to discuss the underlying principles of the universe. In all, four dialogues took place. Each lasted three days, during which each participant was given the opportunity to contribute. One observer recalls with amazement how he saw physicists, academics, and Native and non-Native elders openly engage in complex discussions—while experiencing little difficulty communicating their ideas to the assembly.[6] To this day, a core group of participants continues to meet annually; many of the ideas in this chapter have arisen from those meetings. As a result of these dialogues, the field of Native philosophy has expanded rapidly within a few short decades.

It must be noted that these dialogues did more than bring together a unique cross-section of intellectuals; the ensuing discussions helped articulate in English ideas that for millennia had animated North American Indigenous philosophies. This has become a contentious issue for academics, who maintain that the essence of Indigenous cultures is contained in their languages and that certain Indigenous philosophical concepts are difficult if not impossible to understand without knowledge of those languages. Deloria, however, used to contend that Western ideas often must be injected into "Indian" philosophy in order to thoroughly understand its foundations.[7] While it may be impossible to fully capture the subtleties of Indigenous ways of knowing, approaching these ideas in such a way can offer a starting point for those seeking to further explore similar issues.

Partly as a result of this increased academic attention on Native philosophy, eight North American Native people have obtained a doctoral degree in philosophy. Dozens of other academics are investigating how these philosophies continue to inform Indigenous cultural development.[8] The recently released book *American Indian Thought,* edited by Anne Waters, is the first collection of essays produced by Indigenous scholars examining Native philosophy's tenets. Advocates of this approach—specifically, those who are trying to integrate a Native perspective into their teaching—argue that to understand how individuals in a specific community respond to prevailing political, social, and economic pressures, one must first appreciate how a specific environment has informed a community's philosophical evolution.

Nevertheless, the beliefs long held by mainstream Canadian society are difficult to overcome, especially those beliefs which view Native peoples as lacking the sophistication of European cultures and their structured philosophies. Critics continue to promote a universal approach to understanding genesis, suggesting that Indigenous cultures have always lacked written languages, coherent political structures, and codified rules for social interaction. The notion that there exists a universal way of interpreting one's surroundings is misleading, according to Little Bear, who suggests that an individual comes to know and understand his or her surrounding environment by observing that environment.[9] In essence, how a person comes to know is defined by that person's culture, which in turn influences how that person comes to define reality. Which opens up this question: is it that outlandish to suggest that North American Indigenous peoples developed environmentally specific political, economic, and social philosophies in much the same way as their European counterparts?

Those teaching in Native Studies need to be reminded of the need to constantly challenge beliefs that downplay both the existence of Native philosophy and its importance in highlighting how Indigenous populations have responded to local experiences. Unfortunately, improper conveyance of complex ideas has resulted in Indigenous peoples being portrayed more often than not in rather simplistic ways, in both academic and popular literature. Often lost in this distorted representation of how "Indians" presumably lived are Native perceptions of how events affected their peoples and their intellectual responses—perceptions that merit greater attention. So it is vital that we endeavour to present a Native perspective of events—that is, that we utilize the historic ideas that informed North American Indigenous nations' political, social, and economic cultures before *and* after their first extended contact with non-Native peoples. This is where the

Native Studies discipline comes into play: it is predisposed to utilizing these philosophical tenets to evaluate and better understand how Indigenous peoples have always confronted the social and pathological forces challenging their communities.

Two scholars in particular have expressed concern that the term "Native perspective" "smacks of essentialism, the concept of categorization that presupposes that people must think and act in certain ways because of their ethnic group or gender."[10] Given Canada's cultural and linguistic diversity, it is foolish to suggest that a single Native perspective exists. Yet there are unique ways of understanding events that have demonstrated to me and others that there are culturally specific ways of appreciating what we may have previously considered to be universally accepted ideas. A substantial challenge in writing this book presents itself: is it possible to demonstrate the uniqueness of the various Native perspectives across Canada while also showing "how common themes and similar experiences have shaped" the distinctiveness of Indigenous identities in Canada?[11]

Arguably we in Native Studies must adopt such an approach if we are to accomplish two important objectives: (1) develop a better understanding of how Native leaders responded to pre- and post-contact social, political, and economic forces; and (2) counter the prevailing scholarly ideologies that tend to devalue Indigenous ways of knowing, thus relegating those ways of knowing to the academic periphery and stifling our ability to generate a holistic understanding of events and ideas.

Native Philosophy

It is the landscape that contains the memories, the bones of the ancestors, the earth, air, fire, water, and spirit from which a Native culture has come and to which it continually returns. It is the land that ultimately defines a Native people.

—Gregory Cajete (Tewa)[12]

What is Native philosophy? This is a difficult question to answer owing to its abstract nature. Asking this question is analogous to walking up to an individual in downtown Winnipeg, Montreal, or Yellowknife and asking that person to describe the central tenets of Western philosophy in the time it will take to read this chapter. Perhaps the best place to start is by acknowledging that every society has a bundle of fundamental if not unspoken assumptions about both life and reality, assumptions that in turn guide how people in a society interpret and understand their society's laws, rules, customs, and actions. Since Indigenous occupation predates the arrival of Europeans by 40,000 years according to some estimates, we may conclude that North America has long been home to unique ways of understanding. We are at the same time unable to assume that a universal North American

Indigenous philosophy has ever existed. Why? Because each Indigenous community has always been unique, which makes it impossible to construct an interpretive model that can be used to definitively answer how and why certain communities have responded as they have to various circumstances.

Several obstacles make it difficult to offer blanket explanations for a community's political, social, and economic evolution. An illustration of this difficulty: The Iroquois (Haudenosaunee) of Quebec and southern Ontario were matriarchal (a system where the mother is head of the family). They were also an agricultural people whose members tended to settle in one location for decades, with hundreds of people in any one village. By contrast, the Inuit lived in small, highly mobile communities guided politically and socially by strong male influences and dependent mainly on large game animals and sea mammals.[13] Though explorers and writers during the early stages of contact generally labelled both these societies "Indian," the similarities stop there. To suggest that these two communities had even remotely similar social, political, and economic outlooks would be folly. But *why* were they so different? And what influences led to those differences?

The beginning of our journey into Indigenous philosophies begins with the land. Native and non-Native writers consistently return to the fact that the earth and "Indians" cannot be separated. Land in this case is the heart of Creation. Whereas Western depictions suggest that a god provided humans with the earth as a source of resources for their economic and social utilization, Indigenous scholars tend to present the land as the heart of Creation, a realm where humans are one among a vast array of creatures. In this environment humans are dependent on all of Creation and its various entities for survival (see below). Simply put, the earth is the source of Native identity, the mother to children (humans and other-than-humans), who were assigned responsibilities to act as stewards for all of Creation. It is vital to acknowledge and to try to comprehend this connection in order to better understand the issues relevant to Native Studies and the study of Native issues in Canada.

From a Native perspective, humans were inundated with everything that Creation had to offer, both good and bad. This ranged from fires and floods to low animal counts during hunting seasons to an abundance of medicines, basically everything imaginable. In response to these forces, Indigenous peoples developed unique ways of interacting with Creation, ways that when summed together have been described by the Tewa scholar Gregory Cajete as an ecological philosophy. Specifically, an ecological philosophy is one that takes into account how the local environment influences a person's beliefs, actions, and "approaches to knowing." This approach to knowing in turn led to the evolution of a community-based consciousness founded on hundreds if not thousands of years of observations of, and interactions with, Creation. From this, people developed a keen awareness of the ongoing power of Creation in particular ecosystems and a corresponding view of their role in Creation. This led people to look to the surrounding landscape as the basis of meaning in relation to the unity and the origins of life.[14] As a result of this unique way of understanding Creation, human beings began to measure their existence in terms of how well they ensured the land's health and safety as opposed to wealth and personal gain. It is interesting that in most North American Indigenous communities, this is a central tenet of Indigenous ways of knowing.

One scholar has concluded that philosophies like these are "born of a lived and storied participation with natural landscape and reality." As a result, concepts of time, space, relationships, and language have evolved to reflect people's extended interactions with their physical environment.[15] With this in mind, "the earth and its forces are the living context that instructs Aboriginal teachings and order."[16] Creation, however, was not a universal process: each Indigenous nation occupied a unique ecological region, and this led to the emergence of specific ecological philosophies. Each Indigenous nation in Canada, while adhering to similar beliefs about the land, also expresses unique beliefs that are a function of the ecological context. Detailed economic, political, cultural, and social ideologies have consequently developed, as have distinctive codes of conduct guiding human interaction with other humans, the animals, and the land. The land is recognized as the source of life, provided by the Creator for humans to share with all other living creatures. Again, over time the length and intimacy of interaction with the land has led to a level of knowledge about the local natural order—knowledge that in turn has informed people about their relationship with and responsibilities to Creation and how to interact with all beings properly and effectively.

Because of the diversity of ecological zones, meaning becomes increasingly contextual. Simply put, meaning exists only within the circumstances of personal and community experiences in a specific environment. And since each Indigenous nation's social, political, and economic processes developed within a unique ecosystem, its people came to know by observing and interacting with their environment.[17] In this vein, we run the risk of trivializing or even oversimplifying Native philosophies and ways of knowing. An excellent example of this occurred in the early 1970s, when leaders of the various environmental movements provoked widespread activism characterized by a legion of young men and women portraying Indigenous peoples as the first ecologists.[18] The goal was to impress on contemporary North American society the potential of living in harmony with the environment—just look at how the "Indians" of the past accomplished this goal—but in the process of achieving that goal, complex Native ways of knowing were often ignored, and replaced by unsophisticated representations of "Indians" as mere products of their environment. These historic cultures were presented as instinctive, as living according to natural constraints, rather than as intellectual agents and vigilant students of their surroundings. In their attempts to put forward a positive message, many non-Native activists belittled intricate thought systems and ecological models.

Criticism may also be levelled at those writers who perpetuate romantic notions of pre-contact North America by suggesting that "Native knowledge about the natural world tends to view all—or at least vast regions—of nature, often including the earth itself, as inherently holy rather than profane, savage, wild or wastelands."[19] Two important questions are raised here: How can we as academics ensure that Native philosophies and ways of knowing about the land and Creation are taken seriously? And how can we ensure that complex ideas are not simply transformed into academic constructs declaring an "Indian" connection to the land? We need to think hard about these questions, especially in light of one writer's warning that to step outside the circle is to forget our relations.[20] This is a provocative statement, but what exactly is the circle being described above? And who or what are the relations being discussed?

In recent years the academic study of Indigenous ways of knowing has divided itself into two main schools. One group of scholars tends to focus on what could be described as Native science, contemplating ideas such as constant flux, relationship, and spirit in the context of Indigenous communities and their collective responses to prevailing forces. This group tends to fuse the language and concepts of quantum mechanics with Native ways of knowing. The outflow is ideas that together lay the foundations of Native philosophy. A second group of scholars tends to focus on Indigenous ethics and codes of conduct. These people examine Native values in an effort to discern how Indigenous populations developed social, political, and economic responses to their environment. Each approach has its strengths and weaknesses. When attempts to discern the Native perspective on events engage both schools of thought, it is possible to generate a more holistic understanding of events. This well suits Native Studies, which seeks to develop complex ways of knowing. Indeed, it is difficult to separate the two schools of thought, for ethics are informed by the tenets of Native science whereas the study of Native science is rooted in ethical protocols. In what follows, each will be dealt with accordingly.

ELDERS

Elders approach all issues through the traditional teachings of their culture, teachings seen to emanate from the Creator. Because the knowledge a person receives is given by the Creator, it is considered sacred. As learning continues throughout one's life, so life itself is a sacred ceremony. In our teachings, your spirit lives forever. It is only using this vessel for the period of time it is in this realm on Mother Earth. And when we were placed here on Turtle Island, the Creator promised us forever that life and that love. He promised us all of those things that we would ever need to go to that beautiful place. Everything you will ever need is there for you. If you get sick, your medicines are there. Your food is there with those animals, with the fish, with the bird life. Those trees, those rocks, that water that gives all life, the life blood of our Mother, the Earth, flows in the rivers, lakes and streams and brooks and creeks. That is our lifeblood. You will nourish from that. All life nourishes from that.

Source: Roger A. Jones (Shawanaga First Nation), presentation before the Royal Commission on Aboriginal Peoples, Sudbury, June 1, 1993.

Native Science

The key idea driving the Native science school of thought is that from the environment emerge the ideas that animate cultural processes. More simply put, Creation teaches all ways including people, how to behave. While this may seem a crude statement, Native science focuses on the broader forces from which societal ethics and codes of conduct emerge. According to Little Bear there are five tenets in Native science:[21]

- space/land
- constant motion/flux
- all things being animate and imbued with spirit
- relationship
- renewal

For the purposes of this chapter, all five are examined with the intent of helping the reader understand why political, economic, and social beliefs—to cite just a few examples—developed as they did within a specific landscape. This will also provide the reader with the framework needed to understand how many of these same ideas continue to inform contemporary First Nations, Métis, and Inuit societies. Breaking a holistic mode of thought into categories is a difficult chore, for the tenets of Native science are mutually dependent. It is done here with the understanding that it is impossible to separate these categories from the broader network of ideas being discussed.

Space/Land

Of central importance to Indigenous peoples is the land. As discussed earlier, Creation is the primary source of identity, and identity is the result of years of personal association with a surrounding territory. Land is more than the topsoil on which grass grows, rivers flow, and people subsist. It is Creation—that is, it is the earth, sky, rivers, lakes, and wind, and all of the people, animals, and other physical manifestations of this planet. All of these things we refer to in total simply as the environment. After thousands of years of close association, each Indigenous community has developed a close spiritual connection with the land; in turn, this connection has borne an impressive understanding of the natural environment. This Indigenous knowledge is most often encountered in stories describing how Creation happened. These tales address human evolution; they encapsulate peoples' histories; they hold the instructions that ever since have guided people in their day-to-day activities. Most important, these stories emphasize the need to become and remain socially, politically, and economically adaptable, for all communities and their peoples face an uncertain future.

According to one Ojibwa (Anishinaabe) author writing in the mid-nineteenth century, stories "had an important bearing on the character of the children of our nation."[22] The stories spoke of the importance of leadership, differences between men and women, and the historically tested values that helped ensure balanced and peaceful community relations. So important were stories and songs that many Indigenous peoples came to perceive them as conscious beings with their own powers of thought that could inform humans. Most often, strict rules were closely associated with storytelling, and from the continual recounting of stories a familiarity developed among the people of a community that had long shared the same landscape. In essence, a methodology evolved that permitted an individual to "speak and sing the land," and soon the homeland became everything to an individual.

Those fortunate enough to share in such stories as listeners were being invited to participate in the cycle of Creation occurring within what has been described as a moral universe.

Each Indigenous nation across Canada boasts unique Creation tales and songs specific to the ecological context. The Mi'kmaq communicate that the Great Spirit created Kluskap to help guide the people it created and situated on earth.[23] Among the Blackfoot (Niitsítapi), Napi, the Old Man, whose father and mother were the sun and moon, made the birds and animals while covering the land with grass from which the animals fed. A woman and child were then moulded from clay and taught how to fend for themselves.[24] Sedna, the Inuit goddess, lost each of her fingers to her parents' sharp knives as she attempted to resist their efforts at drowning her. Each of the fingers changed into a swimming creature: a whale, a seal, a walrus, and a salmon. Though now confined to the water beneath the ice, Sedna would ever after be called on as the Inuit provider in times of food scarcity.[25]

Stories and songs contain themes of good and evil, health and illness, hunger and plenty; they offer moral teachings that help shape identity and explain the world. Speaking and singing one's land, because it derived directly from interaction with the surrounding environment, also fulfilled practical roles; for example, it defined territorial boundaries, and it identified the locations of hunting grounds and of areas with good medicine. Stories and songs continue to assist people in mapping out their physical and cultural landscape while further reinforcing personal and affiliated identities that evolve through personal experience and observation. According to one writer, "the Native map enfolds both time and space. It deals in the cycles of the seasons, the movement of game, the time of planting and the time of gathering. Its sets aside time of ritual and time for dance, times of birth, time of naming and times of death and passing away."[26] Or, as another scholar has explained, Indigenous people "story the world."

Constant Motion/Flux

Ongoing interaction with Creation, combined with the need to remain aware of the natural environment's rhythms, compelled the development of impressive powers of observation. This in turn led to heightened ecological and environmental knowledge. It became an accepted fact that humans were at nature's will. Droughts could quickly make the prairies an inhospitable environment, resulting in diminished buffalo herds, poor crops of wild potatoes and turnips, and limited fresh water for both humans and (by the mid-eighteenth century) large herds of horses. Floods in southern British Columbia could overwhelm and displace thousands living in semipermanent villages. Despite the catastrophic nature of these and like events, humans over time discerned patterns and, using a collected knowledge base, began to plan seasonal moves according to these rhythms. For example, rising water levels in the spring were the norm in southern Manitoba, and storms in the autumn signalled to eastern nations that winter was on its way. As predictable as certain events were, the environment was apt to change quickly, thus communities needed to be adaptable in anticipation of the unknown.

Take as an example global warming's potentially devastating effects on traditional Inuit and Innu society. Fixico writes that "by studying the changes of the seasons and observing the lives of animals and plants as a part of nature, native logic became grounded in the central idea of a continuum of events that seemed familiar. . . . Nature repeated itself in a continuous series of cycles and seasons of circular patterns."[27] In sum, patterns were noticed and over time were catalogued, which contributed to the development of Indigenous philosophies, ways of knowing, and unique ecological strategies.

Recurrent rhythms suggested that the world was undergoing constant change, a process that Little Bear has described as Creation remaining in a state of constant flux. Constant change demanded a keen awareness of what was occurring in one's environment if humans were to succeed. Over time this, too, became a guiding tenet among most North American Indigenous peoples—one that if properly acknowledged would enable those peoples to adapt to prevailing albeit constantly changing circumstances. The best known manifestation of this flux is the trickster. Often taking animal form, trickster figures have been described as "wise and foolish, passionate and cruel, chaste and lecherous, potent and petty," and as tending to embrace "the very forces of chaos and mystery that modern science finds most frustratingly intangible and elusive."[28]

Trickster stories are both entertaining and moralistic and have always been useful tools for teachers to describe a universe in constant transformation. One scholar suggests that "what people miss about Trickster stories is that they're talking about a process of flux. They're talking about how things change. They change quickly and dramatically. The Trickster may have outrageous behaviour and then change again. We're teaching our children to have tolerance for change; to understand it, not to fight it."[29] For example, constant motion is represented among the Blackfoot by Napi, a character that "straddles the consciousness of man and that of . . . the Great Spirit."[30] Napi's role is to teach humans about the meaning of existence and how to relate effectively to their surroundings. Simply acknowledging that change happens, though one cannot know when, can be a source of stability. Constant change means regional and by association social imbalance. To contend with change, Indigenous peoples attempt by various means to attain a rough equilibrium. A striving for balance in a world that is constantly transforming itself is evident in all aspects of society—social, ecological, territorial, ceremonial. One result is that each being has responsibilities aimed at trying to create and maintain ecological balance.

All Is Animate and Imbued with Spirit

Creation is powerful. For humans, Creation amounts to an environment in which animals, plants, and even rocks are all sentient beings. Simply put, everything is alive. Centuries of close observation have enabled humans to identify patterns and rhythms as well as fixed interactions among all the beings they have located. Over time these interactions have resulted in the perception that all things are mutually connected and the belief that everything in an ecosystem is animate and imbued with spirit. As explained by Little Bear, if all is animate, including me, then we must all be somewhat alike, imbued with an energy force we call spirit. If all else have spirit, then I can relate to all and all can relate to me, including other humans, animals, plants, rocks, the earth, the sun, the moon, and so on. In other words, all are my relations.[31] All of Creation and its various manifestations, then, are imbued with spirit since all of Creation is of one spirit. This means that all are my relations and that because this is so, I have certain responsibilities to ensure their progress and safety. So relationships must be forged and maintained.

Relationship

The Creator gave meaning to existence, and over time the intimacy of interaction with the land led to a layered understanding of the local natural order. The universe took on a personal nature, one that demanded that each and every entity seek out and attempt to sustain personal relationships with all other entities. To better understand the personal, interrelated nature of Creation, the oft-used example of the spider web is instructional. The web and all of its beings—be it the fly, the strands of the web, or the spider itself—merge to create one living organism. From a personal perspective it may seem possible to travel to any part of that web without coming into contact with other relations such as the spider. From a distance, however, the web is an organism composed of a network of relations, and just like you the spider is itself an intrinsic part of the environment—it represents a relation within the web of life. To ignore the spider is to disregard a relation within Creation that could result in dire consequences. By acknowledging its existence you have accepted this relationship in anticipation of one day coming into contact.[32]

Consequently, relationship is acknowledged as a central tenet, a product of everything mixing together in a constantly changing universe. The relationship between man and the land, for instance, is similar to that of mother to child, of teacher to student; it is one that defines each person in relation to the surrounding environment and all of the beings inhabiting that territory. Responsibilities befall all of Creation, humans and animals both, and those responsibilities must be respected if a community's collective agenda is to be forged. In a universe in constant flux, relationships are apt to change constantly. If strong relationships are to be maintained, those relationships must constantly be renewed. This is done in various ways, but the continuous need to strive for balance demands that each being take a proactive approach to renewing relationships.

It may seem odd to assign animals an active role in maintaining Creation, but a Native perspective suggests that a reciprocal relationship develops with all of Creation. Animals possess their own spiritual powers, so hunters must treat them with proper respect in order to ensure a successful hunt. The following example is from the perspective of the Cree (Nehiyaw) of northern Quebec:

> A successful hunt is not simply the result of the intention and work of the hunter; it is also the outcome of the intention and actions of the animals. In the process of hunting a hunter enters into a reciprocal relationship: animals are given to hunters to meet their needs and wants, and in return the hunters incur obligations to the animals. Thus the Cree conception of hunting involves a complex and moral relationship in which the outcome of the hunt is a result of the mutual efforts of the hunter and the environment. This is a subtle and accurate ecological perspective. It may seem odd that animal kills should be conceptualized as gifts, and it is important therefore to note that Cree do not radically separate the concepts of "human" and "animals." In their everyday experience in the bush they continually observe examples of the intelligence and will power of animals. They express this by saying that animals are "like persons"; they act as if they are capable of independent action, and they are causally responsible for things they do.[33]

The Cree in this instance acknowledge the animals' sacrifice by giving away the food and by following strict rules structured to ensure the conveyance of respect. When the animal spirit has been pleased, it may once again give itself to the humans. When this respect is not forthcoming, animals may no longer come to humans in dreams, enabling them to "spot the herds of caribou that will be crossing the river at a particular point on the following day; they see a group of strangers approaching and know that they will reach their camp in so many days time; they follow spoor on the ground and reach the place where bear is walking."[34]

In addition to this, animals as part of Creation have important lessons to convey. The buffalo taught the Blackfoot and the Cree of Saskatchewan to always confront one's fears by running into the force of a storm. Stories about the consequences of asking for more than you can possibly use or for hoarding game animals are prominent on the Prairies as well as in northern Canada and the eastern woodlands. Native philosophies emphasize that human beings round out the cycle of life, for "nothing whatever depends on our survival."[35] Hence the role Creation bestows on the animals as human guardians.

An Ojibwa story from Manitoba describes how a boy left his village after his father was mean to him. He was subsequently invited to live with a bear. Bear took care of the boy and fed him, aware that when the fish were gone he would have to leave to find food elsewhere. The bear took care of and watched over the boy, whom he called his grandson, until it was time for him to return to the village. This reciprocal relationship had the bear accept his responsibility for the boy's care and the boy accept his dependence on the bear for his survival. Just as the bear saw the boy as one of his relations—which teaches the importance of caring for all of Creation—the boy's relationship with the bear was functionally the same as existed with other human beings.[36] This often overlooked aspect of the Native perspective assigns all beings within Creation responsibility for one another. This way of thinking teaches that an individual prior to hunting must ask the animal being sought to share its life, for that is one of its roles in Creation—an animal giving itself to the human is a responsibility.

Sentience is not reserved for human beings and animals, however. Lamenting the fact that people—especially non-Native folks—no longer look to or accept Creation's guidance, Walking Buffalo (Stoney) from Alberta expressed his frustration: "Did you know that trees talk? Well they do. They talk to each other, and they'll talk to you if you listen. Trouble is, white people don't listen. They never learned to listen to the Indians, so I don't suppose they'll listen to other voices in nature. But I have learned a lot from trees; sometimes about the weather, sometimes about animals, sometimes about the Great Spirit."[37] Corn, beans, and squash shape what the member nations of the Iroquois describe as the Three Sisters, who regularly appear in the related Creation stories. Clearly, the Quebec Cree and the Iroquois of Ontario and Quebec revere animal and plant beings while considering all to be related. This means that it is possible to have a relationship with all—animals and plants included. From an Ojibwa perspective, rocks communicate, and so do water, thunder, hills, and plants; all have what we would describe as consciousness, and as such, they have lessons to convey to humans.

Dreams are viewed as the interface between humans and other-than-humans rather than as visions requiring interpretation. Described as visitors that interact with humans, dreams act to guide, warn, inform, and entertain. In much the same way that time is non-linear, meaning that it is possible to look into the future and past through ceremony, it is equally possible to speak to the ancestors and other spirit beings. Dreams are often employed as doorways into these worlds, thereby enabling individuals to gain power. Dreams are a form of communication between the keepers of the animals and the thoughts of Indigenous individuals. As entities acting in a specific ecological context that makes it impossible to interpret their actions outside a specific territory, dream imagery can be integrated into daily activities. Dreams offer "a direct connection or communion with a landscape that lies outside time and space. The dream may be of immediate practical significance, as when it gives information about the movement of game or the coming of strangers. But it may also stretch down deep into the earth or reach to the remote past of the group. So the dream is constantly reanimating the map and charging the landscape with its power."[38]

Renewal

As the intellectual foundation of the Native mind, the land—or specific pockets of traditional territories across North America—provides the ideas driving each Indigenous nation's intellectual foundation as catalogued in their history and societal norms. Little Bear eloquently describes this phenomenon: "The Earth is where the continuous and/or repetitive process of

Creation occurs. It is on the Earth and from the Earth that cycles, phases, patterns [are] experienced." As a result, "creation is a continuity, and if creation is to continue, then it must be renewed, and, consequently, the renewal ceremonies, the telling and re-telling of the creation stories, the singing and re-signing of songs, which are the humans' part in the maintenance of creation."[39] As suggested, loss of balance in Indigenous societies had significant implications for all regional beings. Community leaders are therefore assigned the task, not of instructing people, but of using their powers of persuasion to try to restore and maintain equilibrium. In this instance, balance serves a holistic, integrating function and is an integral part of the overall process of renewal.

Creation unites existence in all its forms, energies, and concepts as these are found in the visible and spiritual worlds. Thus Creation can be described as an extended kinship network. In this sort of cohesive environment, all beings must maintain their existing relationships with one another. As one Ojibwa writer states, in his language there is "no term for [the separation] of man/nature, or subject/object dichotomy in their language, because there is no nature, or environment, as such, understood to be separate from the self."[40] From a Native perspective, the environment and humans were created as equals. This leads to the truism that "in Creation one is never alone." The regular renewal of relationships becomes an important referent point since it cannot be assumed that life will continue on its present course; after all, everything is constantly changing. Thus renewal becomes important, for failing to renew a relationship may lead to its malfunction. From a more universal perspective, if a community fails to maintain its relationship with the sun, for example, the sun may choose not to rise the next day. This has led many academics to describe Indigenous peoples as strict empiricists who need to witness events before they can acknowledge that an event has occurred. From a Native perspective born of a world of constant change and the need to maintain positive relationships within an animate world, it is foolish to believe that the sun will rise every day, or that the sturgeon will return each spring, or that the caribou will revisit a familiar migration route each autumn, unless an individual becomes directly involved in what he or she is observing. To ensure the maintenance and renewal of these patterns, humans must play a role in the continued maintenance of Creation.

Ceremonies have been developed to aid in renewing relationships aimed at restoring personal, community, and regional balance. They are ways of coming to know, of coming to understanding.[41] Fasting, and making offerings to spirits and animals, are but two examples of ceremonies designed to renew relations. Such events enable the flow of power from one person to another person, animal, or spirit in an attempt to keep all relations strong. They also have a social and political imperative, for a balanced community means that no individual can become more powerful than another. For many Native peoples in Canada, unless an individual becomes directly involved in what he or she is observing, there is no guarantee that the anticipated event will in fact occur.

Through ceremonies, individuals take an active role in ensuring that Creation unfolds as it has before. The distinction between the observer and what is being observed cannot be made, for we cannot speak about nature without also speaking about ourselves. Here the observer plays an important role in creating reality. Such an approach suggests that Native philosophies consider the universe as a living entity, one that should be approached in a personal manner. Thus each society plays an important role in maintaining place and in the harmonious operations of Creation.

Codes of Conduct

The philosophical tenets of Indigenous nations described above provide a window onto this unique world. But how are these ideas executed by Indigenous peoples? More specifically, how do these ideas inform the Creation of beliefs, customs, values, and languages, thereby providing the context that individuals require in order to determine what is and is not socially acceptable? The local environment influences the development of cultural ideals. In this instance, philosophy, customs, values, and the individual all inform the guidelines that arise from "historical marriages or alliances between humans." These in turn can be construed as social contracts that establish reciprocal obligations of kinship and solidarity. But how do these ideas become values that guide daily actions? Values are the means by which a society instructs its members how to act. These codes of conduct are necessary for a good life. Should an individual choose not to subscribe to those codes of conduct, s/he is of course free to leave and take up residence in a neighbouring community; or s/he could seek out supporters and start her/his own community. Those who willingly choose to adhere to local values agree to the community's essential organizing principles. These help generate a commitment to meeting general community and individual needs.

Speaking before the Royal Commission on Aboriginal Peoples (RCAP) in 1992, Ojibwa scholar James Dumont stated: "If we try to understand and sensibly appreciate Native [teachings] we must be willing, first of all, to accept that there is involved here a very special way of 'seeing the world.' Secondly, and a necessary step, we must make an attempt to 'participate' in this way of seeing."[42] The late Mohawk psychiatrist Clare Brant, in his 24 years of practice (mainly in Ontario), identified among his Cree, Ojibwa, and Iroquoian patients familiar behaviours he identified as ethics. He placed these in three main categories: (1) noninterference, (2) emotional restraint, and (3) sharing. He identified four other categories as less influential albeit still important: (4) a notion of time that emphasizes doing things "when the time is right" rather than by the clock, (5) avoiding public expressions of praise, (6) ordering social relations according to complex rules, and (7) learning by doing, or teaching children by encouraging their observing and participation as opposed to direct instruction.[43]

According to the Royal Commission's (1996) authors, "the ethics described in Brant's article are the natural outgrowth of values flowing from the spiritual world view and relationship to the land" described earlier in this chapter. They then added: "The values or beliefs fundamental to this world view include the belief that there is a natural law that cannot be altered by human action and to which human beings must adapt; the obligation to maintain harmonious relationships with the natural world and those to whom you are related; personal responsibility to adhere to strict behavioural codes; and an ethic of sharing, which involves returning gifts to human and other-than-human relations to sustain the balance of the natural order."[44]

To Brant the key ethic was noninterference, which he described as "a behavioural norm of North American Native tribes that promotes positive inter-personal relations by discouraging coercion of any kind, be it physical, verbal, or psychological."[45] According to this ethic, individuals must refrain from telling others what to do. It is attributable to a belief in voluntary cooperation, the purpose of which is to ensure economic and political stability and, thus, community balance. Brant suggested that interrelated behaviours served to suppress conflict in small communities. This is not to imply an absence of rules guiding proper behaviour; nor is it to suggest that people never attempt to sway others' opinion. The goal, rather, is to employ narratives to convey effective messages or, when this fails, to resort to teasing as a means of persuasion and social control. Besides helping maintain balance, noninterference plays a vital role in preparing children for the environment they will be entering.

Inevitably there are moments when action must be taken to benefit the whole group to the detriment of an individual. Such actions are taken, however, to ensure balance. While appearing to contradict the ethic of noninterference, they may be warranted in a communal environment. In such cases, though, it is imperative that individuals maintain their emotional restraint, the second identified ethic; for according to Brant, even though an individual may sense that he or she has been wronged, the community's survival may well depend on that person's restraint. Displays of anger may upset the delicate balance that community members strive so hard to maintain. As well, folks in the community must remain aware that children pattern their behaviour after parents and adults. The size of these communities means that children interact with large numbers of adults regularly, so adults must constantly be aware of who may be watching to see who may indeed be watching them.

Spiritual resources as described above take precedence, though one cannot overlook the importance of meeting material needs. Nevertheless, in most Indigenous societies it is vital to avoid accumulating material possessions, an act that denotes individual weakness. Generosity is from an early age taught to all children, and acts of sharing are actively promoted. Poverty in societies that function this way is rare—those with the most share with those most in need, meaning that wealth is redistributed to the benefit of all. This is not to suggest that accumulated wealth is foreign to Indigenous societies. Among the Blackfoot, for example, the individual with the largest horse herds is a person of authority, owing mainly to his ability to influence political and social dynamics by improving the wealth of others through his generosity. A deep sense of community accountability results, and strong attachments develop. Sharing with all of Creation ensures the renewal of relationships with all beings, human or otherwise. Stories told to children often warn of the consequences of selfish behaviour.

Behaviour is also directly influenced by Indigenous conceptions of time. As Brant relates, North American Indigenous peoples were once "regulated by the seasons—the sun, the migratory patterns of birds and animals," and they "had to depend upon the seasons and nature to supply them with food, with light."[46] This resulted in a relaxed and flexible attitude toward time, an attitude that prevails to this day and that is generally misunderstood by non-Native Canadians. Instead of emphasizing chronological time, Indigenous peoples place importance on events, which reflects a process-oriented approach. Indigenous time is nonlinear, "cyclic, interwoven, and interconnecting in a spiralling and constantly manifesting space–time continuum with no distinct differences between past, present, and future."[47] According to one scholar, "continuity in time connects ancestors with the unborn. Each that has come this way, and each that is yet to come, has a name. We are not born into the family and do not die out of it. Death does not end relationships, and relationships already exist with those who are yet to come." The "spirit world, from which all souls come and to which they return, completes the circle of each lineage" that each "family extends both backwards and forward through time, bridging the physical and spiritual worlds."[48] This implies a responsibility for the living, the dead, and those yet to be born.

In times of death, for example, sharing in other's grief to help lighten the pain is expected, as is providing needed support for those healing. Gratitude is deeply felt even when it isn't outwardly expressed, for acts of sharing are expected. It is something that is expected and an act of respect. Failure to share could irreparably damage reciprocal relationships within Creation. For example, an animal giving itself expects the hunter to show respect by not wasting the meat and by treating the remains properly. Also, gifts are offered to the animals. Failing to show respect could offend the animal spirits, who might believe that humans place a higher value on possessions than on relationships. This helps demonstrate the highly structured nature of Indigenous cultures and the arduous demands placed on each individual to maintain proper social behaviour. Simply put, there are certain ways of doing things that are conveyed through example—an effective way of transmitting to the young how things are to be done.

Contemporary Thinkers

The past three decades have seen a flowering of Native writers utilizing many of the ideas described in this chapter in furtherance of their work. Many of these academics have played an important role promoting grassroots education, while informing non-Native people nationally about the Native perspective on treaty and Aboriginal rights and self-government. As role models they have generated excitement among budding scholars by injecting their work with ideas from the Indigenous past. Several have become intellectual leaders whose work influences Supreme Court Justices, the Prime Minister's Office, and federal and provincial policymakers.

As discussed in the following chapters, this is not a new trend. As early as the mid-1800s, Peter Jones, George Copway, and William Warren were celebrated thinkers and historians.

All three were Ojibwa. In the early to mid-twentieth century, political lobbyists and organizers like Andy Paull (Squamish), the Reverend Peter Kelly (Haida), John Tootoosis (Cree), and Jules Sioui (Wendat) were organizing Native peoples nationally. By the 1960s, internationally renowned thinkers such as Harold Cardinal (Cree) and George Manuel (Shuswap) were strongly influencing the Native–Canada relationship.

In the tradition of these political thinkers, younger scholars had begun to challenge contemporary issues. Emma Larocque (Métis) in literature; Joseph Couture (Cree) and Clare Brant (Mohawk) in psychology; Eber Hampton (Chikasaw), Ernie Benedict (Mohawk), and Verna Kirkness (Cree) in education; Basil Johnston (Ojibwa) in spirituality; and Olive Dickason (Métis) in history—again to name but a few—have all emerged, and in so doing have helped establish an intellectual foundation for future scholars to draw from. Their work has permitted grander intellectual explorations into Native philosophy by Leroy Little Bear (Blood); Native law by James Youngblood Henderson (Chikasaw) and John Borrows (Chippewas of Nawash); communications by Gail Valaskakis (Chippewa); education by Marie Battiste (Mi'kmaq); economic development by Wanda Wuttunee (Cree) and more recently Calvin Helin (Lax Kw'alaams); governance by Taiaiake Alfred (Mohawk); politics by Kiera Ladner (Cree); environmental issues by Leanne Simpson (Missikssauga); and political philosophy by Dale Turner (Temagami First Nation).

The list grows daily. An estimated 30,000 Native students are currently attending university in Canada. It is also important to acknowledge these academics' influence on students who may be returning to their communities or working with governments as policymakers. Slowly but surely the influence of Native thinkers and the Native Studies discipline is being felt, and both will continue to influence future generations about Native philosophy and how the various Native perspectives Indigenous to Canada inform us daily.

NATIVE LANGUAGES

I feel that Aboriginal languages should be recognized as special heritage languages of Canada, so that original inhabitants of this land can develop and maintain their mother tongue for future generations. Aboriginal people were the original people of Canada, and yet their languages have been ignored, denied and treated with disrespect. Many Aboriginal people have lost their mother tongue because of this; therefore, they have been stripped of a very integral part of their identity. Language is the essence of a culture. Languages are vehicles for the transmission of values, culture and literature. They shape perceptions, an understanding of self, culture, heritage and world view. If these languages are lost, they will be lost to the world forever. Of the 53 Aboriginal languages in Canada, experts estimate that within 10 years only three will be in existence: Cree, Ojibway and Inuktitut. Even for these three languages there is a real threat of loss.

Source: Mary Noey, presentation before the Royal Commission on Aboriginal Peoples, La Ronge, Saskatchewan, May 28, 1992.

Conclusion

It is difficult in contemporary American society, and particularly in the highly structured environment of an academic institution, to comprehend the emotional and cognitive understanding of a landscape from which one can draw both physical and spiritual sustenance.

—Clara Sue Kidwell and Alan Velie[49]

In this chapter, striving for balance has been presented as vital in a universe that is "driven by constant interrelationships between spirit and matter"—in other words, that is in a state of constant transformation.[50] Each being is responsible for transferring power to others in an attempt to maintain balance. Doing so involves "a dynamic process of constant adjustment" that helps individuals maintain a multitude of relationships and so preserve community harmony. Trying to understand "the complex nature of natural forces and their interrelationships [is] an important context for Indigenous knowledge and heritage."[51] As we alter our environment, we affect the complex of inter-relationships and in so doing create disharmony.[52] If the network of all a person's relations is stopped or interfered with, imbalances thereby generated could bring Creation to a halt.

Over time these relationships came to embrace values such as respect and reciprocity while promoting the need to develop holistic, sacred approaches to understanding based on observational knowing. What followed was the Creation of culturally specific methodologies that helped people teach the community's youth and thereby ensure the generational trans-ference of community knowledge. The main ideas presented by the Native science school of thought are found in most North American Indigenous communities, which have provided people with the base they need to develop descriptions of the nature of reality. How each community has utilized these philosophical tenets to establish its own understanding of reality is not known. We do know, however, that certain consistencies exist in the codes of conduct of North American Indigenous communities.

This Native perspective has always guided the political, economic, and social processes of Indigenous communities. Accordingly, we must understand these foun-dational ideas before we can comprehend why Indigenous leaders have responded as they have done to prevailing ecological forces, man-made or otherwise. Simultaneously, the Native perspective informs Native leaders, and again one must start to understand these ideas before one can appreciate the scope of Aboriginal self-government and why Native communities fight so hard to maintain control of education, to name just two examples.

FURTHER READING

Battiste, Marie, and Sakej Youngblood Henderson. *Protecting Indigenous Knowledge and Heritage: A Global Challenge.* Saskatoon: Purich, 2000.

Cajete, Gregory. *Native Science: Natural Laws of Interdependence.* Santa Fe: Clear Light, 2000.

Colorado, Pam. "Bridging Native and Western Science." *Convergence* 21, nos. 2 and 3, 1988: 49–67.

Cordova, Viola F. "Approaches to Native American Philosophy." In *American Indian Thought: Philosophical Essays,* ed. Anne Waters. Malden: Blackwell, 2004, pp. 27–33.

Deloria, Jr., Vine. *God Is Red: A Native View of Religion.* Golden: Fulcrum, 1994.

———. *The Metaphysics of Modern Existence.* San Francisco: Harper and Row, 1979.

Ermine, Willie. "Aboriginal Epistemology." In *The Circle Unfolds: First Nations Education in Canada,* ed. Marie Battiste and Jean Barman. Vancouver: UBC Press, 1995, pp. 101–12.

Fixico, Donald K. *The American Indian Mind in a Linear World: American Indian Studies and Traditional Knowledge.* New York: Routledge, 2003.

Henderson, Sakej Youngblood. "*Ayukpachi:* Empowering Aboriginal Thought." In *Reclaiming Indigenous Voice and Vision,* ed. Marie Battiste. Vancouver: UBC Press, 2000, pp. 248–78.

Knudston, Peter, and David Suzuki. *Wisdom of the Elders.* Toronto: Stoddart, 1993.

Peat, F. David. *Lighting the Seventh Fire: The Spiritual Ways, Healing, and Science of the Native American.* New York: Birch Land Press, 1994.

NOTES

1. David Newhouse, "Imagining New Worlds: The Aboriginal Imagination," in *Aboriginal Cultural Landscapes,* ed. Jill Oakes, Rick Riewe, Yale Belanger, Sharon Blady, Kelly Legge, and Patsy Wiebe (Winnipeg: Aboriginal Issues Press, 2004).

2. Vine Deloria, Jr., *The Metaphysics of Modern Existence* (San Francisco: Harper and Row, 1979); idem, *God Is Red: A Native View of Religion* (Golden: Fulcrum, 1994).

3. Deloria, *God Is Red,* p. 65.

4. Deloria, *The Metaphysics of Modern Existence,* p. vii.

5. Ibid., p. viii.

6. Rupert Ross, *Returning to the Teachings: Exploring Aboriginal Justice* (Toronto: Penguin, 1996), p. 115.

7. Deloria, "Philosophy and Tribal Peoples," in *American Indian Thought: Philosophical Essays,* ed. Anne Waters (Malden: Blackwell, 2004), pp. 3–11.

8. Anne Waters, ed., *American Indian Thought: Philosophical Essays* (Malden: Blackwell, 2004).

9. See Leroy Little Bear, "Relationship of Aboriginal People to the Land and the Aboriginal Perspective on Aboriginal Title," in *For Seven Generations: An Information Legacy of the Royal*

Commission on Aboriginal Peoples [CD-ROM] (Ottawa: Canada Communications Group, 1996), cited in Royal Commission on Aboriginal Peoples, *Treaty Making in the Spirit of Co-Existence: An Alternative to Extinguishment* (Ottawa: Canada Communications Group, 1994).

10. Clara Sue Kidwell and Alan Velie, *Native American Studies* (Lincoln: University of Nebraska Press, 2005), p. 9.

11. Ibid.

12. Gregory Cajete, *Native Science: Natural Laws of Interdependence* (Santa Fe: Clear Light, 2000), p. 205.

13. See William N. Fenton, *The Great Law and the Longhouse: A Political History of the Iroquois Confederacy* (Norman: University of Oklahoma Press, 1998).

14. Peter Knudston and David Suzuki, *Wisdom of the Elders* (Toronto: Stoddart, 1993), p. 13.

15. Cajete, "Philosophy of Native Science," in *American Indian Thought: Philosophical Essays,* ed. Anne Waters (Malden: Blackwell, 2004), pp. 45–46.

16. Sakej Youngblood Henderson, "*Ayukpachi:* Empowering Aboriginal Thought," in *Reclaiming Indigenous Voice and Vision,* ed. Marie Battiste (Vancouver: UBC Press, 2000), p. 259.

17. Little Bear, "Relationship of Aboriginal People"; see also Henderson, "*Ayukpachi*"; and Deloria, *God Is Red.*

18. See, generally, David Rich Lewis, "Native Americans and the Environment: A Survey of Twentieth-Century Issues,"*American Indian Quarterly* 19, no. 3 (Summer 1995): 423–50.

19. Knudston and Suzuki, *Wisdom of the Elders,* p.13.

20. Viola F. Cordova, "Approaches to Native American Philosophy," in *American Indian Thought: Philosophical Essays,* ed. Anne Waters (Malden: Blackwell, 2004), pp. 27–33.

21. Little Bear, "Relationship of Aboriginal People."

22. George Copway, *The Traditional History and Characteristic Sketches of the Ojibway Nation* (London: Charles Gilpin, 1850).

23. See, generally, Marion Robinson, *Red Earth Tales of the Mi'kmaq* (Halifax: Nimbus, 2007).

24. Percy Bullchild, *The Sun Came Down: The History* (San Francisco: Harper and Row Publishers, 1985).

25. See, for example, Shelagh D. Grant, "The Sea Goddess Sedna: An Enduring Pan-Arctic Legend From Traditional Orature to the New Narratives of the Late Twentieth Century," in *Echoing Silence: Essays on Arctic Narrative,* ed. John Moss (Ottawa: University of Ottawa Press, 1997), pp. 211–24.

26. F. David Peat, "I Have a Map in My Head," based on a talk given at the Patterns in the Universe conference, Smithsonian Museum, October 1989. [online] http://www.fdavidpeat.com/bibliography/essays/smithson.htm. Last accessed September 3, 2008.

27. Donald K. Fixico, *The American Indian Mind in a Linear World: American Indian Studies and Traditional Knowledge* (New York: Routledge, 2003), pp. 49–50.

28. Knudston and Suzuki, *Wisdom of the Elders*, p. 29.

29. Quoted in Ross, *Returning to the Teachings*, p. 125.

30. Thomson Highway, *The Kiss of the Fur Queen* (Toronto: Doubleday, 1998), p. ii.

31. Little Bear, "Relationship of Aboriginal People," p. 7.

32. Mark A. Dockstator, "Towards an Understanding of Aboriginal Self-Government: A Proposed Theoretical Model and Illustrative Factual Analysis" (LL.D., Osgoode Hall Law School, York University, 1993).

33. Harvey A. Feit, *Hunting and the Quest for Power: The James Bay Cree and Whitemen in the 20th Century* [online] http://arcticcircle.uconn.edu/HistoryCulture/Cree/Feit1/feit1.html. Last accessed August 14, 2008.

34. Peat, *Lighting the Seventh Fire: The Spiritual Ways, Healing, and Science of the Native American* (New York: Birch Land, 1994), p. 79.

35. Ross, *Returning to the Teachings*, p. 61.

36. Thomas W. Overholt and J. Baird Callicott, *Clothed-in-fur, and Other Tales: An Introduction to an Ojibwa World View* (Washington: University Press of America, 1982).

37. Quoted in Deloria, *God Is Red*, p. 90.

38. Peat, *Lighting the Seventh Fire*.

39. Little Bear, "Relationship of Aboriginal People," p. 48.

40. Quoted in Rheault, *Anishinaabe Mino-Bimaadiziwim*.

41. Cajete, *Native Science*, p. 81.

42. James Dumont, "Journey To Daylight-Land through Ojibwa Eyes," in *The First Ones: Readings in Indian/Native Studies*, ed. David Miller (Saskatchewan: Saskatchewan Indian Federated College Press, 1992), p. 75.

43. Clare Brant, "Native Ethics and Rules of Behaviour." *Canadian Journal of Psychiatry* 35 (August 1990).

44. Canada, *For Seven Generations: An Information Legacy of the Royal Commission on Aboriginal Peoples* (Ottawa: Canada Communications Group, 1996).

45. Brant, "Native Ethics and Rules of Behaviour," p. 535.

46. Ibid.

47. John Boatman, *My Elders Taught Me: Aspects of Western Great Lakes American Indian Philosophy* (Lanham: University Press of America, 1992), p. 34.

48. Russel Lawrence Barsh, "The Nature and Spirit of North American Political Systems," *American Indian Quarterly* (Spring 1986): 187.

49. Kidwell and Velie, *Native American Studies*, p. 37.

50. Boatman, *My Elders Taught Me*, p. 11.

51. Marie Battiste and Sakej Youngblood Henderson, *Protecting Indigenous Knowledge and Heritage: A Global Challenge* (Saskatoon: Purich, 2000), p. 43.

52. Peat, *Lighting the Seventh Fire*, p. 168.

CHAPTER

The Land and Indigenous Political Economy

2

When a child began to talk and understand things, one of the very first lessons he or she received was about the Great Spirit. A child would grow up learning about nature and the importance of respecting all things in creation.

—Chief John Snow (Stoney)[1]

No two Indigenous societies are the same politically or economically. This may appear an innocent comment when one considers the differences between, say, the Mi'kmaq and the Tsimshian (Sm'algyax). Located at opposite ends of the continent, these two nations historically employed radically different governance models and economic processes despite living in similar ecological environments. Yet this simple statement challenges centuries of written histories portraying North American "Indians" as largely hunter–gatherers who embraced uniform political and religious beliefs. On the contrary, North American Indigenous populations developed unique political and economic processes specific to their different environments. Various political models were employed. For example, the Iroquois created a bicameral council in which women played influential political roles; also, the Iroquois economy mixed hunting with agriculture to support communities with populations in the thousands. In contrast, smaller bands on the Prairies embraced hereditary leadership models in communities that relied on the buffalo hunt as their primary economic resource.

People may seem similar in how they organize politically and manage local resources; but every society develops its own mechanisms for determining collectively how those resources will be allocated. Questions concerning how much will be produced and how it will be distributed require careful consideration. In present-day Canadian society we employ institutions known as the state and the market to help answer these questions. When we break these concepts down we are simply talking about politics and the economy. Political economy is the study of the science of government—that is, how societies balance the inherent tensions between states and markets. Political economy helps us uncover how particular mixes of political and economic activities emerge and who benefits. This tells us a great deal about how particular societies operate. Such an approach is practical for studying pre-contact North American Indigenous communities, because it can (1) help us discern how the forces of politics and economics influence community development, and (2) inform us how community-based ideologies related to consumption and leadership are structured to help maintain political and ecological balance while ensuring the prosperity of community members.

Political economy from a Native perspective, then, is defined as the study of the environment's influence on Indigenous political institutions and economic ideologies as these respond to prevailing ecological forces and the dynamics associated with Creation. Never forgetting the centrality of the interrelational network, it is imperative that we consider how the actions of individuals in a community influence its overall dynamic and how that one community in turn can affect its neighbours.

Understanding Indigenous Peoples: A Non-Native Perspective

Any group that wishes to be regarded as the authority in a human society must not simply banish or discredit the views of their rivals, they must become the sole source of truth for that society and defend their status and the power to interpret against all comers by providing the best explanation of the data.

—Vine Deloria, Jr. (Standing Rock Sioux)[2]

Perhaps the most important role the Native Studies discipline performs is to provide an alternative sphere of academic influence that is able to challenge prevalent and accepted ideas about Native peoples that originated with European writers, philosophers, jurists, and academics. For this purpose it is vital to break away from non-Native standards of academic exploration. This is because non-Native academics to date are largely responsible for popular portrayals of Native peoples that are in ways quite scathing about pre-contact Indigenous societies. As will be discussed in depth later, the once politically and economically independent nations indigenous to North America came to be framed by non-Native writers as barbarous, savage, and noble, as peoples who were victims of their own inherent inability to socially evolve in their respective environments; this, it was supposed, led to a life that was characterized as little more than nasty, brutish, and short.[3] It is important, however, to acknowledge that these representations were the product of a broader colonial agenda that actively promoted the removal of Indigenous peoples from the lands that settlers desired.[4]

Unfortunately, countering prevailing theoretical frameworks and embedded stereotypes is difficult, for a variety of reasons. Perhaps the most ominous barriers are theories developed by academics seeking answers to lingering questions about Indigenous peoples. Having been trained in intellectual approaches dating back to the seventeenth and eighteenth centuries, modern academics are puzzled by what they view as the unorthodox beliefs of Indigenous peoples. Western researchers seem unaware that these Native societies have for centuries been a reflection of homegrown epistemologies; yet instead of engaging in intensive study to uncover those epistemologies, they develop alternative theories that bear little relation to the actual lived worlds of Native people. Outlandish yet academically accepted theories have proliferated because well-meaning and genuinely curious anthropologists, historians, sociologists, political scientists, and legal scholars are seeking answers to questions they only think are relevant.

Because of these thought processes and similar ones, Indigenous peoples have found themselves classified according to scales that measure societal advances according to Western standards. Moreover, the Western context that Native people have to contend with was born at the height of the Industrial Revolution. As a result, Indigenous peoples were widely perceived as Stone Age tribes slowly progressing toward civilization. To economists these populations were no more than hunters and gatherers engaging in limited trade and with no industry. Political metrics were devised to distinguish peoples in terms of how advanced their social philosophies were; again, Western institutions served as the yardstick. Native development in Canada continues to be measured in terms of Western norms. What is missing from these measures is anything remotely reflecting an Indigenous world view. In particular, except for some research done on the Haudenosaunee Confederacy, there is little mention of the economic and political philosophies that informed most communities. Also missing are the words of the elders and community leaders who could have explained Native societies to Westerners had they been asked. As a result of all this, a colonial mentality that has always "captured" Indigenous culture continues to set the tone when academics and politicians discuss Native peoples.

Ecological Context

As Aboriginal people experienced the forces of an ecosystem, Aboriginal worldviews, languages, consciousness, and order arose. With the elders' calls to return to Aboriginal worldviews, languages, knowledge, and order, we need to re-examine their ecological context. Such an inquiry requires us to learn from the ecosystem as our ancestors did, as well as to learn from our elders' experiences.

—James [Sakej] Youngblood Henderson (Chickasaw)[5]

It is suspicious that these ideas were overlooked or at the very least downplayed by academics and politicians alike, for every society inevitably generates its own political and economic structures to facilitate internal working relationships, which then allow diplomacy between nations to occur. From the West's perspective, political science studies power and coercive force, and economics studies the production, distribution, and consumption of goods and services. Contrast this with pre-contact North American Indigenous political and economic structures, both of which begin with *land*. The recent writings of the legal scholar Sakej Youngblood Henderson are instructive here—especially his discussion of the ecological context, that is, the relationship between the ecological order and Indigenous political and economic traditions. Henderson's central thesis is that specific Indigenous political and economic strategies arose in response to the specific environment.

Critics often oppose new (academic) ideas that challenge accepted beliefs. Many also advocate against adopting these alternative approaches even though "each different way of life makes its own assumptions about the ends and purposes of human existence, about ways by which knowledge may be obtained, about the pigeon-holes in which each . . . sense datum is filled, about what human beings have a right to expect from each other and the gods, about what constitutes fulfillment or frustration. Some of these assumptions are made explicit in the lore of folk; others are tacit premises which the observer must infer by finding consistent trends in word and deed."[6] Since previous theories developed to explain Indigenous political and economic traditions have to date left us with little more than incomplete foundations, embracing theoretical frameworks Indigenous to North America appears a logical step forward toward a more complete understanding.

Henderson borrows from the work of Brazilian social theorist Roberto Unger—specifically, his ideas about context. Unger argues that European notions of nature were crafted by Christian theologians and philosophers and that the outcome was a theory of social phenomena largely removed from nature. This resulted in an *artificial* context, since society was then imagined and ultimately created according to these ideas—that is, in an attempt to escape the state of nature. In other words, the basic ideas that have long guided European thought were constructed as reactions against the natural world.[7] In contrast, Indigenous philosophies were developed according to the rhythms of specific ecological contexts—that is, from a mixture of keen observation and extended interaction with nature, which Henderson describes as a *natural* context.[8] It is foolish to suggest that North American Indigenous societies had no great men and/or women striving to improve their communities; indeed, many imagined greater things for their people. The difference is that their ideas were informed by the natural context and were developed with that context in mind.

It is within this broader ecology that the knowledge base and history of a people emerged. These ways of knowing in turn became the source of Indigenous identities while also providing what was required for people to prosper as a society, both spiritually and materially. The relationship to the natural world that informed their knowledge creation also guided them as they constructed their languages and social philosophies, which in turn were utilized when it came time to establish their governance and economic models. Critics may argue that the resultant social order was a human product. It was, but it also reflected the ecological order. Take Indigenous languages as an example. Today there are an estimated 52 such languages representing 11 language families (ten First Nations plus Inuktitut). But it is estimated that there may have been upwards of 300 languages spoken in North America in the past, and many more dialects that emerged in various ecological contexts.

Speaking with Henderson in the 1990s, the eminent physicist F. David Peat related that in the Mi'kmaq language

> the names of trees are the sound that the wind makes as it moves through their leaves in the fall. The name of the tree is therefore far from arbitrary. It is based upon the direct experience of listening to a specific sound that refers to a particular tree—for each of the different species of trees makes a different sound. It is, moreover, a sound made at that time of the year when the leaves begin to dry, a sound specific to a particular area of Turtle Island [North America] as the salt-laden wind blows in from the Atlantic Ocean.[9]

Peat expands on this, highlighting the fact that the Algonquian languages "with their verbal base, rhythms, and sonic vibrations, are themselves both an expression and manifestation within such a world."[10] Descriptions such as this help us understand why Native leaders nationally struggle to secure the funding needed to ensure language protection and revitalization, for language is an expression of society and culture that contains the stories of the land dating back to Creation. That is why dislocation from one's ecological context vis-à-vis the loss of language can leave an individual feeling disconnected or apart from Creation even when s/he is still living on her/his traditional territory. The loss of language means that the portal into that world is forever closed.

In much the same way that language came to reflect the ecological context, so too did political and economic processes. But then it seems sensible to suggest that the environment shapes not only how people harvest the resources they need to survive and reproduce the culture but also how political processes are formulated to mitigate the associated tensions. Within these ecological contexts an implicit reality unique to the land exists that over time humans recognize through a concentrated interface with Creation. This reality, once acknowledged and built into social processes, allows people and their societies to emerge and their identity to strengthen. Vine Deloria captures this dynamic eloquently when discussing the importance of the land, or Creation, to North American Indigenous peoples. He writes "that a revelation is not so much the period of time in which it occurs as the place it may occur. Revelation becomes a particular experience at a particular place, no universal truth emerging but an awareness arising that certain places have a qualitative holiness over and above other places." He adds that "the universality of truth then becomes the relevance of the experience for a community of people, not its continual adjustment to evolving scientific and philosophical conceptions of the universe."[11]

Note well that while the continent itself may be referred to in and of itself as an ecological context, especially when discussing the ideological differences between, say, European and Indigenous philosophies, there have always been pockets of identity, which suggests that multiple ecological contexts existed from which various cultures emerged. That Canada has six main geographic zones (Arctic, Subarctic, Plains, Plateau, Northwest Coast, Northeast), which in turn can be broken into various subzones, supports the contention that hundreds if not thousands of communities developed in relation to the land, creating along the way vital social processes reflecting these territorial rhythms. So to suggest that Indigenous groups residing within a Prairie environment albeit 200 kilometres apart would have developed identical political and economic ideologies is foolhardy, especially when one considers the fluctuating topography associated with that region.

By way of comparison, the Iroquois (Haudenosaunee) and the Huron (Wendat) of what is today southern Ontario have developed similar confederacy structures in their resource-rich environments, yet striking ideological and procedural differences are evident in these political processes as a result of the geographic distance between them. So, despite several significant commonalities, these two nations are unique—something our study should reflect. Communities adapt to their environment by developing specific economic ways of life, which is not to suggest that Indigenous leaders did not learn through direct contact with their neighbours when developing forms of governance. In sum, the land base itself informs Indigenous political economy. The next section describes some of the differences among Canada's Indigenous nations in terms of political economy.

Politics

Tribal peoples include all forms of life in their body of evidence from the very beginning, so that their concepts must be much more precise and involve considerably more evidence. Their statements must be framed in ways that are applicable not simply to humans but to living creatures.

—Vine Deloria, Jr. (Standing Rock Sioux)[12]

Students in Native Studies will be regularly challenged with ideas and conclusions that mistakenly suggest that Indigenous peoples were little more than aimless wanderers. Take, for example, the work of political scientists Tom Flanagan and Mark Dickerson, who wrote a popular political-science textbook which suggested that groups like the Cree (Nehiyaw) of Saskatchewan and the Dakota of Manitoba were "tribal societies" with "little or no specialized structure of government" evident.[13] Flanagan has since advanced these ideas, claiming that because European civilization was several thousand years more advanced than North American Indigenous nations, "both in technology and social organization," the European colonization of North America was both inevitable and justifiable.[14]

Authors of a recently published international-relations textbook have followed suit by suggesting that "the present-day international system is the product of a particular civilization—Western civilization, centred in Europe"—and that the international system "developed among the European states of 300 to 500 years ago, was exported to the rest of the world, and has in the last century subsumed virtually all of the world's territory into sovereign states." They insist that students studying issues related to Indigenous peoples accept that pre-contact North American cultures "did not have extensive agriculture, large cities, irrigation, and the others trappings of 'civilization'" and that "Indigenous cultures were largely exterminated or pushed aside by European settlers."[15]

Further scrutiny suggests these conclusions to be false and the ideas about North American political traditions to be exaggerated. Most North American Indigenous political traditions embrace a system characterized by an absence of power relations (coercive, hierarchical, authoritative). Importance is placed on maintaining the relationships that develop among all relations (human and nonhuman) occupying the same territory and neighbouring regions.[16] Often defined communally, Indigenous communities did not overtly promote economic competition and the accumulation of material wealth.[17] Instead, spiritual compacts were devised that stressed the importance of balance that "must be made between sources of life, the land, their place, and with the natural entities there."[18] Humans were taught to govern their own personal affairs. For that reason no individual or community-based agency existed in most Indigenous societies, and those that did operate did not have the right to govern others, even should those actions be perceived as not being in the community's best interests. Leadership skills were seen as gifts derived from the Creator and as fostered over time. Each individual enjoyed this power, which was characterized as "the repository of responsibilities rather than a claimant of rights."[19] As a result, all government functions were ruled over by the people, who in turn were guided by Creation.

Kinship rather than geographic boundaries acted as the basis of political philosophies, which emphasized mutual responsibility for all of Creation. In short, it must never be forgotten that how an individual behaves has significant implications for the surrounding world. This connection means many things. None of Creation's manifestations may own the land, since both humans and nonhumans are expected to share the territory in an equitable fashion. Kinship networks also help localize living arrangements; in other words, every entity living within a specific geographic region claims that region as its home. This necessitates accepting coyote, raven, and bear as both neighbours and relations within the broader kinship network. Each feeds the others, educates the others, and interacts with the others. All have responsibilities, and sharing the same place demands the formation of reciprocal relationships. The salmon are uncles to the humans who live on the stream's edge and give up their lives to feed them. To sell or destroy the salmon rather than respect or protect them had serious implications.

The tensions inherent in promoting a combination of autonomy and individual responsibility were admittedly difficult to surmount. Structured protocols were established to help maintain balance. For example, a person who had a grievance or suggestion was provided with a forum to voice his or her concerns, since everyone in the community was responsible for day-to-day governance. Those considered to be commanding or overbearing were often rejected; and public debates were almost always avoided.[20] This prevented emotionally charged discussions and at the same time promoted calm political dialogues leading to a consensus, which would then be announced at a public meeting. Even then, consensus did not mean that community members were bound to the council's decisions. Indeed, no one was forced to accept decisions as binding. If you disagreed, you and other followers could leave the larger community and establish a satellite community; or you choose to abide by the pronouncements while continuing to work behind the scenes, using your diplomatic prowess to effect change.

Public order relied on self-discipline. When this faded or was obscured by emotions, public opinion and ridicule became important mechanisms for compelling an individual back in line, as it were. As products of Creation, humans were imbued with powers that made them equal. This, however, did not make humans more powerful than their non-human relations. As such it was difficult for one leader to emerge to lead or exert control within a community. To achieve rank, one needed to gain respect within the community by building a reputation based on acts of bravery, or by showing wisdom and discretion, or by becoming an object of admiration.[21] Importantly, leaders did not have a treasury or taxes to empower themselves or to coerce others into following their lead. This made it impossible for one person or a small group of individuals to become powerful by accumulating material wealth or by centralizing authority. As a consequence, Indigenous societies established protocols where self-interest could not be separated from the tribal good—the two were inextricably intertwined and virtually identical.

One commonality did develop among North American Indigenous communities: economic independence was acknowledged as a means to ensure individual independence. In this regard, political leaders were powerless to deprive any family of its economic well-being, which made it impossible for them to shift a political balance. This powerlessness, based as it was on a lack of centralized authority and decision-making institutions, was deliberate. Materialism, the basis of the capitalist economy, was viewed by most Indigenous peoples as futile and dangerous madness.[22] Growing political and economic strength within a community was considered natural, whereas using outside political philosophies to shape community political beliefs was considered evil. It is interesting that contemporary research suggests that current Native leaders consider the latter point relevant for two reasons. First, the imposition of the band-council model has coincided with an extended period of socioeconomic depression in Native communities. Second, this model contradicts many of the historic governing processes described above while simultaneously encouraging political ambition and economic greed, both of which were once considered undesirable qualities in individuals.

This is not to suggest that some individuals did not rise to positions of influence—there are accounts of important men and women who rose to leadership positions and whose ideas and words carried tremendous weight within their own nations and those of their neighbours. But these leaders were not the sole decision makers; rather, they were coordinators, peacemakers, teachers, mentors, and role models—and they were comedians who could quickly defuse tense and potentially volatile situations. Such a leader could not tell others what to do but was expected to lead by example, to cajole, tease, or inspire. Here, minimizing differences of opinion was key to successful leadership. To prevent the concentration and abuse of power, most Indigenous nations employed a system of hereditary chiefs to ensure that the people's interests were served. The system succeeded because political successors were trained from a very early age to assume leadership positions.[23]

But not all Indigenous nations were egalitarian, nor did all of them discourage power relations and hierarchical political models. For example, governance systems on the Northwest Coast and on the Plateau revolved around groups of related families utilizing a common territory; or around bands comprising one or several villages, which tended to be occupied in the winter months. Each chieftainship operated mainly at the level of a large village, and in each case a council of elders appointed the chief. These chiefs could usually trace their lineage to an ancestor with the highest rank. These individuals were considered the highest ranking people and as such the most powerful and politically influential. Chiefs were also expected to care for the community by ensuring the well-being of individuals and by formally recognizing rank and prestige. Each family in the community was also ranked, and responsibilities were assigned accordingly.[24]

Economics

Indigenous economics: the science of dealing with the production, distribution, and consumption of wealth in a naturally holistic, reciprocal manner that respects humankind, fellow species, and the eco-balance of life.

—First Nations Development Institute[25]

The philosophies related to the successful production, distribution, exchange, and consumption of goods and services were products of the ecological context. Unlike the first Europeans, North American Indigenous peoples did not emphasize economic innovation or the use of wage labour or entrepreneurship to promote accumulation and societal advancement based on individual wealth or material progress. Individual wealth did exist in many forms, however: some individuals in Plains societies owned large horse herds; and among West Coast groups, individuals would accumulate large amounts of goods, which they would then give away during an elaborate ceremony known as the potlatch. In both cases, accumulation could and did result in political influence. As for regional balance, the ethic of trying to avoid overexploiting the environment was a guiding principle that fostered economic processes and ideologies based on respecting one's surroundings when utilizing resources. Exploitation of resources within traditional homelands did occur; the point is that greater attention was paid to ensuring resource renewal and ecological balance.

Take the fairly balanced Saulteaux economy in Manitoba's Interlake region, a resource-rich area also utilized by the Sioux (Dakota), Assiniboine (Nakota), Chippewa (Anishinaabe), and Cree (Nehiyaw).[26] The Saulteaux accepted that they were stewards of the land. Fish were plentiful, sap was available for sugar production, small game animals such as rabbits were abundant, and a variety of vegetables were grown in local gardens. These resources provided local populations with all their dietary needs.[27] Yet those resources were never harvested to a threshold of scarcity. This meant that natural resources—including birch trees, which were used to build lodges and canoes—remained accessible, as did fur-bearing animals, which were trapped and traded with neighbouring nations.

The Interlake region also served as a "highway" linking local communities. This was important for facilitating inter- and intratribal trade, which was well established and extended throughout North America. Trade accomplished a number of objectives. First, it fulfilled material wants and needs. Contrary to the popular assumption that Native people engaged solely in subsistence economies, human desires propelled trade as much as general needs. Trade also helped maintain political alliances, which were renewed during trade fairs. The extent of continental trade suggests that it was not simply a result of surpluses; rather, it was a systematic and carefully thought-out process. In eastern Canada, for example, a complex trade network was in place: farming communities such as the Huron (Wendat) would trade corn for pelts and dried fish with Ojibwa (Anishinaabe) and Cree (Nehiyaw) from northern Ontario. Luxury items such as copper, exotic furs, and marine shells (including wampum) were also traded, as were cherts, which made their way along various trade corridors.[28]

To the Northeast, the Innu would gather in large groups numbering upwards of 300 people at the mouths of rivers flowing into the St. Lawrence to trade, fish, renew relationships, and participate in ceremonies. In western Canada it was not uncommon for Blackfoot trade parties to make long forays south and east to trade with other nations. Pemmican—a mixture of buffalo, moose, or deer fat and saskatoon berries (or other fruits)—was a popular trade item, as were buffalo robes and handmade weapons such as knives. All of these were exchanged for shells, paint, and religious and secular artifacts.[29]

OOLICHAN TRADE

Oolichan oil was an important item among the Indigenous nations of what is now British Columbia's West Coast and Interior. Known among the Tsimshian (Sm'algyax) as *hali'mootk*, or the saviour fish, oolichan was a species of smelt that, once processed, delivered large quantities of oil. That oil was high in nutritional value (it was used in place of butter); it could also be used to treat various maladies. So it was a popular trade item. One box of grease could garner four blankets or two beaver skins; two boxes had the value of one canoe; a female slave might bring in three boxes. Access to oolichan fishing grounds was often negotiated. Indigenous peoples from the Interior, for example, would travel hundreds of kilometres to trade furs in return for permission to fish. For instance, the Nisga'a would rent out their nets, equipment, and shelter for the fishing season. Travel into the territories, and the movement of grease out of the territories, occurred along trade highways known as "grease trails." Some of the better known travel routes stretched for more than 300 kilometres. These routes were later employed by newcomers to the region, facilitating extended contact and settlement among communities in the Interior.[30]

And in the Northwest and Plateau regions trade was a regular occurrence, one that facilitated the creation and/or maintenance of kinship ties. This fostered regional, political, and economic stability.

A Brief Overview of Ecological Contexts

This section provides an overview of Canada's six geographic regions and their political and economic models, to help readers understand how Indigenous nations in those regions developed as they did.

Arctic[31]

Economics

Canada's Arctic is a dynamic region characterized by rolling hills, Plateaux, rock outcroppings, lakes, and river valleys as well as tundra, Subarctic forests, coastal Plains, mountains, and Arctic seas. Daytime temperatures fall below −50°C in the winter and reach 30°C in the summer. The people of modern-day Nunavut occupy three distinct ecological contexts. In the unbroken expanses of ice that join the region's islands and peninsulas, the winter economy was restricted to "breathing-hole sealing" owing to an absence of large sea mammals. In summer, inland camps were the norm and the focus is on caribou hunting and fishing. Farther south, the hunting of sea mammals such as beluga whales was supplemented by sealing and by following the caribou inland. On the tundra, seasonal caribou hunting is supplemented by fishing. In the northern Northwest Territories the Inuit catch fish and hunt fowl, small game, and caribou from May to November.

The interior and coastal Inuit of Quebec hunt caribou in the spring and fall; this is supplemented with fishing, sealing, collecting seagull and spider eggs, and hunting waterfowl and small game. Because of fluctuating weather patterns, food caches are required into late spring. Limited regional resources have compelled rigid land-management regimes and cultural protocols. Northern populations rely on 140 plant species for food (30 types of ground vegetables, 25 types of root vegetables, 50 different fruits) as well as for other materials (e.g., they harvest barks for beverages and flavourings). The people have developed protocols; for example, they harvest only those plants they really need, and they waste nothing. When gathering medicines, for instance, they make certain not to strip a tree of its bark. Resource management is widespread; for example, it is common to remove plants and animals to another region to ensure their survival.

Politics

The various (i.e., by region) Inuit groups shared certain political and economic characteristics. Most typically, small groups of extended families lived and worked together. In this harsh region the fundamental social law was the obligation to help one's kin. Kinship placed equal importance on both sides of the family (i.e., the mother's and the father's) and was acknowledged through marriage and formal trade relationships that could make the difference between life and death. Men of influence often headed family groups, organized trade, and led hunting groups and ceremonies. Whaling captains had the greatest prestige owing to their capacity to support their crews and thereby secure political influence. The responsibility for hunting, fishing, and building shelter fell to the men; the women cooked, dressed animal skins, and made clothing. Community ridicule was the most common means of social control, though in extreme cases—and only after lengthy deliberation—an offender might be socially ostracized or even put to death. There was an absence of communal legal structure, but people were taught that harming an individual in your community could have grave repercussions by provoking a blood feud.

Subarctic[32]

The Dene occupy the western Subarctic; the Cree, Métis, and Innu occupy the central and eastern Subarctic. The Subarctic encompasses treeless tundra, temperate rain forests (on the Northwest Coast), forested mountains (on the Plateau), grasslands (on the Plains), and woodlands (in the Northeast). Most of the Subarctic, however, is boreal forest consisting of black and white spruce and birch, aspen, pine, fir, poplar, alder, and willow. Caribou and moose are the most important regional resources; these provide meat, as well as hides, bones, and sinews, which are used to make clothing, tents, tools, and (in certain regions) skin boats. The consistent nature of the boreal forest and of Indigenous coping strategies has resulted in similar lifestyles among the various groups that inhabit this region.

Economics

The Subarctic is a fairly forgiving environment that can provide all that people require to survive comfortably. In most of its subregions, the people have needed to develop seasonal rounds—that is, regular territorial movements—in order to secure enough resources. The territory offers large stocks of fish, wild game, and plants. Lodges are built from birch trees, as are canoes for fishing and for shoreline hunting of deer and moose. Furbearing animals are trapped and traded. In the past, an Indigenous nation would often claim a transportation route, charging other nations the equivalent of a modern-day toll for the right to use it. This facilitated interregional communication and trade of items such as chokecherries, sassafras, sumac, hemlock, maple sugar, and Labrador tea were not universally available. Community technologies were adapted to different growing seasons. For example, the Iroquois developed 60 different varieties of beans. In the southern reaches of the Subarctic, various plants were used for food; plants were also used to make sunflower oil and ceremonial rattles. The people practised rotation agriculture and food redistribution.

Politics

This is perhaps the most difficult region to describe because of the diversity of nations and the sheer geographical expanse. This region extends 4500 kilometres from the Yukon River to the Labrador coast and from the Arctic Circle to the Canada–U.S. border. Nations ranging from Ojibwa to Métis to Cree and Innu occupy treeless tundra, temperate rain forest, grasslands, and woodlands. The complexity of governance structures in the Subarctic does not permit a detailed discussion. It can be said, though, that the theory of ecological context is well illustrated by the strong differences among the Subarctic nations' political economies. Even subtle ecological changes have had an impact on how Subarctic peoples have organized themselves.

Northeast[33]

At time of contact there were an estimated 40 nations in the Northeast, who had occupied the region for more than 10,000 years. Local nations included the Eastern and Western Abenaki, the Maliseet-Passamaquoddy, the Mi'kmaq, and the Beothuk. They lived in small villages numbering less than a few dozen houses alongside rivers and other bodies of water, which served their transportation and communication needs. Landscape variations led to distinct and changing settlement strategies and economic processes, as well as population growth and technological development. Rules for hunting and land clearing developed in response to this dynamic environment.

Economics

The economies of the Northeastern Indigenous nations were enormously diverse because of the abundance of accessible resources, which included large and small game animals and fish and fowl. These were supplemented by some farming. Men hunted deer, moose, elk, buffalo, caribou, sea mammals, and various birds; they also fished. The women and older children did the farming and cleaned and preserved produce, game, and fish. Children's participation was viewed as a way to teach them economic and social skills. Local stories and political and economic ideologies were conveyed to children as they interacted with more experienced community members. Trade was important and was facilitated by the extensive network of rivers and tributaries. Coastal communities made long journeys up and down the Atlantic coast. A popular trade item was tobacco, which in times of scarcity was traded for with neighbouring nations. Maple sugar was also popular, and stands of sugar trees were associated with specific families. Acid soils and a short growing season made agriculture difficult. However, wild rice was common and could be stored over long periods to help sustain large populations in case hunting was poor or the winter was long. Communities often moved regularly to follow specific plants such as birch. To the Beothuk, birch was vital—it was used to construct everything from canoes to storage pits and burial sites.

Politics

The variety of nations in the Northeast made for diverse languages, housing types, ceremonies, and kinship patterns. Tremendous emphasis was placed on political autonomy. The different nations were linked by kinship ties but were still independent and not easily coerced into collective action. Village leaders focused on the local populations and their ceremonial activities and internal affairs. One result was a fairly peaceful environment. Regular warfare was not known, though skirmishes sometimes occurred. This means that each group needs to be examined in its own highly specific context, even though all were similar in some ways.

The Plains[34]

Encompassing 1.6 million square kilometres, the northern plains were home to the Blackfoot, Cree, Assiniboine, and Ojibwa. The eastern plains are known for their oak-hickory forest; on the western plains, deciduous trees line the river valleys. Toward the west, arid conditions are the norm and the ground is covered with short grass, with few trees. Temperatures and rainfall vary considerably across the Plains. In pre-contact times their population density was low and nomadism was common. The people sustained themselves by hunting a few common grassland animals and by gathering plants.

Economics

The woodlands to the east and the foothills to the west were home to a variety of animal resources, including moose, elk, white- and black-tailed deer, rabbit, muskrat, and quail. Fish were caught in the rivers. Also available were wild rice, maple sugar, and wild vegetables such as wild turnips. Some corn was grown, and potatoes were quite common. Large stands of trees allowed for semipermanent villages. Cedar was used for posts, pine for ceremonial timbers. Wood was a valuable source of fuel, more so on the western plains, where there were fewer forests or woodlots. Resources grew scarcer toward the west, which meant that the people had to move constantly to find enough of them.

   The Indigenous nations of the central and western plains relied mainly on the buffalo. At one time there were 60 million buffalo in the region. Berries and edible roots were available, but it was the buffalo that provided food, clothing, housing, tools, and other necessities (see Figure 2-1). On the Plains, controlled fires were set periodically; this made the region safer to occupy and encouraged new growth. Large animal herds such as the buffalo and pronghorn helped in the latter process, by spreading seeds in their waste. The Indigenous people also hunted rabbit, deer, dog, bighorn sheep, antelope, wapiti, beaver, and bear. There was a short-lived experiment with agriculture around 1400.

Figure 2-1 Uses for the Buffalo

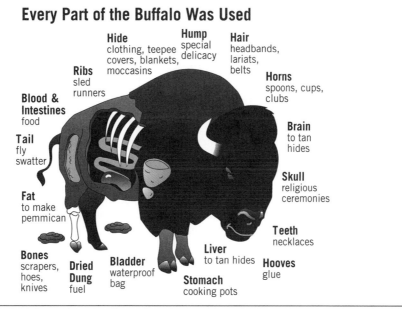

Every Part of the Buffalo Was Used

Hide
clothing, teepee
covers, blankets,
moccasins

Hump
special
delicacy

Hair
headbands,
lariats,
belts

Ribs
sled
runners

Horns
spoons, cups,
clubs

**Blood &
Intestines**
food

Brain
to tan
hides

Tail
fly
swatter

Skull
religious
ceremonies

Fat
to make
pemmican

Teeth
necklaces

Bones
scrapers,
hoes,
knives

**Dried
Dung**
fuel

Bladder
waterproof
bag

Liver
to tan hides

Hooves
glue

Stomach
cooking pots

Source: Arnold, Phyllis et al. *Second regard sur le Canada 6*. Edmonton: Les Editions Duval, 2001. p. 27.

Politics

Political models on the Plains were quite similar between nations, though unique compared to other regions. Small, politically autonomous bands developed their own governing processes. Such bands were often guided (but not ruled over) by a head chief, who likely was chosen through a hereditary process, and by a cluster of secondary chiefs, who achieved their status through their acts of generosity, diplomatic skills, and/or bravery in war. The various chiefs constituted an informal council that was responsible for appointing distinguished warriors to help maintain community order. Bands would govern themselves throughout the year, sometimes gathering for political councils, buffalo hunts, trade, or ceremonies. There was no overarching political structure, so when the bands gathered they camped in a circle with each band occupying its own section, thus expressing its political autonomy. Each band represented a large extended family and was headed by a chief who had been selected based on merit. Most often, merit was earned through generosity in taking care of an extended family. Chiefs did not have the authority to compel others to act, as individuality was valued.

"The Plains" is an all-encompassing label, yet it refers to a highly diverse and constantly changing region.

Among the Assiniboine, the band was the largest political unit. The Plains Ojibwa could trace their origins to the Ojibwa, Ottawa, and Huron communities of what is now Minnesota, Wisconsin, and Michigan. The westward-moving Ojibwa allied with the Cree and Assiniboine once they arrived on the Plains. The Ojibwa divided their time between the Plains and the eastern parklands. On the former, they lived in small bands; on the latter, they lived in larger villages. It is assumed that the Cree moved west in the early eighteenth century as a result of the negative impacts of the fur trade and diseases. By the 1730s many Cree were living on the prairies and fully immersed in the buffalo economy with the Blackfoot. Each Cree band was highly mobile, and membership was extremely fluid. A community chief attracted followers according to his war record, generosity, wealth, and hunting ability. A chief was not so much a political leader as a respected man; a band could have more than one. The leading men of each band formed a community council that was summoned when important decisions were required.

The Blackfoot, who included the Bloods, Peigan, and Blackfoot, were another highly mobile culture that depended heavily on the buffalo. The member nations of the Blackfoot Confederacy had once been small bands of roughly 30 people who claimed their own specific territories within the larger Blackfoot territory. Before they acquired horses in the mid-eighteenth century, the Blackfoot traversed their territory on foot. The horse's arrival ushered in efficient hunting techniques and the expansion of territorial claims. Blackfoot political culture centred on the band, each of which had its own recognized leaders. As with the Cree, Blackfoot leaders had well-established records. It was their task to maintain the community's political, economic, and social stability. Meeting regularly, the chiefs did their best to maintain an open dialogue.[35]

The Plateau[36]

Nestled between the Cascade Mountains and the Rockies, the Plateau region encompasses both forested mountains and desert. It has ten distinct subregions, each with its own topography and geology. It is rich in animal and plant resources. The people enjoy a well-balanced diet and plenty of materials for building homes, which means they can gather in large groups at one site for long periods. The climate swings from severe winters to extremely hot summers. Some of the Plateau has fertile soils, other sections are desert.

Economics

Economic adaptability was the hallmark of the Plateau region. Economies were mixed: salmon were fished on their return from the ocean, roots and berries were harvested, and game animals were hunted in the fall and winter. Furs and skins were used for clothing, blankets, and footwear. The Indigenous peoples developed regular patterns of movement as well as resource-management schemes. Fisheries management involved allowing a number of salmon to escape upstream before the fall fishing season. Then, over several weeks, fishing camps were established where salmon were harvested and processed. Over the same time, kinship ties and political relationships were renewed. Berry picking was regulated and did not begin until the chief granted permission. Deer-hunting fences were used. The long winters with their limited daylight were a time for sewing, making baskets, and carving utensils, tools, and weapons. Also during the winter, stories were told and ceremonial dances and feasts were held, such as the potlatch, during which property rights were transferred and confirmed and the community's wealth was distributed to serve political, social, religious, and economic purposes.

Politics

The Plateau's political culture was characterized by pacifism, egalitarianism, and communal ownership of land. Most often located in its own village or cluster of villages, each household was autonomous. Kinship ties were strong. However, village membership was highly fluid, making it possible to winter with one community and summer with another. Constant movement was also a result of political disagreements. The position of chief was inherited, but the chief's influence depended on community support. The women of the leading families also held high rank; along with the wives and daughters of the chiefs, they undertook leadership roles. Qualities associated with strong leaders included honesty, sound judgement, an even temperament, and good arbitration skills. A group of selected subchiefs held regular councils. Coercive measures such as imprisonment and corporal punishment were not used. Instead, authority was exercised through elaborate divisions of labour and power. When criminal activity occurred, the head chief presided before an open court, where witnesses testified and evidence was presented. If a murder occurred, gifts (as opposed to executing an individual) were often considered sufficient compensation. Punishments ranged from social ostracism to banishment from the community or from particular ceremonies.

Northwest Coast[37]

For eight millennia, the Northwest Coast and what is now the B.C. Interior supported Indigenous population concentrations greater than any other part of Canada. These various groups developed unique lifestyles, sophisticated art, and elaborate ceremonies. The Northwest Coast is a region of extremes that encompasses everything from coastal rain forests to boreal forests, from snow-capped mountains to inland deserts. The climate varies apace. Lakes, rivers, and mountain passes provide excellent travel routes. The various regions offer a tremendous variety of resources, which means that the people, if they wish, can settle in permanent villages for several decades before relocating. In this way, the region's resources have time to replenish themselves.

Economics

It was once common to see permanent villages of large red-cedar-plank houses that were home to hundreds of people representing dozens of families. Canoes stretching 20 metres were carved to assist with the primary economic pursuit: fishing. The various rivers and tributaries provided access to the Pacific and its tremendous game and fish preserves. Northwest Coast economies were mixed and included fishing, harvesting roots and berries, and hunting game animals in the fall and winter. Furs and skins were used for clothing, blankets, and footwear. Land and sea mammals and various bird species supplemented the huge quantities of fish—especially salmon. Fish was the basis of all foodstuffs, including fish oil for cooking, heating, and other purposes. Indeed, fish and other resources were so abundant that there was little need to manage stocks. During the long winters, people occupied themselves by sewing, making baskets, and carving utensils, tools, and weapons. It was also a time for feasting, telling stories, and conducting dances and other ceremonies.

Politics

Northwest Coast systems of governance focused on groups of related families who utilized a common territory. In the winter months, people lived in villages housing one or several bands. Chieftainships operated mainly at the level of large villages; always, a council of elders appointed the chief. Usually, the chief was the individual who could trace his lineage to the highest ranking ancestor. Chiefs were expected to care for the community by ensuring both the well-being of individuals and the formal recognition of rank and prestige. Every family in the community was ranked in much the same way as the chief, and their responsibilities assigned accordingly. Individual families claimed specific rights, which included the right to establish fishing and shellfish-gathering sites and to create dances and ceremonies specific to the family and region. Winter was an important time for socializing: this was when stories were recited, songs were sung, and dances and ceremonies were held. The region's villages were linked by a sense of common history and kinship, and they gathered at various times during the year to renew their political, economic, and social relations. Individual bands possessed varying levels of authority that reflected each chief's level of influence. Regional political processes were fluid and adaptable, and a long history of interactions encouraged leaders to consider broader political associations.

Toward an Iroquois (Haudenosaunee) Political Economy[38]

A focused re-commitment to traditional teachings is the only way to preserve what remains of Indigenous cultures and to recover the strength and integrity of Indigenous nations.

—Taiaiake Alfred (Mohawk)[39]

Studies of political economy tend to obscure how communities fuse ecologically specific political and economic philosophies into operational systems. This section offers an overview of the political economy of the Iroquois (Haudenosaunee) of southern Quebec and southwestern Ontario to show how political economy helps fuse philosophy and ideology with practice.

In historic times, five nations were regularly at war. They were the Onondaga (Onöñda'gega'), the Seneca (Onöndowága'), the Cayuga (Guyohkohnyo), the Oneida (Onyota'a:ka), and the Mohawk (Kanien'kehá:ka). Hearing of these events in Huron country, the Peacemaker carved a great canoe from granite and ventured into Haudenosaunee territory to meet with the leaders of the warring nations. After several failed attempts, the Peacemaker gathered the people together even though they remained skeptical of his self-professed powers. After much talk and negotiations, peace was struck among the various nations. A confederacy was formed known as the Iroquois League or the Haudenosaunee Confederacy. It was agreed that to maintain the peace, all weapons would be gathered and buried beneath a white pine, only to be unearthed when the five nations faced a common enemy. Importantly, the five nations would never use those weapons against one another. This was the heart of the Great Law, which was meant to guide political and social interactions among the five nations. That law also forbade unauthorized entry into homes, and guaranteed freedom of religion to ensure a balanced and stable mind and body. The goal in all this was to foster interaction and humane conduct through speech and thought so that equity and justice would be enjoyed by all peoples.

The Peacemaker likened the Confederacy to a longhouse: the sky was the roof, the earth its floor, and each nation was represented by a fire burning within. So that the five nations would remain at peace while forging strong bonds, the Peacemaker organized the various nations into nine clans: Turtle, Bear, Wolf, Heron, Hawk, Snipe, Beaver, Deer, and Eel. The goal was to create bonds of brotherhood so that people of different clans would view the other clans as kin and therefore family. Compelling individuals to marry outside their clan strengthened these bonds—to do otherwise would have been the equivalent of marrying one's sibling. The confederacy's civil authority was the Grand Council, a 50-seat governing body whose members were headmen selected by the clan mothers of the families that held hereditary political rights to office. Women representing the clans would meet under the leadership of a clan mother to select the Grand Council chiefs. The Grand Council was empowered to treat with foreign nations and to help resolve domestic disputes. The headmen's rights, duties, and qualifications were outlined to them with the understanding that they could be removed from office by the women after three warnings if they failed to perform adequately.

The confederacy was divided into houses occupied by the older brothers the Mohawks and Senecas, who organized as a house, and the younger brothers the Oneidas and Cayugas, who also organized as a house. Issues presented before the Grand Council were first considered by the older brothers, then by the younger brothers. This was equivalent to judicial review—that is, objections could be raised if rulings were considered inconsistent with the

Great Law. If the two sides failed to reach an agreement, the Onondagas were petitioned to cast the deciding vote. Thus the Onondagas served as the Firekeepers. If the brothers reached an agreement, the Onondagas were obliged to confirm the decision irrespective of their own views on the matter. The goal in all of this was to generate a unanimous decision, though the governance structure was designed to mediate issues when unanimity could not be attained. When a large majority favoured a proposal, a second vote was cast, at which time all dissenters were expected to confirm their solidarity with the majority. It must be pointed out that the people were regularly consulted and could halt a proposal at any time under the threat of community-initiated impeachment proceedings.

The Iroquois were stewards to the land base they occupied; but at the same time, they considered those territories to be their property. Property issues were the concern of women, and included the distribution of the common land base to the different clans. The land thus allocated was in turn allocated to different families and households. Most often the land would be redistributed annually, though clans could often request that a reallocation take place once the Clan Mothers' Council gathered. It was imperative that the land be properly cared for. Those who violated these codes were issued a warning by the Clan Mothers' Council. Further violations would result in the redistribution of their landholdings. Responsibility for the land extended to women taking responsibility for planting and cultivating the crops of corn, beans, and squash. Known as the Three Sisters, these three vegetables were the main source of food for the people of the confederacy. To ensure that all clans had access to some cultivable land while keeping animosities to a minimum, certain areas of land were always reserved for the clans' women. The women also engaged in physical labour in the fields, again taking responsibility for planting, farming, and harvesting the crops while also gathering food, raising the children, and maintaining the household.

Men participated in physical labour, though their work was restricted to hunting, trading, warfare, and the manufacture of goods required by the community. Working cooperatively, they organized the hunting parties needed to collect the number of animals needed to feed their communities, which often numbered several longhouses and more than 1,000 individuals. Large groups would organize fishing expeditions made up of dozens of canoes; sometimes, 1,000 fish were caught in one expedition. These food resources helped supplement crops and game animals. The captured game animals and fish were considered common property and accordingly were distributed by either a respected member of the hunting expedition or a community member. This is not to suggest that hunting and fishing expeditions were always cooperative efforts. Still, most members acknowledged that the Haudenosaunee economy operated much more efficiently when people chose to work together. Note well that the men were responsible for community protection; it was they who acted collectively during military actions.

Kinship bonds and the collective nature of economic productivity meant that there was no such thing as trade within the confederacy. But people sought out external trade partners, and the resulting networks permitted the exchange of surplus corn, beans, and squash for wampum (with eastern tribes) and pelts (with northern groups), as well as for other exotic items. It is noteworthy that the clans that established trade routes held exclusive trading rights; in other words, it was possible to establish trade monopolies. Except for this one opportunity for individual enterprise, the community-driven need to ensure balance and well-being took precedence. Within the confederacy, gift giving was the most important mechanism of exchange, based on the concept of reciprocity—that is, gifts were given in response to the demonstrated generosity of clans or neighbouring communities. It was expected that a gift or service of equal or superior quality would be returned as thanks.

Conclusion

For the Indians, land is not purchasable, but it can be shared. Land cannot be purchased because "all my relations" have interests in the land, as humans do.

—Leroy Little Bear (Blood)[40]

The centrality of land to Indigenous political and economic development cannot be understated. The land was more than simply a space to reside. It was the mother, the giver of all life, and it provided everything needed to survive. Relationships and interactions with the land led to the development of regionally unique forms of governance and political and economic ideologies. As the intellectual foundation of the Indigenous mind, the land—or specific pockets of land—became the vital reference point from which Indigenous nations could emerge. Besides hunting and gathering, Indigenous peoples developed intricate economies rooted in their extensive knowledge of agriculture, animal migration patterns, weather cycles, and trade with neighbouring communities. This fostered identity along with the political and economic strategies required to endure in a particular ecological context.

FURTHER READING

Barsh, Russel Lawrence. "The Nature and Spirit of North American Political Systems." *American Indian Quarterly* (Spring 1986): 181–98.

Boldt, Menno, and J. Anthony Long, "Tribal Traditions and European-Western Ideologies: The Dilemma of Canada's Native Indians." In *The Quest for Justice: Aboriginal Peoples and Aboriginal Rights,* ed. Menno Boldt and J. Anthony Long. Toronto: University of Toronto Press, 1985, pp. 333–46.

Cajete, Gregory. *Native Science: Natural Laws of Interdependence.* Santa Fe: Clear Light, 2000.

Ladner, Kiera L. "Governing Within an Ecological Context: Creating an AlterNative Understanding of Blackfoot Governance." *Studies in Political Economy* 70 (Spring 2003): 125–52.

Marule, Marie Smallface. "Traditional Indian Government: Of the People, By the People, For the People." In *Pathways to Self-Determination: Canadians and the Canadian State,* ed. Leroy Little Bear, Menno Boldt, and J. Anthony Long. Toronto: University of Toronto Press, 1984, pp. 36–45.

Weatherford, Jack. *Indian Givers: How the Indians of the Americas Transformed the World.* New York: Random House, 1988.

NOTES

1. Chief John Snow, *These Mountains Are Our Sacred Places: The Story of the Stoney People* (Calgary: Fifth House, 2005), pp. 8–9.

2. Vine Deloria, Jr., *Red Earth, White Lies: Native Americans and the Myth of Scientific Fact* (Golden: Fulcrum, 1997), p. 26.

3. *Thomas Hobbes discussing the natural state of mankind where men would be left to suffer should they fail to progress to more civilized status, in Leviathan, or the matter, forme, and power of a commonwealth, ecclesiasticall and civill* (1651).

4. Robert Williams, *The American Indian in Western Legal Thought: The Discourses of Conquest* (New York: Oxford University Press, 1990). See also Stuart Banner, *How the Indians Lost Their Land: Law and Power on the Frontier* (Cambridge, MA: Harvard University Press, 2005); and John C. Weaver, *The Great Land Rush and the Making of the Modern World, 1650–1900* (Kingston and Montreal: McGill–Queen's University Press, 2003).

5. Sakej Youngblood Henderson, "*Ayukpachi:* Empowering Aboriginal Thought," in *Reclaiming Indigenous Voice and Vision,* ed. Marie Battiste (Vancouver: UBC Press, 2000), pp. 248–78.

6. Clyde Kluckhohn, "The Philosophy of the Navajo Indians," in *Ideological Differences and World Order,* ed. F.S.C. Northrop (New Haven: Yale University Press, 1949), pp. 358–59.

7. The works Henderson specifically references are Roberto Unger, *Passion: An Essay on Personality* (New York: Free Press, 1984); and idem, *Social Theory: Its Situation and Task: A Critical Introduction to Politics, a Work in Constructive Social Theory* (Cambridge: Cambridge University Press, 1987).

8. Henderson, "*Ayukpachi.*"

9. F. David Peat, *Lighting the Seventh Fire: The Spiritual Ways, Healing, and Science of the Native American* (New York: Birch Land, 1994), p. 227.

10. Quoted by Leroy Little Bear, "Aboriginal Paradigms: Implications for Relationships to Land and Treaty Making," in *Advancing Aboriginal Claims: Visions/Strategies/Directions,* ed. Kerry Wilkins (Saskatoon: Purich, 2004), p. 30.

11. Vine Deloria, Jr., *God Is Red: A Native View of Religion* (Golden: Fulcrum, 1994), pp. 80–81.

12. Vine Deloria, Jr., "Philosophy and Tribal Peoples," in *American Indian Thought: Philosophical Essays,* ed. Anne Waters (Malden: Blackwell, 2004), p. 8.

13. Mark O. Dickerson and Thomas Flanagan, *Introduction to Government and Politics: A Conceptual Approach,* 3rd ed. (Toronto: Nelson Canada, 1990), pp. 17–18.

14. Thomas Flanagan, *First Nations? Second Thoughts* (Kingston and Montreal: McGill–Queen's University Press, 2000), p. 6.

15. Joshua Goldstein and Sandra Whitworth, *International Relations* (Toronto: Pearson Longman, 2005), pp. 23–24.

16. Kiera Ladner, "Governing Within an Ecological Context: Creating an AlterNative Understanding of Blackfoot Governance," *Studies in Political Economy* 70 (Spring 2003): 125–52.

17. Menno Boldt and J. Anthony Long, "Tribal Traditions and European–Western Political Ideologies," in *A Quest for Justice: Aboriginal Peoples and Aboriginal Rights,* ed. Menno Boldt and J. Anthony Long (Toronto: University of Toronto Press, 1988), p. 336.

18. Gregory Cajete, *Native Science: Natural Laws of Interdependence* (Santa Fe: Clear Light, 2000), p. 81.

19. Menno Boldt and J. Anthony Long, "Tribal Philosophies and the Canadian Charter of Rights and Freedoms," in *A Quest for Justice: Aboriginal Peoples and Aboriginal Rights,* ed. Menno Boldt and J. Anthony Long (Toronto: University of Toronto Press, 1988), p. 166.

20. Russel Lawrence Barsh, "The Nature and Spirit of North American Political Systems," *American Indian Quarterly* (Spring 1986): 181–98.

21. Boldt and Long, "Tribal Traditions and European–Western Political Ideologies," p. 336.

22. Barsh, "The Nature and Spirit of North American Political Systems."

23. Peter McFarlane, "Aboriginal Leadership," in *Visions of the Heart: Canadian Aboriginal Issues,* ed. David A. Long and Olive P. Dickason (Toronto: Harcourt Brace and Company Canada, 1996), p. 118.

24. See, generally, Douglas Hudson and Marianne Ignace, "The Plateau: A Regional Overview," in *Native Peoples: The Canadian Experience,* 3rd ed., ed. R. Bruce Morrison and C. Roderick Wilson (Don Mills: Oxford University Press, 2004), p. 347.

25. Quoted in Wanda Wuttunee, *Living Rhythms: Lessons in Aboriginal Economic Resilience and Vision* (Kingston and Montreal: McGill–Queen's University Press, 2004), p. 3.

26. Laura Peers, *The Ojibwa of Western Canada, 1780–1870* (Winnipeg: University of Manitoba Press, 1994); Arthur J. Ray, *Indians in the Fur Trade: Their Role as Trappers, Hunters, and Middlemen in the Lands Southwest of Hudson Bay, 1660–1870* (Toronto: University of Toronto Press, 1998).

27. Yale D. Belanger, "'The Region Teemed with Abundance': Interlake Saulteaux Concepts of Territory and Sovereignty," in *Proceedings of the 32nd Algonquian Conference,* ed. J. Nichols (Winnipeg: University of Manitoba Press, 2001), pp. 17–34.

28. Bruce G. Trigger, "Entertaining Strangers: North America in the Sixteenth Century," in *The Cambridge History of the Native Peoples of the Americas,* ed. Bruce G. Trigger and Wilcomb E. Washburn (Cambridge: Cambridge University Press, 1996), p. 329.

29. See, generally, Liz Bryan, *The Buffalo People: Prehistoric Archaeology on the Canadian Plains* (Edmonton: University of Alberta Press, 1991).

30. For a brief overview, see Hillary Stewart, *Indian Fishing: Early Methods on the Northwest Coast* (Seattle: University of Washington Press, 1977).

31. For the information contained in this section, see Renee Fossett, *In Order to Live Untroubled: Inuit of the Central Arctic, 1550–1940* (Winnipeg: University of Manitoba Press, 2001).

32. The information for this section can generally be found in Robert Brightman, *Grateful Prey: Rock Cree Human–Animal Relationships* (Berkeley: University of California Press, 1993); Marie Wadden, *Nitassinan: The Innu Struggle to Reclaim Their Homeland* (Vancouver: Douglas and McIntyre, 2001); Toby Morantz, *The White Man's Gonna Getcha: The Colonial Challenges to the Crees in Quebec* (Kingston and Montreal: McGill–Queen's University Press, 2002); Peter Kulchyski, *Like the Sound of a Drum: Aboriginal Cultural Politics in Denedeh and Nunavut* (Winnipeg: University of Manitoba Press, 2005); Kerry Abel, *Drum Songs: Glimpses of Dene History,* 2nd ed. (Kingston and Montreal: McGill–Queen's University Press, 2005); and Ken S. Coates, *Best Left as Indians: Native–White Relations in the Yukon Territory, 1840–1973* (Kingston and Montreal: McGill–Queen's University Press, 1991).

33. The information for this section can generally be found in Daniel N. Paul, *We Were Not the Savages: A Mi'kmaq Perspective on the Collision Between European and Native American Civilizations* (Halifax: Fernwood, 2000); Cornelius J. Jaenen, *The French Relationship with the Native People of New France and Acadia* (Ottawa: Indian and Northern Affairs Canada, 1984); James [Sakej] Youngblood Henderson, *The Mikmaw Concordat* (Halifax: Fernwood, 1997); Leslie F.S. Upton, *Micmacs and the Colonists, 1713–1867* (Vancouver: UBC Press, 1979); Denys Delage, *Bitter Feast: Amerindians and Europeans in Northeastern North America, 1600–1664* (Vancouver: UBC Press, 1993); Bruce Trigger, *The Children of Aataentsic: A History of the Huron People to 1660* (Kingston and Montreal: McGill–Queen's University Press, 1976); and William N. Fenton, *The Great Law and the Longhouse: A Political History of the Iroquois Confederacy* (Norman: University of Oklahoma Press, 1998).

34. The information for this section can generally be found in Ladner, "Governing Within an Ecological Context"; Mike Mountain Horse, *My People the Bloods* (Calgary: Glenbow Museum, 1979); Joseph F. Dion, *My Tribe the Crees* (Calgary: Glenbow Museum, 1979); John S. Milloy, *The Plains Cree: Trade, Diplomacy, and War, 1790–1870* (Winnipeg: University of Manitoba Press, 1988); Peers, *The Ojibwa of Western Canada;* Peter Douglas Elias, *The Dakota of the Canadian Northwest: Lessons for Survival* (Regina: Canadian Plains Research Centre, 2002); Snow, *These Mountains Are Our Sacred Places;* and Theodore Binnema, *Common and Contested Ground: A Human and Environmental History of the Northwestern Plains* (Toronto: University of Toronto Press, 2004).

35. Ibid.

36. The information for this section can generally be found in Rodney Frey, *Stories That Make the World: Oral Literature of the Indian Peoples of the Inland Northwest, as told by Lawrence Aripa, Tom Yellowtail, and Other Elders* (Norman: University of Oklahoma Press, 1995); Clifford Trafzer, ed., *Grandmother, Grandfather, and Old Wolf: Tamanwit Ku Sukat and Traditional Native American Narratives from the Columbia Plateau* (East Lansing: Michigan State University Press, 1998); Jacqueline Peterson, *Sacred Encounters: Father DeSmet and the Indians of the Rocky Mountains* (Norman: University of Oklahoma Press, 1993); James Teit, *The Salishan Tribes of the Western Plateau* (Lancaster and New York: Annual Report of the Bureau of American Ethnology, 1930); Franz Boas and Alexander Chamberlain, "Kutenai

Tales," Bureau of American Ethnology, Bulletin no. 49 (1918): 1–387; James Teit, "Traditions of the Lillooet Indians of British Columbia," *Journal of American Folk-Lore Society* 25 (1912): 287–371; Alvin Josephy, *The Nez Perce and the Opening of the Northwest* (Boston: Houghton Mifflin, 1965); Harry Robinson, *Native Power: In the Spirit of an Okanagan Storyteller,* comp. and ed. Wendy Wickwire (Seattle: University of Washington Press, 1992); James Teit, "The Shuswap," American Museum of Natural History 4, no. 7 (1909); James Teit, "The Thompson Indians of British Columbia," American Museum of Natural History 11, no. 4 (1900); and Robert J. Muckle, *The First Nations of British Columbia,* 2nd ed. (Vancouver: UBC Press, 2006).

37. The information for this section can generally be found in Wayne Suttles, *Handbook of North American Indians, Vol. 7: Northwest Coast* (Washington: Smithsonian Institution/U.S. GPO, 1990); Jay Miller, *The Tsimshian and Their Neighbours of the Northwest Coast* (Seattle: University of Washington Press, 1984); Ruth Kirk, *Wisdom of the Elders: Native Traditions on the Northwest Coast, the Nuu-chal-nulth, Southern Kwakiutl, and Nuxalk* (Vancouver: Douglas and McIntyre, 1988); Robert M. Galois, *Kwakwaka'wakw Settlements, 1775–1920: A Geographical Analysis and Gazeteer* (Vancouver: UBC Press, 1994); Alan D. MacMillan, *Since the Time of the Transformers: The Ancient Heritage of the Nuu-Chah-nult, Ditidaht, and Makah* (Vancouver: UBC Press, 1999); Wayne Suttles, *Coast Salish Essays* (Seattle: University of Washington Press, 1987); and Muckle, *The First Nations of British Columbia.*

38. The information for this section can generally be found in Fenton, *The Great Law and the Longhouse;* Matthew Dennis, *Cultivating a Landscape of Peace: Iroquois-European Encounters in Seventeenth-Century America* (New York: Oxford University Press, 1993); Gilles Havard, *The Great Peace of Montreal of 1701,* trans. Phyllis Aronoff and Howard Scott (Montreal and Kingston: McGill–Queen's University Press, 2001); Francis Jennings, *The Ambiguous Iroquois Empire: The Covenant Chain Confederation of Indian Tribes with English Colonies, from Its Beginnings to the Lancaster Treaty of 1744* (New York: Norton, 1984); Sally Weaver, "The Iroquois: The Consolidation of the Grand River Reserve in the Mid-Nineteenth Century, 1847–1875," in *Aboriginal Ontario: Historical Perspectives of the First Nations,* ed. Edward Rogers and Donald Smith (Toronto: Dundurn, 1994); Paul Williams, "The Chain" (LL.M. thesis, Osgoode Hall Law School, York University, 1982); Robert A. Williams, Jr., *Linking Arms Together: American Indian Treaty Visions of Law and Peace, 1600–1800* (New York: Routledge, 1997); Gerald F. Reid, *Kahnawa:ke: Factionalism, Traditionalism, and Nationalism in a Mohawk Community* (Lincoln: University of Nebraska Press, 2004); Anthony Wallace, *Death and Rebirth of the Seneca* (New York: Vintage, 1972); and Henry Lewis Morgan, *League of the Ho-de'-No—Sau-Nee Or Iroquois* (New York: Dodd, Mead, 1901).

39. Taiaiake Alfred, *Peace, Power, Righteousness: An Indigenous Manifesto* (Don Mills: Oxford University Press, 1999), p. 29.

40. Little Bear, "Aboriginal Paradigms," p. 37.

3

The Arts

Today, more and more Indians are becoming successful warriors and healers, storytellers and teachers in mainstream society, applying historical values to contemporary situations, proud and certain of their identity, successfully maintaining their culture as adapted to their new situation, and relying on the same spiritual resources that guided their ancestors.

—Jane Ash Poitras (Chipewayan)[1]

Examining the arts produced by Native people is an oft-neglected pursuit. Too often as a result, recognition of the historic and contemporary centrality of Native literature, the performing arts, and visual art is entirely missing from Native Studies textbooks. Most authors tend to emphasize popular fields of study—Aboriginal self-government, economic development, and First Nations, Métis, and Inuit history and policy—to the detriment of evaluating artistic traditions. Arguably this approach is popular because high-profile contemporary issues mix well with political science, Canadian history, and management courses. Also, these issues also tend to provide scholars with a substantial and more diverse base of literature to draw from for their analyses. In comparison, the arts are more abstract, and in the view of many authors they contribute little to broader discussions of sociopolitical and socioeconomic issues. Further scrutiny shows, however, that literature and the performing and visual arts fit neatly into an Indigenous intellectual tradition. Shaped around the spoken, written, and sung word, and artistic images and forms, Indigenous intellectual traditions catalogue history and philosophy in much the same way that songs, visual arts, and written histories offer a glimpse into the Canadian psyche.

Employing a variety of media in unique ways, Indigenous intellectual traditions embrace performance as a personal expression of self and community, as symbols of social identity, or simply as outlets for entertainment and artistic expression. They also demand that spectators analyze abstract ideas that are difficult to appreciate and even more complicated to interpret when trying to reconcile, say, the ideas contained in Thomas King's writings about the importance of Indigenous narrative traditions with the debates about, say, the modern Native self-government movement or Native health and well-being. As happens with all expressions of self and community, critiques are inevitably generated concerning the forces confronting Native communities. Thomson Highway (Cree)[2] has written about the scourge of alcoholism and AIDS, while Richard Wagamese (Ojibwa) has contextualized the forces of identity and modernity in a community seeking closer ties to tradition.[3] Buffy Saint Marie (Cree) and the Aboriginal War Party are musically divergent, but both infuse their music with political and social commentary. And artists such as Joe Tehawehron David (Mohawk) and Rebecca Belmore (Ojibwa) have used their work to discuss Native nationhood and the impact of colonialism on family, friends, and nations, and even themselves.

Too often, ideas and issues related to First Nations, Métis, and Inuit people in Canada are presented as politically charged, as if all dialogues emerging from Native communities are inherently political acts on the part of the author or artist. Alfred Young Man (Cree) has noted that volatile debates about the nature of Native art tend to confound even the most appreciative students.[4] Such debates are rooted in the forces of change in Native societies—since cultural authenticity is historically frozen, any change that injects modern beliefs and/or practices into traditional arts raises protests about corruption or contamination.[5] The dominant society perceives Native culture as best left alone. Yet music, dance, stories, and art are expressions of individuality and artistic talent created for entertainment. It follows that they *must* change if they are to remain culturally relevant for a world that is in constant flux.

Take the CBC's *Dead Dog Café Comedy Hour*, which ran from 1997 to 2000. Largely derived from Governor General's Award–winning author Tom King's *Green Grass, Running Water*, the show combined biting political critiques of contemporary politics with a nonthreatening setting.[6] It also merged the electronic media with a storytelling tradition—and quite effectively. The mythical Dead Dog Café was located in the fictional town of Blossom, Alberta. The program revolved around three "Indians" who were operating a radio station out of a café that served puppy dog stew. A regular segment of the show was Gracie's Authentic Traditional Aboriginal Recipes (including puppy stew, fried bologna, and Kraft Dinner). Another was her conversational Cree lessons, which taught students phrases such as "Please ask the chauffeur to bring the car around" and "How long will we be in court?" The show also offered an authentic "Indian" name generator that automatically created names like Stewart Coffee Armadillo and Rodney Frumpy Cigarette. The blend of satire and real-world situations was innovative—and is sorely missed. The show was cancelled, then revived as *Dead Dog in the City* for 26 episodes in 2006, then cancelled again.

This chapter is unique in that it treats performance arts, literature, and visual arts as core components of Native culture. These forms of cultural expression have always played an important role in contemporary First Nations, Métis, and Inuit communities, where they simultaneously anchor and reproduce contemporary Native culture while offering the reader/observer/listener a path to comprehending the varied responses to colonialism's effects. In keeping with this book's overarching theme of ecological context, it is worth noting the role played by imagination. David Newhouse (Onondaga) has recently written: "The imagination is a key part of being human. I would go so far as to say that without imagination, without the ability to imagine, we are not and cannot be human." More important, he suggests that the imagination furnishes humans with an "ability to create within our own minds and thoughts, a world that we want to exist, that distinguishes us from the rest of the universe. Imagination implies creativity, innovation, an ability to see what is not there." In this way it offers humans the "ability to see the spaces" and to "see underneath the ordinary reality of everyday life."[7]

The imagination, for Newhouse, is the basis of all thought. It informs not only the arts but also broader political, social, and economic discussions centring on Native communities. Being able to imagine new worlds to address identified weaknesses suggests that the ideas informing the Native arts are the same ideas as guide economic-development strategies and self-government debates, for example. From a Native perspective, then, in order to better comprehend politics and economics, one must develop an awareness of the arts. The same can be said of the arts: to grasp what is being presented requires improved understanding of the issues affecting Native communities.

Literature

Some of these stories are most exciting and so intensely interesting that I have seen children during their relation, whose tears would flow most plentifully, and their breasts heave with thoughts too big for utterance. Night after night for weeks have I sat and eagerly listened to these stories. The days following, the characters would haunt me at every step, and every moving leaf would seem to be a voice of a spirit.

—George Copway (Ojibwa)[8]

In 2003, University of Guelph English professor Thomas King was invited to deliver the prestigious Massey Lecture, which he titled *The Truth About Stories: A Native Narrative*. Exploring the importance of oral tradition, and asserting that the truth about stories is "that's what we are," this provocative quintet of essays unravels the essence of stories and their centrality to both individual and community identity.[9] These essay–lectures were originally performed before an audience. It is impossible to discern the audience's reaction; we can only know that reading the book elicits a different experience than had we witnessed King's presentation. Though his work is reduced to typescript on a page, this book is vital for a variety of reasons, not the least of which is King's attempt to reveal writing's power to convey complex topics to an audience seeking to better understand the complexities confronting First Nations, Métis, and Inuit people in Canada. Perhaps most important, King reminds the reader that stories reveal social and moral responsibilities—an underlying theme in a fascinating narrative laced with political overtones reflecting the concerns of Native people nationally. Weaving this subtle tapestry enables King to simultaneously expose Canadian "Indian" policy's negative influence without alienating the non-Native reader. This allows him also to tap into the intricacies of what it is to be Native in Canada while providing readers an untainted glimpse into what is for most an unfamiliar world.

Non-Written Literatures

Written Native literature today continues a tradition dating back 200 years—indeed, back far longer, when one adds oral traditions to the time line. Native literature is an umbrella term for contemporary works by Native authors from communities displaying distinctive means of expression, unique languages, specific philosophical ways of understanding the environment, and culturally specific methods of conveying stories. In its written format, Native literature both maintains and adds to a timeless literary tradition described by a host of academics as oral tradition. Contained within this oral tradition is oral literature, which can be defined as a body of work that a people has preserved and passed on to later generations. It encompasses various formats including stories, songs, rituals, prayers, speeches, histories, anecdotes, and jokes.

Words command great power. The Iroquois (Haudenosaunee) chose their spokespeople according to their oratorical gifts, which suggested their potential political and diplomatic skills. As discussed in Chapter 1, proper prayers helped ensure a successful hunt. Words were also central to promoting healing and spirituality, as well as for speaking the land. In this way words came to be acknowledged as powerful entities that could alter reality in both positive and negative ways. It was believed that to maintain balance, one must discipline one's thought and show proper respect with words in both thoughts and actions. After all, the observer helped create the reality—in other words, improper thoughts could result in imbalance and damage the community. A modern example of the need to respect words is found in Leslie Silko's *Ceremony*. Describing a witchery contest where the assembled participants attempt to outdo one another by telling the most outlandish and horrifying tale possible, one person tells a story about newcomers from another land who will pollute the land and water, introduce diseases, and kill Indigenous peoples out of fear. The other witches, fearing repercussions, ask the individual to rescind the story, only to be told, "It's already turned loose. It's already coming. It can't be turned back."[10] In this instance the words unleash the invasion of Europeans to North America, forever altering the ecological contexts of all Indigenous inhabitants.

Creations stories such as *The Making of Oldman River* are the cornerstone of Indigenous literary traditions. Of these stories there are three categories: (1) the earth diver story, in which, after three previous failed attempts, an animal dives below the recently flooded earth, returning with mud that will be used to once again establish a habitable world; (2) the emergence story, chronicling the movement of all life from an underground cave to the world as we know it; and (3) the two creators story, where the universe is created by two entities who then feud with each other, resulting in a flux-filled environment that is uniquely balanced owing to competing interests. Such stories reflect the origins of a community even though outsiders tend to describe them as myths or, in a standard sense, as fiction. Many stories currently in print should not have been recorded, and field researchers should not simply write down every story they hear without being given the proper permission. This issue confronts those academics who seek to integrate oral histories into their scholarly work.

Stories serve a variety of functions. For example, they provide moral guidelines for living a good life while teaching both the young and the old what is and what is not appropriate behaviour; they provide a sense of identity, "situating community members within their lineage and establishing their relationship with the rest of the world"; and they entertain (and the first two functions do not preclude the third).[11] It is problematic to remove stories from their ecological context, for that context provides the reader/listener with the environmental circumstances they need to know if they are to comprehend what they are reading/hearing.

The accompanying box reprints *The Making of Oldman River,* to demonstrate the importance of placing traditional stories in their ecological context. This version was published in 1985 by the Blackfoot elder Percy Bullchild, who was trying to convey as accurately as possible stories he had heard from the Blackfoot elders about the Creation. He was trying to correct inaccuracies in non-Native histories, which he described as "so false and smearing that it gets me mad."[12] In this trickster story, Napi, the Oldman, as usual is in a difficult situation.

THE MAKING OF OLDMAN RIVER (TRICKSTER STORY)

It was in the Rocky Mountains, as they are called today, in this particular river flows eastward from just south of Franks Slide in the Province of Alberta Canada.

In those early days, a small group of the people would have some sort of trouble among the large camp of people. These small groups, not wanting trouble, would then leave the main camp to go far in another area where they might find a good place to hunt and live for the time being.

This small group of people left the main camp to go find themselves a good hunting area because of a little trouble are rising between them and another clan. This was before the Oldman River came to be, many hundreds of years ago, and this group camped right out in the mountains just south of Frank's Slide (it wasn't a slide then). The camp consisted of about six or seven tipis and only a handful of people. Napi was among them with his sister.

For many happy days this group of people lived happily in those foothills of the Rockies. They hunted each day, everything was plentiful here. The root food, the smaller game of the mountains, many fowls that were edible. They were a happy bunch of people.

The small group and been there for several months, and there were only very few grown boys and girls among them. In fact, there was only Napi as a very young man and there were only about four or five girls, including his sister. These were the teenagers of the camp, and they were in the age to know love with the opposite sex. But with only one young man and five girls, this was a problem for them.

Being no other young men around, the four girls besides Napi's sister began to make plans who would be the first one to get Napi. Napi's sister overheard this and she made her own plans, but she didn't let the other girls in on her plans.

Before the other girls got to Napi, she must put her plans into action. The only way she knew how to do it was to work at nights when he was just so dark and nothing could be seen.

That very night, Napi sister waited until she knew everyone must be asleep. She got up out of her bed and went sneaking into her brother's bed. She woke him up without talking, only hand language to make him understand that she was crawling in bed with him. Napi knew the other girls were after him, and he took it for granted this as one of those other girls. He never once thought it was his own sister that came crawling in bed with him.

It was well toward morning when the girl left Napi's bed, but it was still very dark, nothing could be seen yet. So she was safe.

From then on Napi had company almost every night, only he didn't know who his secret lover was. Thinking it was one of the other girls, Napi would flirt with them all. For several months this went on.

One day when Napi was walking around in the forest, he began to think about who this secret lover of his could be. The more he thought about her, the more he decided to find out somehow. Right away, he began to make a plan. After many plans, Napi finally decided on one good plan. It would take several days of hard work, but he must do it to find out who this girl was.

Whenever the hunters—and Napi was one of them—brought in a big load of fresh meat, all of the women and the girls and children would go down to a nearby lake and wash off the meat and the entrails. It was one of these days that Napi would sneak away from the group and go to his tipi to work on his plan. It took several days like this to complete what he was doing.

Directly under his bed he dug a pit, a deep one that no one could get out of without the help from someone above, on the surface. Napi hid all the telltale dirt in the nearby trees, and whenever the group would come, Napi would fix his bed over this pit and no one was the wiser. Rigged with a rawhide rope trip, he could just pull a little on this rawhide rope and the bed would tip into the deep pit. Everything was ready to catch this secret lover of his.

Napi wasn't one to pull things off. That very night he had the chance to put his trap into action, Not very long after everyone had gone to bed, that secret lover came crawling in bed with Napi again. Through the night they laid there making love. The girl must've had a way to know when it was getting towards morning; she made motions with her hands on Napi's hands to let him know she was leaving. There never were any words from this girl. Napi would talk to her in a very low whisper so no one could hear, but she only answered with her hand language. She was starting to get out of Napi's bed when Napi tripped the trap and down into the pit they both fell. There was no way out for the girl, she had to stay put.

Slowly daylight came, and as it got lighter the girl tried to hide herself with a buffalo robe. Napi let her be until it was light enough to see all over. The girl had the buffalo robe over her, but Napi wanted to know who she was. Slowly he pulled the robe off of her head, to his biggest surprise, he seen the face and body of his sister. He couldn't get mad at her, but he just felt so very cheap. The girl too felt it was so cheap to be with her own brother, making love with each other all this time. Both felt so low, cheap, and dirty that, without knowing it, both were urinating as they stood there gazing at each other.

They urinated and urinated. The pit filled up and the urination began to run down the low spots, and the two still urinated. The urination began to run first as a brook, then a creek, and finally into a river, which channeled down through southern Alberta and became known as the Oldman River, or as the Natives know it, Napi's River.

This was their punishment for knowing each other, Napi and his sister. And the Oldman River is there to remember that a sister and a brother shouldn't get together.

Source: Pages 171–173 from *THE SUN CAME DOWN* by PERCY BULLCHILD. Copyright © 1985 by Percy Bullchild. Reprinted by permission of HarperCollins Publishers.

Perhaps some readers will read this story as exemplifying a dysfunctional society; or some may come away thinking that the Blackfoot regularly practised incest. Neither conclusion could be further from the truth. Yes, the story contains an important lesson about interfamily sexual relations—a moral that, indeed, is found in all the world's cultures. Remember here that to achieve its goals, the trickster repeatedly violates accepted rules of human interaction while fooling those with whom it comes into contact. Remember, too, that tricksters are fallible and often fall prey to their own desires. This helps explain the story's vivid and potentially disturbing portrayal of events. The point is, it is vital to educate children about how to behave properly, and this story does so. Stories are also important renewal mechanisms in the sense that they instruct and remind adults about how to respond most effectively to various situations. Besides warning against vanity, deception, naiveté, and lack of forethought, the tale asserts Blackfoot sovereignty, demarcating the nation's boundaries and guiding individuals to an important point about Creation. Running through the heart of Blackfoot territory is the Oldman River, which is considered sacred and an identifying territorial feature. Thus, seeing the river reminds people they are in their territory, reminds them as well of acceptable social norms, and forever connects the Blackfoot to Creation.

In the beginning, each Indigenous nation had its own unique oral tradition, one that reflected the ecological context that led to the emergence of its own regionally distinctive history and socioeconomic and sociopolitical processes. Each nation also developed its own values and customs, which were embedded in its literary tradition in the form of multiple narratives that presented the nation's understanding of the surrounding world. When these stories are told outside the context of the literary tradition, they often make little sense. Inconsistencies in logic and presentation can baffle and confuse even the most interested reader or listener. The literary tradition of each Indigenous nation tells that nation's story from early times to the present, which suggests that to understand the essence of a given community, an individual must hear all of its stories in the proper context. This often means travelling to specific sites or waiting for hours if not days until a storyteller is ready to speak. From a Native perspective, knowledge is respected and is never provided in a nonchalant manner. There is also an expectation that each listener will engage in the proper protocols before accepting what is viewed as a powerful gift. Some stories are considered to be so powerful that they are not told in public; or they are deemed the property of specific families or clans and as such are told only to specific audiences.

Besides passing down information from generation to generation, storytelling as an artistic tradition helps enhance cultural identity. *The Making of Oldman River* was not originally presented in a written format. Rather, it is one of a corpus of legends and Creation stories, part of an oral literature that provides individual and collective guidance and that catalogues a community's history and social and moral codes. Stories are so vital to a community's survival and continuation that many Native peoples extend them the reverence reserved for powerful beings. Storytellers, then, have an important role: they must convey the tales with sufficient authority that their power is respected, while expressing the emotion and authority required to draw in young audiences. This latter point is important, for not all stories are appropriate to all ages. Also, the repetitive nature of storytelling may bore younger audiences, so it is vital to change how stories are told to keep the audience interested, since each story sets the stage for the next, and over time the stories became increasingly detailed. It is the storyteller's responsibility to gauge the audience and determine how best to get the message across while compelling the audience to become intellectually active and disciplined listeners. Choosing a proper site for telling stories is fundamental, as many tales speak about the territory, serving as interactive history lessons that delineate the region's ceremonial and social properties.

Written Literatures

The stories discussed above have provided the foundations for modern Native authors. Contact with Europeans led to changes in traditional themes. It also introduced the written word, which inevitably led to the first Native-penned writings. Beginning with the late eighteenth-century temperance lectures by the Mohegan Reverend Samson Occum of Connecticut,[13] early Native writings in Canada tended to be produced by individuals who happened to be successful missionaries. Demonstrating an impressive ability to craft detailed regional and community-based histories, many also wrote culturally specific sermons in an attempt to provide political leadership to their communities. Many took it a step further. In Ontario, for instance, Peter Jones wrote a political constitution for his community that integrated colonial and Native customary law.[14] Most of these early writers happened to be from various Ojibwa communities in Ontario and around the Great Lakes. They included Peter Jones the Elder and his son, George Copway, George Henry, Peter Jacobs, and Allen Salt. Between 1850 and the First World War, writers from various communities emerged, the most famous of whom was Pauline Johnson (Mohawk). Johnson, born in 1861 on the Six Nations Reserve nearby Brantford, Ontario, was a critically acclaimed poet who celebrated her heritage and injected a sense of nationalism into her work. She was at her most popular in the 1890s and early 1900s, when she embarked on speaking tours across Canada, the United States, and Britain, dressing for her performances as an "Indian princess."[15]

Pauline Johnson

The Song My Paddle Sings

E. PAULINE JOHNSON

I stow the sail, unship the mast:

I wooed you long but my wooing's past;

My paddle will lull you into rest.

O! drowsy wind of the drowsy west,

Sleep, sleep,

By your mountain steep,

Or down where the prairie grasses sweep!

Now fold in slumber your laggard wings,

For soft is the song my paddle sings.

During these same years, Native writers evolved from regional historians and preachers into journalists, political pundits, and poets. As Native literacy levels improved, they also became more influential. But though Canadians had quickly expressed an interest in Native writers, the fad had subsided somewhat by the end of the nineteenth century. Native individuals continued to write, but, as in the case of Andy Paull (Squamish), their work was often confined to newsprint.[16] The few books produced by Native writers in Canada tended to be life histories or collections of stories; very few community histories were produced, and a literature base was slow to develop. During the mid-1900s it became popular to write about Indians, and a number of non-Native authors came forward to pen short stories or brief biographies about their "Indian" subjects. Rarely did this involve or include as active participants the people being written about. In the 1940s a number of Native-run newspapers appeared in response to the grassroots demand for a Native perspective, which mainstream newspapers were not providing (for more on this, see Chapter 13).[17] During the 1960s a handful of papers emerged that provided a national political voice for Native people. Those years also produced a number of activists, and people like Duke Redbird (Métis), Howard Adams (Métis), Willie Dunn (Mi'kmaq), and Alanis Obomsawin (Abenaki) went on to become prominent writers, musicians/songwriters/performers, and screenwriters and filmmakers.

The late 1960s proved to be an important time in the evolution of Native literature in both Canada and the United States. The 1968 release of N. Scott Momaday's (Kiowa) Pulitzer Prize–winning *House Made of Dawn*[18] opened the door to a host of Native writers, whose work led to what has been described as the Native literary renaissance, a three-decade period during which hundreds of Native authors produced thousands of titles. In Canada the assortment of writing produced by Native writers was remarkable. Dominated initially by nonfiction accounts of daily life in Canada, this work was dismissed as protest literature.

Harold Cardinal (Cree),[19] George Manuel (Shuswap),[20] and Howard Adams (Métis)[21] produced scathing critiques of Canadian "Indian" policy and its lingering effects on Native communities, demanding immediate changes. Later memoirs by Peter Erasmus (Cree-Danish),[22] John Tetso (Dene Tha),[23] and Tom Boulanger (Ojibwa)[24] offered firsthand albeit at times folksy observations of life in Native communities. And previously published or finished-but-not-yet-published manuscripts were finally made available to the reading public. Political veterans like Mike Mountain Horse (Blood)[25] and Joseph Dion (Cree)[26] captured the imagination of readers by drawing them into a period of history that non-Native readers often considered long past.

By the 1980s, Native writers had made their mark both nationally and internationally and had moved forward from historical/political nonfiction to become novelists and poets, playwrights and screenwriters, as well as humorists and newspaper columnists. A cadre of female writers emerged to tell their stories, including Maria Campbell (Métis),[27] Lee Maracle (Métis),[28] Ruby Slipperjack (Ojibwa),[29] Jeanette Armstrong (Okanagan),[30] and Beth Brant (Bay of Quinte Mohawk).[31] Not unlike Cardinal and Adams, for example, these novelists and essayists incorporated autobiographical elements to help readers make sense of Native politics, identity, colonization, and gender discrimination, as well as to celebrate the resilience of Native culture generally and Native women in particular. They were providing a voice to the specific lived experiences of specific Indigenous peoples.[32]

By the 1980s, Native playwrights were also becoming well known. By then, a number of Native theatre companies and theatre schools were able to boast impressive complements of Native actors to perform their works. Thomson Highway (Cree),[33] Daniel David Moses (Delaware-Tuscarora),[34] and Marie Clements (Métis)[35] have written critically acclaimed plays that have been produced outside Native communities—indeed, across the country. Drew Hayden Taylor (Ojibwa) from Curve Lake First Nation nearby Peterborough, Ontario, may well be the most widely produced Native playwright in the world, with 60 mountings of his work, 8 published scripts, and 6 published books of essays, articles, and short stories.[36] Before focusing specifically on Native issues, he was a screenwriter for *The Beachcombers* and *Street Legal*.

This is a necessarily limited overview of Native literature in Canada. Today we see Native-penned novels and screenplays published worldwide, a phenomenon traceable back to eighteenth-century readers' desire for "Indian" biographies. Drawing from a timeless literary tradition, many Native writers have always challenged readers by suggesting that there is more to a story than just words on paper. Indeed, stories merge the storyteller with the story itself and with the audience, and all three with history. As readers and listeners we bring our own life experiences to the story; this requires an act of interpretation, which makes it incumbent on readers to familiarize themselves with the writer's culture to better understand the lesson to be drawn. Similarities and differences with other cultures abound; thus writers try to take the world of the text, the facts, and the world of experience and background and use them to establish a dialogue between objective and subjective reality. At the same time, history cannot be separated out, for history is a blending of the past with personal experience. A broader cultural world exists beyond the written word, and arguably this is where two worlds are ultimately exposed.

Performing Arts

I can sing my land. Can you? The songs of the land are in our languages.

—Elder, quoted in Paul Williams[37]

Performance in North American Indigenous cultures has always taken various forms, including dancing, singing, acting, and historical re-enactments. Performance has always served both sacred and secular purposes, in both public presentations and in spiritual ceremonies held outside the gaze of curious onlookers. In much the same way, stories have been used to catalogue important events and to maintain a sense of tribal history, thereby providing a moral base for the following generations. Indigenous peoples have highly ordered cultures in which structures of meaning emerge from an ecological context that informs the community's sociopolitical and socioeconomic beliefs. These world views are often expressed in the form of dance and song.

Music was formally integrated into all aspects of Indigenous cultures and was an important teaching tool. Music had important ceremonial functions, but it was also for entertainment. In sum, it was an important artistic and religious medium available to all community members. Every North American Indigenous nation had what could be described as its own musical tradition, which included songs specific to local ceremonies and social values. Today, music is considered a readily available, mass-produced commodity for mass consumption, but this was not always so. For Indigenous people, songs were animate beings, acknowledged as gifts of the Creator. Specialized protocols were developed as signs of respect, which meant that songs were often part of particular ceremonies and had to be sung by particular individuals. Singing songs without permission might incur the community's wrath, for songs confirmed and helped maintain relationships with spirit helpers. Songs, like stories, are but one component of a larger musical and spiritual canon—albeit an inseparable one.

Indigenous communities had "specialist" members who were responsible for maintaining ceremonial and religious songs and the musical instruments on which they were played. Still other community members were master musicians and singers, whose gifts were greatly respected. The voice was the most important instrument; when combined in singing groups, those voices could be layered to create complex melodies and harmonies. Drummers often accompanied singers. At one time, only hand-held drums were used; these have since been augmented by large drums around which the drummers and singers perform in a circle. Adding to the texture of the music were rattles and scraping instruments. Songs vary by region as do vocal styles, rhythms, and metres, all of which are related to the stories of Creation and important events that have taken place in an ecological context. The rhythm of a region is captured in these songs, making it possible to discern from the beat where a drum group is from even before the singing begins. Since songs are based on observances of nature, the songs performed by a drum group from the southern prairies will sound quite different from the songs performed by drummers from the Arctic. As the rhythms and stories from each ecological context differ, so too does the music.

In recent years Native music has expanded beyond the confines of Native communities' celebrations. The reasons why vary, but many relate to new recording techniques, the flowering of reserve and community radio stations, speciality programming on the CBC, and the Aboriginal Peoples Television Network (APTN). The result has been increased visibility for Native singers, more and more of whom have been breaking into the mainstream pop charts. The list of these performers is long, and spans both decades and genres. Examples include the roots music of Robbie Robertson from The Band, the blues of George Leach, the country of Shane Yellowbird, and the pop songs of Susan Aglukark. Also, many traditional singers are recording and distributing their music while touring in Native and non-Native communities nationally and internationally. Recognizing these trends, the Juno Awards—Canada's music awards—in 1994 established the Aboriginal Recording of the Year category. In 2001 the Grammy Awards in the United States followed suit, creating the Best Native American Music Album.

Music as a performing tradition can exist on its own, unlike dance, which usually requires music to be effective. That said, music is most powerful when accompanied by dancers.

Susan Aglukark

Traditional Native dances are usually group events; there are few solo dances. The complexity of Indigenous dances does not permit an extensive discussion; suffice to say that some dances are multipart, with a lead dancer coordinating the group. Like songs, dances are closely associated with ceremonies of renewal and healing. Some are celebratory and are performed after a great military victory or a successful hunt, for example. For non-Native Canadians, dance is perhaps the most recognizable aspect of Native culture. As Chapter 5 will discuss, it is interesting that what is today viewed as culturally significant was once outlawed. Obviously, this has changed; today, tourist brochures from Alberta and Saskatchewan show photographs of Native dancers adorned in ceremonial outfits.

More and more non-Native people are attending powwows, which offer a diversity of dancers and singing groups. An example is the Canadian Aboriginal Festival, held at the Rogers Centre in Toronto. At these exhibitions, more than 1,000 North American dancers perform traditional dances for non-Native spectators, while providing an education in the centrality of dancing to Indigenous traditions both religious and secular. For Native people, dance fuses social expression with respect for the ecological context. Dance, for them, is an adaptable medium in a world of constant flux—that is, a manifestation of ongoing Creation.

During the time of first contact, government officials quickly grasped the importance of dances and songs to Native ceremonies. Both were soon banned.[38] For the sake of retaining them, traditional songs and dances were often performed during Christian holidays and observances such as Christmas and Easter. To onlookers, it looked as if Native people were forsaking traditional ways and adopting European culture and beliefs. Later on, songs and dances would be performed at powwows, rather innocuous events to which officials paid little attention. "Powwow" is derived from the Algonquian word *pau wau*, meaning "a gathering of medicine men and spiritual leaders in a curing ceremony." The powwow soon became a social celebration involving feasts, arts and crafts, singing, and dancing.[39] These relaxed gatherings emerged as a means of bringing family and friends together to renew relationships; they were also a chance to sing the songs and dance the dances outlawed by the Canadian government.

At one time, the powwow was the most effective way of bringing Native arts to the masses, be they Native or non-Native. Since then, filmmaking and television have become important media for Native artists. Native people have long been involved in film, most often as extras or bit players in Westerns; rarely would you find a Native actor playing the lead or a character other than an "Indian." Between 1971 and 1991 the only two Canadian actors nominated for an Academy Award were Native: Chief Dan George for his role in *Little Big Man*, costarring Dustin Hoffman; and Graham Greene for his role as Kicking Bird in the Kevin Costner epic *Dances With Wolves*. In a perverse twist, several members of the academy opposed Dan George's nomination on the basis that awarding a Native person an Oscar for playing one of his own was an unfair advantage. Canadian television has also embraced Native productions, as evidenced by *North of 60*, which ran as a series from 1992 to 1998 and also generated five made-for-TV movies between 1999 and 2005; and the comedy *The Rez*, which ran for two seasons until 1997. There have been others.[40] The two shows mentioned launched the careers of many Native actors. After catching his break on *North of 60*, Adam Beach (Ojibwa) landed roles in the Hollywood films *Smoke Signals* (1998), *Windtalkers* (2002), and *Flags of Our Fathers* (2006) before joining the cast of *Law and Order: SVU*.

There is also an impressive tradition of Native documentary and popular filmmakers. Zacharias Kunuk's (Inuit) *Atanarjuat: The Fast Runner* won the Camera d'Or for Best First Feature at the 2001 Cannes Film Festival, along with six Genie awards in Canada, including those for Best Picture and Best Director. Raised on the land in the Northwest Territories, Kunuk has been a filmmaker and video artist for more than 20 years, creating along the

Alanis Obomsawin (© National Film Board of Canada. All rights reserved.)

way several short documentary works and a 13-part television series. He also established the Inuit Broadcasting Corporation in 1983, producing original programming, much of it in Inuktitut; and he cofounded Igoolik Isuma Productions in 1991. *Atanarjuat* is the first feature film to be written and acted entirely in Inuktitut; it retells an ancient Inuit story of how a community cursed by rivalries and intercommunity factionalism was healed after overcoming violent dissention.[41]

But it was Alanis Obomsawin's (Abenaki) path-breaking work that exposed Native filmmakers to Canadians and the international community. Obomsawin started her career with the National Film Board in 1967. Perhaps her best known work is *Kahnesatake: 270 Years of Resistance* (1993), which documents the Oka standoff of the summer of 1990 and is innovative in its presentation—specifically, in its presentation of Mohawk perspectives as she captured them on film during her time in the compound. Obomsawin's personal fight against discrimination and injustice against Native people guides how she interprets events. An Officer of the Order of Canada and a Governor General's Award winner, Obomsawin has produced more than 30 films documenting Native issues (see "Filmography" on the following page).[42]

Many Native filmmakers have successfully used the documentary genre to expose systemic issues confronting Native peoples. Take for example Drew Hayden Taylor's *Redskins, Tricksters, and Puppy Dog Stew*. Combining documentary filmmaking with comedy, Taylor explored this question—"What exactly is Native humour?"—calling on a number of Native individuals working in the field of humour and comedy. Incorporating terrifically candid moments, and exposing the dark side of Native–non-Native interactions, the film shows that Native humour is both a coping mechanism and an extension of the Native tradition of the trickster. For example, Tom King in his interview for the film concluded that "those things that hurt in life, those things that continue to hurt about being Native in North America, I can handle those things through humour. I can't handle those through anger because, if I get angry about something, it just gets away from me. It just consumes me. I've got to keep coming back to humour as my sort of safe position. And I think I can make more of an impact."[43]

The politically charged humour of Dave McLeod, presented at an evening devoted to Native comedy that opened the 2004 Winnipeg Comedy Festival, is an excellent case in point: "Yesterday I went to buy a crayon for my nephew's birthday. But what is the one colour you won't find anymore? Indian Red. That ain't an accident, that ain't a coincidence—that's calculated Crayola genocide."[44] Humour can make non-Native audiences uncomfortable, but it is also an excellent forum for presenting a Native perspective detailing in a minimally confrontational way the impact of centuries of colonization.

Visual Arts

I believe there is something valid called Native art. Although Native art might not be the best way to describe our subject, it is, nevertheless, the only way we can describe it just now. I don't so much see Native art as being in opposition to anything, but rather, that it just is.

—Alfred Young Man (Cree)[45]

Echoing Young Man's words, Anna Lee Walters exclaims: "No word exists in the hundreds of Native American languages that comes close to our definition of art." This forces us to ask: What exactly is Native art? Walters suggests as our starting point the belief that "Indians did not set out to create art for its own sake. In traditional Indian thinking, there is no separation between art and life or between what is beautiful and what is functional."[46] Native peoples did not separate art into secular and sacred, though some art was indeed considered more spiritual. Even those works produced for daily use carried spiritual meaning if they were made in the proper way and from the proper materials. Both were vital to the production of useful products such as protective shields, which were power objects and could literally protect a warrior from harm during battle. A Blackfoot man would advertise his bravery in warfare by painting the story of his exploits on his tipi or on the buffalo robe he wore. As with the performing arts and literary traditions, Native art has deep roots and is still used for a multitude of reasons, from addressing political and social issues to expressing one's culture to simply producing aesthetic pleasure.

"Native art" until recently was an umbrella term coined by non-Native people to describe a variety of forms of material culture produced by North America's Indigenous people. These arts and crafts, as they are colloquially known, have over time ended up in non-Native art collections. And some items may not be art—that determination is in many ways up to the manufacturer, who may or may not be alive, and if alive, is rarely consulted. One critic has described the market for Native art as trafficking in the primitive. What is often lost in all this is the difference between material culture and works of art. The term "primitive" implies that primitive cultures cannot produce art, for that would mean they have an intellectual tradition. Rather, it is concluded, whatever is produced must have a utilitarian function in addition to an aesthetic quality. It follows that everything produced by Indigenous peoples is art. Absent from this logic is the recognition of a Native intellectual tradition that has always embraced art as a means to express culture, thereby revealing the influence of the ecological context.

Native art reflects the environment even while expressing and illuminating social structures and a world view. For thousands of years the Tlingit, Haida, Kwakiutl, and other peoples of the Northwest Coast and the Plateau utilized readily available cedar to craft totem poles, masks, dance rattles, storage boxes, and feasting bowls. The cedar's branches, bark, and roots were flexible and were used to make woven items such as capes, hats, bags, baskets, and mats. The relative abundance of natural resources meant that communities could stay in one place for longer periods and spend less time travelling throughout their territories in search of resources. This meant they had more leisure time to make art. The highly mobile Plains nations had less time for such pursuits. Their art had to be portable, for they had no means to transport bulky materials. Small-scale works included painted shields as well as garments decorated with paint, beads, quills, hair, feathers, and fur. Also, tipis were adorned with images that conveyed stories telling visitors about the residents they would soon be meeting.

The buffalo was to the Plains nations what cedar was to their neighbours in the west. Hides were used to make clothing and shelter; sinews were used to sew items together; horns were used to make jewellery and utensils. Stone was another popular medium in Indigenous traditions. In regions lacking abundant materials, the people relied on caribou, polar bear, salmon, walrus, whale, and seal for art-making materials. Soapstone and copper were prized media for which there was a brisk trade. Many Inuit sculptures ended up in the Nordic countries long before the Europeans founded their colonies along the east coast and the St. Lawrence River in the late sixteenth century.

The material itself reflects the importance of land to the artistic endeavour: if land and culture are one, then art and culture must be fixed. Each Indigenous society's unique understandings of what art represents are embedded in culturally distinct philosophies that have developed in specific ecological contexts. This cultural variability makes it difficult to speak authoritatively about a North American Indigenous artistic tradition in the same way one would discuss neoclassicism, romanticism, realism, impressionism, and symbolism, for instance. Native art has a sense of place that is central to a sense of identity. Native cultures have intimate knowledge of the surrounding environment and its ceremonial sites, places of power, and historical significance, which suggests that Native art, much like Native literature, is an expression of nationalism and by association an expression of sovereignty.

This should not be viewed as an attempt to frame art according to culture area—a time-tested and "anthropologist-friendly" approach to categorization—for neighbouring communities may in fact have unique artistic traditions owing to their own specific social and political orientations. The Plains Cree and Ojibwa are neighbours with similar approaches to art production, yet they are quite different with regard to the types of art they fashion and their choices of media. Aesthetic here is being tied directly to the environment; variables are being merged in ways that are impossible to pinpoint.

Take the work of the late Norval Morrisseau as an example. In 2006 the National Gallery of Canada organized a retrospective of his work—the first time ever that the gallery dedicated a solo exhibition to a Native artist. Morrisseau was born in 1932 on the Sand Point First Nation near Thunder Bay. While studying Creation stories as a young boy he was stricken with tuberculosis and was not expected to live. Following a renaming ceremony during which he was bestowed the name Copper Thunderbird, his grandfather gave him permission to put on canvas his people's stories. Morrisseau helped found the Woodland school of art, which has been described as legend or medicine painting. His work translates Ojibwa beliefs onto canvas for both Natives and non-Natives. His style is unique and quickly identifiable: he uses X-ray anatomy, with spirit power lines radiating from the spines of animals from a ball of radiant spirit power. Originally found on birchbark scrolls detailing Midewiwin rites and on rock petroglyphs (the latter found throughout North America), these features have been adopted by most painters of the Woodland school. At first, Morrisseau's work met with resistance from his community; there was concern that traditional stories were being made available to outsiders through his work.

The work of Norval Morrisseau is unique and ushered in a new school of art known as the Woodlands School. (McMichael Canadian Art Collection 1981.87.1)

Close-up of a section of the pictographs on the eastern shore of the south bay of Darky Lake in Quetico. Another section of this pictograph shows a man with a gun, which makes it one of the few pictographs to which an approximate date can be assigned. This is one of the most beautiful pictographs in Quetico. (Photo © Valerie Jacobs)

Native art is not at all monolithic. Some artists produce traditional art objects, others create modern art in the Western tradition but inspired by traditional motifs. Unlike many of his peers, Morrisseau merged the two traditions. The same can be said of the late Bill Reid (Haida) and Tony Hunt (Kwakiutl), both of whom produced works grounded in what is described as the Northwest Coast tradition, which is most familiar to Canadians from carved totem poles. Just as distinctive is Inuit art, where the principal materials are soapstone, ivory, and bone. The situation of Inuit art is rather unique. In 1949 the federal government, in conjunction with the Hudson's Bay Company, the Canadian Handicrafts Guild, and artist James A. Houston, began encouraging the Inuit to produce and market carvings internationally. Soon after, Houston introduced the Inuit to print-making and to Japanese techniques for drawing on paper. This led to a rapid increase in the popularity of Inuit prints, which are now available as stone cuts, silkscreens, engravings, and etchings.[47]

By the 1960s, Native art was gaining recognition as more than simple arts and crafts; it was now being viewed as legitimate artistic work reflecting the artists' thoughts on nationalism and colonialism, to name but two themes. The work of Allen Sapp (Cree), for instance, offered a window onto his childhood on the Red Pheasant Reserve in Saskatchewan during the 1930s and 1940s. Alan Syliboy's (Mi'kmaq) work is infused with his people's spiritualism. The work of Jane Ash Poitras (Chipewayan) reflects her renewed sense of self and identity and the clash of Native–non-Native cultures. Gerald Tailfeathers's (Blood) art portrays his people's interface with settler society with impressive historical accuracy. And Daphne Odjig (Ojibwa), the only female member of the Woodland school, embraces Creation and spirituality in her work, much as Morrisseau did.

Native art should not be portrayed as an exclusively historic phenomenon. Indeed, Native artists continue to move into uncharted territory with their work. Painters, carvers, performance artists, and digital artists are all embracing a variety of media even while relying on the philosophies of their communities to guide their efforts. A case in point is the innovative work of Brian Jungen (Dunne-za), which challenges the influence of non-Native–produced ethnography over the development of cultural identity. His best known work to date has involved disassembling Nike Air Jordan shoes and reconfiguring them to simulate Northwest Coast masks. In another innovative project, he cut up white plastic deck chairs to construct an enormous suspended whale skeleton. This section is much too brief; far more ground could have been covered. Needless to say, however, Native art's further evolution is assured.

Conclusion

In my view, artistic expression is the internal conversation by which individuals within a culture respond to things that connect them as community.

—Jeannette C. Armstrong (Okanagan)[48]

Today's Indigenous arts are all rooted in Creation, and those roots continue to inform their evolution. In the past, Creation and trickster stories were told to the young even while guiding adults in their daily lives. Those stories are still being told, and have extended themselves into books, radio, CD-ROMs, television, and movies, to name just some of the formats. The same can be said of music and songs and art: it is possible to embrace tradition while employing new technologies to entertain both Native and non-Native audiences; just as it is possible to preserve Indigenous images and ideas for future generations.

FURTHER READING

Armstrong, Jeanette C. "Aboriginal Literatures: A Distinctive Genre Within Canadian Literature." In *Hidden in Plain Sight: Contributions of Aboriginal Peoples to Canadian Identity and Culture,* ed. David R. Newhouse, Cora J. Voyageur, and Dan Beavon. Toronto: University of Toronto Press, 2005, pp. 180–86.

Dickason, Olive Patricia. "Art and Amerindian Worldviews." In *Earth, Water, Air, and Fire: Studies in Canadian Ethnohistory,* ed. David T. McNab. Waterloo: Wilfrid Laurier University Press, 1998, pp. 21–31.

Hoy, Helen. *How Should I Read These? Native Women Writers in Canada.* Toronto: University of Toronto Press, 2001.

Irwin, Rita L., and Ruby Farrell. "The Framing of Aboriginal Art." In *Visions of the Heart: Canadian Aboriginal Issues,* ed. David Alan Long and Olive Patricia Dickason. Toronto: Harcourt Brace, 1996, pp. 57–92.

King, Thomas. *The Truth About Stories: A Native Narrative.* Toronto: House of Anansi, 2003.

McMaster, Gerald. "Contributions to Canadian Art by Aboriginal Contemporary Artists." In *Hidden in Plain Sight: Contributions of Aboriginal Peoples to Canadian Identity and Culture,* ed. David R. Newhouse, Cora J. Voyageur, and Dan Beavon. Toronto: University of Toronto Press, 2005, pp. 140–62.

Miller, Mary Jane. *Outside Looking In: Viewing First Nations Peoples in Canadian Dramatic Television Series.* Kingston and Montreal: McGill–Queen's University Press, 2008.

Murphy, Jacqueline Shea. *The People Have Never Stopped Dancing: Native American Modern Dance Histories.* Minneapolis: University of Minnesota Press, 2007.

Petrone, Penny. *Native Literature in Canada: From the Oral Tradition to the Present.* Toronto: Oxford University Press, 1990.

Taylor, Drew Hayden. *Me Funny.* Toronto: Douglas and MacIntyre 2006.

Young Man, Alfred. "The Metaphysics of North American Indian Art." In *Indigena: Contemporary Native Perspectives,* ed. Gerald McMaster and Lee-Ann Martin. Toronto: Douglas and MacIntyre, 1992, pp. 81–99.

NOTES

1. "Jane Ash Poitras," in *Indigena: Contemporary Native Perspectives,* ed. Gerald McMaster and Lee-Ann Martin (Vancouver and Toronto: Douglas and McIntyre, 1992), p. 167.

2. Thomson Highway, *Kiss of the Fur Queen* (Toronto: Anchor Canada, 1999).

3. Richard Wagamese, *Keeper 'N' Me* (Toronto: Anchor Books, 1994); idem, *A Quality of Light* (Toronto: Doubleday Canada, 1997).

4. Alfred Young Man, "The Metaphysics of North American Indian Art," in *Indigena: Contemporary Native Perspectives,* ed. Gerald McMaster and Lee-Ann Martin (Vancouver and Toronto: Douglas and McIntyre, 1992), pp. 81–100.

5. John W. Friesen and Virginia Lyons Friesen, *Canadian Aboriginal Art and Spirituality: A Vital Link* (Calgary: Detselig, 2006), p. 10.

6. Thomas King, *Green Grass, Running Water* (Toronto: Bantam, 1994).

7. David Newhouse, "Imagining New Worlds: The Aboriginal Imagination," in *Aboriginal Cultural Landscapes,* ed. Jill Oakes, Rick Riewe, Yale Belanger, Sharon Blady, Kelly Legge, and Patsy Wiebe (Winnipeg: Aboriginal Issues, 2004).

8. George Copway, *Traditional History and Characteristic Sketches of the Ojibway Nation* (Boston: 1851), pp. 98–99.

9. Thomas King, *The Truth About Stories: A Native Narrative* (Toronto: House of Anansi, 2003).

10. Leslie Marmon Silko, *Ceremony* (New York: Viking, 1977).

11. Angela Cavendar Wilson, "Power of the Spoken Word: Native Oral Tradition in American Indian History," in *Rethinking American Indian History*, ed. Donald L. Fixico (Albuquerque: University of New Mexico Press, 1997), p. 111.

12. Percy Bullchild, *The Sun Came Down: The History of the World as My Blackfeet Elders Told It* (San Francisco: Harper and Row, 1985), p. 2.

13. See Samsom Occum, *A Choice Collection of Hymns and Spiritual Songs* (New London: Press of Thomas and Samual Green, 1774); idem, *A Sermon Preached at the Execution of Moses Paul, an Indian Who Was Executed at New Haven on the 2nd of September 1772 for the Murder of Mr. Moses Cook, late of Waterbury, on the 7th of December 1771* (New Haven: Press of Thomas and Samual Green, 1774).

14. Mark Walters, "'According to the Customs of Our Nation': Aboriginal Self-Government on the Credit River Mississauga Reserve, 1826–1847," *Ottawa Law Review* 30 (1998–99), pp. 1–45.

15. See Veronica Strong-Boag and Carole Gerson, *Paddling Her Own Canoe: The Times and Texts of E. Pauline Johnson Tekahionwake* (Toronto: University of Toronto Press, 2000); and Betty Keller, *Pauline: A Biography of Pauline Johnson* (Vancouver: Douglas, 1981).

16. Alan Morley, *Roar of the Breakers: A Biography of Peter Kelly* (Toronto: Ryerson Press, 1967).

17. Yale D. Belanger, "The Aboriginal Media in Canada," in *Hidden in Plain Sight: Contributions of Aboriginal Peoples to Canadian Identity and Culture*, Vol. 2, ed. David Newhouse, Cora Voyageur, and Dan Beavon (Toronto: University of Toronto Press, in press).

18. N. Scott Momaday, *House Made of Dawn* (New York: Harper and Row, 1968).

19. Harold Cardinal, *The Unjust Society: The Tragedy of Canada's Indians* (Edmonton: Hurtig, 1969).

20. George Manuel and Michael Posluns, *The Fourth World: An Indian Reality* (New York: Free Press, 1974).

21. Howard Adams, *Prison of Grass: Canada from the Native Point of View* (Toronto: New Press, 1975); idem, *The Tortured People: The Politics of Colonization* (Penticton: Theytus, 1995).

22. Peter Erasmus as told by Henry Thompson, *Buffalo Days and Nights* (Calgary: Fifth House, 1999).

23. John Tetso, *Trapping Is My Life* (Toronto: Peter Martin, 1976).

24. Tom Boulanger, *An Indian Remembers: My Life as a Trapper in Northern Manitoba* (Winnipeg: Peguis, 1971).

25. Mike Mountain Horse, *My People the Bloods* (Calgary and Standoff: Glenbow Museum and Blood Tribal Council, 1979).

26. Joseph Dion, *My Tribe the Crees* (Calgary: Glenbow Museum, 1979).

27. Maria Campbell, *Halfbreed* (Toronto: McClelland and Stewart, 1973).

28. Lee Maracle, *Ravensong* (Vancouver: Press Gang, 1995); idem, *I am woman: a native perspective on sociology and feminism* (Vancouver: Press Gang, 1996).

29. Ruby Slipperjack, *In Search of April Raintree* (Winnipeg: Pemmican, 1983); idem, *Honour the Sun* (Winnipeg: Pemmican, 1987).

30. Jeannette Armstrong, *Slash* (Penticton: Theytus, 1985).

31. Beth Brant, *Mohawk Trail* (New York: Firebrand, 1985); see also idem, *Writing as Witness: Essay and Talk* (Toronto: Women's Press, 1994).

32. Helen Hoy, *How Should I Read These? Native Women Writers in Canada* (Toronto: University of Toronto Press, 2001), pp. 183–201.

33. Thomson Highway, *Dry Lips Oughta Move to Kapuskasing* (Calgary: Fifth House, 1989); idem, *The Rez Sisters* (Calgary: Fifth House, 1992).

34. His produced plays include *Coyote City, Big Buck City, The Witch of Niagara, The Dreaming Beauty, The Indian Medicine Shows,* and *City of Shadows.*

35. Among her ten produced plays: *Copper Thunderbird, Burning Vision, The Unnatural and Accidental Women,* and *Urban Tattoo.*

36. See, for example, Drew Hayden Taylor, *The Night Wanderer: A Native Gothic Novel* (Toronto: Annick, 2007); *Me Funny* (Toronto: Douglas and MacIntyre, 2006); *Funny You Don't Look Like One: Observations of a Blue-Eyed Ojibway* (Penticton: Theytus, 1996). Among his 18 produced plays: *Sucker Falls, The Boy in the Treehouse, Raven Stole the Sun, In a World Created by a Drunken God,* and *Toronto at Dreamer's Rock.*

37. Quoted in Paul Williams, "Corlaer's Moon," in *Relationship of Aboriginal People to the Land and the Aboriginal Perspective on Aboriginal Title,* Vol. 1, ed. Sakej Youngblood Henderson, Tony Hall, Leroy Little Bear, and Paul Williams. Submitted to the Royal Commission on Aboriginal Peoples (RCAP), 1993, p. 68.

38. Katherine Pettipas, *Severing the Ties That Bind: Government Repression of Indigenous Religious Ceremonies on the Prairies* (Winnipeg: University of Manitoba Press, 1994).

39. See Thomas W. Kavanaugh, "Powwows," in *Handbook of North American Indians: Indians in Contemporary Society,* Vol. 2, ed. Garrick A. Bailey (Washington: Smithsonian Institution, 2008), pp. 327–337.

40. Mary Jane Miller, *Outside Looking In: Viewing First Nations Peoples in Canadian Dramatic Television Series* (Kingston and Montreal: McGill–Queen's University Press, 2008).

41. See "Kunuk, Zacharias," in *Current Biography International Yearbook, 2002* (New York: H.H. Wilson, 2002).

42. Jerry White, "Alanis Obomsawin, Documentary Form, and the Canadian Nation[s]," *Cineaction* 49 (1999): 26–36.

43. Drew Hayden Taylor, *Redskins, Tricksters, and Puppy Dog Stew* (Canada: National Film Board, 2000), 55 mins.

44. "Winnipeg Comedy Fest Opens with Native Humour," *CBCNews.ca,* March 26, 2004. [online] http://www.cbc.ca/arts/story/2004/03/24/nativecomedy20040324.html. Last accessed September 1, 2008.

45. "Lawrence Abbott Interview with Alfred Young Man," *Canadian Journal of Native Studies* 16, no. 2 (1996): 332.

46. Anna Lee Walters, *The Spirit of Native America: Beauty and Mysticism in American Indian Art* (San Francisco: Chronicle, 1989), p. 17.

47. See *James Houston, Inuit Art Pioneer.* [online] http://www.houston-north-gallery.ns.ca/jameshouston.htm. Last accessed September 1, 2008.

48. Jeannette C. Armstrong, "Aboriginal Arts in Canada: Points for Discussion," presentation to National Gathering on Aboriginal Artistic Expression, June 17–19, 2002, Ottawa.

HISTORY

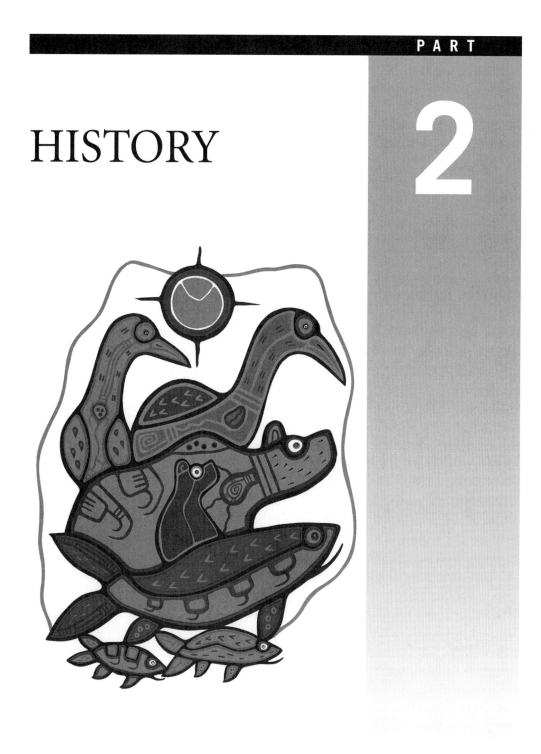

4 Treaties

We heard our lands were sold and we did not like it; we don't want to sell our lands; it is our property, and no one has a right to sell them.

—Sweet Grass (Cree)[1]

I f there is one aspect of First Nations political culture that Canadians identify with, it is the treaty. More than 70 treaties were signed by Indigenous leaders and Crown representatives between 1701 and 1923. Recent opinion polls have found that 80 percent of Canadians believe that several specific treaties, notably those signed in the late nineteenth and early twentieth centuries, should be honoured as binding agreements—up from 75 percent in 2006. Also, 55 percent of Canadians agree that the treaties should be honoured even if they obstruct or prevent economic development in nearby First Nations and non-Native communities.[2] Yet, while acknowledging their existence, most Canadians do not fully comprehend treaties—neither their histories, nor their legal complexities, nor their relationship to the future of Confederation. First Nations people believe that by breaking treaties, the Crown greatly harmed an already difficult political relationship.

Treaties are a common thread running through the history of the Indigenous–European relationship. The early treaties ensuring a peaceful cross-cultural interface led to a brief period of mutual economic growth. But eventually those treaties came to be used by the Europeans as documents of territorial dispossession; still later, in the 1960s, the Europeans tried to dismiss them as relics of the past.

First Nations refuse to allow outsiders to devalue those treaties, which they view as agreements negotiated between sovereign nations. Nor will they allow Canadians to deny their importance when relations between First Nations and Canadians are being defined. That resolve has led to a treaty revival of sorts. Since 1975, 13 modern-day treaties have been negotiated by First Nations with the Canadian government. And First Nations are continuing to forge ahead with self-government discussions and land-claim negotiations. In British Columbia, provincial leaders agreed in 1991 to establish a treaty process with the aim of resolving the outstanding land claims of First Nations provincially. Treaty rights have been recognized and affirmed in Section 35 of the *Constitution Act* (1982) and the Supreme Court of Canada has declared treaties to be not contracts or pacts bound by international law, but unique (sui generis) accords requiring a fair and liberal interpretation[3] that is not restricted to British/Canadian legal frameworks.[4] Yet treaties remain a contentious issue in Canadian politics, in large part because of differences in how First Nations and Canadian officials interpret them. This chapter discusses the Native perspective on treaties, examining several key negotiations framed by the tenets of Native philosophy to draw out the their meaning to First Nations.

Indigenous Treaty-Making Tradition

There was a long and rich history of treaty-making among the Aboriginal nations of the Americas before the arrival of Europeans . . . expanded to include European powers.

—Royal Commission on Aboriginal Peoples (RCAP)[5]

Before contact, North American Indigenous peoples possessed complex political processes. As described in Chapters 1 and 2, Indigenous nations developed unique political ideologies and procedures to reflect their ecological context. One result was that they came to focus on preserving their cultural autonomy, maintaining their political sovereignty, and safeguarding their traditional lands. In defending these, most of them developed processes for engaging with neighbouring peoples to establish political relationships. What emerged was a North American treaty order. Indigenous peoples had various reasons for engaging in politics and diplomacy. As an example, two Indigenous nations claiming sovereign rights to the same territory could go to war to resolve their differences, an expensive option. *Or,* they could form military and political alliances while simultaneously establishing trade guidelines and regional resource-utilization schemes. *Or,* they could negotiate treaties establishing the same things. In sum, Indigenous treaties maintained regional balance and thereby fostered peaceful relationships.

Cultural diversity meant that despite prolonged contact, language barriers existed between even the closest allies. Besides making communications difficult, this forced nations to develop tremendous diplomatic skills based in a common political process, the purpose of which was to reconcile the desires of competing parties. The diplomatic arena for resolving complex diplomatic issues was the council, of which there were various models. Whatever specific form it took, a council's success depended on the willingness of ambassadors to respectfully engage adversaries with the goal of resolving mutual grievances. One result was that elaborate ceremonies developed to ensure a peaceful start to council meetings. For example, those meetings often began with condolence ceremonies to mourn deceased chiefs, acknowledge successors, and ensure that past transgressions would be overlooked. Only then, after the pipe was smoked, did treaty discussions begin.

The process of negotiating a treaty was as important as the outcome. Over several days, grievances were aired and thoughtful responses were presented by each party's delegates.

Delegates were especially interested in the tone of the discussions and carefully assessed their opponents' diplomatic skills. Each side was intent on gaining the diplomatic advantage during negotiations, though never to the point of betraying fellowship or showing disrespect. The promises and affirmations that resulted from good-faith negotiations were considered binding. Because most Indigenous cultures relied on oral histories rather than written texts, negotiations and final agreements had to be committed to memory. This meant that all aspects of the treaty council were open to critique, including the nature of the final agreement and the delegates' actions. Treaty councils ended when the negotiations and resulting agreements were deemed binding and gifts and wampum were exchanged.[6]

Early Treaties in North America

By the sixteenth century, Indigenous peoples already had a long history of treaty diplomacy. This system had existed even before the Europeans developed their own version in the mid-seventeenth century. In other words, the European conquest of North America had been under way for a century before European monarchs adopted the treaty as a mechanism of diplomacy. Contemporary treaties are generally defined as "formal agreements between two or more fully sovereign and recognized states operating in an international forum, negotiated by officially designated commissioners and ratified by the governments of the signatory powers."[7] Treaties developed only after monarchs leading emergent European nation-states set out to develop a set of international principles to regulate their interactions. In the late eighteenth century the Swiss jurist Emmerich de Vattel had defined treaties in *The Law of Nations* as compacts "entered into by sovereigns for the welfare of the State, either in perpetuity or for a considerable length of time" by the highest state authority.[8] The first collection of European treaties was published in 1643, five years in advance of the Treaty of Westfalia, which ushered in the age of international relations. These early European treaties merged the papal bull (a decree from the Pope with international standing) with the treaty (first mentioned in the roll of British Parliament in 1427).[9]

The Europeans desired North American lands, but Indigenous peoples already occupied them, and the international understanding was that occupation conferred perpetual right of use (later referred to as Aboriginal title). Prior to then, the doctrine of discovery had regulated the Europeans' acquisition of territory that was *terra nullius* (unoccupied). At first, that doctrine made no mention of occupied lands *or* their occupants. Over time, various jurists, philosophers, and governments debated strategies ranging from outright denial of Indigenous humanity (in other words, they lacked the attendant rights to land ownership) to full recognition of their *imperium* (liberty) and *dominium* (property).

Writing in 1532, the Spanish jurist Francisco de Vitoria developed a set of principles that were eventually adopted as international law. Specifically, discovery permitted a European monarch to claim the land for the sovereign. Indigenous occupation meant that Aboriginal title existed, and such title could be extinguished one of three ways: (1) if the land was later abandoned, (2) if a just war was waged on infidels, or (3) if sanctioned negotiations led to a formalized treaty acknowledging a land sale.[10] The latter became the most popular approach. In other words, the Indigenous peoples were acknowledged as property owners with full dominion over their territories, which included the right to exclude others from those lands. In effect, the Europeans' willingness to enter into treaties with Indigenous leaders amounted to an acknowledgment that Indigenous peoples were sovereign political entities. International norms of treaty making were thus forged on the understanding that treaties were binding and inviolable.

In North America, Indigenous peoples engaged in trade with European sailors, who found a diversity of Indigenous governance models and economic processes. The newcomers quickly determined that to solidify their economic position, they would have to establish political alliances with Indigenous communities while engaging in commerce with them. Increasing competition among the British, French, and Dutch in North America quickly forced this idea into practice. The growing cultural diversity, however, made it difficult to develop a universal approach to negotiations with Indigenous peoples. To facilitate negotiations, the Europeans integrated aspects of North American treaty diplomacy; this allowed delegates to streamline their treaty-making procedures to better reflect regional diplomatic etiquette. Those seeking a political accord often had little knowledge or understanding of the other party's traditions or beliefs. To address this, a unique treaty diplomacy was created, one that integrated elements of Indigenous and European treaty-making traditions. The old North American treaty order was thus adapted into a unique amalgam of Indigenous and British, Spanish, French, and Dutch approaches to treaty making.[11]

Indigenous leaders were accustomed to complex political machinations and viewed European allies as useful for helping them advance their own claims. One can assume that in much the same way that European traders sought political and economic advantage through alliances with Indigenous leaders, those Indigenous leaders saw advantages to cultivating allies among the newcomers. Because they enjoyed economic and military supremacy, Indigenous leaders early on could strongly influence negotiations by deciding where and when negotiations would take place and which issues would be debated. In the spirit of promoting balance and acknowledging all relations, Indigenous peoples viewed treaties an important means for formalizing relationships that encompassed respect for cultural values, customary practices, and political traditions. Take, for example, the Mi'kmaq of eastern Canada. In 1610, following contact with the French, the Great Mi'kmaq chiefs Membertou and Messamouet and members of their extended families established an alliance with the Catholic Church, representing an arrangement the Mi'kmaq relied upon for protection from the French monarchic authority.[12]

This was more than a general political agreement, however. Mi'kmaq philosophies informed the negotiations, and the French and Mi'kmaq emphasized effective working relationships. The concordat led to the founding of a North American Mi'kmaq republic; at the same time, it codified Mi'kmaq independence and embraced the union of Indigenous and

European spiritual leaders. Far from accepting outright a foreign system of governance, the Mi'kmaq leaders employed those European philosophical and theological tenets they deemed useful. Later on, the French monarch would wave this peace treaty at rival European powers as proof that it owned what is now much of Nova Scotia. For the purposes here, the point is that the concordat confirmed a relationship of alliance between the Mi'kmaq and the French Crown and that it should be viewed as one of the first in a continuum of treaties stretching into the twenty-first century.[13]

The Mi'kmaq Concordat is an excellent example of two parties voluntarily meeting to apply sanctions on themselves. It also demonstrates how treaty-derived rights evolved in North America. However, as Indigenous societies gradually lost their military, economic, and demographic superiority, the treaty order became transformed. In the beginning, treaties had been considered nation-to-nation agreements bound by everything discussed during negotiations; slowly, however, non-Native delegates compelled a subtle shift away from these principles until the focus was on written documents as the norm. Also, when resolving interpretive disputes, it would be the written summaries of the promises made during negotiations that non-Native leaders referred to. Nevertheless, Indigenous leaders continued to rely on what was said during negotiations and on the oral promises as comprising the treaties. Furthermore, though non-Native leaders disagreed, Indigenous peoples upheld the belief that they remained sovereign and in control of their territories and natural resources. The gradual appropriation of the treaty process enabled European powers to undermine the existing treaty order in a way that sustained legal expansion into Indigenous territories. In this way they were able to achieve their empire-building aspirations.

Treaty Making in Canada

The sound of the rustling of the gold is under my feet where I stand; we have a rich country; it is the Great Spirit who gave us this; where we stand upon is the Indians, property, and belongs to them. If you grant us our requests you will not go back without making the treaty.

—Ojibwa (Anishinaabe) Chief to Treaty Commissioners, Treaty 3, 1873[14]

At first, the North American treaty order was based on the process of sovereigns engaging one another in diplomatic negotiations to establish mutual agreements classified as treaties. But non-Native delegates slowly began to take control of the treaty process. Indigenous leaders, however, continued to promote the integrative aspects of treaties in order to draw non-Native people into their kinship networks. This approach is evident in each of Canada's four eras of treaty making: (1) first contact to the Royal Proclamation (1763), (2) post–Royal Proclamation to Confederation (1867), (3) post-Confederation to the Natural Resources Transfer Agreements (1930), and (4) the modern treaty period (1975–present). The Native perspective on these agreements could be similarly listed: "compact" (embracing category 1), "contract" (embracing category 2), and "covenant" (combining categories 3 and 4).

Many words have been used to describe treaties: compacts, covenants, conventions, memorandums of understanding, and so on. As Jim Miller points out, though treaties and agreements tend to be characterized as sacred covenants, different categories of treaties developed in different periods, reflecting the general tenor of indigenous–European relations during each era. To describe more precisely the nature of the treaty relationship, Miller breaks the treaty order into three phases. Initially there were compacts—that is, informal agreements establishing economic relationships and military alliances. Except for some highly visible inter-nation negotiations such as the Treaty of Albany (1664), the Great Peace of Montreal (1701), and the Treaty of Niagara (1764), this type of agreement predominated from contact until just after the Royal Proclamation of 1763.

Toward the end of the end of the eighteenth century and into the early nineteenth, land-based treaties emphasizing land cessions and sales came to dominate treaty making. The contract period is aptly named, for these treaties more resembled land transactions than nation-to-nation agreements. During the final phase, which began in the 1870s, agreements began taking the form of covenants. These treaties were three-party affairs that included the Creator. Thus, any promises made were made before the Creator and were binding once all participated in a pipe ceremony. Since the Creator was party to the agreement, unilateral alterations to the treaty are not permitted. This meant that to update the terms of the agreement, the three parties would have to re-engage with one another.[15]

So perhaps it is not strange that the contract phase followed George III's now famous Royal Proclamation of 1763, which declared all lands west of the Appalachians Mountains to be British sovereign territory reserved for the Native people's use and benefit. In the spirit of maintaining strong relationships and ensuring the acknowledgment of past treaties, Indigenous leaders were reluctant to permit colonial officials to arbitrarily ratify legislation affecting their political autonomy. The Crown caved in to aggressive lobbying and invited Native leaders of the Great Lakes and the upper Ohio Valley to attend a conference at Niagara in 1764. There would be discussed principles for governing Native–Crown relations. It was hoped this would help establish "the framework by which the parties would relate to one another."[16] In July and August around 2,000 chiefs representing two dozen Indigenous nations from Nova Scotia to as far south as Mississippi and as far north as the Hudson Bay watershed met at Niagara Falls both to clarify the proclamation's provisions and to renew political relationships.

The contract stage that followed the Royal Proclamation was profoundly detrimental to Indigenous interests, mainly because colonial leaders were beginning to aggressively try to displace Indigenous peoples from their lands, or to outright dispossess them, so that those lands could be opened to settlement. To meet settlers' demands, British officials in Canada were seeking parcels of Quebec land, offering in exchange demarcated reserves, gifts, and one-time cash payments. In their efforts to secure quick agreements, they often drew up incomplete and inaccurate treaties that were poorly interpreted to Indigenous leaders. There had been a time when treaties helped develop hybrid policies and codes of law that were applicable to all parties. But now, in the 1780s, Indigenous leaders in eastern Canada and Ontario and Quebec were expressing dismay at Britain's failure to respect these agreements. Clearly, the colonial understanding of treaties as contractually approved land sales was at odds with Indigenous understandings of treaties as mutually beneficial nation-to-nation agreements.

After the War of 1812, Indigenous peoples were no longer considered military allies or viable trade partners. Rather, they were viewed as economic liabilities who depended on the annuities and gifting provisions as codified in past treaties. They were also seen as barriers to territorial development and westward expansion. So in 1830 the British established a policy that made Indigenous people wards of the Crown. Put another way, they were abandoning the treaty order in favour of promoting Indian integration into the colonies' European social fabric.

The Numbered Treaty Periods, 1871–77 and 1899–1921

Canadians generally can equally be considered participants in the treaty process, through the actions of their ancestors and as the contemporary beneficiaries of the treaties that gave the Crown access to Aboriginal lands and resources.

—RCAP[17]

Between first contact and Confederation, 123 treaties and land surrenders were negotiated with First Nations. Treaties were a popular approach in the United States as well: between 1778 and 1871 the U.S. Senate ratified treaties with one or more Native groups on 367 separate occasions.[18] Many of these treaties involved Indigenous people near the Canadian border. Indeed, some of them actually involved Indigenous leaders from Canada. Overall, then, treaties were a very common mechanism for establishing political relationships between Indigenous leaders and settlers. In Canada, however, treaty making declined in importance, at least until 1850. That year, in response to reports of violence between settlers and Indigenous people and Ojibwa requests to "formalize their relationship with the government by means of a treaty, even to the extent of being willing to leave the amount of compensation for the government to decide,"[19] an Ontario MLA (Simcoe) named William B. Robinson was appointed treaty commissioner. He was dispatched to Sault Ste. Marie to finalize what would become two treaties with the regional Indigenous peoples surrounding Lakes Huron (38 men present) and Superior (9 men present). Conforming to the Royal

Proclamation's land-surrender provisions, which required public negotiations with the Indigenous delegates prior to their lands being sold to a Crown agent, a £2,000 payment was made, partnered with the following promises: a perpetual annuity of £500 for the Superior Ojibwa and £600 for the Huron peoples; the creation of protected reserves; and freedom to continue regional hunting and fishing (see Figure 4-1).[20]

The Indigenous leaders of the region were well versed in treaty diplomacy, having been involved with the treaty order since first contact with the French and British in the seventeenth century. So it is logical to assume that on entering negotiations, the Indigenous delegates envisioned a discussion between sovereigns that would lead to mutually beneficial agreements. Colonial officials, however, employed this treaty model to extinguish Aboriginal title, challenging the previously accepted notion that Indigenous people had attendant rights of land ownership and imperial recognition of their *imperium* and *dominium*. They had also become selective regarding which peoples they would engage in treaties. Take, for example, events as they unfolded on the West Coast. Between 1851 and 1859, the colonial governor James Douglas negotiated treaties with 14 Indigenous communities where settlement had begun or was anticipated.[21] The communities leaders willingly engaged in negotiations during which they surrendered traditional lands in their entirety on the understanding that each treaty would make their village sites and enclosed fields available for their use, so that they would be able to freely "hunt over the unoccupied lands, and to carry on fisheries as formerly." Reserve sites were established on the promise that traditional means of subsistence would be permitted to continue.[22] But plans for treaties with the mainland Indigenous peoples were never promoted, and to this day the vast majority of B.C.'s Native peoples have never signed a treaty with the Crown.

Those who did not sign treaties benefited from the legal framework acknowledging Indigenous peoples as imbued with the inherent right to self-government as well as various Aboriginal rights related to territorial occupancy. And federal officials begrudgingly accepted treaty signatories as First Nations with an inherent albeit limited right to self-government. Yet as mentioned, the Crown failed to sign treaties in most of B.C. (the exception being Vancouver Island) as well as Quebec, and the territorial North. This suggests that regional Aboriginal title remains as yet 'unextinguished'; it also suggests that according to the Royal Proclamation, non-Native ownership of land is prohibited until a treaty has been formalized and the land has been ceded to the Crown. To address this, the Comprehensive Land Claims process was launched in 1973 to resolve the underlying question of title.

In some cases, such as that of the Lubicon Cree of Alberta, certain groups of people were overlooked during regional treaty commissions (the Lubicon were away hunting). Since neighbouring groups signed the treaty, Aboriginal title to the land was extinguished and control of natural-resource development was assigned to the province, which then leased out traditional Lubicon lands to forestry and mining interests.[23]

The failure to implement the treaties according to the spirit and intent of the negotiations is yet another a significant issue. This will be discussed in more detail below.

Figure 4-1 Historical Indian Treaties

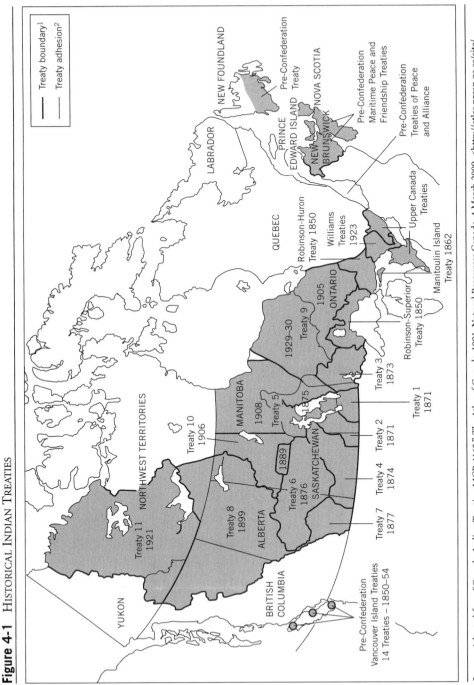

Legend:
— Treaty boundary[1]
— Treaty adhesion[2]

YUKON

NORTHWEST TERRITORIES

Treaty 11
1921

Treaty 10
1906

BRITISH
COLUMBIA

ALBERTA

Treaty 8
1899

Pre-Confederation
Vancouver Island Treaties
14 Treaties – 1850–54

Treaty 7
1877

Treaty 6
1876

1889

SASKATCHEWAN

Treaty 4
1874

MANITOBA

1908

Treaty 5

1875

Treaty 2
1871

Treaty 1
1871

Treaty 3
1873

1929–30

Treaty 9

1905

ONTARIO

QUEBEC

LABRADOR

NEW FOUNDLAND

Robinson-Superior
Treaty 1850

Robinson-Huron
Treaty 1850

Williams
Treaties
1923

Manitoulin Island
Treaty 1862

Upper Canada
Treaties

PRINCE
EDWARD ISLAND

NEW
BRUNSWICK

NOVA SCOTIA

Pre-Confederation
Treaty

Pre-Confederation
Maritime Peace and
Friendship Treaties

Pre-Confederation
Treaties of Peace
and Alliance

Source: Adapted from "Canada, Indian Treaties, MCR 4162." *The Atlas of Canada.* 1991. Natural Resources Canada. 4 March 2009. <http://atlas.nrcan.gc.ca/site/english/maps/archives/5thedition/historical/mcr4162>.

Treaties 1 to 7 (1871–77)

The negotiations leading to Canada's acquisition of Rupert's Land (see Figure 4-2) for £300,000 from the Hudson's Bay Company in 1868 resulted in an Imperial order-in-council cautioning that "any claims of Indians to compensation for lands required for purposes of settlement shall be disposed of by the Canadian Government in communication with the Imperial Government; and the Company shall be relieved of all responsibility of them."[24] Canada had already accepted sole responsibility for "Indians and lands reserved for Indians" under Section 91(24) of the British North America Act (1867), and in 1868 it established the Department of the Secretary of State to supervise Native peoples. Federal officials around this time were in general agreement that westward expansion would be necessary to extend Canada's claims to sovereignty in an effort to stop the Americans from annexing what today is Alberta and Saskatchewan. Treaties were considered an effective means to protect Native peoples and to extinguish their existing Aboriginal title, thereby promoting westward expansion and Canadian sovereignty.

Canadian officials were, however, not prepared to immediately enter into treaty negotiations. Their focus at the time was on nation building in central and eastern Canada. By this time, Native peoples were open to treating with the Crown, mainly because of the influx of settlers; Indigenous leaders feared that their people would soon be overrun, and many told

Figure 4-2 RUPERT'S LAND

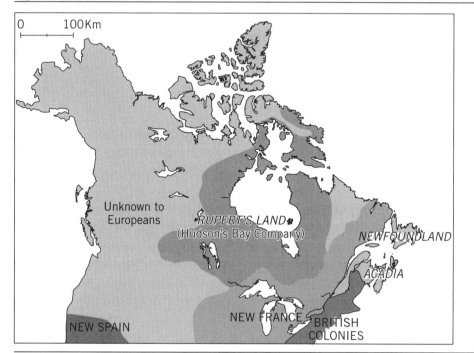

Source: Adapted from "The Rupert's Land Map by Weldon Hiebert." *Centre for Rupert's Land Studies.* 2000. University of Winnipeg. 4 March 2009. <http://uwwebpro.uwinnipeg.ca/academic/ic/rupert/index.html>.

Crown officials that they desired treaty negotiations. An excellent example of this involves the Saulteaux of central Manitoba, who in 1871 petitioned the Crown for a formal treaty. In the same document they expressed an interest in selling their lands in return for a protected reserve. In return for this, they demanded protection of their fishing and hunting rights as well as the right to cut timber in the region.[25] Eventually the government acquiesced, after being pressured by Native leaders, settlers, and politicians. Canada at this point was not acknowledged as a sovereign entity (a status it would not receive until 1931); so it was the British Crown that negotiated the treaties, with Canadian observers often on hand. The Crown adopted the Robinson model for the two sets of Numbered Treaties (1871–77, 1899–1921). Under the resulting written terms, which Native leaders argue failed to integrate the negotiations' discussions and resulting oral promises, in exchange for ceding vast tracts of land, the Native leaders received protected reserves. They believed this would enable their people to remain economically independent while continuing their traditional pursuits. They also received up-front payments and perpetual annuities (many of which have long ceased being distributed), along with further government assistance in the form of schools to ease the transition to European society, which it was expected would soon be flourishing in former Native homelands.[26]

By July 1871 the treaty commissioners had completed negotiations for what would become Treaties 1 and 2. Five more treaties would follow over the next six years—which was breakneck speed, compared to the modern-day pace of such negotiations. An account of each treaty is not possible here, because of the drawn-out process by which—so Canadian officials claim—the Native peoples voluntarily ceded their land in Manitoba, Saskatchewan, and Alberta. Doubts about this have led in recent years to significant debate as to what the treaties actually represent. First Nations leaders insist that these treaties are nation-to-nation agreements assigning responsibilities to the signatories that last in perpetuity; Canadian officials insist that the treaties are simple land cessions. The central and common article of the Victorian treaties (Treaty 1 is an exception) provides as follows:

> And the undersigned Chiefs and head men, on their own behalf, and on behalf of all other Indians inhabiting the tract within ceded, do hereby solemnly promise and engage to strictly observe this treaty, and also to conduct and behave themselves as good and loyal subjects of Her Majesty the Queen.
>
> They promise and engage that they will, in all respects, obey and abide by the law: that they will maintain peace and good order between each other, and between themselves and other tribes of Indians, and between themselves and others of Her Majesty's subjects, whether Indians, Half-breeds, or whites, now inhabiting or hereafter to inhabit any part of the said ceded tract, and that they will not molest the person or property of any inhabitant of such ceded tract, or the property of Her Majesty the Queen, or interfere with or trouble any person passing or travelling through the said tract, or any part thereof: and that they will assist the officers of Her Majesty in bringing to justice and punishment any Indian offending against the stipulation of this treaty, or infringing the law in force in the country so ceded.

Like their eastern cousins, it is likely that western Native leaders were well versed in the treaty-order practices—the Cree (Niheyaw) from Ontario had attended the Great Peace at Montreal in 1701, and their relatives from Saskatchewan and Manitoba had travelled to the Treaty of Niagara in 1764. Native perspectives on the Numbered Treaties vary, but one thing is for certain: the treaties established the rules for cultural interaction and the sharing of territory; that much was substantiated by the Treaty Commissioner himself, Alexander Morris. The wording of the aforementioned key provision found in all Numbered Treaties only strengthens the view that the Crown intended to establish working relationships with Native leaders to open their territory to settlers seeking to *share* the land with its original inhabitants.[27] Treaties were also used to extend the monarchy's protection to western Native peoples battling an influx of settlers and whisky bootleggers, initially improving Native lives.[28]

Under the written provisions of the Numbered Treaties, which the Canadian government insists is the proper interpretation, the First Nations agreed to cede their territories to the Crown in exchange for the following benefits:

1. Reserves were to be established within the ceded territories for the exclusive use and benefit of the First Nations signatories.
2. Small cash payments were to be given to the members of First Nations signatories. Thereafter, annuity payments would be given to them and their descendants.
3. In the prairie treaties, farming implements and supplies were promised as an initial outlay. Thereafter, hunting and fishing materials such as nets and twine were to be furnished on an annual basis.
4. Rights to hunt, fish, and trap over the ceded territories were guaranteed.
5. The government was to establish and maintain teachers and schools on the reserves.
6. Flags, medals, and suits of clothing were to be given to the chiefs and headmen of each band.
7. In Treaty 6, a "medicine" chest for the use of the First Nations was to be provided.

From the Native perspective, the treaties guaranteed certain rights that were to be enjoyed by the First Nations signatories in perpetuity:

1. First Nations retained their sovereignty over their people, lands, and resources both on and off reserve, subject to some shared jurisdiction over the lands known as "unoccupied Crown lands." This was understood as recognition of the right to self-government.
2. The Crown promised to provide for First Nations economic development in exchange for the right to use the lands covered by treaty.
3. The treaties promised revenue sharing between the Crown and First Nations.[29]

It is clear that federal officials saw the treaties as mechanisms for opening the West to settlement, thereby securing Canadian hegemony. The same can be said for Treaties 8 to 11, through which between 1899 and 1921 the Canadian government obtained land in northern Ontario, Saskatchewan, B.C., and the Northwest Territories and Yukon.

Treaty Proceedings at Smith's Landing (Fort Smith), NWT, July 17, 1898.

Once confined to reserves, the First Nations discovered that the treaties lacked political punch and that their political status was diminished. Canadian officials began interpreting the treaties rigidly, relying on the written summaries of the negotiations instead of being guided by the spirit and intent of the negotiations. Over time, rations diminished. When problems arose, cost cutting was implemented. Eventually the annuities contained in the Numbered Treaties were unilaterally consolidated into an annual $5 payment which is still in effect today. This also goes against the Native perspective of treaties as binding covenants not apt to arbitrary alteration. In 1930, Canada passed the Natural Resource Transfer Act (NRTA), which conveyed control of all Crown lands, minerals, and other natural resources to the three Prairie provinces. In return, those provinces agreed to certain promises concerning Native land use—promises that obliged the provincial governments to respect the right of Indians to hunt, trap, and fish "for food at all seasons of the year on all unoccupied Crown land and other land to which they have a right of access."[30] Native leaders also consider this transfer of authority an unacceptable alteration of the treaties signed with the Queen and an overt transgression that further undermined the spirit and intent of the treaty relationship.

This new jurisdictional arrangement enabled provincial officials to implement hunting and fishing legislation applicable to Native people. Yet under Treaty 6, for example, unoccupied Crown lands were defined as all Crown lands not taken up for settlement, mining, and lumbering, and game preserves were not specifically identified. More and more often, debates over treaty interpretation have ended up in Canadian courts. In 1999, in an attempt to clarify treaty arrangements and to determine how to implement treaty provisions to the satisfaction of the parties involved, the Supreme Court of Canada developed the following legal guidelines:

1. Aboriginal treaties constitute a unique type of agreement and attract special principles of interpretation.

2. Treaties should be liberally construed and ambiguities or doubtful expressions should be resolved in favour of the aboriginal signatories.

3. The goal of treaty interpretation is to choose from among the various possible interpretations of common intention the one which best reconciles the interests of both parties at the time the treaty was signed.

4. In searching for the common intention of the parties, the integrity and honour of the Crown is presumed.

5. In determining the signatories' respective understanding and intentions, the court must be sensitive to the unique cultural and linguistic differences between the parties.

6. The words of the treaty must be given the sense which they would naturally have held for the parties at the time.

7. A technical or contractual interpretation of treaty wording should be avoided.

8. While construing the language generously, courts cannot alter the terms of the treaty by exceeding what "is possible on the language" or realistic.

9. Treaty rights of aboriginal peoples must not be interpreted in a static or rigid way. They are not frozen at the date of signature. The interpreting court must update treaty rights to provide for their modern exercise. This involves determining what modern practices are reasonably incidental to the core treaty right in its modern context.[31]

The Williams Treaties (1923) were the last treaties to be signed in Canada before a five-decade moratorium on treaty negotiations. Involving the Chippewa of Rama, Christian Island, and Georgian Island, and the Mississauga of Rice Lake, Mud Lake, Scugog Lake, and Alderville, these treaties were intended to settle disputes arising from earlier treaties and the outstanding land claims of Native leaders not involved with the pre-Confederation Robinson treaties. Disputes nevertheless characterize these treaties, owing to the Ontario government's insistence that Native signatories ceded not only their lands but all off-reserve hunting, fishing, and trapping rights. This interpretation was upheld by the Supreme Court of Canada in 1994.[32] It seems foolish to suggest that signing the treaties represented an agreement by Native leaders to renounce practices central to their cultural, religious, and economic survival.[33] Clearly, the Court thought differently and pronounced accordingly.[34]

Modern Treaty Making

Why should the Cree people have had to negotiate for something that all other non-Native Canadians take for granted? The James Bay Agreement was negotiated as an out-of-court settlement of our aboriginal claim to Northern Quebec. As I said earlier Quebec is in court trying to invalidate our treaty. If the court does invalidate the Agreement, I hope that Quebec will also remove the dams and dykes from our rivers and restore the waters to the Eastmain River that used to flow by my community. The Crees were lied to when we signed the James Bay Agreement.

—Ambassador Ted Moses (Cree)[35]

After the historic treaty period, there was a 52-year break before the next Native–Crown treaty negotiations, which were held in 1975 and led to the James Bay and Northern Quebec Agreement. The modern treaty period was thus born. Modern-day treaties are just as complex as the ones negotiated in the past. At first glance, the actual negotiations are similar enough: Crown and Native delegates meet to discuss issues of concern with the intention of reaching an agreement both sides can sign. In terms of ideology, however, the modern-day process is significantly different. The two sides do not come to the table as political or economic equals, and most Native delegates admit that they are negotiating in an effort to mitigate their communities' present-day socioeconomic difficulties. Moreover, modern treaties focus almost exclusively on outstanding land claims (see Figure 4-3)—little else penetrates the process. As a result, modern treaties take an inordinate amount of time to complete, and at a cost of millions.

Modern-day treaties are framed as land claims and self-government agreements. The latter focus on jurisdiction in relation to neighbouring non-Native communities (see Chapter 10). Whatever they are called, they are still all treaties. Two types of claims dominate negotiations: specific land claims and comprehensive ones. Specific land claims result from past grievances related to the administration of Indian lands and other assets, as well as the fulfillment of

Figure 4-3 MODERN TREATIES IN CANADA

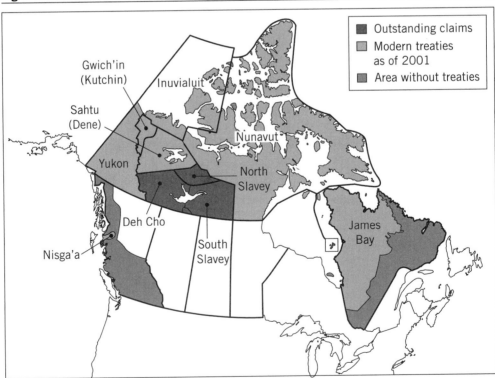

Source: Adapted from "First Peoples: Treaties." *The Canadian Atlas Online.* Canadian Geographic. 15 December 2008. <www.canadiangeographic.ca/atlas/themes.aspx?id=first&sub=first_issues_treaties&lang=En>.

treaties. Thus they are retrospective in considering the treaties' written terms. Comprehensive land claims aim to resolve claims to Aboriginal title in areas of Canada that have not been addressed by treaty or other legal means. Negotiations have two objectives: to establish certainty of title to lands and resources; and to enhance economic development and socioeconomic opportunities for Native communities. Alternative dispute resolution models have recently emerged. In B.C., for instance, a provincial Treaty Commission has been established to expedite comprehensive claims that have arisen because no treaty with the Crown exists to start with. In Saskatchewan, the Office of the Treaty Commissioner (OTC) is a tripartite negotiating body established to reconcile multiple treaty perspectives into mutually acceptable agreements.

The James Bay and Northern Quebec Agreement, 1975[36]

The James Bay Cree and the federal government signed the James Bay and Northern Quebec Agreement (JBNQA) in 1975. This was the first treaty produced in what has become known as Canada's modern treaty period. All of the lands that comprise the JBNQA area were at one time within the demarcated region known as Rupert's Land. In 1870, by Imperial order-in-council, Crown officials in an unprecedented decision agreed to formally obtain Indian title to the lands through treaty. Two boundary extensions in 1898 and 1912 (the Quebec Boundaries Extension Act) resulted in the transfer of territorial title to the Province of Quebec. The Extension Act obliged provincial officials to acknowledge Indian title and to negotiate a proper treaty to extinguish said title and recognize Native cultural rights. Specifically, "The province of [Quebec] will recognize the rights of the Indian inhabitants in the territory above described to the same extent, and will obtain surrenders of such rights in the same manner as the Government of Canada has heretofore recognized such rights and has obtained surrender thereof and the said province shall bear and satisfy all charges and expenditure in connection with or arising out of such surrenders."[37] Yet Quebec refused to act immediately to negotiate a treaty, even though Native people continued to utilize the vast region.

There was initially limited outside interest in the region, so little thought was given to Aboriginal rights in Quebec until provincial officials in the mid-1960s began researching the region's hydroelectric potential. In 1971 the Province of Quebec announced its intention to begin developing the James Bay hydroelectric project, which would entail blocking and sometimes diverting rivers in the James Bay drainage basin. Subsequently, the province established the James Bay Development Corporation to develop all of the territory's resources, including hydroelectricity, forestry, mining, and tourism. It did so, however, without consulting the region's 10,000 Cree and 5,000 Inuit. They discovered only through media reports that their homeland was destined to be flooded.

The Cree quickly mobilized, and in 1972 the newly formed Quebec Association of Indians petitioned the Quebec Superior Court for an injunction to stop all construction in the region. The injunction was granted on the grounds that the Province of Quebec had failed to settle all outstanding land claims. This decision was overturned within days, once again opening the region to hydroelectric development. Many Native leaders optimistically viewed the decision as affirming their claims and once again lobbied the provincial government for a land-claims resolution. By 1974 the Cree and Inuit of northern Quebec, the governments of Canada and Quebec, and the Quebec Hydro-Electric Commission had concluded an agreement-in-principle, which led to the signing of the JBNQA in November 1975. Early in the negotiations, the Cree formed the Grand Council of the Cree (of Quebec), with one chief and leaders from each of the eight Cree communities comprising the organization's board of directors. An executive group of four regional leaders was then selected, whereupon the Grand Council took over negotiations. Even though they represented the Cree people in negotiations, the Grand Council was not empowered to act without consulting the people at the community level. Simply put, the Cree people remained the final decision makers.

The JBNQA total compensation package amounted to $225 million, to be paid over 20 years to the Cree Regional Authority, and the Makivik Corporation on behalf of the Inuit, by the federal and Quebec governments. This modern-day treaty settled all outstanding Native land claims in northern Quebec dating back to 1912. It also defined Native rights and established regional land-use regimes for both Native and non-Native people in the region and among local, regional, provincial, and federal governments. The Cree retained 3,100 square miles of territory; the Inuit retained more than 8,000 square kilometres of settlement land, in addition to exclusive harvesting rights over an additional 16,000 square kilometres of land.

The JBNQA extinguished Aboriginal title to 965,600 square kilometres of land. Under the JBNQA, the territory was divided into Category I, II, and III lands. Category I lands are for the exclusive use and benefit of Native people. Category II lands belong to the province, but Native governments share in the management of hunting, fishing, and trapping, as well as tourism development and forestry. Native people have exclusive hunting, fishing, and trapping rights on these lands. Category III lands are a special type of Quebec public lands, where Native and non-Native people may hunt and fish subject to regulations adopted in accordance with the JBNQA. The agreement requires the province to monitor the environmental and social impacts of development. Committees have been established to advise governments on environmental issues, policies, and regulations. Each committee comprises federal, provincial, and Native representatives.

The JBNQA also recognizes a form of Aboriginal self-government. Inuit communities have been incorporated as municipalities under Quebec law, with municipal powers delegated by Quebec legislation. The Kativik regional government has been established under provincial legislation, and the province has established the Cree Regional Authority to assist in creating services for Cree communities. Cree and Inuit school boards have been established as part of the agreement; these have a special mandate and unique powers enabling them to adopt culturally appropriate educational programs. The federal government and Quebec jointly fund the school boards, with Canada paying one-quarter of the Inuit budget and three-quarters of the Cree budget. A coordinating committee of federal and provincial representatives and Native delegates has been established to administer, review, and regulate wildlife harvesting, while ensuring that Native rights to hunting acknowledged in the agreement are not abused.

Land Claims: Specific and Comprehensive

The Supreme Court of Canada in 1973 recognized Aboriginal rights to the land based on Aboriginal title. In *Calder,* the Nisga'a of B.C. were seeking title to nearly 22,000 square kilometres of land lost on a legal technicality. The Court, however, ruled that an Aboriginal right to land exists and that such rights are based on an Aboriginal community or group's traditional use and occupancy of a land base. In response to the anticipated flood of similar grievances related specifically to abrogations of treaty promises, a specific-claims policy was established. Since 1973, 1,279 specific land claims had been filed: 489 of these have been concluded, and 790 are outstanding. This is an expensive process. Between 2006 and 2007 the federal share of the specific claims cases that were settled amounted to $15,785,881.[38] Comprehensive claims were defined at the time as negotiated settlements that are needed to clarify the rights to lands and resources for Native groups lacking a treaty relationship with Canada or where extinguishment of Aboriginal rights is questionable. Under the Comprehensive Claims Policy (1987), the following criteria must be met:

1. The Aboriginal group is, and was, an organized society;

2. The organized society has occupied the specific territory over which it asserts Aboriginal title since time immemorial. The traditional use and occupancy of the territory must have been sufficient to be an established fact at the time of assertion of sovereignty by European nations;

3. The occupation of the territory by the Aboriginal group was largely to the exclusion of other organized societies;

4. The Aboriginal group can demonstrate some continuing current use and occupancy of the land for traditional purposes;

5. The group's Aboriginal title and rights to resource use have not been dealt with by treaty; and,

6. Aboriginal title has not been eliminated by other lawful means.[39]

Several comprehensive claims have been resolved; dozens more are currently awaiting adjudication and processing by the Indian Claims Commission (est. 1991). The following is a complete list of final agreements regarding comprehensive land claims achieved to date:

2006. Nunavik Inuit Land Claims Agreement

2005. Labrador Inuit Land Claims Agreement

2003. Kluane First Nation—Final Agreement

2003. Tlicho Agreement (signed August 25, 2003)

2002. The Ta'an Kwach'an Council Final Agreement

1999. Nisga'a Final Agreement

1998. Tr'ondëk Hwëch'in Final Agreement

1997. Little Salmon/Carmacks Final Agreement

1997. Selkirk First Nation Final Agreement

1993. Sahtu Dene and Métis Comprehensive Land Claim Agreement (effective 1994)

1993. Umbrella Final Agreement between the Government of Canada, the Council for Yukon Indians, and the Government of Yukon

1993. Vuntut Gwitchin First Nation Final Agreement (effective 1995)

1993. Champagne and Aishihik First Nations Final Agreement (effective 1995)

1993. Teslin Tlingit Council Final Agreement (effective 1995)

1993. Nacho Nyak Dun First Nation Final Agreement (effective 1995)

1993. Nunavut Land Claims Agreement

1992. Gwich'in Comprehensive Land Claim Agreement

1984. Western Arctic Claim—Inuvialuit Final Agreement

1978. The Northeastern Quebec Agreement

1975. James Bay and Northern Quebec Agreement and Complementary Agreements (effective 1977)

To provide a clearer context regarding the details of these agreements, those resolved include:[40]

The James Bay and Northern Quebec Agreement (1975). This was the first comprehensive claim to be settled, and was followed by the *Northeastern Quebec Agreement,* signed in 1978. These agreements compensated the region's 19,000 Cree, Inuit, and Naskapi to the tune of $230 million and granted them ownership to more than 14,000 square kilometres of land. They also assigned exclusive hunting and trapping rights to an additional 150,000 square kilometres.

The Inuvialuit Final Agreement (1984). This settlement provided 2,500 regional Inuvialuit in the western Arctic with 91,000 square kilometres of land and $45 million in compensation paid out over 13 years. It also guaranteed hunting and trapping rights as well as equal participation in the management of wildlife and the environment. Also, it established a $10 million Economic Enhancement Fund and a $7.5 million Social Development Fund.

The Gwich'in Agreement (1992). This agreement provided the Gwich'in with about 24,000 square kilometres of land in the northwestern Northwest Territories and 1,554 square kilometres of land in Yukon. In addition, they will receive a nontaxable payment of $75 million to be paid over 15 years, a share of resource royalties from the Mackenzie Valley, subsurface rights, hunting rights, and a greater role in the management of wildlife and the environment.

The Nunavut Land Claims Agreement (1993). Detailed in Chapter 6 on the Métis and Inuit, this agreement is the largest comprehensive claim in Canada. Under this agreement, in 1999 the federal government divided the Northwest Territories in two to create the new territory of Nunavut.

The Council for Yukon Indians (1993). In 1993, 14 Yukon First Nations signed an Umbrella Final Agreement with the federal government and the Yukon Territorial Government. It sets out the general terms for the final land-claim settlements in the territory. Around the same time, final land-claim agreements were reached with four of these First Nations—the Vuntut Gwitchin First Nation, the Champagne and Aishihik First Nations, the Teslin Tlingit Council, and the First Nation of Na-cho Ny'a'k Dun—who also negotiated self-government agreements giving them more control over land use on settlement lands and greater authority in areas such as language, health care, social services, and education.

Premier Glen Clark and Nisga'a Tribal Council President Joe Gosnell shake hands after signing the Nisga'a Final Agreement in Terrace B.C. Tuesday, April 27, 1999. The historic ratification of the Nisga'a Treaty and Nisga'a Constitution won a majority vote by the Nisga'a Nation on November 6, 1998 after 113 years of negotiation.

The Sahtu Dene and Métis Agreement (1994). This settlement provided the Sahtu Dene and Métis with 41,437 square kilometres of land, a share of resource royalties from the Mackenzie Valley, and guaranteed wildlife harvesting rights. It also ensured their participation in decision-making bodies dealing with renewable resources, land-use planning, environmental impact assessments and reviews, and land and water use regulations. Finally, it provided $75 million over 15 years.

B.C. Treaty Commission and the Nisga'a Treaty

In 1991 the B.C. treaty process was launched following the recommendation of the B.C. Claims Task Force that land claims and governance issues be dealt with in a non-coercive environment of open communication between First Nations and provincial leaders.[41] A set of 19 principles was developed to guide future treaty negotiations, and an independent body, the B.C. Treaty Commission (BCTC), was created to serve as the "keeper of the process"—that is, to ensure adherence to those principles. The BCTC would also:

- coordinate the start of negotiations;
- assess the readiness of the parties (Canada, B.C., and First Nations) to negotiate;
- monitor the progress of negotiations;
- allocate funds to enable First Nations to participate in negotiations; and
- prepare and maintain a public record of the status of negotiations.[42]

Unfortunately, the principles established were vague, and little thought was given to expanding the BCTC's mandate beyond promoting treaty negotiations. This lack of common understanding of what the process represents has been problematic. Nevertheless, over the last 14 years the six-stage process has produced one ratified agreement and one initialled final agreement (see box).[43] Currently in B.C., 58 First Nations are participating in the provincial treaty process at 48 negotiating tables. Seven tables are now at the fifth stage (final agreement) of negotiations, and 40 are at the fourth stage (agreement-in-principle). It is up to First Nations to decide how they organize themselves for the purposes of treaty negotiations. This means that at some tables a single First Nation is represented, while at others there are two or more. Final agreements have been concluded with the Tsawwassen, Maa-nulth, and Lheidli T'enneh First Nations and are now being ratified. There are, however, 198 provincial First Nations communities, not including the 36 chartered Métis communities. In other words, fewer than one-third of the province's First Nations are currently participating in the treaty process.

There are various issues that upset First Nations. One is the cost: the province's government spends $52 million a year on negotiations and has assigned 140 staff to them, whereas many small First Nations communities have no more than $1.5 million annually to spend and only a handful of researchers to assist with their claims.[44] Also, the process is time intensive. Since the process was officially launched in 1993, $1.1 billion has been spent on it, yet only one claim has been ratified. A Fraser Institute report indicates that the Tsawwassen First Nation agreement provides that 300-member band with more than 700 hectares of prime land in Delta, south of Vancouver, along with a $14 million cash settlement and accompanying self-government provisions and fishing rights. Yet the agreement states that 38 issues in that agreement require further consultation.[45]

B.C. SIX STAGE TREATY PROCESS

Stage 1—Statement of intent to negotiate

A First Nation files with the BCTC a statement of intent to negotiate with Canada and the province. The statement of intent:

- identifies the First Nation's governing body and the people that body represents;
- shows that the governing body has a mandate to enter the treaty process;
- describes the geographic area of the First Nation's traditional territory in B.C.; and
- identifies any overlaps in territory with other First Nations.

Stage 2—Readiness to negotiate

The Treaty Commission must convene an initial meeting of the three parties within 45 days of receiving a statement of intent. For most First Nations, this will be the first time they have ever sat down at a treaty table with representatives of Canada and the province. This meeting allows the Treaty Commission and the parties to exchange information, consider the criteria for determining the parties' readiness to negotiate, and generally identify issues of concern. Each party must demonstrate that it has:

- a commitment to negotiate;
- a qualified negotiator who has been given a clear mandate;
- sufficient resources to undertake negotiations; and
- a ratification procedure.

In addition, the First Nation must have a plan for addressing any issues of overlapping territory with neighbouring First Nations. The governments of Canada and B.C. must have a formal means of consulting with other parties, including local governments and interest groups.

Stage 3—Negotiation of a framework agreement

The three parties negotiate a framework agreement that states the issues to be negotiated, the goals and procedures, and a timetable. The federal and provincial governments engage in public consultations at the regional and local levels. The parties also establish a public information program, which will continue throughout the negotiations.

Stage 4—Negotiation of an agreement-in-principle

The three parties examine in detail the issues identified in the framework agreement with the goal of reaching an agreement-in-principle. The agreement-in-principle identifies a range of rights and obligations, which are to constitute the basis for the treaty. The parties also begin to plan for the treaty's implementation.

Stage 5—Negotiation to finalize a treaty

Technical and legal issues are resolved to produce a final agreement that embodies the principles outlined in the agreement-in-principle. The treaty formalizes the new relations among the parties. Once signed and formally ratified, the final agreement becomes a treaty.

Stage 6—Implementation of the treaty

Plans to implement the treaty are put into effect or phased in as agreed. Long-term implementation plans need to be tailored to specific agreements. The table remains active in order to oversee implementation of the treaty.

Source: "Six-Stages: Policies and Procedures." *BC Treaty Commission.* 2007. 18 September 2008. <http://www.bctreaty.net/files/sixstages.php>. Reprinted with permission.

The Nisga'a Treaty

The Nisga'a Treaty concluded by the Nisga'a Tribal Council (NTC) and the federal and provincial governments on July 15, 1998, was the first modern treaty negotiated in B.C., though this was not done through the BCTC.[46] As far back as 1887 the Nisga'a had been demanding treaty negotiations as well as recognition of their Aboriginal title and right to self-government. In 1968 the NTC petitioned the B.C. Supreme Court to rule on its claim that the Nisga'a had never surrendered their land base and still possessed Aboriginal title to their territory. In 1973 the Court finally rendered the *Calder* decision (Calder was the name of the late Nisga'a chief), which formally acknowledged the Aboriginal right to land. In 1976 the federal government initiated treaty negotiations with the NTC; in 1990 the province joined these talks. The public was kept well informed of events; between 1991 and 1998, federal and provincial negotiators held 250 consultations and public-information meetings in northwestern B.C. As passed into law on May 11, 2000, the Nisga'a Treaty provided the Nisga'a with:

- $196.1 million (in 1999 dollars);
- 2,019 square kilometres of land;
- an average yearly allocation of 44,588 sockeye salmon, 11,797 coho salmon, 6,330 chum salmon, 6,524 chinook salmon, and 4,430 pink salmon, protected by the treaty;
- a commercial yearly allocation of 28,913 sockeye and 88,526 pink salmon under an agreement that is not part of the treaty;
- limited allocations of moose, grizzly bear, and goats, for domestic purposes;
- $11.8 million to enhance participation in the general commercial fishery;
- $10.3 million in Canada's contribution to the Lisims Fisheries Conservation Trust (to which the Nisga'a provide $3.1 million);
- transition, training, and one-time funding of $40.6 million;
- a water reservation for domestic, agricultural, and industrial purposes;
- authority to operate their own government, and the power to make certain laws; and
- funding to help deliver health, education, and social services to First Nation members and other area residents.[47]

Concerns about the treaty's viability and utility have been raised by both provincial officials and members of the Nisga'a community. During the ratification process the Reform Party (now the Conservative Party) declared that it would do everything in its power to delay treaty ratification, though little resulted from this resistance. Then in 2005 two Nisga'a elders petitioned the B.C. Supreme Court to declare the treaty unconstitutional, on the basis that it was destroying hereditary governance and culture. The case was thrown out in 2006, the Court having ruled that the plaintiffs had not properly prepared their case. Then, the following October, the B.C. Court of Appeal reactivated the case. As of this writing, the Court of Appeal had yet to rule on the petition.

Office of the Treaty Commissioner (OTC)

The OTC was established in 1989 to help resolve issues surrounding treaty land entitlement (TLE) in Saskatchewan. It is an independent body that provides a forum for the Federation of Saskatchewan Indian Nations (FSIN) and the federal government to discuss treaty issues, with the Province of Saskatchewan acting as an independent observer. On the assumption that the Crown–First Nations treaties of the 1870s are the basis of existing relations between First Nations and the federal and provincial governments, the OTC facilitates dialogue about jurisdictional issues. It does so through "exploratory tables" that examine issues related to health, education, and justice. What began as an interesting idea in 1989 had by 1996 evolved into a five-year agreement under which the commissioner was given an augmented role—one that has since been renewed. Central to the OTC's work is the acknowledgment of First Nations' right to self-government, and the respect thereby accorded. The OTC's mandate includes:

- building a forward-looking relationship, one that started with the signing of the treaties in Saskatchewan;
- reaching a better understanding of what the treaties actually mean and of the results expected from the exploratory treaty discussions; and
- exploring the requirements and implications of treaty implementation, based on the views of the two parties.[48]

The OTC has done much to settle hundreds of millions of dollars in TLE claims in Saskatchewan. TLE refers to land that Canada and the provinces owe specific bands under the terms of the treaties. After the Numbered Treaties were signed, reserves were immediately surveyed, with land to be distributed at a rate of 640 acres to each family of five. The task of surveying was made difficult, however, by issues such as fluctuating band populations and nefarious surveyors. As a result, errors occurred.[49] It is worth noting that Section 10 of the NRTA compelled the provinces to fulfill their treaty land obligations.[50] Provincial officials acknowledged the need to resolve northern treaty issues; they were less concerned about southern First Nations issues, often assuming that TLE obligations had been met. In the early 1970s the Federation of Saskatchewan Indians identified 1 million acres owed to five northern and ten southern bands.[51] Between 1968 and 1973, Saskatchewan set aside nearly 185,000 northern acres for TLE claims.[52] Several fits and starts occurred prior to the 1991 implementation of the Treaty Land Entitlement Framework Agreement, which, as of 1992, 25 First Nations had signed, entitling them to receive about $516 million over 12 years to purchase 1.95 million acres of land to add to their reserves.[53]

The OTC was forced to close its doors briefly in March 2007 when its mandate expired. However, Indian and Northern Affairs Canada (INAC) took quick steps to ensure its continued operations, and in June of the same year, Indian Affairs Minister Jim Prentice appointed Bill McKnight as the new Treaty Commissioner.

Figure 4-4 INQUIRY AND MEDIATION PROCESSES

	The Inquiry Process	The Mediation Process
	The following is the process that was followed to conduct an inquiry, up to November 27, 2007.	
	Initial Request for Inquiry	**Preparation for Mediation**
Stage 1	The Commission reviews the First Nation's request for an independent inquiry and, if it agrees to accept the specific claim for review and assessment, a panel of three Commissioners is formed to hear the inquiry. (Activity now ceased)	The Commission reviews the claim being negotiated and brings representatives of the negotiating parties together face to face to discuss the issues and terms of the negotiation and mediation protocol agreements.
	Preparation for Inquiry	**Negotiation Process**
Stage 2	Briefing material is prepared and sent to all of the parties in advance to facilitate discussion. Counsel for both parties are asked to state the issues to be addressed by the inquiry, from which the Commission staff will attempt, in consultation with counsel for the parties, to generate a single list of issues. A planning conference is held among the parties and their counsel. In many instances, the need for further research is identified. If there is no consensus by the parties on a single list of issues, this matter is placed before the panel for decision. (Activity now ceased)	The Commission facilitates discussions on compensation, assists the parties by coordinating the gathering of information including land appraisals and joint loss-of-use studies, and monitors the parties' decisions and undertakings.
	Staff Visit and Community Session(s)	**Settlement**
Stage 3	Commissioners and staff attend a session or series of sessions in the First Nation's community to hear directly from Elders and other knowledgeable members of the First Nation. In some instances, expert witnesses may be called upon to present evidence or testimony and are subject to cross examination by the other party. (Activity now ceased)	When and after the negotiating parties reach an agreement in principle, lawyers for the First Nation and Canada work together to draft a final settlement agreement, which is initialled by the negotiators and ratified by both parties.
	Written and Oral Submissions	**Final Mediation Report**
Stage 4	Both parties present submissions to the panel.	The Commission reports to the federal government, the First Nation and the public on the outcome of the negotiation.
	Commissioners' Final Report	
Stage 5	The panel of Commissioners considers the evidence, testimony and submissions presented and issues a final report that contains its findings and recommendation that the Minister of Indian Affairs accept the specific claim for negotiation, or that the Minister of Indian Affairs not reconsider the decision to deny the specific claim.	

Source: Courtesy the Indian Claims Commission.

Conclusion

Treaties are sacred promises and the Crown's honour requires the Court to assume that the Crown intended to fulfil its promises. Treaty rights can only be amended where it is clear that effect was intended.

—*R. v. Badger,* Supreme Court of Canada (1996)[54]

Canadians tend to view treaties as documents outlining certain promises of a historical period long passed. From a Native perspective, however, treaties are pacts negotiated on a nation-to-nation basis, most often in the presence of the Creator. In other words, the promises made in treaties are not simply between parties—they involve Creation and cannot be altered unilaterally. That said, treaties always reflect a moment in time, and the ones in effect today reflect a relationship between Indigenous peoples and the Crown that was always likely to change. In that sense, all treaties are transitional, for they speak to relationships as they existed at the time of signing. It follows that treaties must sometimes be renegotiated if they are to properly address parties' changing relationships. All of that aside, the nation-to-nation aspects of treaties cannot be ignored, for First Nations leaders firmly believe that their participation in negotiating them was akin to diplomacy with foreign nations and that the French and British, by entering into talks, were recognizing the fact that Indigenous nations had sovereign political status.

FURTHER READING

Henderson, Sakej Youngblood, "Treaty Governance." In *Aboriginal Self-Government in Canada: Current Trends and Issues,* ed. Yale D. Belanger. Saskatoon: Purich, 2008.

——— . *The Mikmaw Concordat.* Halifax: Fernwood, 1997.

Lerat, Harold. *Treaty Promises, Indian Reality: Life on a Reserve.* Saskatoon: Purich, 2005.

Miller, J.R. *Lethal Legacy: Current Native Controversies in Canada.* Toronto: McClelland and Stewart, 2004.

Morris, Alexander. *The Treaties of Canada with the Indians of Manitoba and the Northwest Territories.* Toronto: Fifth House, 1991.

Ray, Arthur J., Frank Tough, and Jim Miller. *Bounty and Benevolence: A History of Saskatchewan Indian Treaties.* Montreal and Kingston: McGill–Queen's University Press, 2000.

Treaty 7 Elders and Tribal Council with Walter Hildebrant, Sarah Carter, and Dorothy First Rider. *The True Spirit and Intent of Treaty 7.* Montreal: McGill–Queen's University Press, 1996.

Wicken, William C. *Mi'kmaq Treaties on Trial: History, Land, and Donald Marshall Jr.* Toronto: University of Toronto Press, 2002.

Woolford, Andrew. *Between Justice and Certainty: Treaty Making in British Columbia.* Vancouver: UBC Press, 2005.

NOTES

1. Alexander Morris, *The Treaties of Canada with the Indians* (Toronto: Fifth House, 1991), p. 170.

2. Norman Greenway, "Canadians Display Concern About Aboriginal Issues: Poll," *Saskatoon Star-Phoenix,* June 23, 2007, A17.

3. *Simon v. The Queen* [1985] *2 S.C.R.* 387.

4. *R. v. Badger* [1996] *1 S.C.R.* 771.

5. Canada, "Restructuring the Relationship: Vol. 2," in *For Seven Generations: An Information Legacy of the Royal Commission on Aboriginal Peoples,* CD-ROM (Ottawa: Canada Communications Group, 1996).

6. For an excellent description of the purpose of and diplomacy associated with what the author described as international conferences, see Gilles Havard, *The Great Peace of Montreal of 1701: French–Native Diplomacy in the Seventeenth Century* (Kingston and Montreal: McGill–Queen's University Press, 2001), pp. 20–26.

7. Francis Paul Prucha, *American Indian Treaties: A History of a Political Anomaly* (Berkeley: University of California Press, 1994), p. 2.

8. Emmerich de Vattel, *The Law of Nations, The Classics of International Law,* ed. James Brown Scott (Washington: Carnegie Institution of Washington, 1916), p. 160.

9. Sharon O'Brien, "Indian Treaties as International Agreements: Development of the European Nation State and International Law," in *Treaties with American Indians: An Encyclopedia of Rights, Conflicts, and Sovereignty,* ed. Donald L. Fixico (Santa Barbara: ABC-CLIO, 2008), p. 50.

10. Ibid.

11. Vine Deloria, Jr., and Raymond DeMallie, *Documents of American Indian Diplomacy: Treaties, Agreements, and Conventions, 1755–1979,* Vol. 1 (Norman: University of Oklahoma Press, 1999), p. 103.

12. James [Sakej] Youngblood Henderson, *The Mikmac Concordat* (Halifax: Fernwood, 1997).

13. Ibid.

14. Morris, *The Treaties of Canada with the Indians,* p. 64.

15. For this detailed discussion, see J.R. Miller, "Compact, Contract, Covenant: The Evolution of Indian Treaty Making," in *New Histories for Old: Changing Perspectives on Canada's Native Pasts,* ed. Ted Binnema and Susan Neylan (Vancouver: UBC Press, 2007), pp. 66–91.

16. John Borrows, *Recovering Canada: The Resurgence of Indigenous Law* (Toronto: University of Toronto Press, 2002), p. 125.

17. Canada, "Looking Forward, Looking Back," in *For Seven Generations.*

18. There are six more whose status is questionable. See Prucha, *American Indian Treaties,* p. 1.

19. Olive Patricia Dickason, *Canada's First Nations: A History of Founding Peoples from Earliest Times* (Toronto: McClelland and Stewart, 1991), p. 253.

20. Phil Bellfy, "Robinson-Superior Treaty (First Robinson Treaty)" and "Robinson-Huron Treaty (Second Robinson Treaty)," in *Treaties with American Indians: An Encyclopedia of Rights, Conflicts, and Sovereignty,* ed. Donald L. Fixico (Santa Barbara: ABC-CLIO, 2008), pp. 334–35.

21. Dennis Madill, *British Columbia Treaties in Historical Perspective* (Ottawa: Research Branch, Corporate Policy, Indian and Northern Affairs Canada, 1981), p. 8.

22. Cole Harris, *Making Native Space: Colonialism, Resistance, and Reserves in British Columbia* (Vancouver: UBC Press, 2002), p. 26.

23. See, generally, John Goddard, *Last Stand of the Lubicon Cree* (Toronto: Douglas and McIntyre, 1991); and Dawn Martin-Hill, *The Lubicon Nation: Indigenous Knowledge and Power* (Toronto: University of Toronto Press, 2008).

24. Peter A. Cumming and Neil H. Mickenberg, eds. *Native Rights in Canada,* 2nd ed. (Toronto: General, 1974), p. 148.

25. Frank Tough, *As Their Natural Resources Fail: Native Peoples and the Economic History of Northern Manitoba, 1870–1930* (Vancouver: UBC Press, 1996); and Yale D. Belanger, "'The Region Teemed with Abundance': Interlake Saulteaux Concepts of Territory and Sovereignty," in *Proceedings of the 32nd Algonquian Conference,* ed. J. Nichols (Winnipeg: University of Manitoba Press, 2001), pp. 17–34.

26. See Morris, *The Treaties of Canada with the Indians;* and Arthur J. Ray, Jim Miller, and Frank Tough, *Bounty and Benevolence: A History of Saskatchewan Treaties* (Kingston and Montreal: McGill–Queen's University Press, 2002).

27. James [Sakej] Youngblood Henderson, "Implementing the Treaty Order," in *Continuing Poundmaker's and Riel's Quest: Presentations Made at a Conference on Aboriginal Peoples and Justice,* ed. Richard Gosse, James [Sakej] Youngblood Henderson, and Roger Carter (Saskatoon: Purich, 1994), pp. 52–62.

28. Mark Dockstator, *Toward an Understanding of the Crown's Views on Justice at the Time of Entering into Treaty with the First Nations of Canada* (Saskatoon: Office of the Treaty Commissioner, 2001); and Hugh Dempsey, *Firewater: The Impact of the Whiskey Trade on the Blackfoot Nation* (Calgary: Fitzhenry and Whiteside, 2002).

29. Norman Zlotkin, "Interpretation of the Prairie Treaties," in *Beyond the Nass Valley: National Implications of the Supreme Court's* Delgamuukw *Decision,* ed. Owen Lippert (Vancouver: Fraser Institute, 2000), p. 185.

30. See Thomas Isaac, Aboriginal Law: Cases, Materials, and Commentary (Saskatoon, SK.: Purich Publishing, 1999), p. 313.

31. Writing in dissent in *R. v. Marshall* [1999] *3 S.C.R.,* Justice McLachlin summarized the prior case law regarding the principles governing treaty interpretation.

32. Peggy J. Blair, *Lament for a First Nation: The Williams Treaties of Southern Ontario* (Vancouver: UBC Press, 2008).

33. Andrew H. Fisher, "Hunting, Fishing, and Gathering," in *Treaties with American Indians: An Encyclopedia of Rights, Conflicts, and Sovereignty,* ed. Donald L. Fixico, (Santa Barbara: ABC-CLIO, 2008), pp. 147–48.

34. *R. v. Howard* [1994] *2 S.C.R.* 299.

35. Briefing by Ambassador Ted Moses on Indigenous Issues for the Heads of Foreign Posts External Affairs, Canada. [online] http://www.gcc.ca/archive/article.php?id=60. Last accessed September 10, 2008.

36. The information used for this section can be found in Yale D. Belanger, "James Bay Cree and Northern Quebec Agreement," in *Encyclopedia of American Indian History*, Vol. 2, ed. Bruce E. Johansen and Barry M. Pritzker (Santa Barbara: ABC-CLIO, 2008), pp. 565–68.

37. Bruce Clark, Native Liberty, Crown Sovereignty: The Existing Aboriginal Right of Self-Government in Canada (Kingston & Montreal: McGill-Queen's Press, 1990), p. 118.

38. In Bradford Morse, "Regaining Recognition of the Inherent Right of Aboriginal Governance," in *Aboriginal Self-Government in Canada: Current Trends and Issues*, 3rd ed., ed. Yale D. Belanger (Saskatoon: Purich, 2008), p. 58.

39. Canada, *General Briefing Note on the Comprehensive Land Claims Policy of Canada and the Status of Claims* (Ottawa: Comprehensive Claims Branch, Indian and Northern Affairs, 2007). [online] http://www.ainc-inac.gc.ca/al/ldc/ccl/pubs/gbn/gbn-eng.pdf. Last accessed December 6, 2008.

40. The data used to compile each of these brief overviews can be found at Canada, *General Briefing Note on the Comprehensive Land Claims Policy of Canada and the Status of Claims*

41. See Andrew Woolford, *Between Justice and Certainty: Treaty Making in British Columbia* (Vancouver: UBC Press, 2005).

42. B.C. Treaty Commission, "Six-Stages: Policies and Procedures". [online] http://www.bctreaty.net/files/sixstages.php. Last accessed September 3, 2008.

43. B.C. Treaty Commission, "First Nations and Negotiations" [online] http://www.bctreaty.net/files/nations_negotiations.php Last accessed September 3, 2008.

44. See "Treaty Process in Jeopardy After Vote," *Caledonia Courier*, April 4, 2007, p. 1.

45. James Keller, "B.C. Native Treaty Process Has Cost $1 Billion with Little Success: Report," *Daily Bulletin*, July 29, 2008, p. 7.

46. For an overview of this process, see Tom Molloy, *The World Is Our Witness: The Historic Journey of the Nisga'a into Canada* (Calgary: Fifth House, 2006).

47. Canada, *Fact Sheet: The Nisga'a Treaty* (Ottawa: Indian and Northern Affairs, 2008). [online] http://www.ainc-inac.gc.ca/ai/mr/is/nit-eng.asp. Last accessed December 6, 2008.

48. Office of the Treaty Commissioner, "Treaty Governance". [online] http://www.fsin.com/treatygovernance/treatytable.html. Last accessed September 5, 2008.

49. Brenda McLeod, "Treaty Land Entitlement in Saskatchewan: Conflicts in Land Use and Occupancy in the Witchekan Lake Area" (M.A. thesis, University of Saskatchewan, 2001).

50. Ibid., p. 192.

51. Noel Dyck, "The Negotiation of Indian Treaties and Land Rights in Saskatchewan," in *Aborigine Land and Land Rights*, ed. Nicolas Peterson and Marcia Langton (Canberra: Australian Institute of Aboriginal Studies, 1983).

52. Richard Bartlett, "Native Land Claims: Outstanding Treaty Land Entitlements in Saskatchewan, 1982–89," in *Devine Rule in Saskatchewan: A Decade of Hope and Hardship*, ed. Leslie Biggs and Mark Stobbe (Saskatoon: Fifth House, 1990), p. 138.

53. Treaty Land Entitlement. [online] http://www.fnmr.gov.sk.ca/lands/tle. Last accessed August 26, 2008.

54. *R. v. Badger* [1996], p. 33.

The *Indian Act* and Indian Affairs in Canada

5

I am often asked whether it would be better to change the existing Indian Act or to eliminate it entirely. Will we still need the Indian Act once our right to self-government is recognized and our treaties are implemented? I believe we will need some federal legislation to make clear the obligations the federal government bears towards First Nations peoples. This is radically different from an Indian Act that continues to allow a minister and some bureaucrats to tell people who they are, what they can do, or how they must live. This arrangement is a colonial relic.

We would all like to see it disappear.

—Ovide Mercedi (Cree)[1]

irst contact for Indigenous peoples was a strange event. By then, they were long established on their territories and had developed time-honoured economic, political, and social processes, so the sight of bedraggled newcomers who in many cases needed their help to survive did not initially inspire awe. Slowly, however, the Europeans established themselves and began working closely with Indigenous peoples, especially in terms of economy. Yet no matter how powerful their new neighbours became, and no matter how hard those neighbours tried to extend their political and legal authority beyond their communities, Indigenous leaders adhered to the belief that their nations were independent.

The best indicator of this belief is found in the two-row wampum, the *gus wen tah*, which laid the foundations for early treaties and agreements made with the Europeans. The two-row wampum was developed by Indigenous leaders as they sought peaceful coexistence with the European settlers. They wanted a relationship that emphasized Indigenous political sovereignty and economic agency. Embodying the principles of sharing, mutual recognition, respect, and partnership, the two-row wampum signified that Indigenous peoples and Europeans were two autonomous nations, each vested with its own political authority.[2]

The two-row wampum belt has three parallel rows of white beads separated by two rows of purple. These symbolize two paths, or two vessels travelling together down the same river of life. On one side is a birchbark canoe representing Indigenous interests; on the other side is a ship carrying Europeans. The two vessels represent the laws, customs, and beliefs of each group. In this scenario it is possible for both peoples to travel side by side down the river, each in their own boat, without directly or negatively influencing the other. This suggests that working and living together in the same environment is possible. Also reflected in the belt is the idea that neither side will try to steer the other's vessel—to do so might result in a collision of cultures and cause each vessel to capsize, its occupants possibly left to perish. The two rows have been described as symbolizing the nation-to-nation relationship between the Native people and the Crown, autonomous parties that are at the same time linked by a shared ecological context (the bed of white beads).

The European perspective on events differs quite dramatically. First of all, the settlers brought their own laws, which they then adapted to new colonial environments. Second, the Europeans brought the preconceived notion that Indigenous peoples were barbaric—a notion that was only strengthened by what they perceived as a lack of structured religions and land-use strategies. On that basis, they developed laws and forcibly extended them into Indigenous communities. The impact was like a fatal disease. Later on, these laws were amended to compel Indigenous people to leave their communities for villages and towns. Indigenous leaders resisted this overt attempt to draw their people into foreign legal structures, but to little avail—the myriad laws and bureaucracies established specifically to address Indigenous peoples' needs encouraged colonial leaders to forget that Native people were their political and economic equals. This chapter talks about how Europeans, while continuing to sail their own vessel and simultaneously signing treaties with Indigenous leaders, began steering that of the Indigenous people, with disastrous consequences for the latter.

The Antecedents of Canadian Indian Policy

The Indian Act did a very destructive thing in outlawing the ceremonials. This provision of the Indian Act was in place for close to 75 years and what that did was it prevented the passing down of our oral history. It prevented the passing down of our values. It meant an interruption of the respected forms of government that we used to have, and we did have forms of government be they oral and not in writing before any of the Europeans came to this country. We had a system that worked for us. We respected each other. We had ways of dealing with disputes. We did not have institutions like the courts that we are talking about now. We did not have the

massive bureaucracies that are in place today that we have to go through in order to get some
kind of recognition and some kind of resolution.

—Judge Alfred Scow (Kwakiutl)[3]

European laws mentioning North America's Indigenous peoples date back to the early seventeenth century. Laws were employed by colonial officials in their efforts to secure political authority; slowly and relentlessly, those laws subverted Indigenous governance structures and social and political philosophies. Prior to those laws, relations between Indigenous peoples and European settlers had been based on treaties and economic and military alliances. Then in 1755 the first Indian Department was established in British North America. Sir William Johnson and John Stuart were appointed the first two superintendents of the British Indian Department in British North America. Eight years later, in 1763, to preserve peaceful relations between settlers and the Indigenous populations of the increasingly volatile Ohio Valley, King George III made a Royal Proclamation that established a legal framework for Indian Department officials. The proclamation declared all land west of the Appalachians to be Indigenous hunting territory; in other words, European settlement was prohibited there. The same document barred colonists from engaging Indigenous leaders in land negotiations; in part this was a response to past frauds and abuses by colonists.

The 1763 proclamation also went far to establish the legal regime that British leaders would later use to lay claim to all of North America. It acknowledged the Indigenous right of occupancy in traditional territories, but it also declared that trade was to proceed according to Imperial regulations and that the British Parliament was to be solely responsible for protecting Native people and their lands. Finally, it required the Crown to ensure peaceful relations between settlers and Indigenous people and to protect Indigenous lands from expropriation. The purpose of this was to prevent local Native groups from being entirely dispossessed.[4]

It might appear that the Royal Proclamation was solely concerned with protecting Indigenous land rights, and in many ways that was its purpose. The reasons for enacting it, however, had more to do with establishing new, legal means to remove Indigenous peoples from lands coveted by settlers. For example, the Royal Proclamation, though it protected Indigenous lands, at the same time set out a land-surrender formula—a formula that in years to come would be utilized during the Robinson-Huron Treaties (1850) and the Numbered Treaties (1871–77, 1899–1921). Nevertheless, by the late eighteenth century the Crown was sure it had purchased sufficient territory to provide settlement lands for American Loyalists and other immigrants to Canada. This seemed to end any need to strictly interpret or adhere to the proclamation and related Indian laws. In the early nineteenth century, however, dramatic events transformed military and economic relations between Indigenous peoples and the Crown. In particular, after the War of 1812 ended,

Indigenous peoples were no longer viewed as an important military force and were abandoned as allies.[5] Even worse, the Crown desired more Indigenous lands for agricultural settlement. As will be discussed later, the British Parliament soon began framing its relationship with Indigenous peoples as one of a guardian protecting its wards. And soon after that, it began establishing inclusive laws to "protect" Indigenous peoples.

The declining military importance of Indigenous peoples also meant that the British could begin distancing themselves from past treaty relationships, especially those that emphasized equality between peoples. Decisions about Indigenous peoples were now being made in London by politicians rather than in the field by informed officials. As a result, the British policy of acknowledging Indigenous peoples as equals morphed into a policy of "civilizing" Indians. This civilization policy was meant to turn Native people away from "savagery" and "barbarism" and promote their progress (slow, no doubt) towards civilization.[6] Model farms and villages were to be constructed near non-Native communities so that Indigenous people could observe "civilizing" influences. Soon, though, this emphasis on example gave way to legal mechanisms whose purpose was to accelerate the pace of the civilizing project.

This new approach was more expensive than the old one, however. So in 1828, Major-General H.C. Darling—the military secretary to the Governor General, and later Chief Superintendent of Indian Affairs for Upper Canada—produced the Darling Report, which recommended that expenditures be slashed, which—ironically—necessitated increased short-term funding for the Indian Department. It was suggested that additional monies for Indigenous education and farming would inevitably lead to the founding of permanent communities. Falsely convinced that Indigenous peoples were wanderers by nature who lacked structured governments and established economies, colonial officials set out to permanently settle Indigenous communities. The hope was they would then be easier to govern. The seeds of what would five decades later become Canada's official reserve policy are evident in all of this; so are the fundamentals of Canada's future Indian policy.[7]

The parallel policies of assimilation and protection dovetailed into one overarching Canadian civilizing policy that eschewed the need to interact with Indigenous leaders. Now that Indigenous people had been turned into wards who must be protected and civilized, the British Parliament was responsible for legislating on *behalf* of them, instead of negotiating *with* them. Take, for example, the *Crown Lands Protection Act* of 1839, which classified lands appropriated from Aboriginal peoples as being for the residence of "certain Indian tribes" as Crown lands.[8] This was an important step in the formal codification of the guardian/ward relationship, and one that would guide treaty negotiations in the 1870s. It was followed in 1844 by the report of the Bagot Commission, which recommended centralized control over colonial Indian affairs.[9]

Contrary to the popular portrayal of Indigenous leaders as silent observers, many of them aggressively voiced their displeasure at the Crown's failure to acknowledge pre-existing Aboriginal rights.[10] For example, these leaders cited the Royal Proclamation of 1763 in arguing that they had not sold their lands to the Crown and that the right of possession remained in place.[11] Note that Indigenous populations were now being referred to in legal discourse and legislation as separate from mainstream colonial society. As a result of all this, as well as heavier reliance on reserves and aborted experiments with industrial schools (beginning with the Mohawk Institute in 1829), Indigenous peoples found themselves increasingly cut off from Canadian society, both physically and ideologically, as separate legal and social spheres would continue to evolve in opposition to Indigenous desires to partici-pate as partners in the creation of what would become Canadian Confederation in 1867.

The *Indian Act* (1876)

Potentially representing the final solution to the white society's Indian Problem, they use coop-eration of Native leaders in the design and implementation of such systems to legitimize the state's long-standing assimilationist goals for Indigenous nations and lands.

—Taiaiake Alfred (Mohawk, Kahnawake)[12]

By 1850, colonial officials were attempting to consolidate the myriad Indian laws into two parallel acts designed to deal with the infiltration of settlers into Indigenous-held territories. "An Act for the better protection of the Lands and Property of the Indians in Lower Canada" and "An Act for the protection of the Indians in Upper Canada from imposition and the property occupied or enjoyed by them from trespass and injury" transferred responsibility for leasing Indian lands and collecting rents to the Commissioner of Indian Lands. The same two acts defined who was and was not an Indian.[13] Initially these laws were implemented to pro-tect Indigenous people from fraud and other abuses. It is interesting, though, that the overar-ching goal—assimilation—was always left unstated. All the same, the point of the legislation was clear enough: remaining an Indian was no longer to be an option. A Native person who wanted to become civilized in the eyes of the law would have to formally renounce his heritage, for the two categories—Indian and civilized—were mutually exclusive. From this point on, laws aimed specifically at Indians in Canada were termed civilizing laws.

Nowhere was this more apparent than in "An Act to encourage the gradual Civilization of the Indian Tribes in this Province, and to amend the Laws respecting Indians" (1857), the first colonial law to state bluntly that assimilation was the Crown's key policy toward Native people. From now on, Native people who were capable of managing their own affairs were eligible for enfranchisement. The legislation established separate legal status for Indigenous populations, identifying them as wards under Canada's guardianship and emphasizing that the legal categories of Indian and citizen could not coexist. The Gradual Civilization Act (short title) was also the colonial government's first attempt to seize control of Indians from Westminster—a move that encountered little resistance. Colonial politicians were now empowered to enact Indian laws and policies without having to obtain permission from Britain.[14] Legislative activity increased. In 1859, Canada passed the Civilization and Enfranchisement Act, which consolidated all previous Indian legislation. In 1860, authority over Indians and Indian lands was formally transferred to the colonial legislature, which by then had embraced a policy of civilization—a policy that would remain until Indigenous peoples had embraced colonial (i.e., European) social norms.

In keeping with this now established approach to Indian policy, the Fathers of Confederation accepted responsibility for "Indians, and lands reserved for the Indians" under Section 91(24) of the *British North America Act* (1867). Canada made its first independent foray into Indian law in 1869, when it passed the "Act for the Gradual Enfranchisement of Indians and the Better Management of Indian Affairs." This legislation assumed that assimilation was inevitable and introduced the concept of nonhereditary, municipal-style government to the reserves. The previous year had seen the founding of the Indian Affairs Branch as one of four branches of the Department of the Secretary of State for the Provinces. In 1873, Indian Affairs was transferred to the Department of the Interior, once that department was established. Among federal officials, who were now involved in time-consuming and expensive treaty negotiations, this was seen as an appropriate move. For a few brief years (1871 to 1876), no further Indian legislation was written.

Then in 1876 the *Indian Act* was passed. It consolidated and amended all previous statutes related to Indigenous peoples and their government-delegated rights. It also provided for the administration of three key areas: (1) the allocation of reserve lands, (2) the definition of "Indian" status, and (3) the granting of enforcement authority to the federal government. The *Indian Act* was and remains a comprehensive piece of legislation with the authority to control almost every aspect of Native life, depending on how rigidly Indian Affairs officials choose to interpret its provisions. Early on, Indian Agents posted in or near reserve communities to administer the *Indian Act* were granted significant jurisdiction over Indians. They were ex officio justices of the peace.[15]

Provisions of the *Indian Act* forced an end to traditional governance practices, which were replaced by municipal-style councils. Traditional ways of selecting leaders, including by heredity, were outlawed. Indian Agents were granted extraordinary administrative and discretionary authority to enforce the new act. An enfranchisement process was adopted that entitled qualified individuals to full citizenship—but only after relinquishing their ties to their community. Note that the *Indian Act* was viewed as a stopgap; that is, once Native people had been absorbed into Canadian society, it would have outlived its usefulness.[16] Since Canada's Indigenous people never were absorbed, the *Indian Act* to this day is the legislation that all governments cite in their interactions with Native peoples.

Besides giving up one's culture, enfranchisement required individuals to meet a number of standards. For example, they had to obtain an education, and they had to be of strong moral character. In this way the *Indian Act* distinguished between Status and Non-Status Indians. Status Indians, who were registered with the federal government as Indians under the terms of the *Indian Act,* were eligible for minimal government services. Non-Status

Indians were not registered and therefore were not eligible for government programs. Clearly, the government's ultimate goal was to eliminate the category of Status Indians and thereby end their responsibility for all Native people. Section 12(1)b of the act was the cornerstone of this approach. Accordingly, an Indian woman who married a non-Indian man under the act had her status taken away from her; her children would also lose their status.[17] In 1880 the act was amended so that an Indian who obtained a university degree was automatically enfranchised. A further amendment in 1933 empowered Canadian officials to arbitrarily enfranchise Indians who met the *Indian Act's* qualifications.[18] Not until 1951 were these offending criteria removed from the act. Many individuals nevertheless remain convinced that the federal government wanted to rid itself of the Indian problem by eliminating the Status Indian category.

Native leaders expressed their displeasure even if overt resistance to the act was limited. There were various reasons for this reticence. Indigenous leaders in the East lacked the military power to compel the government to alter its Indian policies. The nations of the West were another story. Indeed, Crown officials agreed to negotiate treaties in an effort to remain at peace with the Plains peoples, in particular the Blackfoot (Niitsítapi) (see Chapter 4).

By the 1870s, epidemics had reduced Canada's Native population to about 125,000, even while the Canadian population as a whole was growing steadily, from 3.625 million in 1870 to 4.185 million in 1879.[19] This demographic shift reduced the military strength of Indigenous nations; more important, it left most Native communities struggling bleakly to cope with the attendant loss of Indigenous knowledge. In the East, most communities were surrounded by non-Native society; in the West, the steady expansion of European settlement was destabilizing Indigenous economies. European society was converging on Native peoples from all directions. The impact would be calamitous.

Native Participation in Formulating the *Indian Act*

Following the War of 1812, colonial authorities began interfering directly with the internal autonomy and sovereignty of several Indigenous nations. They did so by destroying traditional structures of governance and institutionalizing their own "puppet" governments, which were supposed to aid in the goal of "civilizing" the Indian, politically, economically, socially, and religiously.

—Kiera Ladner (Cree)[20]

The contemporary view is that Native leaders watched helplessly from the sidelines while the federal government imposed the *Indian Act*. Actually, several Native leaders associated with the Grand General Indian Council of Ontario and Quebec (GIC) reviewed and commented on various drafts of the act. Impressed with the GIC's political standing in the communities it claimed to represent, the Secretary of State for the Provinces, Joseph Howe, prefaced the 1870 Indian Branch Report by stating that a "good deal of diversity of opinion exists among many of the more intelligent Indians, as to some clauses of the laws by which their affairs are regulated." He also indicated that "certain resolutions were passed, to which due weight will be given, should the Indian laws be revised."[21]

The GIC's involvement in the *Indian Act* was part of a broader Indigenous strategy to establish a political dialogue with Canadian officials—a strategy that failed for several reasons. First, beyond commenting on the act's provisions, the GIC had little influence in the process. Second, the hoped-for political dialogue failed to develop. Third, Indian Affairs officials believed that the organization spoke for Canadian Indians. This may not have appeared to be a problem at the time, but it initiated a trend that had federal officials seeking out a Native political organization to speak for Native people to the exclusion of band council chiefs and influential community leaders. Appreciative of the GIC's efforts, Indian Affairs paid most of its operating expenses prior to its third conference, at Sarnia in 1874. David Laird, the Superintendent-General of Indian Affairs, again enlisted the GIC to critique federal Indian policy by contributing $300 to help defray delegates' travel expenses.[22] Soon after, the GIC's first vice president, William Wawanosh, indicated that it was "high time" Native people were placed on "equal footing" with other Canadians.[23]

The GIC responded by offering two enfranchisement schemes. The Reverend Allen Salt (Ojibwa) proposed assimilation without taking into account the paradoxical nature of Indian land ownership and Indian advancement, for "so long as land, a citizen's greatest asset, remained inalienable, he could not participate in the economic life of the country to his greatest extent."[24] Dr. Peter Edmund Jones (Ojibwa), a medical doctor and one-time community Indian Agent, and the son of noted Methodist missionary and author Peter Jones, developed a scheme that would automatically exempt the wives and children of enfranchised Indians from the *Indian Act*. After much debate, "a large majority" accepted Jones's proposal without amendment. This led to its inclusion, in an altered form, in the 1876 *Indian Act*.[25] On receiving a copy of the new *Indian Act* complete with these recommended changes, the GIC delegates voiced their approval. In August, the Grand Council President the Reverend H.P. Chase received a letter from Laird expressing his "gratification" that the GIC had accepted the act. Laird further informed GIC leaders of his willingness to work with the organization; in theory, this would have permitted delegates to guide both the evolution and the philosophical underpinnings of Indian legislation. In other words, federal officials were seeking their wards' advice about how best to facilitate their own cultural absorption into Canadian society.

Criminalizing Native Culture in Canada

The *Indian Act* took direct aim at Native peoples' lifestyles, making it illegal in many respects to be an Indian. Two examples are especially instructive, for they demonstrate how the act was used to undermine Native societies and thereby compel assimilation. The first was the banning of the potlatch; the second was the banning of the Sundance.

In 1884 the *Indian Act* was amended to prohibit the potlatch, a ceremony among the West Coast nations that marked important events such as the appointment of chiefs. It involved individuals giving away their possessions.[26] Penalties for violating the act's potlatching provision ranged from two to six months in jail. By that point, the *Indian Act* was already being applied to alter traditional governance and land-use regimes. This new approach was a direct assault on cultural practices. The ban on such practices provided officials with useful leverage for civilizing Indians.[27] The primary strategy here was for Indian Agents to harass potlatch participants; not until 1922 was anyone actually arrested for taking part in one (see box). In 1895 the *Indian Act* was again amended to criminalize the Sundance among the Blackfoot and the Thirst Dance among the Cree and Saulteaux. All three are Plains peoples. Specifically, it was now illegal to give away property or mutilate one's own body. However, the dancers were immune from prosecution. Both bans were removed from the *Indian Act* in 1951.

DAN CRANMER'S POTLATCH

A potlatch was an important economic, political, and legal institution among Northwest Coast nations. It was used to confer leadership positions, to celebrate successful political negotiations with a neighbouring nation; to redistribute wealth to community members in need; to bestow an individual with a hereditary name; and for occasions of birth, marriage, and death. It was outlawed in 1884, but not until 1913 did some officials (by no means all) work up the nerve to try enforcing the ban. Several attempts to end the practice followed. They failed, owing to uneven enforcement; many Indian Agents were not at all certain the law was legitimate. Meantime, Native people found ways to circumvent the law. For example, potlatches could be held during the Christmas season to coincide with mainstream society's "giveaways." Such was the case with Dan Cranmer's potlatch, held on Christmas Day of 1921. Having been alerted to the celebration, Indian Agents and local police arrested more than 50 attendees. In February 1922, 49 people were convicted and sent to jail in Vancouver. In all, 22 were sentenced to two months in prison, 4 were sentenced to six months, and 23 were given suspended sentences after agreeing to renounce potlatching and to hand over their ceremonial regalia to officials.[28]

Residential Schools:
A Mechanism of Assimilation

To the approximately 80,000 living former students and all family members and communities, the Government of Canada now recognizes that it was wrong to forcibly remove children from their homes, and we apologize for having done this. We now recognize that it was wrong to separate children from rich and vibrant cultures and traditions, that it created a void in many lives and communities, and we apologize for having done this. We now recognize that in separating children from their families, we undermined the ability of many to adequately parent their own children and sowed the seeds for generations to follow, and we apologize for having done this. We now recognize that far too often these institutions gave rise to abuse or neglect and were inadequately controlled, and we apologize for failing to protect you.

—Prime Minister Stephen Harper, apology to residential school survivors, June 11, 2008[29]

Federal officials came more and more to view Indigenous people as uncivilized and inherently criminal. So they devised the residential-school system to assist their acculturation. The schools were loosely patterned on the Carlisle Indian Industrial Schools in the United States. Canada's residential schools included industrial schools, boarding schools, student residences, hostels, and billets. They were founded in every province except New Brunswick and Prince Edward Island. Canadian officials had taken responsibility for educating Native children since 1842. Then in 1857, the *Gradual Civilization Act* set aside funds for schools that would teach English to Native people. By 1874 a formal school system had been established to educate Native people so as to ease their transition into mainstream society. With the *Indian Act* (1876), the federal government accepted responsibility for Native children's education, though not until 1883–84 did the first schools open in western Canada, at Qu'Appelle, High River, and Battleford. These early schools were largely ad hoc institutions. In 1892, by order-in-council, formal regulations were established for residential schools. From that point on they were funded by a federal-grant arrangement in the amount of $110 to $145 per student per year (for church-run schools) and $72 per student (for day schools).[30]

Native leaders railed against what they saw as an assimilation project, yet many also acknowledged the value of a "white" education, which in any case had been promised them under the treaties they had signed. However, the treaties' unwritten provisions had called for community-based educational norms, which the residential schools did anything but reflect. Indeed, Canadian officials built the residential schools far from reserve communities so that students had to leave their community each fall to attend them. The distance from the community was meant in part to discourage children from fleeing. Entering the school was a traumatic event: the children had their hair shorn, and their clothing was replaced with work clothes. In most residential schools, students were forbidden to speak their own language and could be severely punished if caught doing so. Religious studies were interspersed with mainstream curricula. Children were expected to work in the fields to offset the costs of their education.[31] By the time the system was shut down in the 1980s, more than 150,000 children had attended 132 residential schools. The last federally operated residential school, in Saskatchewan (Gordon Indian Residential School), closed its doors in 1996.

In June 2008 Prime Minister Stephen Harper formally apologized for the residential-school policy, admitting that "the treatment of children in these schools is a sad chapter in our history."[32] The apology had been a long time coming. Most residential-school survivors

At a ceremony in the House of Commons on June 11, 2008, AFN Chief Phil Fontaine (right, wearing headdress) watches as Prime Minister Stephen Harper officially apologizes for more than a century of abuse and cultural loss involving Indian residential schools.

tended to keep silent about their horrific experiences as did those who cited positive experiences. By the 1970s, however, more were speaking openly to the press about their suffering and demanding that the federal government acknowledge the damage wrought. In the 1980s tales of sexual and other forms of abuse at residential schools began to appear in the media. In 1990 this led Phil Fontaine, then National Chief of the Assembly of Manitoba Chiefs (AMC), and currently the Grand Chief of the Assembly of First Nations (AFN), to go public about the abuse he had experienced in a residential school. He, too, demanded a formal apology. Several lawsuits were launched; support groups were formed. In 1996 the Royal Commission on Aboriginal Peoples (RCAP), in its Final Report, demanded a public inquiry to investigate and document residential school abuses. The following year the AFN initiated discussions with the federal government and school survivors; these resulted in a public statement of regret by Indian Affairs Minister Jane Stewart in January 1998. An Aboriginal Healing Foundation was created, and $350 million fund was set aside for survivors.[33]

On June 11, 2008, Prime Minister Stephen Harper finally delivered the apology that Native people had been demanding since the 1970s. In doing so he admitted the Canadian government's culpability, though he also described the residential-school model as "joint ventures with Anglican, Catholic, Presbyterian, and United churches." His apology was detailed:

- "Indian residential schools separated over 150,000 aboriginal children from their families and communities";
- "Two primary objectives of the residential school system were to remove and isolate children from the influence of their homes, families, traditions and cultures, and to assimilate them into the dominant culture";
- "Today, we recognize that this policy of assimilation was wrong, has caused great harm, and has no place in our country";
- "The government now recognizes that the consequences of the Indian residential schools policy were profoundly negative and that this policy has had a lasting and damaging impact on aboriginal culture, heritage and language";
- "The legacy of Indian residential schools has contributed to social problems that continue to exist in many communities today";
- "The government recognizes that the absence of an apology has been an impediment to healing and reconciliation."[32]

Yet many residential school survivors believed that notwithstanding the statement of regret, the funding for curative programs, and the prime minister's formal apology, the true story of residential schools had been disregarded. In response, a Truth and Reconciliation Commission (TRC) was established June 1, 2008, as part of the Indian Residential Schools Settlement Agreement reached in September 2007 (see box). The TRC has been tasked with writing a complete historical record about the schools' policies and operations based on research examining the conditions that gave rise to those schools. It is hoped that the report will provide First Nations, Inuit, and Métis survivors the opportunity to share their experiences, thereby drawing all Canadians into a process of truth, healing, and reconciliation. As stated on the TRC website, "when the average Canadian hears the experiences of former students . . . this will bring about a new understanding, and hopefully a better relationship between all Canadians."[34] In October 2008 Commissioner and former Supreme Court Justice Harry LaForme resigned, citing undue political interference from the Assembly of First Nations, in particular Grand Chief Phil Fontaine, whom he claimed was attempting to influence the TRC to abandon reconciliation in lieu of a more inflexible political orientation.

INDIAN RESIDENTIAL SCHOOLS SETTLEMENT AGREEMENT (IRSSA)

In May 2006 an agreement-in-principle accepted by the Government of Canada became the Indian Residential Schools Settlement Agreement (IRSSA). It was submitted to the courts in nine jurisdictions across Canada for approval, which was given on March 23, 2007. A five-month "opt-out" period lasted until August to enable former students to determine whether they would seek inclusion in the IRSSA. Those who opt out are not eligible for the Common Experience Payment, nor are they eligible to enter the Independent Assessment Process. In such cases, litigation is the only avenue available to those still seeking resolution of their claims. A proviso has been included indicating that should more than 5,000 former students opt out, the agreement can be declared null and void.

The Department of Indian Affairs

Between 1755 and 1830 the Department of Indian Affairs (DIA) was a branch of the military. A civilian Department of Indian Affairs replaced it, largely to facilitate the purchase and sale of Native lands in Upper Canada. Then in 1844, responsibility for Indian Affairs was transferred to the Province of Canada from the Imperial authorities. In 1868 the Department of the Secretary of State was established. One of its portfolios was the supervision of Native peoples. This arrangement lasted until 1873. Indian Affairs achieved the status of a separate department in 1880 through an amendment to the *Indian Act*. However, it was still under the direction of the Minister of the Interior, who now held the secondary title of Superintendent-General of Indian Affairs.

The DIA's mandate was to "civilize" Canada's "Indians" through assimilation. In 1881 the *Indian Act* was amended to strengthen the authority of Indian Agents. They now had the powers of justices of the peace, which meant they could prosecute Native people and sentence them for violating a provision of the *Indian Act*. The *Indian Advancement Act* of 1884 imposed *Indian Act* provisions on band councils. Around the same time, the department issued individual allotment tickets, which placed pressure on Canadian Native leaders to subdivide previously protected reserves in various regions of Canada. The following year yet another amendment to the act strengthened government control over reserve elections by granting the Indian Agent final say over election results in the event of a tie. Later that same year, the act was amended (again) to permit the Superintendent-General of Indian Affairs to determine who would or would not be recognized as a band member.

For cost-cutting reasons, Indian Affairs was often restructured over the next five years as federal officials attempted to facilitate Native people's assimilation into mainstream society. This resulted in the creation of several distinct branches, reflecting the expanded nature of the department's activities. In 1936, however, the department was dissolved and responsibility for Indian Affairs was transferred to the Department of Mines and Resources, where a subdepartment was established: the Indian Affairs Branch (IAB). The IAB included the following components: field administration, a medical welfare and training service, reserve and trust services, and a records service.[35] Over the next three decades, responsibility for Indian Affairs was transferred a number of times; between 1949 and 1966 it was actually located within the Department of Immigration and Citizenship.

In 1964, R.F. Battle was appointed Assistant Deputy Minister of Indian Affairs and he spearheaded a restructuring of the branch. This was followed by the formation of three new directorates: the Development Directorate, responsible for establishing and coordinating social, industrial, and resource development; the Education Directorate, responsible for establishing and carrying out education policy; and the Administration Directorate, responsible for dealing with Indian lands and estates, membership, records management, field administration, and secretariat and support services. To herd all of these new cats, on June 16, 1966, the Department of Indian Affairs and Northern Development (DIAND) was established by the *Government Organization Act*. DIAND was responsible for administering Indian Affairs in Canada. This involved reconciling the socioeconomic interests of an increasingly suspicious and militant Native leadership with myriad legislation and the agendas of federal, provincial, and territorial bodies.

Besides administering Indian and Inuit affairs, DIAND was responsible for developing national parks and managing Canada's wildlife. Arthur Laing, a Progressive Conservative, was appointed minister; E.A. Côté was appointed deputy minister to oversee the department's five branches. Legislation assigned Indian Affairs responsibility for Indian and Inuit affairs and for the residents of Yukon and the Northwest Territories as well as their resources. In an attempt to improve accountability to their clientele, the department established nine regional Indian Affairs offices across Canada. Two years later, DIAND announced that it was restructuring again. It established an "Indian–Eskimo" Bureau to provide advisory services and to liaise with field staff responsible for departmental programs. Within DIAND, four directorates were created: policy and planning, administration, development, and education. Clearly, the Indian Affairs bureaucracy was increasing at an alarming rate.

In 1970 the Economic Development Branch was created to help Native peoples achieve economic self-sufficiency, and the Indian Economic Development Fund was established. That same year the Membership Division began a policy of transferring local administration of the membership function to First Nation bands, and the federal government began funding various Native groups and associations to research treaties and Aboriginal rights. In 1972, spurred on by the National Indian Brotherhood's (NIB) demands for greater autonomy over educational programs, DIAND launched a devolution program that transferred responsibility for education to Native communities.[36] Devolution became central to DIAND's philosophy and is still popular today.[37]

Today, Indian and Northern Affairs Canada (INAC) has two mandates: (1) Indian and Inuit Affairs, and (2) Northern Affairs. Responsible for meeting the federal government's constitutional, treaty, political, and legal responsibilities to the First Nations, the Inuit, and northerners, INAC's mandate is all-encompassing; that mandate is derived from the *Indian Act,* territorial acts, and legal obligations arising from Section 91(24) of the *British North America Act* (1867). This is a significant level of responsibility that entails providing a broad range of services. This suggests that INAC officials should be working closely with First Nations, the Inuit, the Métis, and northerners, as well as other federal departments and agencies and the provinces and territories.

INAC delivers basic services such as education, social assistance, housing, and community infrastructure to Status Indian and Inuit communities. It also administers reserve lands, oversees elections of First Nation councils, registers entitlement to Indian status and First Nation membership, and administers First Nation trust funds and, sometimes, the estates of individual Native persons. On top of all this, it negotiates land claims. According to the INAC website, the department's priorities include these: recognition of greater program and political authority of First Nations and territorial governments by establishing a framework for the effective implementation of the inherent right of self-government; specific initiatives to implement self-government; continued devolution to territories of program administration; and helping First Nations and Inuit peoples strengthen their communities.

In many respects, INAC's mandate in 2009 reflects basic Indian policy of the late 1860s, when the first federal political branch was assigned responsibility for Indian affairs. Arguably, INAC's unstated goal remains to facilitate the physical and cultural absorption of Status Indians, Inuit, and Métis into mainstream Canadian society. In other words, paternalism is still an operating philosophy. Guided by the *Indian Act,* INAC exerts significant control over Canada's First Nations. For instance, Section 6 of the act still *permits* INAC to determine who is or is not an Indian in Canada. This has cut off a number of Native people from government programs. And through Section 81, INAC can limit the powers of band councils. Overall, despite INAC's self-professed interest in promoting self-government, it continues to control most aspects of First Nations life in Canada.

Revising the *Indian Act* (Again)

Due to colonial and provincial policy, the Nisga'a were denied their rights to traditional territories and were prohibited by federal law from seeking legal recourse to protect our lands. The government even introduced special legislation declaring that further activity leading towards the resolution of the land question would be illegal. Native people were prohibited from discussing land rights questions. Legislation in 1927 made it illegal for natives to raise money to pursue land claims, and illegal for a lawyer to help them with land claims.

—Rod Robinson (Sim'oogit Minee'eskw)[38]

By the late nineteenth century the *Indian Act* was being referred to in DIA dispatches to field agents in relation to questions of land use and ownership, health regulations, tribal government elections, and justice issues. The *Indian Act* was open to amendment whenever a situation developed that was not already dealt with in the existing act's provisions. For instance, an 1881 amendment made it illegal for Indians to sell their agricultural produce without an Indian Agent's permission (see box). This provision was extended in 1941 to all Indians in Canada regarding the sale of furs and wild animals. As mentioned, amendments in 1884 outlawed the potlatch; and 11 years later, on the Plains, the Sundance was made illegal. A 1914 amendment forbade Indians to wear Native costumes in any dance, show, exhibition, stampede, or pageant without the DIA's permission. A 1920 amendment made residential-school attendance compulsory and set out penalties for parents who refused to part with their children. And a 1927 amendment made it illegal for Indians to raise money to hire a lawyer to pursue land claims against the government. The attached box represents but a handful of *Indian Act* amendments made between 1880 and 1951.

By the 1940s, Canadian officials reluctantly admitted that the enfranchisement policy had failed. The House of Commons Special Committee on Reconstruction (1943) confirmed officials' fears while highlighting poor on-reserve living conditions. This led to a Special Joint Committee of the Senate and House of Commons (SJC), which sat from 1946 to 1948. The *Indian Act* was the catalyst for debate. The SJC held 128 sessions, heard 122 witnesses, including 31 Native leaders, and published 411 written briefs. It called for the

Indian Act to be thoroughly overhauled; the goal of this complete remake was to help Native peoples gradually advance themselves from wardship to citizenship.[39] In 1951, when the new *Indian Act* was unveiled, many of its more restrictive provisions had been repealed, such as those concerning the potlatch and the Sundance. Generally, though, the new act was little more than a recycled version of the old one, the main difference being that the 1951 act strengthened the power of provincial laws over Native people.[40]

Few significant changes to the *Indian Act* were implemented over the next 15 years. Then in 1969, soon after being elected, Prime Minister Pierre Trudeau (Liberal) proposed its repeal. Citing his "just society" mandate, he made the case that eliminating the act would bring an end to the social and economic inequalities faced by Native people; it would do so by terminating both special status for Native people and federal responsibility for Indian Affairs. However, opposition to Trudeau's plan within the Native community was so strong that the White Paper proposing it was withdrawn in 1971.

The next major change to the *Indian Act* was in 1985 with the passing of Bill C–31 (see below). This bill removed many of the discriminatory provisions of the *Indian Act*, especially the ones that discriminated against women. It also changed the meaning of "Status Indian" and for the first time permitted limited reinstatement of Indians who in the past had been denied their status, or had lost status and/or band membership. Finally, it allowed bands to make their own membership rules.

INDIAN ACT AMENDMENTS

1881. *Amended* to make officers of the Indian Department, including Indian Agents, legal justices of the peace, able to enforce regulations. The following year, Indian Agents were granted the same legal powers as magistrates. *Amended,* as well, to prohibit the sale of agricultural produce by Indians in the Prairie provinces without an appropriate permit from an Indian Agent. This prohibition is still included in the Indian Act, though not enforced.

1884. *Amended* to prevent elected band leaders who had been deposed from office from being re-elected.

1884. *Amended* to prohibit religious ceremonies (potlatch).

1894. *Amended* to remove band control of non-Natives living on reserve. This power now rested exclusively in the hands of the Superintendent-General of Indian Affairs.

1905. *Amended* to allow Aboriginal people to be removed from reserves near towns with more than 8,000 residents.

1906. *Amended* to allow 50 percent of the sale price of reserve lands to be given to band members, following the surrender of that land.

1911. *Amended* to allow municipalities and companies to expropriate portions of reserves, without surrender, for roads, railways, and other public works. Further *amended* to allow a judge to move an entire reserve away from a municipality if it was deemed "expedient." These amendments were also known as the *Oliver Act.*

1914. *Amended* to require Indians in the West to seek official permission before appearing in "Aboriginal costume" in any "dance, show, exhibition, stampede or pageant."

1918. *Amended* to allow the Superintendent-General to lease out uncultivated reserve lands to non-Aboriginals if the new leaseholder would use it for farming or pasture.

1920. *Amended* to allow the DIA to ban hereditary rule of bands. Further *amended* to allow for the involuntary enfranchisement (and loss of treaty rights) of any Status Indian considered fit by the DIA without the possession of land (previously required for those living off reserve). Repealed two years later, but reintroduced in a modified form in 1933.

1927. *Amended* to prevent any lawyer from pursuing Native legal claims without a special licence from the Superintendent-General. This effectively prevented any First Nation from pursuing Aboriginal land claims.

1930. *Amended* to prevent a pool hall owner from allowing entrance to any Native person who "by inordinate frequenting of a pool room either on or off an Indian reserve misspends or wastes his time or means to the detriment of himself, his family or household." The owner could face a fine or a one-month jail term.

1936. *Amended* to allow Indian Agents to direct band council meetings, and to cast a deciding vote in the event of a tie.

1951. Amended to allow the sale and slaughter of livestock without an Indian Agent permit. *Amended* to allow Status women to vote in band elections. *Amended* to allow attempts to pursue land claims (this had been forbidden). *Amended* to allow certain religious ceremonies, such as the potlatch and Sundance (i.e., ones that had previously been banned). *Amended* to compulsorily enfranchise First Nations women who married Non-Status men (including Métis, Inuit, and Non-Status Indians, as well as non-Aboriginal men), thus removing their status and that of any children from the marriage.

1961. *Amended* to end the compulsory enfranchisement of men or bands.

1985. *Amended* to allow First Nations women the right to keep/regain their status even after marrying out, and to grant status to the children (but not grandchildren) of such a marriage. This amendment was also known as Bill C–31. According to this act, a child of a Status/Non-Status marriage would retain status, but if his/her child in turn married a Non-Status or another Status/Non-Status child, their children would not be granted status. Blood quantum was disregarded, or rather, it was replaced by a two-generation cutoff clause, and full-blood/half-blood categories were replaced with categories 6–1 (full status) and 6–2 (half status).

2000. *Amended* to allow band members living off reserve to vote in band elections and referendums.

Source: Copyright © 2008 Wikipedia.

Bill C–31

The legal system of Canada is now coming into increased contact with First Nations. Yet the Canadian legal system constructs gender in a very different way; in it, gendered exclusions are not unusual. In my view, the failure to take account of gender in litigating First Nations land or governance issues leaves us vulnerable to another round of colonial intrusions, this time at the hands of the judiciary. This outcome will be harmful to all First Nations citizens, not just the women.

—Patricia A. Monture (Mohawk)[41]

With the 1857 *Gradual Civilization Act*, married Indigenous women and their children lost their status if their husband/father lost status. This set in motion a process whereby a woman's legal identity was directly tied to her marital status. The difference between Status and Non-Status Indians is on the surface difficult to tell. A Status Indian refers to a person recorded as an Indian in the Indian Registry, whereas a Non-Status Indian refers to a person of Indian ancestry who is not registered as an Indian. Individuals have often been left off treaty or band lists at the time of enrollment, or they have been removed from the Indian Registry according to the *Indian Act's* enfranchisement provisions. This approach was integrated into the *Indian Act* of 1876. According to Section 12(1)(b) of that act, a woman marrying a non-Indian man would lose her status. Also, marrying an Indian from another community would result in the transfer of the woman's membership from her home community to her husband's.[42]

Yet being married to an Indian man did not ensure continuation of a woman's status. During this period, any Indian who voluntarily enfranchised lost his or her status; so did any Indian who earned a university degree, who practised medicine or law, or who entered the Christian clergy. This meant, for example, that the wife of a man who obtained a university degree would have her status revoked, and moreover, she could regain it only by marrying another Status man. The resultant sexual discrimination affected Native women and their children in a number of ways. Besides not being able to reside in their home community, share in its collective property, and be buried on reserve, Non-Status women were no longer protected by the *Indian Act* and lost the right to hunt and fish. Education and health benefits were also unavailable. On top of all this, until 1951, women were prohibited from running for elected positions (chief, band councillor) and were not even permitted to vote.[43]

The 1951 *Indian Act* amendments removed the discriminatory section; however, the general ethos remained in place. In two Supreme Court of Canada cases heard simultaneously in 1973, the Court ruled that, whatever the complaints, Parliament had the power to determine who was an Indian and who was not.[44] In response, Sandra Lovelace of the Maliseet First Nation of New Brunswick petitioned the United Nations International Human Rights Committee, claiming that the *Indian Act* violated the International Covenant on Civil and Political Rights. On July 30, 1981, Canada was found in breach of Native women's rights—an embarrassing decision that led officials to reassess the legislation. Later that year the Governor General decreed that Indian bands would be permitted to remove themselves from 12(1)(b). A mere 19 percent of all bands chose to suspend the offending section in protection of women's rights.

Four years later, the government formally amended the *Indian Act*. These amendments, known as Bill C–31, took effect in 1985 and were designed to remedy the discriminatory provisions. Three key changes were introduced:

- The reinstatement of Registered Indian status. This mainly affected women who had lost their eligibility for registration through provisions in earlier versions of the *Indian Act*. The amendments also provided for the first-time registration of many children;
- The introduction of new rules governing entitlement to Indian registration for all children born after April 16, 1985 (Section 6); and
- The new right of First Nations to develop and apply their own rules governing membership (Section 10).

As a result of Bill C–31, 174,000 individuals have been registered. About 106,000 of these cases have involved the regaining of status. The rest are from births since 1985.[45] Bill C–31 did not eliminate discrimination; more accurately, it deferred it from one generation of women to their descendants. Also, a band's right to determine membership was constrained, in the sense that the act compelled bands to restore membership to women who had been stripped of Indian status and band membership through marriage to non-Indian men. Furthermore, "with the 1985 amendments, popularly known as Bill C–31, came new policies. In section 6, Bill C–31 created two classes of registration: 6(1) designates individuals deemed to have two parents with Indian status, while section 6(2) lists individuals with only one registered parent. For women to register their children, they now must disclose the father's identity and prove his Indian status"[46] (see Figure 5-1).

The results of Bill C–31 have been described as chaotic. Though status has been returned to countless women, the percentage of women and their children with status continues to decline, in part because the Crown retains responsibility for determining status. The Native Women's Association of Canada (NWAC) has condemned Bill C–31, arguing that Native women are being forced to contend with more exclusive membership codes and/or self-government agreements with like provisions. Also, the influx of Bill C–31 women and their children back to their home communities has strained local resources to the point that on returning, animosities often develop. Lifetime residents often look unfavourably on returning individuals, who demand a percentage of pre-established budgets, leaving less available per person. Another problem is that land and housing are not available for returnees. Finally, since Bill C–31 was enacted, there have "been hundreds of cases being litigated in the courts. These cases deal with membership issues, status issues and continued discrimination and sexual discrimination within Bill C–31."[47]

Figure 5-1 How to Trace Indian Status

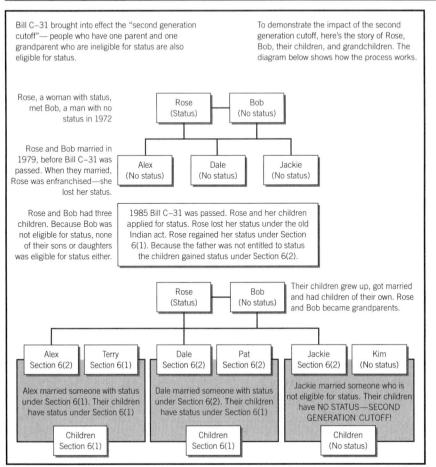

Bill C–31 brought into effect the "second generation cutoff"— people who have one parent and one grandparent who are ineligible for status are also eligible for status.

To demonstrate the impact of the second generation cutoff, here's the story of Rose, Bob, their children, and grandchildren. The diagram below shows how the process works.

Rose, a woman with status, met Bob, a man with no status in 1972

Rose (Status) —— Bob (No status)

Rose and Bob married in 1979, before Bill C–31 was passed. When they married, Rose was enfranchised—she lost her status.

Alex (No status)   Dale (No status)   Jackie (No status)

Rose and Bob had three children. Because Bob was not eligible for status, none of their sons or daughters was eligible for status either.

1985 Bill C–31 was passed. Rose and her children applied for status. Rose lost her status under the old Indian act. Rose regained her status under Section 6(1). Because the father was not entitled to status the children gained status under Section 6(2).

Rose (Status) —— Bob (No status)

Their children grew up, got married and had children of their own. Rose and Bob became grandparents.

Alex Section 6(2)   Terry Section 6(1)   Dale Section 6(2)   Pat Section 6(2)   Jackie Section 6(2)   Kim (No status)

Alex married someone with status under Section 6(1). Their children have status under Section 6(1)

Dale married someone with status under Section 6(2). Their children have status under Section 6(1)

Jackie married someone who is not eligible for status. Their children have NO STATUS—SECOND GENERATION CUTOFF!

Children Section 6(1)   Children Section 6(1)   Children (No status)

Source: Courtesy of Mother of Red Nations Women's Council of Manitoba.

HOW TO LOSE STATUS, PRE-BILL C–31

Marriage to a non-Indian. If a registered Indian woman married a non-Indian, she automatically lost her Indian status. She was no longer considered an Indian as defined by the *Indian Act;* neither were any of her children if they were born after her marriage.

Enfranchisement. Before April 17, 1985, a person could apply to give up his or her Indian status for various reasons, including to gain the right to vote in a federal election. Until 1960 the only way Indians could vote in federal elections was by giving up their Indian status.

Foreign residence. An Indian who lived outside Canada for more than five years lost his or her Indian status.

Source: The Indian Register. Ottawa: Indian and Northern Affairs Canada, July 2003. http://www.ainc-inac.gc.ca/br/is/tir-eng.asp. Reproduced with the permission of the Minister of Public Works and Government Services Canada, 2008.

First Nations Governance Initiative

We must create our own institutions, under our own authority, consistent with our own culture and values.

—Roberta Jamieson (Six Nations of Grand River)[48]

The most recent attempt to revise the *Indian Act* was announced in April 2001 by then–Indian Affairs Minister Robert Nault. The proposed revisions, the *First Nations Governance Act* (FNGA), generated significant opposition from the Assembly of First Nations (AFN) as well as other Native organizations nationally. Soon after, two additional bills were tabled: Bill C–6, the *Specific Claims Resolution Act;* and Bill C–19, the *First Nations Fiscal and Statistical Management Act.* Arguably when read together, the three acts seem designed to establish First Nations communities as municipalities. Bill C–6 assigned the federal government responsibility for funding First Nations research to pursue claims and also implemented procedural guidelines for specific claims. The FNGA (Bill C–7) aimed to legally entrench a definition of Aboriginal self-government, whereas Bill C–19 called for the creation of an institutional framework to provide First Nations with the means to address on-reserve economic development and fiscal issues; this would enable First Nations governments to generate their own financing through property taxes and structured borrowing.

Criticism of the proposed act was vocal and detailed. These were particular concerns:

- *Elections and leadership selection.* The new legislation did not take into account the rights of First Nations to elect their leaders according to custom, traditions, and hierarchy.
- *Legal standing and capacity.* Many First Nations can already enter into contracts, sue, be sued, and create corporations. The proposed legislation would have further incorporated First Nations into the Canadian political framework, without consideration of their inherent right to self-government.
- *Powers and authorities.* The legislation included procedures for passing bylaws, which was an infringement on the Aboriginal right to self-determination. First Nations seeking to develop community-based systems of justice and legal institutions acknowledged that Native enforcement officers require training that is unaffordable. It was recommended that the penalties collected from the enforcement of bylaws go directly to Native legal institutions.
- *Financial and operational accountability restrictions on First Nations' spending.* This had the potential to inhibit the amount of money spent on Native interests. Also, Native Canadians had faith in their ability to govern their own financial institutions and believed that further government interference would undermine Aboriginal self-government.[49]

Unlike the federal government's FNGA, which would apply to all First Nations in Canada, the proposed fiscal-institutions legislation was intended to be "opt-in." There was a concern among Native groups that establishing more government agencies would only strengthen Ottawa's already significant jurisdictional authority over First Nations. Also, this self-government model might confer a right, but it was a delegated right that did not make fiscal responsibility any easier to develop. In effect, Native people were being told to quickly develop more stable and functional governance structures—even though mainstream Canadians, through their European forbears, had taken centuries to do the same. This attempt to establish greater legislative control over all of Canada's First Nations is revealing. It seems that the federal government perceives the right of Aboriginal self-government to be not inherent but rather a product of legislation formulated to streamline existing governing processes. Native groups responded harshly to Nault's plans, and in 2004 Bill C–7 was permitted to lapse.

Bill C–6 (the *Specific Claims Resolution Act*) and Bill C–19 (later Bill C–20; the *First Nations Fiscal and Statistical Management Act*) were both granted Royal Assent, however. As to the former, the Federation of Saskatchewan Indian Nations (FSIN) had particular concerns, including these:

- The bill limits access to the tribunal to claims under $10 million for determining both validity and compensation. There would not even be access to nonbinding recommendations for claims over $10 million, which leaves no option for claims over the cap that cannot be settled through negotiation, other than litigation. Currently all claims, regardless of size, can ask for a nonbinding recommendation by the Indian Claims Commission. This option disappears under the bill. At the very least all claims should have access to the tribunal for validation purposes.
- The bill allows the federal government to indefinitely delay responding to First Nations claims. This is one of the most significant problems of the current system. Interest and costs count toward the cap on the tribunal, so the federal government is actually rewarded for delay.
- The bill does not allow for independent appointments. All appointments and renewals are to be made by Cabinet, solely on the minister's recommendation.
- The bill narrows the definition of a specific claim even from that of the current policy. Bill C–6 would exclude obligations arising under treaties or agreements that do not deal with land and assets, as well as unilateral federal undertakings to provide lands or assets.[50]

The FSIN was joined by, among others, the AFN in lobbying against the legislation. In 2005, two years after it received Royal Assent, the new Minister of Indian Affairs, Andy Scott, announced that Bill C–6 would not be implemented.[51]

Bill C–23 created four First Nations institutions: the First Nations Tax Commission (FNTC), the First Nations Finance Authority (FNFA), the First Nations Financial Management Board (FNFMB), and an institute of First Nations Statistics (FNS). The FNTC is a ten-member board that guides First Nations governments in establishing and maintaining fair and efficient First Nations property tax regimes. The FNFA raises capital by issuing bonds on behalf of its member First Nations governments. The proceeds of the bond issues are used by First Nations to build community infrastructure such as sewers, roads, and water mains. The FNFMB is to provide financial-management-system certification for First Nations that choose to apply for a property-tax–secured loan from the First Nations Finance Authority. Finally, the FNS is a centre of statistical expertise that provides information for the above-mentioned fiscal institutions to conduct their work. It also is designed to improve the overall quality of First Nations information, and improves the statistical capacity in First Nations communities. Each institute is slowly establishing its presence nationally. It is too soon to say how well they are all doing.

Conclusion

So they accepted a treaty, for the future of the women and children, to have a home, a home base. Then the Indian Act came in and they had to get a permit to leave the reserve. That was to discourage the assembly of our people. . . . But what's happening now is the Chiefs have all the say of the Indian Act, not the band, not the community, no more.

—Wilf Tootoosis (Saulteaux)[52]

From a Native perspective, the *Indian Act* is troubling in many ways. It is difficult if not impossible to integrate community concerns into the existing legislation. Not only that, but the act itself is considered a vestige of a colonial period that Native leaders have no desire to relive. The act denies the importance of the treaties to the nation-to-nation relationship that Native leaders insist exists; it also enables the federal government to dictate band governments' operations, among other important issues. Indian and Northern Affairs Canada (INAC) is widely perceived as an outdated approach to dealing with Native leaders, who consider their people one of Canada's three founding nations. Most Native leaders desire a model akin to the two-row wampum belt, where each party guides its own vessel down the river without interfering with the other. Such a model will not come about until the *Indian Act* and the Indian Affairs bureaucracy are dismantled.

FURTHER READING

Fiske, Jo-Anne. "Constitutionalizing the Space to Be Aboriginal Women: The *Indian Act* and the Struggle for First Nations Citizenship." In *Aboriginal Self-Government in Canada: Current Trends and Issues*, ed. Yale D. Belanger. Saskatoon: Purich, 2008.

Jamieson, Kathleen. *Indian Women and the Law in Canada: Citizen's Minus.* Ottawa: Minister of Supply Services Canada, 1978.

Leslie, John, and Ron Maguire. *The Historical Development of the Indian Act.* Ottawa: Treaties and Historical Research Centre, Department of Indian Affairs and Northern Development, 1978.

Milloy, John S. "The Early *Indian Acts:* Developmental Strategy and Constitutional Change." In *As Long as the Sun Shines and Water Flows: A Reader in Canadian Native Studies,* ed. Antoine S. Lussier and Ian L. Getty. Vancouver: UBC Press, 1983.

Pettipas, Katherine. *Severing the Ties That Bind: Government Repression of Indigenous Religious Ceremonies on the Prairies.* Winnipeg: University of Manitoba Press, 1994.

Ponting, J. Rick, and Roger Gibbins. *Out of Irrelevance.* Toronto: Butterworths, 1980.

Tobias, John. "Protection, Civilization, Assimilation: An Outline History of Canada's Indian Policy." In *As Long as the Sun Shines and Water Flows: A Reader in Canadian Native Studies,* ed. Antoine S. Lussier and Ian L. Getty. Vancouver: UBC Press, 1983.

Shewell, Hugh. *"Enough to Keep Them Alive": Indian Welfare in Canada, 1873–1965.* Toronto: University of Toronto Press, 2004.

NOTES

1. Ovide Mercredi and Mary Ellen Turpel, *In The Rapids: Navigating the Future of First Nations* (Toronto: Penguin, 1994), p. 95.

2. John Borrows, *Recovering Canada: The Resurgence of Indigenous Law* (Toronto: University of Toronto Press, 2002), pp. 148–50, 159–60.

3. Chief Alfred Scow, Kwicksutaineuk Tribe, in *Royal Commission on Aboriginal Peoples* (RCAP), National Round Table on Aboriginal Justice Issues, Ottawa (November 26, 1992).

4. See, generally, Stuart Banner, *How the Indians Lost Their Lands: Law and Power on the Frontier* (Cambridge, MA: Harvard University Press, 2007).

5. See George G.F. Stanley, "The Indians in the War of 1812," in *Sweet Promises: A Reader on Indian–White Relations in Canada,* ed. J.R. Miller (Toronto: University of Toronto Press, 1991), pp. 105–24.

6. See Robert F. Berkhofer, *The White Man's Indian: Images of the American Indian From Columbus to the Present* (New York: Vintage, 1979), p. 76.

7. John Leslie, "The Bagot Commission: Developing a Corporate Memory for the Indian Department," *Canadian Historical Association Historical Papers* 17, no. 1 (1982): 31–52.

8. *An Act for the Protection of the Lands of the Crown in this Province from Trespass and Injury R.S.U.C. 1792–1840* (1839, c. 15.)

9. Leslie, "The Bagot Commission," p. 31.

10. Janet E. Chute, *The Legacy of Shingwaukonse: A Century of Native Leadership* (Toronto: University of Toronto Press, 1998).

11. John Goikas, "The *Indian Act:* Evolution, Overview, and Options for the Amendment and Transition," in *For Seven Generations: An Information Legacy of the Royal Commission on Aboriginal Peoples* [CD-ROM] (Ottawa: Canada Communications Group, 1996).

12. Taiaiake Alfred, *Peace, Power, Righteousness: An Indigenous Manifesto* (Toronto: Oxford University Press, 1999), p. 3.

13. John Leslie and Ron Maguire, *The Historical Development of the Indian Act* (Ottawa: Treaties and Historical Research Centre, Department of Indian Affairs and Northern Development, 1978).

14. John Sheridan Milloy, "The Era of Civilization: British Policy for the Indians of Canada, 1830–1860" (Ph.D. Diss., Oxford University, 1979).

15. See, generally, John Peter Turner, *The North-West Mounted Police, 1873–1893* (Ottawa: E. Cloutier, King's Printer, 1950).

16. Mark Dockstator, *Toward an Understanding of the Crown's Views on Justice at the Time of Entering into Treaty with the First Nations of Canada* (Saskatoon: Office of the Treaty Commissioner, 2001).

17. Kathleen Jamieson, *Indian Women and the Law in Canada: Citizen's Minus* (Ottawa: Minister of Supply Services Canada, 1978).

18. Sharon Helen Venne, *Indian Acts and Amendments 1868–1975: An Indexed Collection* (Saskatoon: University of Saskatchewan Native Law Centre, 1981).

19. "The Sustainability Report: Canada's Population." [online] http://www.sustreport.org/signals/canpop_ttl.html. Last accessed September 5, 2008.

20. Kiera L. Ladner, "Rethinking the Past, Present, and Future of Aboriginal Governance," in *Reinventing Canada,* ed. Janine Brodie and Linda Trimble (Toronto: Canadian Scholars Press, 2003).

21. *Report of the Indian Branch of the Secretary for the Provinces* (printed by Order of Parliament) (Ottawa: I.B. Taylor, 1870).

22. Richard R.H. Leuger, "A History of Indian Associations in Canada" (M.A. thesis, Carleton University, 1977), p. 71.

23. Quoted in Yale D. Belanger, "Seeking a Seat at the Table: A Brief History of Indian Political Organizing in Canada, 1870–1951" (Ph.D. diss., Trent University, 2006), p. 69.

24. Norman D. Shields, "Anishinabek Political Alliance in the Post-Confederation Period" (M.A. thesis, Queen's University, 2001), p. 52.

25. Quoted in Belanger, "Seeking a Seat at the Table," p. 70.

26. For a discussion of the potlatch, see Elizabeth Furniss, "The Carrier Indians and the Politics of History," in *Native Peoples: The Canadian Experience,* ed. R. Bruce Morrison and C. Roderick Wilson (Toronto: Oxford University Press, 2004), pp. 198–222; and Douglas Hudson,

"The Okanagan Indians," in *Native Peoples,* ed. R. Bruce Morrison and C. Roderick Wilson, pp. 353–76.

27. Katherine Pettipas, *Severing the Ties That Bind: Government Repression of Indigenous Religious Ceremonies on the Prairies* (Winnipeg: University of Manitoba Press, 1994).

28. Tina Loo, "Dan Cranmer's Potlatch: Law as Coercion, Symbol, and Rhetoric in British Columbia, 1884–1951," *Canadian Historical Review* 73, no. 2 (1992): 125–65.

29. Canada, *House of Commons Debates* 142, no. 110, 2nd Session, 39th Parliament (June 11, 2008), pp. 6849–57.

30. J.R. Miller, *Shingwauk's Vision* (Toronto: University of Toronto Press, 1998); and John S. Milloy, "*A National Crime*": *The Canadian Government and the Residential School System, 1879–1986* (Winnipeg: University of Manitoba Press, 1999).

31. See Miller, *Shingwauk's Vision.*

32. Canada, *House of Commons Debates,* pp. 6849–50.

33. For an overview of the literature examining these events, see Scott Trevithick, "Native Residential Schooling in Canada: A Review of the Literature," *Canadian Journal of Native Studies* 18, no. 1 (1998): 49–86.

34. Indian Residential Schools Truth and Reconciliation Commission, "Truth, Healing, Reconciliation." [online] http://www.trc-cvr.ca/pdfs/20080818eng.pdf. Last accessed September 10, 2008.

35. For a discussion of how Native leaders dealt with DIAND, see Peter McFarlane, *Brotherhood to Nationhood: George Manuel and the Making of the Modern Indian Movement* (Toronto: Between the Lines, 1993).

36. Jean-Paul Restoule, "Aboriginal Education and Self-Government: Assessing Success and Identifying the Challenges to Restoring Aboriginal Jurisdiction for Education," in *Aboriginal Self-Government in Canada: Current Trends and Issues,* 3rd ed., ed. Yale D. Belanger (Saskatoon: Purich, 2008), pp. 373–92.

37. Yvonne Pompana, "Devolution to Indigenization: The Final Path to Assimilation of First Nations" (M.A. thesis, University of Manitoba, 1993).

38. Rod Robinson, "Nisga'a Patience: Negotiating Our Way into Canada," in *Nation to Nation: Aboriginal Sovereignty and the Future of Canada,* ed. John Bird, Lorraine Land, and Murray MacAdam (Toronto: Irwin, 2002), p. 189.

39. Belanger, "Seeking a Seat at the Table," specifically Chapter 9: "Indian Attempts to Re-establish Political Relationships: The Special Joint Senate-House of Commons Committee, 1946–48," pp. 299–344.

40. See Goikas, "The *Indian Act.*"

41. Patricia A. Monture, "The Right of Inclusion: Aboriginal Rights and/or Aboriginal Women?" in *Advancing Aboriginal Claims: Visions/Strategies/Directions,* ed. Kerry Wilkins (Saskatoon: Purich, 2004), p. 53.

42. Jamieson, *Indian Women and the Law in Canada.*

43. Ibid.

44. John Whyte, "The Lavell Case and Equality in Canada," *Queen's Quarterly* 81 (1974): 28–42.

45. Jo-Anne Fiske and Evelyn George, *Seeking Alternatives to Bill C–31: From Cultural Trauma to Cultural Revitalization Through Customary Law* (Ottawa: Status of Women Canada, 2006), p. 21.

46. Ibid., p. v.

47. Native Women's Association of Canada, "Aboriginal Women and Bill C-31: An Issue Paper." [online] http://www.nwac-hq.org/en/documents/nwac.billc-31.jun2007.pdf. Last accessed September 19, 2008.

48. Quoted in "Fontaine Leads Assembly of First Nations," *CBCNews.ca,* June 17, 2003. [online] http://www.cbc.ca/canada/story/2003/07/16/afn_vote030716.html. Last accessed September 10, 2008.

49. *"The First Nations Governance Act,"* *CBCNews.ca,* July 2, 2004. [online] http://www.cbc.ca/news/background/aboriginals/indianact.html. Last accessed August 17, 2004.

50. Federation of Saskatchewan Indian Nations, "Lands and Resources: Specific Claims." [online] http://www.fsin.com/landsandresources/specificclaims.html. Last accessed September 12, 2008.

51. Phil Fontaine, "*Specific Claims Resolution Act* Will Not Be Implemented: A Victory for First Nations," *Assembly of First Nations Bulletin* (November 2005). [online] http://www.turtleisland. org/discussion/viewtopic.php?p=6349&sid=3a8c163c69d47007b9cbd7d049b70b74. Last accessed September 12, 2008.

52. Peter Kulchyski, Don McCaskill, and David Newhouse, *In the Words of the Elders: Aboriginal Cultures in Transition* (Toronto: University of Toronto Press, 1999), p. 339.

6 The Métis and Inuit

Métis have been referred to as a living bridge between Aboriginal and Non-Aboriginal cultures. At one meeting, the Métis Commissioner, Paul Chartrand, pointed out that bridges have to expect to be walked on by both sides. In another context, Métis could also be described as living treaties between Indian and non-Aboriginal cultures. Both of these images help to explain why Métis is so hard to define. Like mercury, the concept of Métis identity is at once fluid and elusive.

—Martin F. Dunn (Métis)[1]

It is imperative to include the Métis and the Inuit in any study of Native people as they are regularly situated outside of contemporary narratives discussing Canada and Native peoples generally. Yet separately they provide compelling histories. The Inuit have for millennia called Northern Canada and the Arctic Circle home. By comparison, the Métis are recent arrivals to North America; descendants of Native and European cultures, they are found across Canada. The Métis are fiercely independent, an attitude born of frequent alienation from both Native and non-Native communities. Territorial isolation led the Inuit to develop ecologically specific concepts of nationalism. Despite their social presence, not until 1880 and 1939, respectively, were the Métis and the Inuit acknowledged in the *Indian Act* or by the Supreme Court of Canada as Indians.[2] And only recently have they been acknowledged as an integral part of Native history generally. This combined legislative, physical, and ideological exclusion is an overarching theme in Métis and Inuit history.

The 2006 census showed that of the 1,172,790 people who identified themselves as an Aboriginal person, 389,785 reported that they were Métis and 50,485 reported that they were Inuit.[3] The Métis and Inuit assert nationhood and distinct culture status based on their distinct languages, unique economies, and enduring political and social philosophies. In 1982, Canada amended its constitution to recognize the Inuit and Métis along with the First Nations as the country's Aboriginal peoples. The Métis and Inuit have always worked at nation building in unique ways, yet little has happened in terms of the federal government acknowledging the Métis' inherent rights to land and self-government. Without doubt the Inuit have fared better; in 1992 they reached a deal with Ottawa that led to the creation of Nunavut and a territorial government in 1999. Meanwhile, the Métis struggle in many

Figure 6-1 Métis Identity Population by 2001 Census Subdivision

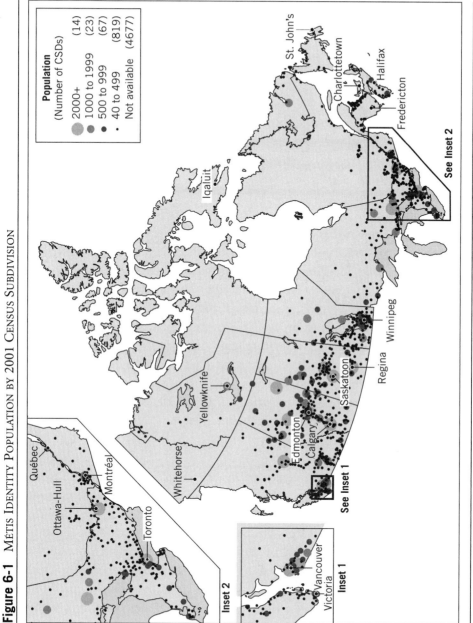

Population
(Number of CSDs)

2000+ (14)
1000 to 1999 (23)
500 to 999 (67)
40 to 499 (819)
Not available (4677)

Inset 1

Inset 2

Source: Adapted from Statistics Canada, "Thematic Maps, 2001 Census," Catalogue No. 92F-0173-XIE2001000, released October 29, 2002, URL: http://geodepot.statcan.ca/Diss/Maps/ThematicMaps/aboriginal/National/Cda_Aborig_Metis_Ebw_f1.pdf.

ways for political recognition. This chapter provides a brief history of each people, to prepare for an analysis of Métis and Inuit nation building.

Métis: Nationally

Society segregates and isolates Métis as rigidly as it does Reserve Indians and, like them, most halfbreeds see themselves as separate from the white mainstream world. There is no independent halfbreed society separate from the Indian Nation: the Métis are part of the total native world.

—Howard Adams (Métis)[4]

The Métis are often presented as a western people who originated in Manitoba's Red River region and then migrated west into Saskatchewan and Alberta in the late nineteenth century.[5] While somewhat accurate, the Métis as a people predate the Red River Colony (founded in 1816) and today are found in almost every province and territory. Métis ancestors include the Cree (Nehiyaw) and Ojibwa (Anishinaabe), the British and French, and Orkneymen and Scottish Highlanders. During the early days of the fur trade the French monarch encouraged French settlers to marry Indigenous women, for this would help expand the colonies without depleting France's population, which was falling as a result of warfare and disease.[6] Similarly, Native kinship systems promoted intermarriage with outsiders so as to foster economic networks and community-based affiliations. This section provides brief sketches of the Métis' evolution in the various geographic areas, both east and west.

Labrador

Prior to Jacques Cartier's voyages to eastern Canada and up the St. Lawrence River in the 1530s, European fishers had long been exploiting regional stocks in and around modern-day Labrador and Newfoundland. Some of them tried to establish communities, which led to interaction with local Indigenous populations. Over time, children were born who were Inuit/Innu *and* European in ancestry. By the early 1700s, permanent communities had developed in the region that displayed unique cultural and social characteristics. Economically, Labrador Métis communities were similar to the neighbouring Inuit and Innu communities, in that they relied on seasonal harvesting of the sea and land base. Social cleavages are evident to this day; 20 Labrador Métis communities have developed that are geographically removed from local Inuit and Innu communities. The federal government has refused to acknowledge the existence of the Labrador Métis. However, in 1996 the Royal Commission on Aboriginal Peoples (RCAP) concluded that the Labrador Métis "are an Aboriginal people within the meaning of section 35. They display the social and geographic distinctiveness, the self-consciousness and the cohesiveness of a people, along with an unmistakably Aboriginal relationship to the natural environment."[7]

The Atlantic Provinces

As in Labrador and Newfoundland, mixed-ancestry communities of Mi'kmaq/Maliseet and French/British developed that chose to live apart from local Indigenous communities and British and French settlements. These Métis communities mixed their rich ancestral traditions into a unique Métis culture, the foundation of which was shaken after the Acadians were expelled by the British between 1755 and 1763. The Métis overcame these events by relocating to modern-day Nova Scotia and New Brunswick, where fishing, hunting, and trapping formed the basis of their economy. The Métis also participated in regional politics, most notably through the Maliseet and Mi'kmaq treaties. Unlike the latter two, the Métis chose not to negotiate as a collective. Instead, those who participated represented their families. The Métis were eventually accepted as a separate Aboriginal people by provincial leaders, though the practice of engaging individual Métis in treaty negotiations was soon abandoned. New Brunswick officials in particular considered the Métis to be Indians and aggressively promoted their cultural assimilation.[8]

Quebec

The western Métis trace their origins to communities that developed in Quebec and Ontario following Métis movement inland. The first French *coureurs de bois*, located in the lower St. Lawrence, travelled west seeking furs and through marriage were gradually integrated into Indigenous kinship networks. Eventually, mixed-ancestry communities appeared, as did a discernable Métis culture. The fur trade and pressure from the newly emergent colonial governments in the United States and Canada led to further westward migration. As the RCAP concluded, when "talking about the French element of the Métis Nation, it may be useful to think of the Métis culture as having been conceived in Quebec, gestated in Ontario and born on the western plains."[9] The growth of the French Métis was facilitated by a French policy that promoted intermarriage between francophone settlers and Indigenous women; this enabled the French to assert territorial sovereignty without increasing emigration from France. The quick ascension of the Métis in Quebec has been attributed to the creation of local laws and governance norms based on a mix of Indigenous and European beliefs to make up for the lack of European institutions.

Ontario

The French authorities encouraged westward movement as a way to replenish diminished fur stocks and sustain the fur trade. One result was that more and more *coureurs de bois* began living near—and eventually in—Native communities, where they married Native women. As these mixed families established their own communities, a number of permanent Métis settlements appeared around the Great Lakes, near present-day Detroit, Chicago, Green Bay, Michilimackinac, and Sault Ste. Marie. Sault Ste. Marie in particular was an important hub of the regional fur trade. That area was largely under Métis control from the late 1600s to the mid-1800s. By 1830 there were 53 Métis communities in the Great Lakes region. Most of these would be forced farther west in search of economic opportunities and a Métis homeland.[10]

MICHIF

One of the more unique aspects of Métis culture is the language, Michif. It is estimated that only 500 Michif speakers remain in North America, one-third the number who spoke the language at the turn of the century. They are located mainly in a scattering of communities in Saskatchewan, Manitoba, North Dakota, and Montana. Developed originally in the 1700s, Michif has been described as a trade language to help Cree, Algonquian, and Sioux speakers from Ontario and Manitoba interact with one another. The result was the emergence of a mixed language that largely follows the grammatical rules of spoken Cree while integrating a large vocabulary of words from the French language. Several dialects of Michif exist that include unique blends of Dene and Sioux with French and English. In comparison to the development of other languages, Michif emerged rather quickly.[11]

The Birth of the Métis Nation

The concerted and sustained political actions of the Métis secured their official recognition, not only in military reactions, but in executive and legislative actions, including negotiations that led to the birth of the province of Manitoba in 1870, and later in legislation that purported to deal with their Aboriginal rights which was implemented only in the west and northwest from 1885 to 1921.

—Paul Chartrand (Métis)[12]

By the late eighteenth century the Métis were beginning to settle in large numbers in the Red River region (Winnipeg). They were establishing farms, hunting buffalo, and acting as regional trade agents. The latter endeavour placed them in competition with the Hudson's Bay Company (HBC). In 1814, Governor Miles MacDonnell responded with the Pemmican Proclamation, which prohibited the export of pemmican, an important trading good for the Métis during these, their foundational years. Years of tensions came to head in 1816 at the Battle of Seven Oaks, which to this day is identified by many as the moment the Métis nation was born. Several Métis and Native combatants led by Métis leader Cuthbert Grant defeated an armed HBC force, killing 21, including its leader, Governor Robert Semple. A Métis–HBC treaty was quickly negotiated, ending hostilities. Soon after, Métis resistance fighters began referring to themselves as *"la nouvelle nation"*—the new nation.[13]

The Métis were developing into a socially unique and economically vibrant people. They diversified their economy to include farming, hunting, fishing, and trapping. They

Métis camp (1874).

also opened small businesses and served as trade agents. The region experienced an economic boom in the 1840s, largely owing to the biannual bison hunt. There was a June hunt to help pay off HBC debts, followed by an autumn hunt to secure provisions for the long winters. Before 1816 these hunts had been small-scale affairs involving a handful of family groups. The growing demand for meat, pemmican, and hides led to an escalation of the hunt, and by 1820 more than 540 individuals were heading west to participate in it. Twenty years later, 1,630 were participating, bringing with them 1,210 Red River carts. Before leaving, the group would choose ten captains, who would be assigned ten soldiers each. The chosen guide would be given the camp flag, which, once raised, meant that the guide was the chief of the expedition. Only after the flag was lowered did the captains' and soldiers' duties begin. This was, in essence, a police force that was responsible for enforcing laws and carrying out summary judgments. Besides protecting the caravan from attack, the force guaranteed property against theft while people were engaged in the hunt.[14]

The "Rules of the Hunt" were developed to govern large numbers of prairie Métis buffalo hunters (see box). Those rules amounted to a fluid governing structure that could be adapted to fit different contexts as they arose. These rules for governing thousands on the open grasslands evolved into a self-government model. We cannot overemphasize the importance of this

---

THE LAW OF THE PRAIRIE (RULES OF THE MÉTIS BUFFALO HUNT, RECORDED IN 1840)

1. No buffalo to be run on the Sabbath Day.
2. No party is to fork off or lag or go before (to hunt bison) without permission.
3. No person or party to run buffalo before the general order.
4. Every captain, with his men, in turn to patrol camp and keep guard.
5. For the first trespass against these laws, the offender is to have his saddle and bridle cut up.
6. For the second offence, his coat is to be taken off his back and be cut up.
7. For the third offence, the offender is to be flogged.
8. Any person convicted of theft, even to the value of a sinew, to be brought to the middle of the camp, and the crier is to call out his or her name three times, adding the word "thief" each time.[15]

Source: "The Report of the Commission on the Métis Laws of the Hunt." *Manitoba Métis Federation.* 2002. 9 March 2009. <http://www.mmf.mb.ca/publications/mmf_comgt_report_final.pdf>.

---

system, especially during the late nineteenth century, when the Métis were moving into western Canada and founding a multitude of prairie settlements. In these new communities it was important to quickly establish rules of democratic governance, and those rules were developed from the Rules of the Hunt. Over time this approach to governance evolved into a political philosophy that guides the Métis to this day. Fundamental to that approach is the right to self-government.[16]

Métis economic and political success exacerbated existing Métis–HBC animosities. In 1849 the HBC cited its governing authority to convict Métis trader Guillaume Sayer for violating the Rupert's Land trade monopoly provisions, which dated back to the 1670 Royal Charter. During the trial a massive demonstration took place outside the courtroom, which influenced the judge to waive any penalty.[17] By then, the HBC trade monopoly was no longer enforceable. The new absence of trade restrictions allowed the Métis to become more economically and politically entrenched; meanwhile, the HBC was withdrawing from the region—an indication that the fur trade was petering out. The Métis were in much better economic shape, because of their diversified economy. Even so, the mix of political ideologies and cultural backgrounds among the Métis soon proved too difficult for their leaders to surmount, and French and English factions began vying for control. The Métis were briefly united in 1869 by a collective sense of outrage directed at the federal government's new western-expansion policies, which ignored Métis sovereignty. On top of that, Ottawa was refusing to consult the Métis while it was negotiating to purchase Rupert's Land from the HBC. The Métis, led by Louis Riel, decided to block the land surveyors' access to the Red River Colony, on the basis that they threatened to establish a new land allocation system.[18]

The Métis quickly formed a provisional government in February 1870, after a party of Canadian officials attempted to infiltrate their territory. Concerned that their landholdings and powers of self-governance were being threatened, Riel sent three delegates to Ottawa to negotiate the region's entry into Confederation. *The Manitoba Act,* 1870, created the Province of Manitoba and offered Canadians a glimpse of what Métis nationalism looked like. That act provided for the protection of specific rights of Red River residents, guaranteed that French would be taught in Roman Catholic schools, offered Crown protection of settled and related common lands, and allocated 1.4 million acres of land to ensure the perpetuation of Métis communities in Manitoba.[19]

The Manitoba Act sounded quite progressive. Nevertheless—as RCAP would detail in its 1996 report—it did not stop problems from arising. Specifically, verbal promises that had been made to the Manitoba Métis in 1870 were never fulfilled. Furthermore, the benefits bestowed under that act, as well as the *Dominion Lands Act,* were delayed so long that their value was eroded by an influx of new settlers. Because settlers now had access to former Métis lands, many Métis felt compelled to migrate even farther west. As well, the provisions of the *Dominion Lands Act* were being imposed on the Métis without negotiation, and the bulk of the land assigned to them was too far from where they actually lived to be of practical use to them. So, too, were the government offices that processed the land transactions.[20]

Figure 6-2 SCRIP

These were not the Métis' only difficulties. Despite being elected three times in succession to Parliament, Riel never took his seat as an MP. Perhaps most harmful to the Métis, however, was the failure of the scrip process. Scrip was a promissory note that could be exchanged for the same value in land (see Figure 6-2). In the beginning, Métis children of family heads were issued 240 acres, whereas family heads themselves were allocated $160 in the form of scrip. In the mid-1880s those individuals not included in the original 1.4 million acre allocation who still had a claim were issued scrip.[21] The process was complicated by a provision that forced individuals to file an application with a federally appointed land commissioner. These applications, known as *Manitoba Act* affidavits, contained all the information needed for the Métis to obtain the allotted lands. The whole process was ill conceived, as evidenced by the blatant discrimination the Métis experienced at the hands of land commissioners, along with government fraud and frequent shortages of land. The process resulted in the Métis being dispossessed of hundreds of thousands of acres of land, which were later earmarked for settlers.[22]

Asserting Métis Self-Government

The Métis never had and never will have anything to do with the theory of individual outrage or conspiracies against individual persons. The theory and practice of the Métis revolts was based on a revolutionary democratic movement against the forces [of] a decadent monopoly which stood as a barrier to the realization of progress and freedom. That was the task of the two

---

CHAPTER 6   The Métis and Inuit

Métis rebellions. Only an ignoramus or idiot can confound conspiracies and terrorism with the policy of the Métis movement which was based on the promotion of a mass democratic movement.

—James Brady (Métis)

After the events of 1869 and the failed land distribution, thousands of Métis migrated into northern Manitoba and west into Saskatchewan and Alberta and formed what are now well-known communities such as Batoche, Duck Lake, and Buffalo Lake. In 1875, several others from Red River established themselves at Lewistown, Montana—one of the oldest continuously occupied Métis settlements in Montana.[23] Angered at their dispossession, people of the village of St. Laurent near Batoche implemented a community-based governance process. On December 10, 1873, Gabriel Dumont was acclaimed president and eight councillors were elected. Monthly meetings were scheduled, during which the councillors determined that they would act as a local police force to enforce 28 laws, which were patterned largely on the Rules of the Hunt. Those laws set out the council's duties, regulated contracts (e.g., agreements made on Sunday were null and void), and authorized the raising of funds through a household tax, which was not to exceed £1 per month. Also, the council had the authority to impose fines on community members found guilty of breaking community laws; the highest fine was set at £3. Finally, laws related to labour relations were agreed upon.[24]

Though St. Laurent was successful, a number of Métis found the transition to farming difficult, and relations with non-Native communities problematic. All of this hindered self-government efforts. Riel was living in exile in Montana after fleeing Canada in the mid-1870s, but he kept himself informed of his people's plight, and in the autumn of 1884 he returned to Canada. With the support of Dumont and several high-ranking Métis leaders, he and his supporters prepared a petition, which they sent to Ottawa in March 1885, and which declared a provisional Métis government. A ten-point Bill of Rights (see box) was attached to the petition, along with specific demands, the central one being acknowledgment of the Métis Nation.[25] But times had changed since 1869: the Métis were no longer the majority population, and the North-West Mounted Police (NWMP) were only a few days' travel from most prairie Métis communities. Not dismayed, Métis forces occupied Duck Lake and on March 26 repelled a NWMP advance. Federal officials quickly raised a militia and within 30 days had gathered a force numbering more than 3,000 (eventually more than 5,000). Several battles ensued, and the Métis were vanquished by

Louis Riel and the Provisional Métis Government

MÉTIS BILL OF RIGHTS

1. That the Halfbreeds of the North-West Territories be given grants similar to those accorded to the Halfbreeds of Manitoba by the Act of 1870.

2. That patents be issued to all half-breed and white settlers who have fairly earned the right of possession of their farms.

3. That the provinces of Alberta and Saskatchewan be forthwith organized with legislatures of their own, so that the people may no longer be subject to the despotism of Mr. Dewdney.

4. That in these new provincial legislatures, while representation according to population shall be the supreme principle, the Métis shall have a fair and reasonable share of representation.

5. That the offices of trust throughout these provinces be given residents of the country, as far as practicable, and that we denounce the appointment of disreputable outsiders and repudiate their authority.

6. That this region be administered for the benefit of the actual settlers, and not for the advantage of the alien speculator.

7. That better provisions be made for the Indians, the parliamentary grant to be increased and lands set apart as an endowment for the establishment of hospitals and schools for the use of whites, Halfbreeds, and Indians at such places as the legislatures may determine.

8. That all the lawful customs and usages which obtain among the Métis be respected.

9. That the Land Department and the Dominion Government be administered as far as practicable from Winnipeg, so that settlers may not be compelled as heretofore to go to Ottawa for the settlement of questions in dispute between them and the land commissioner.

10. That the timber regulations be made more liberal, and that the settler be treated as having rights in this country.

Source: "Bill of Rights." *Back to Batoche*. 2006. Virtual Museum of Canada. 4 March 2009. <http://www.virtualmuseum. ca/Exhibitions/Batoche/html/about/index.php>.

overwhelming numbers. By the end of May 1885, resistance had ended and most of the Métis and Native leaders had been arrested.[26]

For his part in the action, Louis Riel was tried for high treason at Regina. He attempted to convince the jury that he was insane, but his efforts were undermined by his impressive final summation. Found guilty, Riel was hanged with 11 other participants, bringing to a close the treaty period of the 1870s. The 1885 defeat led to a Métis diaspora into Canada's western and northern reaches. In less than five decades the Métis had evolved from fur-trade agents into an economic powerhouse. They had brought about the Province of Manitoba's creation as a Métis territory only to be dispossessed of their lands. Then, in one last attempt to create a territorial land base, they had been defeated militarily and left destitute by the federal government, abandoned to secure their own future.

Métis Association of Alberta

... you know what an enquiry of individuals would result in. A collection of data, irrational, inconsistent, worthless to our cause and in all probability detrimental to our movement. I base this opinion on my knowledge of the Métis people, their limitations and . . . psychology. . . . I am absolutely opposed to this type of inquiry.

—Malcolm Norris (Métis), expressing his concern about the Ewing Commission (1934)[27]

The failed scrip process and the 1885 defeat left the Métis alienated from Canadian society as well as from many First Nations communities on the Plains. Some Métis joined with Cree, Ojibwa, and Dene communities, but Métis living conditions remained poor. In 1895, Father Lacombe petitioned the federal government to establish St-Paul-de-Métis in northern Alberta. This was a farming colony designed to assist the Métis in becoming self-sufficient farmers. The experiment failed, and the lands were eventually opened to settlement. In the early twentieth century the Métis again tried their luck at dry-land farming and hunting and trapping, but life in tents on road allowances was more common. Lacking schooling, medical services, and social relief, malnutrition quickly took hold after hunting and trapping failed, and government remedial measures for Indians generally ignored the Métis. The Natural Resources Transfer Agreements (NRTA) of 1930 made the situation even worse—living conditions deteriorated further, and because the Métis were not acknowledged as Indians, their hunting, trapping, and fishing rights were not protected.

After decades of government inaction, the Métis formed a regional political organization to address the issues they faced. It immediately became clear that the fledgling organization had support after several meetings were each attended by some 200 Métis representing six communities. At one meeting in 1932 a petition was drawn up and signed by 500 Métis, who demanded that the Alberta government provide their communities with (1) assistance in obtaining land, (2) improved education and health care, and (3) free hunting and fishing permits.

The organization was named the Métis Association of Alberta (MAA) and was guided by 32 councillors. Métis leaders began utilizing the organization to reassert their political and territorial claims and to fight for their members' economic, educational, and medical well-being. Malcolm Norris and James Brady in particular were key figures promoting Métis nationalism and the benefits of collective action. Convinced that a strong and centralized executive speaking for the Métis community would result in organizational legitimacy and compel federal and provincial officials to meet with them, the MAA members established a network of locals responsible for reporting to the central executive, whose task was to communicate the Métis' collective concerns to the government.[28]

Brady, Norris, and the MAA executive travelled extensively, seeking the support not only of Alberta Métis, but also of local MLAs and MPs, church officials, and medical doctors—

Alberta Métis Association's Provincial Executive Committee, Edmonton, Alberta (March 1935): Front row, L-R: Malcolm Frederick Norris, Edmonton; Joseph Francis Dion, Gurneyville; James Patrick Brady, Lac La Biche. Back row, L-R: Peter Cecil Tomkins, Grouard; Felix Callihoo, St. Paul.

whoever might sympathize with their cause. By 1933 the MAA could claim 1,200 members in 41 locals and had drafted a governing constitution. In 1934 the MAA's efforts were rewarded when the provincial government established the Ewing Commission to investigate Métis social conditions. Afforded the opportunity to speak before the commission, Norris demanded recognition of non-extinguished Métis land rights. Provincial officials rejected those demands, claiming that Métis rights had been extinguished by the scrip system. Little came of the proceedings, except for a set of recommendations implemented under the aegis of the *Métis Betterment Act* (1938). Specifically, a system of farm colonies was established on Crown land governed by elected advisory boards and overseen by provincially appointed settlement supervisors. Consideration was given to providing the Métis with special harvesting rights. Education was dealt with by the recommendation that boys be educated in math, writing, and agriculture; girls would be taught homemaking skills.[29]

A joint Métis–government committee selected lands that today constitute eight settlements with a total land allocation of 505,857 hectares (1.25 million acres). Vested with the Province of Alberta, these lands were revocable by order-in-council; also, subsurface rights were under provincial jurisdiction. Each settlement elected a five-person board and created a constitution approved by the Indian Affairs Minister. The Lieutenant Governor established each settlement's game laws to control Métis resource harvesting and non-Native access to settlement lands. The original goal of establishing a cooperative management style had broken down by the 1950s, however. Organizational authority gradually devolved to the settlements, but the new leadership was hampered by a public-administration complex that was tough to both comprehend and navigate. In response to all this and to growing fears that the province would explore for resources on Métis lands, a task force was established in 1972. It recommended that an improved self-government model be devised and that land be set aside in perpetuity for the benefit of the Métis.

Modern Métis Politics

Foreshadowing current political times, fashioning membership criteria proved to be problematic for Métis nationalism. In 1940 a Métis person was defined in terms of blood quantum: to be Métis, you had to have at least one-quarter Indian blood. Norris proposed that Métis be defined as any person with a drop of Indian blood in his veins who had not yet

The blue infinity flag represented the Métis as early as 1816 and is still flown by the Métis Nation today. The infinity symbol signifies the joining of two cultures and the existence of a people forever.

Thomas (Gray Coyote) Daigle gestures to government workers watching from the windows of the Centennial Building in Fredericton in October 1999. Daigle was part of a protest led by 100 of the Nation of Acadian Métis Indians, who were angered at being left out of negotiations from the Marshall decision.

assimilated into Canadian society. The Ewing Commission rejected this definition, responding that a Métis had to look like an Indian, live like an Indian, and prove Indian ancestry.[30] The *Constitution Act* (1982) mentioned "Métis" but did not define the term. The lack of a formal definition suggested to some that recognition of Métis rights hinged on who acted first to define those rights. This drove a wedge between the Métis and the First Nations: the latter could claim treaty and Aboriginal rights, and this tended to alienate the western Métis and other Métis populations in Labrador, Quebec, and Ontario, who lacked similar rights. Today the Métis National Council (MNC; and see below) represents Métis organizations in Ontario, Manitoba, Saskatchewan, Alberta, and British Columbia. In 2002 it declared that "Métis means a person who self-identifies as Métis, is of historic Métis Nation Ancestry, is distinct from other Aboriginal Peoples and is accepted by the Métis Nation."[31]

Currently, Métis communities compete with one another at the provincial and municipal levels for various federal funding arrangements. Unlike in 1869, however, there is no common issue to rally universal Métis support. Instead the Métis rely on various political organizations to pursue what have become increasingly region-centred political agendas. Nevertheless, those organizations have done much to define Métis identity and to promote general Métis political needs and desires. For example, the Federation of Métis Settlements was formed in 1977 and launched a legal challenge against the Province of Alberta, accusing provincial officials of misappropriating resource revenues that should have been secured in trust under the *Métis Betterment Act* (1938). In response, in 1982 the MacEwan Committee launched a series of negotiations, during which it produced reports to identify key issues. Those reports led to corrective provincial resolutions that highlighted Métis suggestions for responding to their identified concerns.

All the same, the province could not account for the lost revenues, suggesting that they had been absorbed into general provincial revenues. The Métis agreed to halt litigation in return for a properly negotiated settlement, and an agreement was reached in 1990, followed by legislation to enhance each Métis settlement's political and economic autonomy. Fee simple title was transferred to the centralized Métis Settlements General Council government, the *Betterment Act* was replaced, and an improved self-government process was established. In 1990, 77 percent of voters supported the Métis Accord. Today about 7,000 Métis in eight settlements operate councils that are empowered to pass bylaws relating to land, membership, governance, and similar matters. This makes the Métis Settlements Canada's only legislated, land-based Métis government.[32]

The Métis National Council

The Métis National Council (MNC) is the national voice of the Métis Nation. It was founded in 1983 to ensure (1) that the Métis were represented at the First Ministers' Conference on constitutional and Native affairs, and (2) that they participated in full in the process of asserting their inherent rights to self-government and self-determination. The MNC is structured according to local, regional, provincial, and national circumstances. The local structures vary with local needs and with their relationships to provincial structures. All Métis in any given community have the right to participate in local meetings, votes, and elections. Regardless of their level of activity, every Métis has a right to participate in the local organizations.

Today the MNC comprises five provincial Métis organizations: the Métis Provincial Council of British Columbia, the Métis Nation of Alberta, the Métis Nation of Saskatchewan, the Manitoba Métis Federation, and the Métis Nation of Ontario. Within each provincial association are regional councils made up of the local or community councils. The regional councils have constitutions. The five provincial associations are the most important component of this structure and the focus of most political attention. While the approach varies from province to province, the associations belonging to the MNC are expected to represent all Métis in the political life of the organization.

The provincial councils or boards are chosen in general and provincewide elections in which every Métis has the right to vote. These elections are held by secret ballot, at regular intervals, in communities throughout the province. High electoral participation rates are the norm, which means that the leaders are comfortable speaking for their constituents. The MNC has a Board of Governors made up of the presidents of provincial Métis associations and the National President. The board oversees the affairs of the MNC, assisted by a small permanent secretariat located in Ottawa. The board holds meetings every two months; general assemblies are held once a year and are attended by the elected leaders of the provincial boards and councils.[33]

The MNC, in conjunction with the University of Alberta's School of Native Studies, is currently engaged in the Métis Archival Project (MAP). That project is digitizing archival records relating to Métis communities to help reconstruct the historical geography, demography, and economy of the Métis Nation. The documents range from scrip applications to river-lot claims, censuses, and claim registers. All of these are being input into a database and made available for analysis. Perhaps the most innovative aspect of this project is the digitization of documents associated with the scrip process—in particular, scrip applications, which at the time asked detailed questions about a claimant's family and occupation and thus contain important genealogical, geographical, and economic information about early Métis communities.[34] So far, only the Section 31 *Manitoba Act* affidavits and the 1901 Census document series are thoroughly represented on the public website. Small samples of the Northwest "Half-breed" Scrip Applications, the 1881 Census, and the 1891 Census document series are also included. The interactive database enables individuals to search the digitized archives, conduct genealogical research, and construct a family tree.[35]

The Métis Nation Accord and Canada's Courts

In 1992, B.C., Alberta, Saskatchewan, Manitoba, Ontario, the MNC, provincial Métis organizations, and the federal government signed the Métis Nation Accord, which called on all signatories to negotiate Métis self-government. However, that accord was directly tied to the Charlottetown Accord's proposed comprehensive changes to Canada's constitution. In other words, the Métis Accord would only take effect if the Charlottetown Accord was enacted. The Métis Nation Accord would have extended First Nations political participation and representation in Canada. It would have formally recognized the Métis right to self-government. It would have signalled a commitment on Canada's part to address the appropriate roles and responsibilities of governments relating to the Métis. As a significant first step in relationship renewal between the federal government and the Métis Nation, the accord would have been an impressive political accommodation and would have gone far to resolve many legal questions and outstanding issues, including the definition of "Métis." Among other things, the accord would have

- established tripartite self-government negotiations among the federal government, Métis governments, and the respective provincial governments;
- committed financial resources to the negotiations;
- committed governments to negotiate a land and resource base for Métis;
- committed governments to enumerate the Métis and establish a central registry;
- committed governments to devolve programs and services to the Métis, provide transfer payments to Métis governments, support programs and services, and preserve existing funding and services already provided to the Métis; *and*
- committed governments to preserve and protect Métis settlements in Alberta.

Had the Charlottetown Accord passed, the Métis Nation Accord would have been a modern-day treaty binding the federal government, all provinces west of Ontario, and the Métis Nation. It would have compelled the provincial and federal governments to negotiate self-government agreements, lands and resources pacts, the transfer to Métis of a portion of Aboriginal programs and services, and cost-sharing agreements relating to Métis institutions, programs, and services. But in 1992 the Charlottetown Accord was rejected in a national referendum.

The sting of Charlottetown's failure left the Métis Accord's signatories unwilling to consider multilateral discussions. This left the Métis with few options. The Métis may continue to pursue recognition of their nationhood rights in the courts; or they may remain on the political periphery while provincial and federal officials engage in jurisdictional wrangling. Litigation has sometimes succeeded. In 2004, for example, after more that a decade of battling, the Supreme Court of Canada (SCC) acknowledged that the Métis possessed Aboriginal rights. A Métis father and son, Steve and Roddy Powley, had been charged in 1993 with hunting moose without a licence and with unlawful possession of moose meat, contrary to Ontario's *Game and Fish Act*. In 1998, after a two-week trial, the trial judge ruled that the Métis community of Sault Ste. Marie had an existing Aboriginal right to hunt. The decision, which was later upheld by the SCC, is considered an important advance in the continuing saga of Métis nation building.[36]

The Inuit and Nunavut

The Métis are still seeking acknowledgment of their nationhood status. The Inuit have already attained a significant level of self-government. On April 1, 1999, after nearly 25 years of negotiations, Nunavut became Canada's third territory.

The Inuit trace their territorial occupation back for thousands of years. Yet their claims were long ignored by Canadian officials intent on establishing northern sovereignty. In the 1940s, with American forces stationed in the eastern Arctic and potential American sovereignty claims on the horizon, the RCMP began stationing officers throughout the Arctic to strengthen Canada's sovereignty. Soon after, Ottawa began developing an Inuit policy and attempting to settle the Inuit (who were assumed at the time to be nomads) into small, easily accessible communities. This was an extension of the "civilizing" mission (see Chapter 5).[37]

In the mid-1960s, in response to the steady infiltration of non-Native people from the south and the imposition of federal programs, the North's Native people and Inuit founded the Indian and Eskimo Association (IEA) to research Indigenous people's rights and to fight for territorial land claims. The IEA's goal was to strengthen Inuit social, economic, and political influence by wresting decision-making powers from the federal government. Following two IEA meetings in late 1970 and early 1971, the Inuit Tapirisat Corporation (ITC) was established. Its declared goals were (1) to secure Inuit land title, (2) to establish resource-management protocols with the federal government and other outside interests and (3) to ensure that the Inuit played a role in regional policy formulation, program design, and land and resource allocation.[38] The ITC also proposed that a separate territory be created, to be called Nunavut ("Our Land" in Inuktituk).

As chance would have it, Aboriginal title was just starting to emerge as a significant legal and political issue. In 1973, the *Calder* case forced Aboriginal land title into national awareness, the SCC having acknowledged that Aboriginal rights were pre-existing even if they had not been specified in the Royal Proclamation of 1763. In other words, a separate system of Aboriginal rights existed. The SCC had found that Aboriginal title arose from long-term use and continuous occupancy of the land by Native peoples before first contact with the Europeans.[39] Until that point, Canadian officials had been either oblivious to or wilfully ignorant of Native and Inuit title; they were no longer allowed to be either. Clearly, Ottawa would have to develop a flexible policy for defining and recognizing Aboriginal rights.

Federal officials responded by suggesting that such a policy could be crafted but that it would compel extinguishment of Aboriginal title for Native groups who had never signed a treaty—including the Inuit. In 1973 the Canadian government implemented a new, comprehensive land-claims policy, under which a successful claimant group would receive defined rights, compensation, and other benefits in exchange for relinquishing rights relating to the title claimed over all or part of the land in question.[40] The Inuit surmised that to achieve their goals, they would need research to bolster their claims. So they hired a team to conduct an unprecedented Inuit land-use and occupancy study in Ketikmeot and Keewatin and on Baffin Island. The resulting database would be based on oral history—specifically, on elders' stories, which contained information about everything from preferred hunting areas to favoured sites for collecting medicines.[41]

This research provided the Inuit with the data they needed to press their claims and to draw proposed boundaries for the new territory. To pursue the land-claim negotiations, the Northwest Territories (NWT) Inuit Land Claims Commission (ILCC) was formed. In 1977, after extensive consultations in northern Inuit communities, the ILCC submitted its proposal to Ottawa. In *Speaking for the First Citizens of the Canadian Artic*—a necessarily simpler version of the ITC's previous proposal—the ILCC presented its vision.[42] Though the negotiators were able to build a consensus on a general agenda, the complexity of the overall process was becoming evident to everyone involved. For example, while the land-claim component was well received, negotiations ground to halt after the federal government rejected the Inuit request that political development be discussed first. This delay proved fatal to the ILCC, which disbanded in 1979 and was replaced by the Nunavut Land Claims Project (NLCP).

In 1979, as the land-claims process ebbed, the federal Electoral Boundaries Commission executed a recommendation to divide the NWT, with the new eastern district (Nunatsiaq) roughly corresponding with the proposed boundaries of Nunavut. Though it had not been directly involved since 1977, the ITC closely scrutinized the claims process. At

Figure 6-3 Inuit Identity Population, 2001 Census

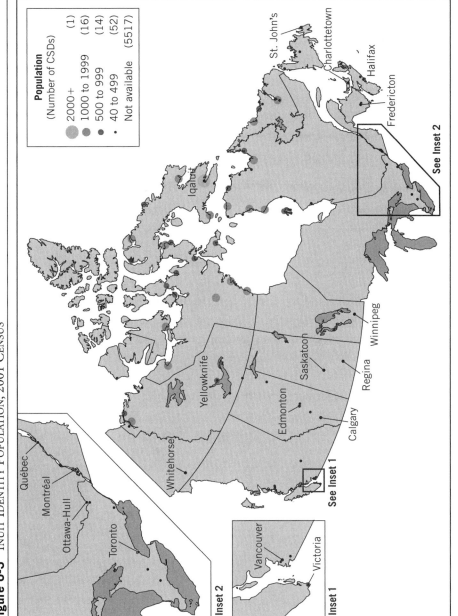

Population
(Number of CSDs)

2000+	(1)
1000 to 1999	(16)
500 to 999	(14)
40 to 499	(52)
Not available	(5517)

St. John's

Charlottetown

Halifax

Fredericton

See Inset 2

Iqaluit

Winnipeg

Saskatoon

Regina

Yellowknife

Edmonton

Calgary

Whitehorse

See Inset 1

Inset 2

Québec

Montréal

Ottawa-Hull

Toronto

Inset 1

Vancouver

Victoria

Source: Adapted from Statistics Canada, "Thematic Maps, 2001 Census," Catalogue No. 92F-0173-XIE2001000, released October 29, 2002, URL: http:// geodepot.statcan.ca/Diss/Maps/ThematicMaps/aboriginal/National/Cda_Aborig_Inuit_Ec_f1.pdf.

its 1979 meeting, the ITC drafted "Political Development in Nunavut," a proposal that incorporated the best aspects of all past proposals. It sought four guarantees: (1) Inuit ownership rights over portions of land rich in nonrenewable resources, (2) Inuit decision-making power over the management of land and resources within the settlement area, (3) Inuit financial indemnity and royalties from resources developed in the area, and (4) a commitment from Ottawa to negotiate self-government once a land claim had been finalized. The ITC reaffirmed that land-claims resolutions must be accompanied by the NWT's division to permit Nunavut's creation and to enable the implementation of Inuit governance. A 15-year implementation schedule was adopted after ITC delegates voted unanimously to pursue Nunavut's creation.[43] In March 1981 the NWT Legislative Assembly responded, ordering a plebiscite to resolve the issue.

Previously unwilling to consent to Inuit demands, the Indian Affairs Minister, John Munro, announced his government's intention to accept both the plebiscite's results and the NWT Legislative Assembly's decisions in relation to the territorial population's wishes. However, three preconditions to division were set out: (1) settlement of Inuit land claims would have to be reached prior to the proposed division, (2) a boundary separating the east and west of the territories would have to be approved by the NWT residents, and (3) an accord would have to be reached defining the basic structural arrangements of the new Government of Nunavut. Around this time the Inuit benefited from a second timely event (the first having been *Calder*): the *Constitution Act* was repatriated, and its Section 35(3) protected land claims "that now exist by way of land claims agreements or may be so acquired." This suggested that any final land-claim agreement would be constitutionally protected. In April 1982, 56 percent of NWT voters favoured division; in the eastern Arctic, where the Inuit population was highest, nearly 80 percent supported the proposal.[44]

Working Toward a New Territory

Following the plebiscite, a structured proposal was developed to assist in the creation of a new territorial government. In an attempt to obtain a grassroots perspective, the newly formed Constitutional Alliance of the Northwest Territories (CA) established two forums to permit debate and planning: the Nunavut Constitutional Forum (NCF) for the eastern Arctic, and the Western Constitutional Forum (WCF) for the western Arctic. In 1982, in anticipation of significant revenues from mineral extraction, the Tunngavik Federation of Nunavut (TFN) was formed; it succeeded the ITC as the agent responsible for pursuing land-claims negotiations on behalf of the Inuit in Nunavut. Within a year of replacing the TFN, the Nunavut Implementation Commission had drafted a comprehensive working proposal, "Building Nunavut." A revised and expanded edition followed two years later.

The negotiations yielded early successes, mainly agreements over the Inuit role in wildlife management, offshore rights, and resource management. A decade of negotiations followed during which countless subagreements were reached. Then in 1985 the Coolican Task Force Report was released, which led to a revised federal land-claims policy that recognized Inuit decision-making authority in relation to joint-management boards, resource revenues, and offshore areas.[45] This important step forward pleased the Inuit and various affiliated organizations participating in the negotiations. The same year, the final report of the Royal Commission on the Economic Union and Development Prospects for Canada was released. It suggested that a new territory in the eastern Arctic would make Canada's North "more governable."[46]

Perhaps the most controversial issue was where exactly to place the new territory's boundaries. In the wake of a new land-claims policy and the Royal Commission, the Inuit negotiators refused to accept federal offers that failed to consider a separate Inuit territory. Acknowledging this sticking point, federal officials decided to pursue the final land claim, promising that a new Inuit territory would be established. Then it was discovered that the original 1979 boundary ran through traditional lands claimed by the Inuit in the eastern Arctic as well as those claimed by the Dene–Métis in the western Arctic. Negotiations to resolve this issue broke down in 1985 after the Dene–Métis refused to ratify a tentative agreement reached by the NCF and WCF. But eventually an agreement was reached, and was formalized in the Nunavut Political Accord and signed in April 1990 by the federal government, the NWT Government, and the TFN.

In 1991 the task of drawing a boundary was assigned to John Parker, the former NWT commissioner. He came up with an initial proposal that was disputed at first, but later adopted in a territorywide plebiscite. With the boundary issues resolved, the Inuit called for Nunavut and its government to be directly incorporated into the final claims agreement. Federal officials were wary of creating a public government through a land-claims process that was meant to serve a population that included a non-Native minority. A compromise was reached, by which a provision was placed in the claim that would enable the creation of the new territory and government.

Other events influenced the negotiations. In 1976 the Inuit from Inuvialuit decided to break away from the Nunavut process and negotiate the first comprehensive land-claim settlement in the NWT. All parties paid close heed to the Iqaluit Agreement, which assigned the Inuvialuit surface-ownership rights to 60,000 square miles of land as well as certain subsurface rights to another 8,000 square miles of land. Special harvesting rights and environmental protections were extended them, as was participation in a number of comanagement regimes. Federal support for economic-development initiatives and for a social-development fund was also included. Financial compensation in the amount of $45 million was to be paid out in annual installments until 1997. Also, the Inuvialuit would have to be consulted as the Nunavut process moved forward. This was followed by a proposal that the western part of the new territory be formed according to the Inuit land-claim settlement area and the Dene–Métis and Inuvialuit claim settlement areas.[47]

Reaching an Agreement

After years of complex negotiations, an agreement-in-principle was reached in 1990. Two years later a single-line boundary between the claims settlement areas was accepted in a plebiscite. That boundary was accepted by the NWT government, the TFN, and the federal government for inclusion in the Nunavut Political Accord. In December 1991, negotiations among Canada, the NWT, and the TFN over a political accord also achieved a deal. The Inuit referendum was held November 3 to 5, 1992. As it turned out, 69 percent voted in favour of the land-claims agreement, which Parliament then passed. The agreement later received Royal Assent. On May 25, 1993, federal, territorial, and Inuit representatives signed the land-claims agreement, which had been initiated almost 20 years earlier (see box). This enabled the transfer of more than $1.1 billion to the Inuit.[48]

The land claim was ratified and enacted by the Canadian Parliament through two pieces of legislation: the *Nunavut Land Claims Agreement Act,* ratifying the settlement; and the *Nunavut Act,* establishing Nunavut as a territory with its own government. In the six months following the *Nunavut Act,* the recently established Nunavut Implementation Commission worked with federal officials and various Inuit organizations to develop recommendations concerning the location of Nunavut's capital, administrative structures, and operating and financing procedures for the Nunavut Legislative Assembly. The commission's final 100-page report provided 104 recommendations regarding the Government of Nunavut's political structure.[49]

The 1993 land claim settlement was the largest in Canadian history. It provided the Inuit with ownership to 354,055 square kilometres of land, mineral rights to about one-tenth of that area, and a financial settlement of $1 billion to be paid out over 14 years. As part of the deal, the Inuit agreed to abandon their claims to all other northern lands. Nunavut exercises the same territorial powers and responsibilities as the NWT.[50] However, because the Inuit make up 85 percent of the population, Indigenous interests dominate territorial governance.[51]

In 1995, Iqaluit was chosen as Nunavut's capital—the location of ministries, financial administration, and related functions. Over the next four years, federal and territorial officials worked to organize Nunavut's government. Ottawa appointed Jack Anawak as Nunavut's interim commissioner; his task was to create a functional government before Nunavut officially was "born." In 1998, *Nunavut Act* amendments were adopted by Parliament; after they received Royal Assent, on February 15, the people of Nunavut headed to the polls to elect 19 members to the new Legislative Assembly. On April 1, 1999, Nunavut and its new government were constituted, and the Nunavut flag and coat of arms were unveiled.

After Nunavut's residents elect their MLAs, the latter elect a premier, a speaker of the assembly, and an executive (Cabinet), all by secret ballot. Nunavut's government has ten departments, each headed by a minister. Those MLAs lacking ministerial portfolios form the opposition. Territorial elections are held every five years. Also, one MP and one senator represent Nunavut federally.

FEATURES OF THE AGREEMENT

- Title to approximately 354,055 square kilometres of land, with mineral rights to 35,406 of them.
- Equal representation of Inuit and government on a new set of wildlife-management, resource-management, and environmental boards.
- The right to harvest wildlife on lands and in waters throughout the Nunavut settlement area.
- Capital-transfer payments of $1.148 billion, payable to the Inuit over 14 years, along with a $13 million Training Trust Fund.
- A share of federal royalties for Nunavut Inuit from oil, gas, and mineral development on Crown lands.
- Where Inuit own surface title to the land, the right to negotiate with industry for economic and social benefits from the development of nonrenewable resources.
- The right of first refusal on sport and commercial development of renewable resources in the Nunavut Settlement Area.
- The creation of three federally funded national parks.
- The inclusion of a political accord that provides for the new Territory of Nunavut and, through this, a form of self-government for the Inuit of Nunavut.[52]

Source: Adapted from Nunavut Act (1993, c. 28). Not the official version.

More than $1.1 billion in compensation money passed from the federal government to Nunavut over a 14-year period that ended in 2007. The money was managed by the Nunavut Tunngavik Incorporated (NTI), a highly centralized organization composed of an annual General Assembly (48 delegates), a ten-member Board of Directors that meets quarterly, and an Executive Committee that meets monthly. The General Assembly approves the annual budget and can increase or restrict spending. It can also modify programs and services if two-thirds of the delegates agree. The Board of Directors meets to review and evaluate the Executive Committee's decisions. Six of the ten board members come from Regional Inuit Associations, which gives significant weight to regional interests on the board. The Executive Committee is the most powerful cog in the machine. The Inuit beneficiaries elect the four-member committee that meets monthly to implement the decisions approved by the General Assembly, while supervising the NTI's day-to-day operations.[53]

The Nunavut Land Claim Agreement's (NLCA) purview extends to various components of Nunavut's political structure. For example, (1) it provides for representative hiring of Inuit within government, (2) it outlines preferential procurement policies for Inuit firms, (3) it requires that an Inuit Impact and Benefit Agreement be performed before major development projects are implemented, and (4) it ensures greater Inuit control over natural resources and the right to harvest.[54] The Government of Nunavut incorporates Inuit values and beliefs into a government model and conducts most of its business in Inuktitut

(Nunavut's other official languages are English and French). The Government of Nunavut is decentralized, with nearly 700 staff divided among Iqaluit and ten other communities. It is anticipated that decentralization will provide Nunavut's three regions with equal decision-making authority. It will also extend new jobs to as many areas as possible.

Conclusion

Having so long held this country as its master and so often defended it against the Indians at the price of blood, we consider it not asking too much to request that the Government allow us to occupy our lands in peace.

—Gabriel Dumont (Métis)[55]

The stories of the Métis and the Inuit are slowly being played out in public political forums. For the Métis, research is providing the data needed to discuss the ill-conceived scrip system (which is still reverberating), the political flowering in the 1930s, and the daily struggle to have their Aboriginal rights acknowledged and respected. The Inuit, by contrast, have largely been a footnote in Canada's nation-building narrative. Nunavut, because it is so isolated, remains peripheral to the rest of Canada. The Métis and the Inuit are similar to the extent that for both, nation building has depended on Canada's willingness to come to the negotiating table; only then has either group been able to forge ahead with its political agenda. The Inuit have achieved territorial status and general self-governing authority; they have also experienced the growing pains associated with those responsibilities. Despite prolonged efforts, the Métis have yet to achieve the same level of self-governance. A key difference between the two groups relates to solidarity: the Inuit were able to develop a unified front in pursuit of their demands; the Métis remain politically fragmented. That fragmentation is today an issue that Métis leaders must find ways to address, for it has enabled federal officials to distance themselves from Métis issues. The same can be said of federal officials who cite Nunavut's territorial status in an effort to remain distant during what has at times been a difficult transition period. Both people's stories are still being written.

FURTHER READING

Métis

Adams, Howard. *Prison of Grass: Canada from the Native Point of View*. Toronto: General, 1975.

Campbell, Maria. *Half-Breed*. Halifax: Goodread Biographies, 1973.

Bell, Catherine E. *Alberta's Métis Settlement's Legislation: An Overview of Management of Settlement Lands*. Regina: Canadian Plains Research Centre, 1994.

Dobbin, Murray. *The One-and-a-Half Men: The Story of Jim Brady and Malcolm Norris, Métis Patriots of the 20th Century.* Vancouver: New Star, 1981.

Ens, Gerhard. *Homeland to Hinterland: The Changing Worlds of the Red River Métis in the Nineteenth Century.* Toronto: University of Toronto Press, 1996.

Flanagan, Thomas. *Louis David Riel: Prophet of the New World.* Toronto: University of Toronto Press, 1979.

Peterson, Jacqueline, and Jennifer S.H. Brown. *The New Peoples: Being and Becoming Métis in North America.* Winnipeg: University of Manitoba Press, 1985.

Woodcock, George. *Gabriel Dumont.* Peterborough: Broadview, 2003.

Inuit

Dahl, Jens, Jack Hicks, and Peter Jull, eds., *Nunavut: Inuit Regain Control of their Lands and Their Lives* Copenhagen: International Work Group for Indigenous Affairs, 2000.

Henderson, Ailsa. *Nunavut: Rethinking Political Culture.* Vancouver: UBC Press, 2007.

Légaré, André. "The Nunavut Tunngavik Inc.: An Examination of Its Mode of Operation and Its Activities." In *Natural Resources and Aboriginal People in Canada: Readings, Cases, and Commentary,* ed. Robert B. Anderson and Robert M. Bone. Concord: Captus, 2003, pp. 117–37.

———. "The Process Leading to a Land Claims Agreement and Its Implementation: The Case of the Nunavut Land Claims Settlement." *Canadian Journal of Native Studies* 16, no. 1 (1996): 139–63.

McPherson, Robert. *New Owners in Their Own Land: Minerals and Inuit Land Claims,* 3rd ed. Calgary: University of Calgary Press, 2005.

Timpson, Annis May. "'Hey, That's No Way to Say Goodbye': Territorial Officials' Perspectives on the Division of the Northwest Territories." Canadian Public Administration 49, no. 1 (2006): 80–101.

NOTES

1. Martin F. Dunn, "The Definition of Métis: A Double-Edged Blade." [online] http://www.othermetis.net/Papers/Dunn/Definition/2-Id&Def.html. Last accessed September 2, 2008.

2. Re *Eskimo* [1939] *2 D.L.R.* 417.

3. Statistics Canada, "Aboriginal Peoples in Canada in 2006: Inuit, Métis and First Nations," 2006 Census, Cat. no. 97-558-XIE (Canada: Minister of Industry, 2008), p. 6.

4. Howard Adams, *Prison of Grass: Canada from a Native Point of View* (Toronto: New Press, 1975), pp. ix–x.

5. George F.G. Stanley, *The Birth of Western Canada: A History of the Riel Rebellions* (Toronto: University of Toronto Press, 1960).

6. Olive Patricia Dickason, "From 'One Nation' in the Northeast to 'New Nations' in the Northwest," in *The New Peoples: Being and Becoming Métis in North America,* ed. Jacqueline Peterson and Jennifer J.H. Brown (Winnipeg: University of Manitoba Press, 1985), pp. 19–36.

7. Canada, "Perspectives and Realities, Vol. 4," in *For Seven Generations: An Information Legacy of the Royal Commission on Aboriginal Peoples*, CD-ROM (Ottawa: Canada Communications Group, 1996).

8. Ibid. See also Olive Patricia Dickason, *Louisbourg and the Indians: A Study in Imperial Race Relations, 1713–1760* (Ottawa: Supply and Services Canada, 1976).

9. Ibid.

10. Jacqueline Peterson, "Many Roads to Red River: Métis Genesis in the Great Lakes Region, 1680–1815," in *The New Peoples: Being and Becoming Métis in North America*, ed. Jacqueline Peterson and Jennifer J.H. Brown (Winnipeg: University of Manitoba Press, 1985), pp. 37–42.

11. Peter Bakker, *A Language of Our Own: The Genesis of Michif, the Mixed Cree–French Language of the Canadian Métis* (Toronto: Oxford University Press, 1997); and Ted J. Brasser, "What Is Michif? Language in the Métis Tradition," in *The New Peoples: Being and Becoming Métis in North America*, ed. Jacqueline Peterson and Jennifer J.H. Brown (Winnipeg: University of Manitoba Press, 1985), pp. 231–42.

12. Paul L.A.H. Chatrand, "Background," in *Who Are Canada's Aboriginal Peoples? Recognition, Definition, and Jurisdiction* (Saskatoon: Purich, 2002), p. 19.

13. See, generally, J.M. Bumsted, *Fur Trade Wars: The Founding of Western Canada* (Winnipeg: Great Plains, 1999); Lyle Dick, "The Seven Oaks Incident and the Construction of a Historical Tradition, 1816–1970," *Journal of the Canadian Historical Association* 2 (1991): 91–113; and Harry W. Daniels, *We Are the New Nation (Nous Sommes La Nouvelle Nation): The Métis and National Native Policy* (Ottawa: Native Council of Canada, 1979).

14. Lawrence Barkwell, "Early Law and Social Control Among the Métis," in *The Struggle for Recognition: Canadian Justice and the Métis Nation*, ed. Samuel Corrigan and Lawrence Barkwell (Winnipeg: Manitoba Métis Federation, 1991), p. 15.

15. Manitoba Métis Federation, "Towards a Métis Co-Management Framework Agreement: The Report of the Commission on the Métis Laws of the Hunt." [online] http://www.mmf.mb .ca/publications/mmf_comgt_report_final.pdf. Last accessed September 15, 2008.

16. Larry Chartrand, "'We Rise Again': Métis Traditional Governance and the Claim to Métis Self-Government," in *Aboriginal Self-Government in Canada: Current Trends and Issues*, 3rd ed., ed. Yale D. Belanger (Saskatoon: Purich, 2008), pp. 145–57.

17. Ted D. Regehr, "The Pierre-Guillaume Sayer Trial," in *Encyclopedia of the Great Plains,* ed. David J. Wishart (Lincoln: University of Nebraska Press, 2004), p. 461.

18. The literature examining Riel and the events of 1869–70 is significant, and these events at this point are accepted.

19. D.N. Sprague, *Canada and the Métis, 1869–1885* (Waterloo: Wilfrid Laurier University Press, 1988).

20. Ibid. See also Canada, "Perspectives and Realities."

21. For this general listing see Lawrence Barkwell, "Metis Rights and Land Claims: An Annotated Bibliography." [online] http://www.mmf.mb.ca/publications/Metis.Rights.and.Land.Claims.pdf. Last accessed September 13, 2008.

22. See, for example, Ken Hatt, "The North-West Rebellion Scrip Commissions, 1885–1889," in *1885 and After: Native Society in Transition*, ed. F. Laurie Barron and James B. Waldram (Regina: University of Regina, Canadian Plains Research Centre, 1986), pp. 189–204.

23. Martha Harroun Foster, *We Know Who We Are: Métis Identity in a Montana Community* (Norman: University of Oklahoma Press, 2006); and Vern Dusenberry, "Waiting for a Day That Never Comes: The Dispossessed Métis of Montana," in *The New Peoples: Being and Becoming Métis in North America*, ed. Jacqueline Peterson and Jennifer J.H. Brown (Winnipeg: University of Manitoba Press, 1985), pp. 119–36.

24. See, generally, George Woodcock, *Gabriel Dumont*, ed. J.R. Miller (Peterborough: Broadview, 2003); Mike Brogden, "The Rise and Fall of the Western Métis in the Criminal Justice Process," in *The Struggle for Recognition: Canadian Justice and the Métis Nation*, ed. Samuel Corrigan and Lawrence Barkwell (Winnipeg: Manitoba Métis Federation, 1991), pp. 39–61; and Stanley, *The Birth of Western Canada*.

25. In Alexander Begg, *The Creation of Manitoba* (Toronto: Hunter, Rose, 1971).

26. See Blair Stonechild and Bill Waiser, *Loyal till Death: Indians and the North-West Rebellion* (Calgary: Fifth House, 1997).

27. Quoted in Murray Dobbin, *The One-and-a-Half Men: The Story of Jim Brady and Malcolm Norris, Métis Patriots of the 20th Century* (Vancouver; New Star, 1981), p. 103.

28. Murray Dobbin, "Métis Struggles of the Twentieth Century," *New Breed* (August–November 1978); and Dobbin, *The One-and-a-Half Men*, p. 77.

29. Catherine Bell and Harold Robinson, "Government on Métis Settlements: Foundations and Future Directions," in *Aboriginal Self-Government in Canada: Current Trends and Issues*, 3rd ed., ed. Yale D. Belanger (Saskatoon: Purich, 2008), p. 264.

30. In Dobbin, *The-One-and-a-Half Men*, in particular Chapter 6: "The Ewing Commission: An Inquiry into the Condition of the Half-Breed Population of Alberta," pp. 88–105.

31. Métis National Council, "Who Are the Métis?" [online] http://www.metisnation.ca/who/definition.html. Last accessed September 13, 2008.

32. Tom Pocklington, *The Government and Politics of the Alberta Métis Settlements* (Regina: Canadian Plains Research Centre, 1991), pp. 150–51.

33. The information for the last two paragraphs can be found at the Métis National Council website: http://www.metisnation.ca

34. Scott Lingley, "Research Road Trip Takes Students to the Heart of Métis Culture," University of Alberta Research Services Office. [online] http://www.rso.ualberta.ca/news.cfm?story=38280. Last accessed September 15, 2008.

35. See http://metisnationdatabase.ualberta.ca/MNC/about.jsp

36. For information on the Métis Nation Accord, see Indian and Northern Affairs Canada, "Proposed Métis Nation Accord." [online] http://www.ainc-inac.gc.ca/ap/pubs/sg/cg/cj5d-eng.pdf. Last accessed December 9, 2008. For the Powley decision, see *R. v. Powley* [2001] *OJ* No. 607.

37. For this general discussion, see Ailsa Henderson, *Nunavut: Rethinking Political Culture* (Vancouver: UBC Press, 2007).

38. Ibid., p. 24.

39. *Calder v. Attorney-General of British Columbia,* [1973] S.C.R. 313. For an academic assessment of the decision and its continued validity, see Hamar Foster, Heather Raven, and Jeremy Webber, eds., *Let Right Be Done: Aboriginal Title, the Calder Case, and the Future of Indigenous Rights* (Vancouver: UBC Press, 2007).

40. See Canada, "Fact Sheet: Comprehensive Land Claims" (Ottawa: Indian and Northern Affairs Canada, 2008). [online] http://www.ainc-inac.gc.ca/ai/mr/is/lnd-clms-eng.asp. Last accessed December 9, 2008.

41. Milton Freeman, *Inuit Land Use and Occupancy Project: A Report* (Ottawa: Thorne Press, 1976).

42. Henderson, *Nunavut: Rethinking Political Culture*, pp. 96, 98.

43. See, generally, Jack Hicks and Graham White, "Nunavut: Inuit Self-Determination Through a Land Claim and Public Government," in *Nunavut: Inuit Regain Control of their Lands and Their Lives,* ed. Jens Dahl, Jack Hicks, and Peter Jull (Copenhagen: International Working Group for Indigenous Affairs, 2000), pp. 30–118.

44. See Henderson, *Nunavut: Rethinking Political Culture,* pp. 146–47.

45. Canada, *Living Treaties: Lasting Agreements* (Ottawa: Queen's Printer, 1985).

46. Canada, *Royal Commission on the Economic Union and Development Prospects for Canada* (MacDonald Commission)(Ottawa: Queen's Printer, 1985); see also Keith G. Banting, "Royal Commission on the Economic Union and Development Prospects for Canada," in *The Canadian Encyclopedia.* [online] http://www.thecanadianencyclopedia.com/index.cfm?PgNm=TCE&Params=A1ARTA0002515. Last accessed September 13, 2008.

47. Canada, *The Western Arctic Claim: The Inuvialuit Final Agreement* (Ottawa: Indian and Northern Affairs Canada, 1984). [online] http://www.ainc-inac.gc.ca/al/ldc/ccl/fagr/inu/wesar/wesar-eng.pdf. Last accessed December 9, 2008.

48. For a timeline of events, see Hicks and White, "Nunavut: Inuit Self-Determination Through a Land Claim and Public Government?" pp. 94–96.

49. See Henderson, *Nunavut: Rethinking Political Culture,* pp. 104–9.

50. Hicks & White, "Nunavut," p. 58.

51. Andre Légaré, "The Nunavut Tunngavik Inc.: An Examination of Its Mode of Operation and Its Activities," in *Natural Resources and Aboriginal People in Canada: Readings, Cases, and Commentary,* ed. Robert B. Anderson and Robert M. Bone (Concord: Captus, 2003), p. 119.

52. Canada, "Agreement Between the Inuit of the Nunavut Settlement Area and Her Majesty the Queen in Right of Canada." [online] http://caid.ca/NunLan1993.pdf. Last accessed December 9, 2008.

53. Légaré, "The Nunavut Tunngavik," pp. 120–23.

54. Henderson, *Nunavut,* pp. 105–6.

55. Quoted in Thomas Flanagan, *Louis "David" Riel: "Prophet of the New World,"* rev. ed. (Toronto: University of Toronto Press, 1996), p. 134.

Native Military Traditions and the Canadian Forces

7

Now that peace has been declared, the Indians of Canada may look with just pride upon the part played by them in the Great War, both at home and on the field of battle. They have well and nobly upheld the loyal tradition of their gallant ancestors who rendered invaluable service to the British cause in 1775 and 1812 and have added thereto a heritage of deathless honour which is an example and an inspiration for their descendants.

—Edward Ahenakew (Cree)[1]

The last great Indian war in Canada took place between the Cree (Nehiyaw) and the three member nations of the Blackfoot (Niitsítapi) Confederacy in late October 1870 near what is today downtown Lethbridge, Alberta. The Blackfoot (Siksika), North Piikuni (Peigan), and Blood (Kainai), who had all been ravaged by smallpox, were attacked by a Cree war party seeking to take advantage of their traditional enemies' weakened state. Within hours of the first attack, the three Blackfoot nations had defeated the Cree aggressors, who, while trying to retreat, lost close to 300 warriors.[2] For a variety of reasons, this battle was the last in a long and storied history of intratribal military encounters in Canada—encounters that predated European contact. Soon after, the Blackfoot succumbed to the lingering effects of the whisky trade. Also soon after, in 1874, the North-West Mounted Police (NWMP) (est. 1873) was dispatched to the prairies. That European-style police force was by definition anti-Métis and anti-Native (see Chapter 9). The NWMP had been founded in part to strengthen Canada's political hold on western Canada through the imposition of European legal norms. All other Indigenous nations suffered similar fates as federal officials promoted assimilation policies designed to dismantle traditional practices. Warfare and martial ideologies were among those practices targeted.

American scholarship has produced a significant body of work examining warfare between the Americans and Native peoples. In contrast, there has been little study of Indigenous warfare in Canada. For instance, the last Blackfoot/Cree war was the culmination of decades of conflict. While the battles have been well catalogued both chronologically and in terms of battle sites, the reasons for those events still elude us. Were Blackfoot/Cree relations inherently violent? Or were those relations generally peaceful, with warfare a sometime anomaly? Important questions such as these are typically overlooked; too often, the emphasis is on the "warrior ethic," on Indigenous warfare as a byproduct of hostile cultures interacting, on colourful episodes in Indian history, or (in the case of the Métis in 1885) on an important moment in Canada's nation-building narrative.[3] As historian Jim Miller suggests, however, warfare among Indigenous peoples had a variety of objectives and did not specifically represent "the manifestation of some insatiable blood-lust."[4] Simply put, that warfare served a variety of purposes. Unfortunately, a detailed examination of Native warfare in Canada, and of First Nations participation in the Canadian Forces in later times, is lacking.

Pre-Contact Warfare

Warriors are men who are there to protect, to look after the people. . . . It was the men who protected and took care of people, they are protectors. They were not there to fight, but if they had to they would fight, but they were there mainly to protect the people.

—Eva McKay (Dakota Sioux)[5]

Before Confederation, Indigenous leaders and their peers viewed their communities as independent political entities operating their own distinctive political economies. As happens in all communities, a military ideology soon developed as each Indigenous nation sought not only to protect its territories, but also to acquire wealth and maintain its cultural viability. As one result, participation in social and religious activities came to be closely linked to warfare— specifically, with demonstrated acts of bravery in battle. This was so in all Indigenous nations: military activity was an important feature of politics and a manifestation of nationhood that had multiple objectives. At the same time, directly related to warfare was diplomacy: Indigenous leaders would try talking with their neighbours in order to avoid battle, for it made more sense to maintain peaceful relations with neighbouring nations than to fight.

Warfare had a variety of roles in pre-contact Indigenous societies. It was a means for acquiring personal wealth, protecting tribal hunting grounds from neighbouring nations, and obtaining status within one's community. Children were raised to see war as an opportunity to acquire fame and wealth; as a result, warfare become an integral part of most Indigenous nations' political economy. Demonstrated prowess as a warrior was requisite to gaining acceptance into various societies, several of which specifically required men to distinguish themselves in battle.[6] Indigenous nations fought with each other for various reasons, which included revenge, security, honour and pride, to control trade, and to obtain desired possessions. They sometimes fought simply for the sake of fighting—that is, young men sought prestige, honour, and proof of military prowess by engaging members of neighbouring nations in skirmishes. Revenge was perhaps the best known reason for engaging another nation in battle. "Reprisal warfare" helped communities cope with the loss of citizens or resources. In such cases, warriors often returned with resources and prisoners. Most prisoners were soon adopted into the community, though some were executed.

Indigenous nations fought wars for different reasons and in different ways than Europeans. European warfare was mainly about territorial expansion and utilized universal military strategies and techniques. In contrast, Indigenous warfare rarely involved land acquisition. It was also smaller in scale and intermittent, and different weapons were used. Warriors were raised from an early age to embrace self-discipline and, once ready for combat, engaged the enemy often armed with only a bow—which, admittedly, had a range of 150 metres and was highly effective at short range—or with a wooden club or axe for hand-to-hand combat. Warriors were also taught to think for themselves in battle. The war chiefs were specialists who during times of peace were not dominant individuals; but when the peace was broken, their role in protecting homelands and preserving lives became all-important. They employed various strategies, which included utilizing small, lightning-fast groups that were able to withdraw before a counterattack could be mounted. War parties were able to travel upwards of 60 kilometres each day on limited rations. Quick retreats were employed to avoid being surrounded and to allow the war party to regroup and change strategy. This was an effective way to save lives while whittling down European forces, whose approach to warfare emphasized precise formations.[7]

On the Plains, most nations adopted the practice of counting coup for times when battles were not available. The specific manner of counting coup differed from nation to nation; often it involved stealing horses from an enemy's camp. Derived from the French word *coup*, meaning a "stroke" or "blow," counting coup was a means to humble one's enemies while proving one's bravery, all without incurring the loss of life. Because gaining personal honour in battle was the greatest achievement a warrior could claim, the potential for loss of life was high—young men seeking prestige often initiated aggressive encounters or large-scale battles. Counting coup became a celebrated act that brought more prestige than killing.[8]

Many scholars have attempted to understand pre-contact Indigenous military behaviour. One of the more important theorists is the ethnologist John Ewers, who argued that the roots of intertribal warfare can be found in the very nature of tribalism. He suggested warfare was fuelled less by specific causes than by a potent combination of ethnocentrism and xenophobia borne of the belief that "each Plains tribe thought of themselves as 'the people' . . . making them inherently distrustful of and aggressive towards outsiders." Ewers's argument is based on two suppositions: (1) that intertribal warfare was much easier to start than to end, and (2) that certain tribes seem to have been enemies since time immemorial.[9]

PRE-CONTACT WARFARE

In the 1690s, for the first time in decades, the Blackfoot were at war. The Cree in the east were peaceful, the Kootenays in the foothills traversed the territory, and the Beaver in the north were also at peace. The war this time was with the Shoshoni, who lived across the Bow River, the dividing line between the two nations. During this period there were no horses, plenty of resources, and plenty of room to move.

The trouble started during a children's game, one in which a leather ball stuffed with deer hair was dropped in the middle of a playing field and the teams kicked, passed, and ran until one side crossed the goal line. During the competition a Shoshoni boy was hurt. His father retaliated by clubbing the Blackfoot boy to death. An old Blackfoot man sat down and threw up his hands, a sign that he did not want to fight. He, too, was killed by the Shoshoni. The Shoshoni left for their side of the river. Peace was at an end.

The following spring the Blackfoot organized a huge war party to go out against the Shoshoni. Travelling south, they came within sight of the Bow River, where across the way they saw the Shoshoni encampment, near a ford known as Ridge Under Water. The two sides stared each other down until the Shoshoni challenged the Blackfoot to fight.

A young man, White Clay, who yearned for greater respect, was downstream. He had been left out of the war party, but now he slipped into the water carrying nothing but a stick between his teeth. The Shoshoni jeered, since he had no weapon. He goaded the Shoshoni chief to fight him in the river, until the chief grabbed his spear and jumped in.

White Clay backed off as though afraid; into the deeper water they waded until the Shoshoni chief hurled his spear. The deep water hurt his aim, and White Clay deflected the spear with his stick. White Clay picked up the spear and killed the chief, who was trapped in the deep water. The Blackfoot cheered and met White Clay downstream.

Days later, the war party returned home as heroes and White Clay was acknowledged as a warrior.[10]

Source: Dempsey, Hugh Aylmer. *The Amazing Death of Calf Shirt and Other Blackfoot Stories: Three Hundred Years of Blackfoot History.* Calgary: Fifth House Publishers, 1994. pp. 17–27. Reprinted by permission of Fitzhenry & Whiteside. Copyright Fitzhenry & Whiteside.

These are intriguing points, even if he glosses over a number of salient issues, in particular the influence that the history of each group played in informing specific Indigenous military ideologies. For example, Ewers rarely investigates the concepts of "enemy" and "alliance," and even when he does, it is more to emphasize how various groups employed warfare as a means to maintain regional or political balance, or the status quo. For Ewers, past entrenched hatreds based on old injustices and wrongdoings were enough to explain why Indians went into battle. Unfortunately, his hypothesis does not address either Native diplomacy or military beliefs and ideologies.

Post-Contact Warfare

Indigenous people historically allied themselves with European powers—with the French and British and later the Canadian government. This theme arches over the history of Native/Canadian relations. For instance, when engaging Indigenous peoples as trade partners and military allies, the French were compelled from early days to ensure successful settlement strategies. For their part, British officials came to accept this need, sometimes integrating Indigenous protocols into their diplomacy with Indigenous leaders.[11] All the while, Indigenous leaders jealously guarded their independence, choosing when and with whom to enter into political arrangements. It was not uncommon for leaders to side with the strongest force, and this compelled European powers to provide gifts in order to attract Indigenous leaders into military alliances.[12] These gifts were practical measures that, if sufficient, guaranteed Indigenous survival during those times of scarcity that resulted directly from fighting for various European powers.

These military alliances were often direct byproducts of economic alliances established during the fur trade. In their attempts to remain economically linked, Indigenous leaders often sided with their trade partners following a declaration of war. Take, for example, the Huron, who were allies of the French, and the Iroquois (Haudenosaunee), who leaned toward the British. These two Native confederacies often found themselves at war with each other after one of their allies declared war on the other. The economic benefits of these alliances at first outweighed the losses; however, rising economic competition led to an increase in both the frequency and viciousness of warfare.[13]

Indigenous leaders often tested the political waters before forming alliances with neighbouring Indigenous communities. The Mi'kmaq, for example, became military allies to the Iroquois Confederacy in 1725, all the while remaining important military allies of the French. They went so far as to occupy Prince Edward Island to help defend eastern Canada from France's enemies.[14] The Iroquois benefited from similar military relationships; in particular, they secured commercial privileges from their French and British allies, which led to their participation in both the American Revolution and the War of 1812.[15] They were most interested, however, in the economic benefits of allying with European powers.

The Iroquois often allied themselves with the British. The Mohawk chief Joseph Brant fought for Britain as a teenager during the Seven Years' War (1755–63).[16] In 1775, he and 1,500 Iroquois supported Britain during the American Revolution. The repercussions of that allegiance were pronounced: after Britain was defeated, Brant and his followers were no longer welcome in the United States, and this compelled them to migrate to Ontario.[17] In 1784, as a reward for their allegiance, and as compensation for the territory lost to the Americans in New York State, General Frederick Haldimand handed the Mohawks a tract of land six miles on either side of the Grand River in Ontario (675,000 acres). When the War of 1812 began, the Mohawks once again took Britain's side. In 1813, during the Battle at Beaver Dams, 180 men from Quebec combined with 200 men from the Six Nations of Grand River to thwart American incursions into Canada.[18]

Right from first contact, the Europeans realized that they needed alliances with Native peoples if they were going to make significant political inroads and penetrate the continent's interior. Perhaps the most important example of the importance of Indian allies was during the Seven Years' War, when the Mohawks strengthened the British militias, allowing them to defeat France. In 1812, Indian allies of the British led by Tecumseh filled a military void that the newly arrived Loyalists could not and in all likelihood saved Upper Canada.[19] Between 1793 and 1814, Indigenous men were awarded 96 Military General Service Medals for helping Britain; this foreshadowed Native people's participation in the First and Second World Wars as well as in Korea.[20] A lasting U.S.–British peace eventually came about. British victories on the North American continent, however, diminished the economic significance of Indigenous peoples, for after the victories, the British came to see them as impediments to territorial expansion and development. Not long after, in 1830, Canada established a formal Indian policy that recognized Indians as wards, thereby significantly altering the relationship between Indigenous and European people (see Chapter 4).

Intratribal warfare increased, as did the incidence of skirmishes. This had a number of causes, including the constant movement of non-Native traders and settlers into the western territories, and the introduction of the horse to Plains Indian culture. Slow but relentless settlement pushed Indigenous populations from their traditional territories and onto neighbouring lands. Early examples of this were the Huron–Iroquois wars of the seventeenth century and, later, the fighting that developed in the "*pays d'en haut*" (middle ground) during the eighteenth century.[21] Strained political relations resulted, and fighting broke out between those who were being pushed from their territories and those whose lands were being encroached upon as a result. Most literature frames this movement as reflecting the aggressive tendencies of warlike cultures seeking to acquire land and resources; there is little understanding in the literature regarding the centrality of these lands to Creation and Native peoples' identity.

Such theories remain extremely problematic. For instance, historical scholarship on the rise of the Plains Cree during the late eighteenth century and the early 1800s concludes that the westward movement was spurred by economic concerns and by the acquisition of the horse and the gun.[22] This forced movement was due in part to a constantly growing population, which in turn led to the displacement of neighbouring nations such as the Blackfoot, the Dakota Sioux, and the Assiniboine through threat of war. The universal need to secure essential resources was also a dominant factor—indeed, the one that caused most tribal conflicts. This settler-induced migration invariably forced changes in military ideologies and practices, because of European encroachment on lands that had been occupied by eastern Native peoples.[23] The second influence was the introduction of the horse, most obviously among the member nations of the Blackfoot Confederacy in what is now southern Alberta. The member nations of the Blackfoot Confederacy were organized into small bands, typically no larger than 30 people, with each band a self-governing and self-sufficient entity that occupied a demarcated territory for its exclusive benefit. Each community fended off parties that challenged its territorial boundaries—especially if they were Cree or southern Shoshoni. Before they acquired the horse in the mid-eighteenth century, the Blackfoot nations had traversed their territory on foot—a period of limited mobility known as the "dog days." The horse was a technological revolution of sorts, in that it permitted the development of more efficient hunting techniques and enabled the Blood and Peigan to expand their territorial resource claims. That in turn led to their acquiring guns from the French, as a result of which the Blood quickly positioned themselves as the dominant force on the northwestern Plains.

A rapid and aggressive period of economic expansion followed: the Blackfoot Confederacy pushed the Shoshoni to the southwestern corner of the Montana territory, at the same time forcing the Flathead and Kootenai across the Continental Divide. This was followed by the rapid displacement of the Cree farther north and east. By the end of the eighteenth century, the Blackfoot Confederacy controlled much of the Montana territory as well as modern-day Alberta and western Saskatchewan.

Post-Confederation Military Dismantling

From the outset of this colossal struggle the Red Man demonstrated his loyalty to the British Crown in a very convincing manner. Patriotic and other war funds were generously subscribed to, and various lines of war work participated in at home. The Indian was not subject to the compulsory Military Act passed in 1917. Certain treaties with the Great White Father stipulated that they would lay down their weapons of war and fight no more. Therefore, any participation the Red Man had in the struggle of 1914 was one hundred per cent voluntary.

—Mike Mountain Horse (Kainai)[24]

The Numbered Treaties negotiated between 1871 and 1877 resulted in the cession of what is modern-day Manitoba, Saskatchewan, and Alberta to the Crown. This in turn brought Indigenous warfare largely to an end. All of the treaties promised annuities as well as protection of the last remaining buffalo herds. The Crown's promises to protect traditional economies were accompanied by promises of education for Native populations, as well as farming and ranching assistance for Native people on reserves. In return, the Plains nations agreed to cede vast tracts of land to the Crown. They also agreed to stop going to war with Canada, the Crown, and neighbouring nations. Native leaders viewed these treaties as nation-to-nation agreements establishing rules of conduct for cultural interaction (including the sharing of territory); the Crown saw the treaties differently—as vital to promoting the peaceful settlement of the West and as a means of avoiding war. During this period the American government was spending $20 million annually to fund its Indian wars, which were aimed at land acquisition; whereas Canada was allocating $19 million annually for federal operations.[25] As a cost-cutting measure, treaties clearly made economic sense.

In particular, Crown and federal officials feared that the Cree, Sioux, and Blackfoot might join together in a large military force capable of severely limiting if not outright arresting westward expansion and settlement. So in 1871, Canada sent treaty commissioners to Manitoba, tasked with securing the peace and friendship of the western nations. Avoiding hostilities and maintaining peaceful relations were clearly important goals, as outlined in the following passage from Treaty 7:

> They promise and engage that they will, in all respects, obey and abide by the Law, that they will maintain peace and good order between each other and between themselves and other tribes of Indians, and between themselves and others of Her Majesty's subjects, whether Indians, Half Breeds or Whites, now inhabiting, or hereafter to inhabit, any part of the said ceded tract; and that they will not molest the person or property of any inhabitant of such ceded tract, or the property of Her Majesty the Queen, or interfere with or trouble any person, passing or travelling through the said tract or any part thereof, and that they will assist the officers of Her Majesty in bringing to justice and punishment any Indian offending against the stipulations of this Treaty, or infringing the laws in force in the country so ceded.[26]

This main provision was found in each of the Numbered Treaties (albeit sometimes worded differently). Clearly, the Crown intended to establish working relationships with western First Nations and (to a lesser extent) Métis leaders. The goal in this was to promote cultural interaction for the purposes of opening tribal lands to settlers wishing to *share* the territory with its original inhabitants.[27] Besides allowing the Crown to extend its jurisdiction into the West, the First Nations leaders were promising to never raise arms against the Crown. And since they were making that promise in the presence of the Creator, it could never be broken.[28] This helps explain why the Canadian government never experienced the level of resistance and outright aggression exhibited by Indian leaders during this period in the United States. By signing the treaties, First Nations leaders were agreeing to never go to war against the Crown or its Dominion government, and this promise was to be kept even in the face of increasingly harsh assimilation policies.

This provision tested the mettle of even the most peaceful Native leaders. By the 1880s, for instance, First Nations were declining to take up arms against the Crown or the NWMP despite dreadful conditions—leaders continued to maintain the peace. Leaders such as Red Crow from southern Alberta resisted Sitting Bull's requests for military support prior to his 1876 annihilation of General George Custer's cavalry regiment at Little Big Horn. Red Crow also resisted the calls of Métis leaders Gabriel Dumont and Louis Riel for help during the events of 1885. Indeed, most Native leaders resolved not to act when confronted with the horrific social and economic conditions facing First Nations and Métis communities after the Crown broke its word to care for its newly acquired wards. And most of them maintained peaceful relations with the Crown even after the Métis violently confronted the Canadian government. In the years since, the literature has generally portrayed the Métis as villainous and aggressive malcontents who led an ill-conceived military assault against the Crown that resulted in their leader, Louis Riel, being hanged for treason.[29] Recent scholarship has been challenging these ideas and presenting a more comprehensive account on what drove the Métis to resist.

Lingering questions keep us from developing a better understanding of Métis martial ideologies and military strategies. For example, the renowned historian Jim Miller asks "why the southern Indians, who were even worse off than those in the Saskatchewan country, failed to take up arms; why so few of the more northerly Indians resorted to violence; why leaders such as Poundmaker and Big Bear appeared to have exerted themselves to minimize bloodshed; and why they ultimately surrendered—all these were discomfiting questions that [have] not [been] addressed by a treatment of the events of 1885 as the clash of two frontiers." We will have to interrogate these issues if we hope to challenge what Miller has described as a "distorted perception of what occurred at Red River in 1869 and in the Saskatchewan country," which, he argues, "set the pattern for most later accounts of these clashes."[30] It is interesting that Métis contributions to the literature have gone largely unexplored except for a handful of academic studies and agency reports.

The fallout of 1885, combined with a strengthened military presence in the West in the form of an augmented NWMP force, led Native leaders to conclude that military action would be ill advised, even if it did not violate the spirit and intent of the treaties. By the late 1880s, Canadian officials were convinced that First Nations and Métis populations had begun their transition from independent political entities to wards of the state under federal guardianship. This demanded that members of First Nations communities alter facets of their political economy as it related to warfare. Many beliefs and practices were necessarily abandoned in the face of an assimilation program which dictated that Native people adopt the norms of mainstream Canadian society. This no doubt was a significant blow to communities that were well versed in the language of military diplomacy and whose leaders utilized such diplomacy to forward their political agendas.

Also preventing First Nations from confronting the Crown about broken treaty promises was the promise to never raise arms against the Crown. This rendered First Nations leaders for all intents and purposes impotent, unable to employ an aspect of their traditional culture that had once been prominent. Canadian Indian military historiography has grappled with only a handful of these issues, suggesting that more research is required. It is, however, safe to say that these changes were destabilizing, and that when combined with new federal policies they led to significant changes to how military endeavours were in the end conceptualized by Native leaders.

World Wars One and Two

The attack on traditional Native military culture waned as fewer nations warred with one another or threatened to raise arms against Canada. When the First World War began in 1914, federal officials were astonished at the level of Indian volunteerism: 4,000 of a potential 11,500 Indian men enlisted.[31] Most would not see action until after 1916—they were initially turned away as unacceptable. But after 1916, the need for soldiers meant that Indians were now acceptable recruits, and many enlisted soon after. At one point, a Native battalion was proposed; the proposal died after being resisted by other battalion commanders. Unfortunately, participating as treaty allies of the British Crown did not result in equal treatment. Many Native recruits found the Canadian military a racist environment that centred out minority recruits.[32] This clouded the Canadian understanding of where Native people fit into Canadian society, including the military.

Impressive participation rates notwithstanding, federal officials still believed that Native people could contribute more. So the *Indian Act* was amended to permit alienation of reserve lands to augment the Greater Production Campaign. In all, nine bills to revise the act were presented to the House of Commons between 1914 and 1930, to increase the powers of the Deputy Superintendent-General of Indian Affairs (DSGIA) while permitting greater access to Indian lands in western Canada.

Canadians were being asked to cut back on food, fuel, labour, and transportation. Facing the threat that soldiers might starve, and with the war's fate presumably in the hands of western farmers, in early 1918 the federal government shifted its attention to acquiring even more parcels of reserve land. This achieved two primary federal objectives. On the one hand, the land would be turned over to agricultural production to boost the war effort. On the other, and more insidiously, the Greater Production Campaign provided the Canadian government the leverage to eliminate Indian reserves by legally permitting the acquisition of upwards of 30,000 acres of "idle" land and resources, which could then be conscripted for the war effort. Most leases created according to these terms were finalized without Native leaders' permission. In all, minimal land was acquired during the Greater Production Campaign: fewer than 85,000 acres were alienated, at a selling price of $1,012,890. This paltry wartime profit must be weighed against the economic dislocation experienced on many reserves, especially on the prairies.[33] For example, the once prosperous Blood reserve cattle-ranching operation never recovered after its herds were removed without compensation.[34] Though technically the monies were held in trust for distribution to individuals, that payout was made during an especially harsh period of fiscal retrenchment, one that resulted in reduced parliamentary appropriations to Indian Affairs beginning in 1916.

The assault on reserve land continued with the *Soldier Settlement Act* (1919), another *Indian Act* amendment, which enabled the Canadian government to acquire still more reserve lands. In an attempt to smooth the progress of western settlement, future prime minister Arthur Meighen devised a scheme that rewarded returning veterans with access to homesteads and farmlands alienated by the federal government from western Canada's First Nations reserve communities. First Nations and Métis war veterans were not eligible for consideration because of conflicting *Indian Act* legislation excluding them from acquiring private landholdings on reserves. The reason: it would have conflicted with the 1906 amendment that "no Indian or non-treaty Indian resident in the provinces of Manitoba, Saskatchewan, Alberta, or the Territories shall be held capable of having acquired or of acquiring a homestead or pre-emption right under any Act respecting Dominion lands."[35] As a result, many First Nations and Métis veterans were disqualified from acquiring alienated reserve land allocations, to which non-Native veterans were entitled at low interest rates no less. Yet by 1923, one-fifth of the 30,604 soldier-settlers had walked away from their land.

Mohawk Lieutenant Fred Ogilvie Loft expressed his dismay after his release from military service, during which he had watched Native and non-Native soldiers and officers work together. Native veterans, he said, found that on their return to Canada, "their service did not put them on an equal footing with their white comrades. . . . [A]ll too many Indian ex-soldiers discovered that, despite their years of service at the front, they were no closer to enjoying the rights that they had ostensibly fought to defend."[36] Native veterans were exposed to poor treatment on their return home, in spite of Deputy Superintendent-General of Indian Affairs Duncan Campbell Scott's enthusiastic declaration that the war had had transformative effects. Loft's message, if at the time ignored, was straightforward: since Native people "fought, bled and died for the great cause the simple recompense they ask is a just and fair dealing for themselves at the hands of the governments, greater in the future than had [been] obtained in the past."[37] Yet the Minister of Pensions and National Health determined in 1932 that the War Veterans' Allowance did not apply to Native people living on reserves because they were akin to any other individual living on a reserve: "such men are wards" of Indian Affairs. It was later determined that Indian Affairs would extend settlement privileges to Native veterans. Yet not until 1936 would Native veterans enjoy benefits equivalent to those received by non-Natives under the *War Veterans Allowance Act* and the Last Post Fund.

During the Second World War, Native people again volunteered at impressive rates (though at lower rates than during the First World War). About 3,090 Native men and women saw action out of a total population of close to 125,000. In all, 213 died and 93 were wounded in the Canadian Forces' three service branches. Education requirements barred many from enlisting, leading 46 to sign on with the American forces.[38] Native people also contributed $23,596.71 to the war effort.[39] Once again, Native people also came under pressure in terms of federal conscription policies. During the conscription debates, Department of Justice officials defined Native people as British subjects and therefore liable for military service. As well, the *War Measures Act* was utilized to override the 70-year-old treaties. Thomas A. Crerar, Minister Responsible for the IAB at the Department of Mines and

Resources, added fuel to the fire by suggesting that "the government has the right to acquire property under the *War Measures Act*."[40]

More important, Native people were still not viewed as allies. They were still considered government wards even though they were participating in the Canadian Forces. The very idea that they were wards of the Crown was anathema to those who believed in Indian nationhood—an idea that was now developing grassroots support. Ignoring the sanctity of the treaties was problematic in many ways, and so, too, was the IAB withholding trust monies as a means to coerce support for the war effort. The Canadian Forces were not responsible for conscripting Native people directly, but as a beneficiary of federal Indian policy, Native people viewed it harshly, as federal officials pushed to secure recruits who likely would have volunteered on their own.

This is supported by one of the few projects to examine Native participation in the Canadian Forces during the Second World War—an oral history survey that probed the reasons why Saskatchewan Indians volunteered during that conflict. Reasons given included these: to escape poverty, because the wife would be entitled to her husband's allowance, and out of loyalty to the Crown borne of treaty relationships.[41] Two more reasons: anger about oppression, and feelings of isolation from both mainstream Canadian society and other reserve community members. Yet on returning, "there was much animosity directed toward the veterans in their home communities that has not been recorded in the secondary literature."[42] It has been posited that "the government acknowledged that the war helped bring nations into their own by broadening the outlook on life for Indians who had served overseas, as well as the home-front. The government further believed that this change indicated a willingness to understand and to get to know the white man's ways through education."[43] The problem with this view is that it fails to recognize the following:

- The Canadian public's attitude toward Aboriginal people changed significantly after the war.
- Native people had a work ethic even before the war.
- Indian participation in the war effort did not signal a new attitude among Native people; rather, it was another example of them adapting to a situation.[44]

It was not only Native men who served. As many as 72 Native women served overseas during the two wars. The reasons women cited for enlisting were not that different from those of the men even if their experiences differed dramatically. First Nations and Métis women generally found that their lack of education blocked their access to desired posts as well as to advanced rank. There was also gender discrimination; however, one study found that most did not claim racism to be an issue. It is interesting that the residential school experience, which resulted in poor educational levels that thwarted professional advancement, was beneficial in one way—the regimented nature of residential schools eased the transition to military life during basic training.[45]

Native Participation in the Canadian Forces

What is clear ... is the pride and dignity of the veterans, feelings that have been tried and tested by their long time sense of neglect. Perhaps our most important task is to ensure that the valuable contribution of the veterans and their families is fully recognized and acknowledged. As the years pass, the number of veterans grows fewer and fewer and the need for a resolution of the issues more urgent.

—Standing Senate Committee on Aboriginal Peoples, 1995[46]

At present, 1,275 First Nations, Métis, and Inuit are serving in the Canadian Forces (CF). That is about 1.4 percent of all enlistees. The CF is attempting to recruit and sustain Native representation at 3 percent, to reflect national workforce demographics.[47] As described above, the participation of First Nations and Métis soldiers in the CF is a historic fact that until recently has been ignored by federal officials. It is also an issue that is poorly understood by Canadians in general. Over the past decade the CF has made a conscious effort to recognize Native contributions to the military. In 1989 the Standing Senate Committee on Aboriginal Peoples was established, as a response to the lobbying efforts of Native veterans, who were demanding federal consideration of the poor treatment of both Native and Métis veterans following their return from the First and Second World Wars and the Korean conflict. Its 1995 report was preceded by one year the release of final report of the Royal Commission on Aboriginal Peoples (RCAP) was released (see box). While it echoed the Senate Committee's account, its authors also urged that the Canadian government own up to its unacceptable treatment of Native and Métis veterans and acknowledge the contributions of these two groups to the Canadian Forces: "The military must recognize its living presence in Aboriginal communities and acknowledge that Aboriginal and military attitudes towards one another are rooted in the past, discussed in the present, and shaped in the future."[48]

Ottawa Memorial to Aboriginal War Veterans

Post-1951 Military Participation

The post-1951 era is arguably the least understood period in the history of First Nations, Métis, and Inuit CF participation. Little in the way of published statistics exists detailing associated CF participation in Korea or Vietnam. As such, post-1951 Native CF participation could be characterized as "hidden participation." Perhaps the best example of this is the Canadian Rangers. Formed in 1947, its role was to "provide a military presence in those sparsely settled northern, coastal and isolated areas of Canada that cannot conveniently or economically be provided for by other components of the Canadian Forces." The Rangers were modelled after the Pacific Coast Militia Rangers (PCMR), formed in August 1942 and

Ranger Roger Hitkolok on sovereignty patrol near Eureka, Nunavut

made up of volunteer citizen-soldiers assigned to defend the western coastline through local patrols and to utilize guerrilla tactics to resist an enemy invasion. By war's end the PCMR comprised 14,849 British Columbians in 126 companies.[49] The protection afforded the West Coast was deemed invaluable. After the war, similar concerns about protecting Canada's northern sovereignty were raised. It was proposed that a cost-effective force consisting of Native people, who made up a small minority of the PCMR, be established to provide a first line of defence in the event that Canada's northern sovereignty was challenged.

This new force, the Canadian Rangers, was established in 1947. In the tradition of the PCMR, it recruited unpaid volunteers, who would carry out their military duties as part of their civilian life.[50] Eventually, annual training exercises alongside professional soldiers became a mainstay of Canadian Ranger capacity building. Cost-cutting measures of the 1960s took their toll on the Canadian Rangers until Pierre Trudeau's renewed interest in northern sovereignty breathed new life into the program. The Rangers were also an appropriate venue in support of new initiatives aimed at improving Native CF participation. One scholar has concluded: "By virtue of their disparate locations, Canadian Ranger patrols are representative of Canada's geographical and cultural diversity and their presence makes an important contribution to the assertion of Canada's 'national interests' in northern, isolated and coastal communities."[51] There are currently 165 patrols across Canada encompassing 4,000 Canadian Rangers—a number that is expected to increase to 4,800 by 2008.[52]

At times volunteers have not been available, which has led the Canadian government to devise alternative schemes for enhancing regional sovereignty. In 1953, for example, the Liberal government relocated several Inuit 2,000 kilometres north into the High Arctic to establish Canadian communities in an effort to enhance northern sovereignty. Concerned about American and Greenland government challenges to existing regional sovereignty owing largely to a lack of occupancy, the federal government sent the Inukjuak at Port Harrison to Grise Fiord and Resolute rather than Iqaluit or Baker Lake. These populations were needed in this particularly harsh region to buttress sovereignty claims. The reality was that the Canadian government viewed this largely as a human experiment to see how successful southern Inuit people could adapt to northern climes. Unprepared for the change in climate, and removed from their ecological context, the Inuit found the transition a difficult one. Many starved, and disease became rampant. The Canadian government chose to withhold rifles, fishing gear, and tent-repairing materials so that the resettled Inuit would not become dependent on federal assistance. Despite intense lobbying by Inuit leaders, the

Canadian government refuses to acknowledge the Inuit role in strengthening Canadian sovereignty in the High Arctic.[53]

Today, attempts to increase First Nations, Métis, and Inuit CF participation have taken the form of the Northern Native Entry Program, which was established in 1971 and expanded into the CF Aboriginal Entry Program in the late 1990s. This program offers Native peoples "the opportunity to explore military careers before making the commitment to join." There is also the Bold Eagle Initiative, established in 1991, which is meant to improve the self-confidence of Native youth through a structured program of militia training that embraces cultural awareness. Finally, the Sergeant Tommy Prince Initiative has been implemented to increase the numbers of "Aboriginal soldiers in the infantry, and in trades to which Aboriginal tradition, culture and often life experience make them particularly well suited."[54]

A recent report identified a troubling incident in which two Bold Eagle participants and eventual CF members who participated in the Tommy Prince Training Initiative were centred out owing to their cultural background. Sergeant Thomas George Prince (1915–77) was one of the most decorated noncommissioned officers in Canadian military history; he was awarded 11 medals in all—including the Military Medal and Silver Star (U.S.). The Native members of the initiative were regaled with Prince's exploits as their commanders attempted to generate a sense of unity.

What occurred later in basic training was disturbing. A 23-year-old former CF member claimed that Tommy Prince's heroics were undercut by a non-Native warrant officer's portrayal of Prince as a "big Native war hero" who "died a drunk in the street . . . like a drunk in the gutter." He added that a warrant officer stated: "You won't hear this in a manual or history books or anything about Tommy Prince, 'cause he was a sergeant and he had eight guys under him. He would use those eight guys as decoys and the Koreans would start shooting at them and he'd go up and start sniping guys."[55] Prince, it has since been identified, suffered from posttraumatic stress disorder (PTSD) and was not operating at peak efficiency during this period. The point is that the name Tommy Prince, which had helped galvanize these young Bold Eagle recruits, had by the program's end become a source of embarrassment and shame for them.

Sergeant Tommy Prince (right), M.M., 1st Canadian Parachute Battalion, with his brother, Private Morris Prince.

The idea of managing Native participation in Canadian society is, arguably, a barrier to improved Native CF participation. Picking up on an earlier theme, Native lands, be they reserve or traditional territories, are still desired by the CF. The most notable and recent example was the low-level flying over Labrador and Quebec that disturbed caribou migratory patterns and that negatively affected the Innu's traditional economy.[56] It has been suggested that similar CF activities—including the activities of foreign military allies training in Canada on, above, or near First Nations, Métis, and Inuit lands—may be an infringement of Aboriginal and treaty rights.[57] Though pressure is still being exacted on Native leaders for land surrenders, the CF's presence has diminished in this regard. Overall, there has been a long and complex history of both positive and negative interactions between the CF and Native leaders, one that continues to influence contemporary First Nations, Métis, and Inuit leaders.

Perhaps most disturbingly, this interface is more often presented not as interactive but as confrontational. The best known incident was the Oka Crisis of 1990, when members of the Kahnawake First Nation barricaded their reserve from construction workers seeking to expand a nine-hole golf course from Oka Township onto a burial ground surrounded by sacred pine trees. The resulting 79-day standoff cost Canadian taxpayers $500 million owing in part to the deployment of the CF (see below for more detail). Oka represents the most visible moment of Native/CF acrimony, though historically it was not the first time that Canadian politicians or military leaders considered using the military to quell an Indian uprising. In January 1946, Native Brotherhood of British Columbia (NBBC) declaration formally reclaimed "the province and declared the white men 'wards of the state' and their right to vote taken away." Under the leadership of Chief William Scow, the NBBC wired its proclamation to B.C. Premier John Hart after reports that the provincial government planned to extend the vote to the Chinese and East Indians but not to "the original Canadians." The NBBC declared early on that this was a publicity stunt "in their battle to gain the right to vote." The proclamation integrated Canadian-imposed prohibitions that restricted Indian freedoms with Canadian cultural norms. Premier Hart responded favourably, acknowledging the proclamation and promising to consider the issue of Indian voting privileges. Even so, Major-General F.F. Worthington, general officer commanding Western Command, responded to this threat by offering his services "in the event that 25,000 west coast Natives went on the warpath."[58]

A more recent example was the release of a Department of National Defence (DND) draft counterinsurgency manual identifying international terrorist threats that had the potential to strain CF/Native relations further. The reason: First Nations were identified as potential threats to national security. In particular, "radical Native American organizations such as the Mohawk Warriors Society are listed in the training manual as insurgents, alongside other insurgent groups."[59] Within days of this report, Defence Minister Gordon O'Connor announced that references to radical Natives would not appear in the aforementioned counterinsurgency manual; however, the damage had been done.

Modern-Day Warrior Responses to Canadian Actions

That radical Native people still worry Canadian officials at a time of active CF recruiting seems contradictory, and seems, moreover, to fly against all the political and social advances made by Native people in recent years. Images of aggressive and bloodthirsty savages continue to pervade Canadian society—images that often date back to the Europeans' first arrival in North America and that are seen daily in movies and on TV programs. More innocuously, many sports teams embrace the Indian's strength in their names (e.g., Washington Redskins, Atlanta Braves, Chicago Black Hawks).[60] The result has been the unconscious internalization by most Canadians of the Indian as warrior.

Warrior societies continue to operate in First Nations communities, though we must be careful when making generalizations, for not all First Nations claim these groups. The Sto:lo in British Columbia are a good example. Sto:lo men do not see themselves as archetypal warriors. One study suggests that many serving in the Second World War found it difficult to live up to the warrior stereotype, for it compromised traditional Sto:lo values.[61] Warrior societies were for the most part intended to be peacekeeping forces. This helped the community remain spiritually oriented. Also, the older members trained the younger men while helping improve their self-control. Most important, the young men were taught that a true warrior desires peace and community stability. The societies inculcated what was identified in the 1980s as the warrior tradition or ethic: an aspect of the Native world view that informed a specific response to war and outside aggression.

This image has taken a beating in recent decades as self-proclaimed warriors from various communities nationally have initiated confrontations with Canadian governments in their fight for recognition of Aboriginal and treaty rights. Between 1981 and 2000, an estimated 266 protests of active resistance occurred nationally that involved more than 120 First Nations communities.[62] An unfortunate byproduct is that the role of traditional warrior societies in Native communities is often obscured by the responses of what could be described as frustrated individuals seeking recourse for the ill treatment of their people. Many of these incidents have led to police intervention. One case in particular, the Oka Crisis in 1990, resulted in the Canadian Forces being despatched for only the third time since 1969 to quell a domestic disturbance.[63] It began on July 11 when the Mohawk Warriors barricaded the road into their community to stop the Oka golf course from being expanded onto Kanesatake lands. Fearing the devastation of several sacred white pine trees and the violation of an ancestral burial site, the warriors held off an advance by the Sûreté du Québec (SQ), during which one officer was killed, and later an advance by the RCMP. After several more officers were hurt and it was evident that the SQ had lost control of the situation, Quebec Premier Robert Bourassa on August 14 requested that the army be mobilized.

More than 2,500 regular and reserve troops were put on notice. On August 20 they arrived at the blockade. As described by observers, the SQ had established a 1-kilometre

Figure 7-1 SITES OF MAJOR NATIVE PROTESTS, 1973–2008

perimeter separating police from the protesters. On their arrival, the army reduced this to 5 *metres*. Many face-to-face confrontations between masked Mohawk warriors and Canadian soldiers occurred. In the meantime, additional troops and heavy equipment mobilized in and around Montreal while CF-116 reconnaissance aircraft conducted missions over Mohawk territory, gathering intelligence. A negotiated end to the protest was signed on August 29; on September 26 the warriors surrendered and were arrested as they attempted to simply stroll past CF soldiers, who were caught unawares. The blockade led developers to shelve the golf-course project.

The image of the warrior seeking justice against Canadian impropriety continues to galvanize young Native individuals nationally. That same year, after several years of legal battles with Alberta that were slowly being resolved in the Peigans' favour, a group calling itself the Lonefighters Society contacted southern Alberta media outlets demanding an immediate halt to local dam construction. The press release described the Lonefighters Society as the protector of the Peigan way of life. According to Peigan elders and a prominent historian, the Lonefighters clan was a distinct and still operational political entity. Specifically, the Lonefighters were vital for "when people had family disputes, they would not take their problems off to different clans—they tried to solve their problems right in that clan, amongst themselves."[64]

The media identified the newly minted Lonefighters followers as an ancient albeit dormant clan recently resurrected.[65] However, traditional Lonefighters clan members and Peigan Women delegates both denounced the upstart Lonefighters as little more than a splinter group that was improperly using the Lonefighters name. The Peigan Women in particular demanded an immediate halt to their agitation, claiming that they lacked community support.[66] The media quickly turned on the Lonefighters, framing their actions as those of young reserve malcontents who were unwilling to engage provincial politicians in what should have been a peaceful dialogue.

IMPROVING RELATIONS

A recent study examining Native attitudes toward the CF and the reasons for forsaking the Canadian military to join the American forces was telling. Compared to the U.S. Marine Corps and the U.S. Army, both of which boast impressive numbers of North American Indian recruits, CF has attracted few Native participants. Recently the CF has launched a research program to determine why Native people across Canada fail to enlist. One recent study among the Kainai in southern Alberta produced interesting results which demonstrate not only that the CF can sometimes be culturally insensitive, but also that Native people still adhere to culturally specific notions of warfare that at times do not match the CF's agenda.

The study demonstrated that a warrior ethic is evident among Kainai young men, who desire to engage in battle to become a warrior in honour of their ancestors. The problem is that the only battles available to demonstrate their bravery require that they fight what they describe as another man's war. Also, the type of warfare and the reasons for engaging in battle are different than in the past; thus, joining the CF today does not mean that the same battlefield will result. Furthermore, the Kainai philosophy of warfare is linked to homeland. To protect their territory is a great honour, whereas the Canadian reasons for engaging in battle are not related to protecting homeland, or about proving bravery. From a Native perspective, engaging in war requires a reason—it cannot be simply to fight. As a result, participating in the CF satisfies a variety of agendas, from honouring past warriors to gaining the necessary battlefield experience to join a religious society. The difficulty is getting this experience without taking a battle to people who bear no animosity toward you and your people.

Many who participated in the study were critical of Canada's treatment of Native people and suggested that they consider themselves and their people to be a nation trapped within a nation. Here, the battle is political, leaving many to question those joining the CF, the military force of an oppressive regime that refuses to acknowledge Native political beliefs and objectives. Such a situation suggests that the true warrior needs to remain at home to protect the community at this tenuous time in history.

This keeps many interested individuals from joining the CF, for to do so would result in their having to leave their community, leaving no one to protect the homeland against Canadian encroachment or even outright invasion. This is often viewed as the last step toward Canada taking over reserve lands for good. So, most informants expressed a reluctance to enlist: they saw the CF as another means of assimilating into Canadian society, and they believed that a real warrior protects his or her family.

Others drew an interesting parallel between the colonial project as practised in Canada (where Indians were forced to surrender their homelands, give up their political processes, and stop speaking their language) with what is occurring in Afghanistan and Iraq. To many, CF participation would mean participating in the repression of the language, government, and culture of another group of Indigenous people. As a member of the CF, it was concluded, you, too, would be playing the role of oppressor. This question was put: "Why do I, a Kainai warrior, want to engage in the same colonial enterprise that resulted in our current living conditions?" Some worried that joining the CF would be an abdication of personal independence and/or individuality. This also reflects the fear many Native people have toward signing papers. Consider that signing documents like Treaty 7 in September 1877 resulted in the loss of land and freedom.

The lack of federal recognition of Native CF contributions is troublesome to many. It was suggested that the desire to see Ottawa's recognition of past CF acts and the bravery exhibited by Native people in general would go a long way toward generating goodwill. The idea of renewing the historic yet currently dormant military relationship with Canada was an important theme in the study. It was suggested that receiving recognition for these deeds would be an honour. Another problem associated with enlisting had to do with a lack of resources: it is expensive to travel from the reserve to an urban centre, and few recruiters enter the reserve. For those who understand military protocol, they stressed that Native people are shy and easily intimidated and that the CF should consider adjusting its policies to acknowledge and accommodate this cultural difference, thereby ensuring that the Kainai CF experience will succeed. In sum, it is time for the CF to learn and understand Native ways.

Conclusion

We have the right to claim and demand more justice and fair play as a recompense for we, too, have fought for the sacred rights of justice, freedom and liberty so dear to mankind.

—Frederick Ogilvie Loft (Mohawk)[67]

Native peoples have a prominent history of military relationships with neighbouring nations and with Canada. Yet there has been little research on Native CF contributions, and less still on Native participation in the First and Second World Wars, the Korean War, or postwar Canada. It was 1979 before two reports were released highlighting the role that Native people have played in the CF. There have been a handful of academic studies; beyond those, our understanding of Native CF participation is derived mainly from reports commissioned by governments or Native veterans' groups. In addition, Métis CF contributions have gone unnoticed. Too few historians have taken the time to interview Canadian Native veterans. We need to evaluate the impact of these historic events while determining through the eyes of these veterans and community members how the ripple effects of history influence contemporary Native individuals when they decide whether to join the CF.

Arguably, these factors have helped shape the existing Aboriginal–Canada relationship, especially when framed by a federal agenda aimed at facilitating the rapid assimilation of Indians into Canadian society. The literature has failed to determine whether these tensions have been exacerbated by the federal government's historic lack of recognition of Native CF contributions. The question is this: did these events engender within Native society a belief that their participation in any facet of mainstream society, in particular their participation in the CF, would be potentially destructive? The impact of a number of federal policies aimed at appropriating reserve lands during the two world wars and beyond suggests that Native people came to acknowledge that their military participation could ultimately lead to territorial dispossession. The lack of recognition afforded Native veterans was a contributing factor.

FURTHER READING

Belanger, Yale D., and Billy Wadsworth. "'It's My Duty . . . to Be a Warrior of the People': Kainai Perceptions of and Participation in the Canadian and American Forces." *Prairie Forum* 33, no. 2 (2008): 297–322.

Dempsey, James. *Warriors of the King: Prairie Indians in World War I.* Regina: Great Plains Research Centre, 1999.

Fallen Hero: The Tommy Prince Story. Kelowna: Filmwest Associates, 1999, 45m.

Gaffen, Fred. *Forgotten Soldiers.* Penticton: Theytus, 1985.

Innes, Robert A. "'I'm on Home Ground Now. I'm Safe': Saskatchewan Aboriginal War Veterans in the Immediate Postwar Years, 1945–1946." *American Indian Quarterly* 28, nos. 3 and 4 (2004): 685–718.

Lackenbauer, P. Whitney. *Battle Grounds: The Canadian Military and Aboriginal Lands.* Vancouver: UBC Press, 2007.

———. "'A Hell of a Warrior': Sergeant Thomas George Prince." In *Profiles of Canadian Military Leadership,* ed. Bernd Horn. Kingston: Canadian Defence Academy Press, 2006, pp. 95–138.

Lamouche, Carrielynn. "The Face of Service: Alberta Métis in the Second World War." In *For King and Country: Alberta in the Second World War,* ed. Ken Tingley. Edmonton: Provincial Museum of Alberta, 1995, pp. 33–38.

MacFarlane, John, and John Moses. "Different Drummers: Aboriginal Culture and the Canadian Armed Forces, 1939–2002." *Canadian Military Journal* 6, no. 1 (2005): 25–32.

Obomsawin, Alanis. *Gene Boy Came Home.* Canada: National Film Board of Canada: 2007. 24m 31s.

Secoy, Frank Raymond. "Changing Military Patterns on the Great Plains, 17th Century Through Early 19th Century." In *Monographs of the American Ethnological Society*. New York: J.J. Augustin, 1953.

Sheffield, R. Scott. *The Red Man's on the Warpath: The Image of the "Indian" and the Second World War*. Vancouver: UBC Press, 2004.

White, Richard. *The Middle Ground: Indians, Empires, and Republics in the Great Lakes Region, 1615–1815*. Cambridge: Cambridge University Press, 1991.

York, Geoffrey, and Loreen Pindera. *People of the Pines: The Warriors and the Legacy of Oka*. Toronto: Little, Brown, 1991.

NOTES

1. Edward Ahenakew, speech to the Annual Meeting of the Woman's Auxiliary, Prince Alberta, Saskatchewan June 16, 1920.

2. Hugh Dempsey, *The Amazing Death of Calf Shirt and Other Blackfoot Stories: Three Hundred Years of Blackfoot History* (Calgary: Fifth House, 1994), pp. 119–37.

3. See George F.G. Stanley, *The Birth of Western Canada: A History of the Riel Rebellions* (Toronto: University of Toronto Press, 1960); and, more generally, idem, *Canada's Soldiers: The Military History of an Unmilitary People*, 3rd ed. (Toronto: Macmillan of Canada, 1974).

4. J.R. Miller, *Skyscrapers Hide the Heavens: A History of Indian–White Relations* (Toronto: University of Toronto Press, 2004), p. 77.

5. Peter Kulchyski, Don McCaskill, and David Newhouse, *In the Words of the Elders: Aboriginal Cultures in Transition* (Toronto: University of Toronto Press, 1999), p. 308.

6. Yale D. Belanger and Billy Wadsworth, "'It's My Duty … to Be a Warrior of the People': Kainai Perceptions of and Participation in the Canadian and American Forces," *Prairie Forum* 33, no. 2 (2008): 297–322.

7. For this discussion, see John Moses, with Donald Graves and Warren Sinclair, *A Sketch Account of Aboriginal Peoples in the Canadian Military* (Ottawa: Minister of National Defence Canada, 2004).

8. Stan Hoig, *Tribal Wars of the Southern Plains* (Norman: University of Oklahoma Press, 1993).

9. John Ewers, "Intertribal Warfare as the Precursor of Indian–White Warfare on the Northern Great Plains," *Western Historical Quarterly* 6, no. 4 (1947): 397, 398.

10. In Dempsey, *The Amazing Death of Calf Shirt*, pp. 17–27.

11. See, generally, Gilles Havard, *The Great Peace of Montreal of 1701: French–Native Diplomacy in the Seventeenth Century*, trans. Phyllis Aronoff and Howard Scott (Kingston and Montreal: McGill–Queen's University Press, 2001).

12. Richard White, *The Middle Ground: Indians, Empires, in the Great Lakes Region, 1650–1815* (Cambridge: Cambridge University Press, 1991).

13. Havard, *The Great Peace of Montreal of 1701*.

14. Royal Commission on Aboriginal Peoples, *For Seven Generations: Looking Back, Looking Forward: False Assumptions and a Failed Relationship* (Ottawa: Queen's Printer, 1996), in particular Chapter 5: "Stage Two: Contact and Co-operation."

15. See, for example, Alan Taylor, *The Divided Ground: Indians, Settlers, and the Northern Borderland of the American Revolution* (New York: Vintage, 2006).

16. See John Jakes, *Mohawk: The Life of Joseph Brant* (New York: Macmillan, 1969); and Isabel Kelsay, *Joseph Brant, 1743–1807: Man of Two Worlds* (New York: Syracuse University Press, 1984).

17. Barbara Graymont, *The Iroquois and the American Revolution* (Syracuse: Syracuse University Press, 1972).

18. Jon Latimer, *1812: War with America* (Cambridge, MA: Harvard University Press, 2008).

19. Reginald Horseman, "Tecumseh," in *Encyclopedia of the War of 1812,* ed. David Stephen Heidler and Jeanne T. Heidler (Annapolis: Naval Institute, 2004), pp. 504–5.

20. See Janice Summerby, *Native Soldiers, Foreign Battlefields* (Ottawa: Veterans Affairs/Government of Canada, 1993).

21. White, *The Middle Ground.*

22. John S. Milloy, *The Plains Cree: Trade, Diplomacy, And War, 1780 to 1870* (Winnipeg: University of Manitoba Press, 1990).

23. See, for example, Bruce Trigger, *The Children of Aataensic* (Kingston and Montreal: McGill–Queen's University Press, 1976); and White, *The Middle Ground.*

24. Mike Mountain Horse, *My People the Bloods* (Calgary and Standoff: Glenbow Museum and the Blood Tribal Council, 1989).

25. Rodney C. McLeod, *The North-West Mounted Police and Law Enforcement, 1873–1905* (Toronto: University of Toronto Press, 1976), p. 3.

26. Alexander Morris, *The Treaties of Canada with the Indians of Manitoba and the Northwest Territories* (Toronto: Fifth House, 1991).

27. James [Sakej] Youngblood Henderson, "Implementing the Treaty Order," in *Continuing Poundmaker's and Riel's Quest: Presentations Made at a Conference on Aboriginal Peoples and Justice,* ed. Richard Gosse, James [Sakej] Youngblood Henderson, and Roger Carter (Saskatoon: Purich, 1994), pp. 52–62.

28. J.R. Miller, "Compact, Contract, Covenant: The Evolution of Indian Treaty Making," in *New Histories for Old: Changing Perspectives on Canada's Native Pasts,* ed. Ted Binnema and Susan Neylan (Vancouver: UBC Press, 2007), pp. 66–91.

29. Blair Stonechild and Bill Waiser, *Loyal Till Death: Indians and the North-West Rebellion* (Calgary: Fifth House, 1997).

30. J.R. Miller, "From Riel to Métis," in *Reflections on Native–Newcomer Relations: Selected Essays,* ed. J.R. Miller (Toronto: University of Toronto Press, 2004), pp. 38–39.

31. James Dempsey, "Problems of Western Canadian Indian War Veterans After World War One," *Native Studies Review* 5, no. 2 (1989): 1.

32. James W. St. G. Walker, "Race and Recruitment in World War I: Enlistment of Visible Minorities in the Canadian Expeditionary Force," *Canadian Historical Review* 70, no. 1 (1989): 4.

33. Fred Gaffen, *Forgotten Soldiers* (Penticton: Theytus, 1985), pp. 36–38.

34. Robert N. Wilson, *Our Betrayed Wards: A Story of "Chicanery, Infidelity, and the Prostitution of Trust'"* (Montreal: Osiris, 1973).

35. Dempsey, *Warriors of the King*, p. 77.

36. Jonathan F. Vance, *Death So Noble: Memory, Meaning, and the First World War* (Vancouver: UBC Press, 1997), p. 259.

37. F.O. Loft, *Women's Century* (ca. 1920), p. 6; quoted in Yale D. Belanger, "Seeking a Seat at the Table: A Brief History of Indian Political Organizing in Canada, 1870–1951" (Ph.D. diss., Trent University, 2006), pp. 152–53.

38. James Dempsey, "Alberta's Indians in the Second World War," in *For King and Country: Alberta in the Second World War*, ed. Ken Tingley (Edmonton: Provincial Museum of Alberta, 1995), p. 39.

39. Ibid., p. 43.

40. Ibid., p. 41.

41. Robert A. Innes, "'I'm on Home Ground Now. I'm Safe': Saskatchewan Aboriginal War Veterans in the Immediate Postwar Years, 1945–1946," *American Indian Quarterly* 28, nos. 3 and 4 (Summer and Fall 2004).

42. Ibid., 696.

43. Dempsey, "Alberta's Indians in the Second World War," p. 49.

44. Innes, "I'm on Home Ground Now," pp. 698–99.

45. Grace Poulin, "Invisible Women: Aboriginal Servicewomen in Canada's Second World War Military," in *Aboriginal Peoples and the Canadian Military: Historical Perspectives*, ed. P. Whitney Lackenbauer and Craig Leslie Mantle (Ottawa: Canadian Defence Academy, 2007).

46. Canada, The Aboriginal Soldier After the Wars: Report of the Senate Standing Committee on Aboriginal Peoples (Ottawa: The Senate of Canada, 1995).

47. Victoria Edwards, "Don't Mention It! The Oka Crisis and the Recruitment of Aboriginal Peoples," paper presented at the Conference for Defence Associations Institute, November 13 and 14, 2002.

48. P. Whitney Lackenbauer, "Aboriginal Claims and the Canadian Military: The Impact on Domestic Strategy and Operations," paper presented at the Conference for Defence Associations Institute, November 13 and 14, 1998.

49. For an overview of the PCMR, see Kerry Steeves, "The Pacific Coast Militia Rangers, 1942–1945" (M.A. thesis, University of British Columbia, 1990).

50. See, generally, Larry Dignum, "Shadow Army of the North," *Beaver* (Autumn 1959): 22–24.

51. P. Whitney Lackenbauer, "Politics or Race, Gender and Sex," in *Aboriginal Connections to Race, Environment, and Traditions*, ed. Jill Oakes and Rick Riewe (Winnipeg: Aboriginal Issues, 2006), pp. 3–16; see also idem, "The Canadian Rangers: A 'Postmodern' Militia That Works," *Canadian Military Journal* (Winter 2005–06): 49–60.

52. These statistics are available at http://www.army.forces.gc.ca/LF/ENGLISH/7_5_1_1.asp. Last accessed June 13, 2008.

53. For this story see, generally, Shelagh Grant, *Errors Exposed: Inuit Relocations to the High Arctic, 1953–1960,* report submitted to the Royal Commission on Aboriginal Peoples (RCAP); and Peter Kulchyski and Frank Tester, *Tammarniit (Mistakes): Inuit Relocation in the Eastern Arctic, 1939–1963* (Vancouver: UBC Press, 1994).

54. John MacFarlane and John Moses, "Different Drummers: Aboriginal Culture and the Canadian Armed Forces, 1939–2002," *Canadian Military Journal* 6, no. 1 (Summer 2005): 25–32.

55. Belanger and Wadsworth "It's My Duty …," pp. 26–27.

56. Marie Wadden, *Nitassinan: The Innu Struggle to Reclaim Their Homeland* (Toronto: Douglas and McIntyre, 1991).

57. Alex Weatherstone, "Fiduciary Duty in the Relationship of Aboriginal Peoples to the Canadian Military" (LL.M. thesis, University of Ottawa, 1993).

58. Quoted in Belanger, "Seeking a Seat at the Table."

59. Joseph Quesnel, "Aboriginals Listed as Terrorists and Insurgents Says Fontaine," *Canada's First Perspective,* April 2, 2007.

60. Daniel Francis, *The Imaginary Indian: The Image of the Indian in Canadian Culture* (Vancouver: Arsenal Pulp, 1992).

61. Keith Thor Carlson, "Sto:lo Soldiers, Sto:lo Veterans," in *You Are Asked to Witness: The Sto:lo in Canada's Pacific Coast History,* ed. Keith T. Carlson (Chilliwack: Sto:lo Heritage Trust, 1997), pp. 126–38.

62. Rima Wilkes, "A Systematic Approach to Studying Indigenous Politics: Band-Level Mobilization in Canada, 1981–2000," *Social Science Journal* 41 (2004): 450.

63. The other two times the CF was activated were during the 1969 Montreal police strike and during the October Crisis of 1970 involving the FLQ.

64. Four Directions Teachings.com, "Piikuni Blackfoot Elders: Dr. Reg Crowshoe and Geoff Crow Eagle." [online] http://www.fourdirectionsteachings.com/blackfoot_bio.html. Last accessed May 24, 2008.

65. Cy Gonick, "Save the Oldman River," *Canadian Dimension* (December 1991).

66. "Peigan Women Oppose Protest; They Want 'Splinter Group' to Stop Bid to Divert Oldman River," *Edmonton Journal,* August 12, 1990, A7.

67. Quoted in Stan Cuthand, "The Native Peoples of the Prairie Provinces in the 1920s and 1930s," in *Sweet Promises: A Reader on Indian–White Relations,* ed. J.R. Miller (Toronto: University of Toronto Press, 1991), pp. 382–83.

POLITICAL ECONOMY

8 Political Organizing in Canada

We present this brief with the sincere hope it will help all interested parties to formulate a plan or policy whereby the status of the Canadian Indian will be improved and may the day soon come when the Indian will lift his head, knowing that he can meet his fellow countrymen as man to man, knowing that his rights will never be molested, knowing that he can enjoy not only some but all benefits of true democracy in this country—the land of his birth. We represent an organization that is non-political and non-sectarian. We will work in harmony and in cooperation with any body, party or organization that is interested in the welfare and advancement of the Indian in Canada.

—Joe Dreaver, Federation of Saskatchewan Indians[1]

Native political organizing in Canada is a time-tested phenomenon. Dating back to 1870, Native organizations are unique political entities that occasionally collaborate to press the federal government for the recognition of Aboriginal rights. Most Native organizations—the Assembly of First Nations (AFN), the Union of Ontario Indians, and the Federation of Saskatchewan Indian Nations (FSIN), to name a few of the more than 4,000 estimated political organizations—are independent lobby groups acting on behalf of constituents with unique and specialized needs. Many of these organizations have in recent years assumed responsibility for service-delivery and economic-development initiatives both on and off reserve. All the same, all their leaders face a universal barrier: the need to fuse community-based political needs and hopes with the demands of operating within the various levels (federal, provincial, municipal) of the broader Canadian political system. This historic tension has proven fatal to many political organizations; even so, the belief in traditional knowledge and historic organizing techniques continues to propel contemporary leadership.

Native political organizations are nothing new. Even before extended first contact in the late sixteenth century, the first peoples of North America had in place complex systems of governance based on spiritual, political, and social principles that had evolved over millennia. After first contact, foreign belief systems significantly challenged these political processes and ideologies. Native leaders nevertheless proclaimed their people to be independent nations with long-established precise protocols for maintaining efficient local governance and inter-nation political diplomacy and trade. The organizing and political models were diverse; but underlying these was a shared political world view that led Native leaders to form organizations to counter assimilation-driven European policies. This chapter chronicles the rise of Native political organizations in Canada.

Pre-Contact Organizing

Native people were organizing themselves even before the sixteenth century. They faced a need to bring together nations whose territories overlapped; this encouraged meetings where the different groups tried to promote peaceful relations that would ensure regional balance. Two organizational systems were generally employed. The first system (see Chapter 2) was intertribal and locally focused: each community found various means to address its internal social, political, and economic concerns. The second system, which is the focus of this chapter, was intratribal, involving two or more nations gathering to consider regional political and economic issues. Owing to an assortment of concerns and agendas associated with large, multi-nation meetings, a flexible, discussion-based model—the council—evolved. Councils were highly adaptable. They were not exclusive to any culture, and they worked well in larger political settings where thorny political issues needed to be dealt with, such as territorial rights and regional trade. Indigenous nations held regularly scheduled councils, where relationships were renewed and alliances were reaffirmed.

Associated with councils was a unique diplomacy adhered to by participating Indigenous groups. In eastern Canada, for instance, generally the process went something like this. First, an invitation for a council was extended to all interested parties weeks in advance; the invitation identified the meeting's location and the issues to be discussed.

The Six Nations Hereditary Council meets in 1898.

Second, before travelling to the council, each participating community's ambassadors prepared for the upcoming dialogues. Third, after all the delegates arrived at the location, two days were allotted for rest before the council convened. Fourth, ceremonies of condolence were carried out to mourn deceased chiefs, confer successors, and ensure that past transgressions would be overlooked. Only then did the fifth stage take place: participants smoked the pipe to create an atmosphere of peace. After all of that, a series of meetings began during which key issues were discussed. Responses to grievances were not expected until the day after they were aired; this gave delegates time to consider the questions and to refocus themselves after emotionally charged debates. If a resolution evaded the participants, the council dissolved itself. The delegates then exchanged gifts and returned home, anticipating a future diplomatic gathering.[2]

Confederacies soon developed based on these regular meetings. A confederacy allowed two or more nations to merge politically in furtherance of mutual goals; in this way was acknowledged the utility of developing strength and political unity based on superior numbers. Confederacies also allowed sovereign nations to maintain political and economic ties. Many such confederacies, such as the Blackfoot (Niitsítapi) Confederacy and the Iroquois (Haudenosaunee) Confederacy, date back centuries. Others, though, were fleeting: nations would merge to resolve animosities and avoid warfare, only to disperse soon after. For the purposes of this section, a brief overview of six confederacies will be provided.

Blackfoot Confederacy. Member nations included the Peigan (South Piikuni), North Peigan (North Piikuni), Blood (Kainai), and Blackfoot (Siksika), as well as, until 1861, the Gros Ventres. These member nations shared a common culture and relied economically on the buffalo hunt. They were known for their military strength, which led the Canadian government to pursue treaty negotiations rather than military intervention as the means to open the West to settlement.

Council of the Three Fires. Located in modern-day Indiana, Michigan, and Ontario, this confederacy was less formal than the Blackfoot Confederacy. Its member nations—the Pottawatomi, Ottawa, and Ojibwa—united for political and military purposes. It maintained and renewed its relationships as protocol demanded, though the fur trade often led to tensions and hostilities among them.

Huron–Wendat (Wyandot) Confederacy. This confederacy comprised five nations and is believed to have been founded in the 1600s. It met several times a year to discuss political developments, engage in trade and ceremonies, arrange hunting, fishing, and trading expeditions, and replace deceased chiefs. It was in constant battle with the Iroquois Confederacy. The political stability provided by the confederacy model enabled the Huron–Wendat to challenge Iroquois political and military supremacy for years.

Iroquois (Haudenosaunee) Confederacy. Dating back to at least the fifteenth century, the Iroquois Confederacy originally included five nations: Mohawk, Oneida, Onondaga, Seneca, and Cayuga. The Tuscarora joined in 1721. When the nations entered into council to debate important issues, all perspectives were heard before decisions were rendered. The confederacy operates to this day in Ontario, Quebec, and New York.

Seven Nations of Canada. This alliance, also known as the Seven Fires, comprised the Iroquois, Hurons, Abenakis, and Anishinaabe. Originally allied with the French, the Seven Nations became an important ally of the British during the American Revolution and the War of 1812.

Wabanaki Confederacy. Located in eastern Canada's Maritime provinces and the State of Maine, the Wabanaki Confederacy included the Mi'kmaq, Maliseet, Passamaquoddy, and Penobscot nations. It focused its energies on diplomacy, war, and trade. Formed to prevent European encroachment, the confederacy eventually extended its ranks to include the Ottawas in an advisory capacity, as well as the Mohawks of Kahnawake and Kanesatake. The confederacy was formally dismantled in 1862, though the member nations remain friends and allies.

Wabash Confederacy. This short-lived military alliance (1785–95) was formed to resist American incursions into Indian Territory. It included the Hurons, Shawnees, Delawares, Miamis, Kickapoo, and Kaskaskia, as well as the Council of the Three Fires and the Six Nations of the Grand River. These nations had from time to time established informal alliances. The threat of unchecked American expansionism led to this confederacy's formation. The Battle of Fallen Timbers in 1794 and the Treaty of Greenville in 1795 brought about the Confederacy's demise.

Many of these alliances were quite successful. Yet each faced many obstacles to smooth operations. For instance, various sovereign nations comprised the confederacies mentioned above. Each nation promoted a unique social, political, and economic vision. Take for example the Iroquois Confederacy. Within it were five separate nations (Mohawk, Oneida, Onondaga, Cayuga, Seneca), which were intrinsically linked but lacked a centralized government. Each nation had its own leaders, its own territories, and its own political and economic needs. There is no doubt that councils helped maintain ties and (it was hoped) strengthen relations among the member nations, neighbouring Indigenous groups, and European representatives. But inter- and intratribal factionalism challenged this confederacy, making it difficult to establish consensus in council. This could be a weakness, for the confederacy would not act in unison without consensus.[3]

Most of the aforementioned confederacies emerged after European contact. Typically, an alliance of nations was viewed as an effective counterweight to the Europeans' growing political, economic, and military presence. During the negotiations leading to the Great Peace of Montreal in 1701, Six Nations leaders met with the French and 1,300 representatives of 40 Indigenous nations extending from the Maritimes to the Great Lakes and from James Bay to southern Illinois. At Montreal they all gathered to establish peaceful relations. The French were already resorting to Indigenous diplomacy in their dealings with various groups. Relying on their understanding of Indigenous protocol, and desiring to expand their colonies to the west, the French initiated a highly structured, month-long ceremony and general council, in the course of which the Great Peace was established among the Iroquois, the French, and the Indigenous nations of the Great Lakes.[4] In an effort to come to one mind, all parties reached an accommodation that established a pact that resulted in (1) peaceful relations through the renewal of regional Indigenous alliances, and (2) the formal integration of the French into what was largely an Indigenous agreement. After speeches were made, the treaty was signed and the Indigenous leaders offered the peace pipe.

Councils and confederacies operated well past the seventeenth century, and the Iroquois Confederacy is still operational. As to why Indigenous people past and present chose to organize, the answer is straightforward: to challenge European hegemony and outsiders' claims on Indigenous lands and resources. The challenges associated with organizing large groups of Indigenous peoples remained significant and in most cases debilitating. Besides inter- and intratribal factionalism, culturally specific ideologies drove Indigenous politics, and these proved difficult to overcome. The Mohawk and the Ojibwa of southern Ontario are a good example. Both had a time-honoured political strategy of engaging neighbouring political powers; for both, this resulted in a long history of treaty relationships. But at the same time, the two nations were unique politically, which made it hard for them to unite in a common cause. The Mohawk political structure was centralized, with a council of chiefs chosen and directed by the clan mothers. The Ojibwa system relied on experienced community members rising to respond to important leadership issues.

Changes in the early nineteenth century's political environment forever transformed the atmosphere of political interactivity: Native peoples came to be viewed as little more than policy and legislative relics. In 1805, in their efforts to maintain allegiance to historic ways of engaging neighbouring nations, Ojibwa leaders sought a treaty with the Indian Department in return for Crown protection. In 1837, 1846, and 1853, large councils were held to consider common political issues. Ojibwa political activities often extended beyond writing petitions and forwarding requests for treaty negotiations to colonial officials. From 1826 to 1847 the Ojibwa at Credit River, led by the Ojibwa Methodist missionary Peter Jones, fashioned a community constitution and legal rules that combined customary with non-Native judicial concepts, thereby securing a degree of cultural and national continuity. According to Jones' great-great-grandson, the legal scholar John Borrows, the missionary "sought control in Canada amidst changing circumstances" while accepting that his people "could benefit from the promises of non-Native education, employment, housing and medicine."[5] Clearly, the Ojibwa were not above fusing political ideologies and negotiating with their political neighbours, so long as it was done according to the understanding that concessions were needed to establish political relationships.[6]

The Mohawks, on the other hand, never wavered in their belief that they were a nation and treaty signatory with the British Crown. Claiming independent status within their own territory, they also asserted that the Royal Proclamation of 1763 had recognized Native land ownership and had established the criteria for future treaty relationships. In other words, their leaders maintained that treaties made with the British were nation-to-nation pacts. As such, they did not believe that political organizing was necessary to obtain an official audience with fellow treaty signatories. After they were compelled to relocate to Quebec and southwestern Ontario following the American Revolution, Mohawk community leaders tried in vain to convince colonial officials, in the spirit of the Covenant Chain, to become political contemporaries through formalized relationships. They also tried to promote a council with Canadian officials to renew the terms of the Crown treaties—albeit only if their own terms remained. The desired meeting never materialized.

The First Wave of Native Organizing in Canada: 1870 to 1918

When my great-great-grandfather placed his name and totemic symbol on a treaty that surrendered 500,000 acres in southern Ontario, he did not assent to assimilation. He sought control in Canada amidst changing circumstances. He knew that Chippewa/Anishinabek culture could benefit from the promises of non-Aboriginal education, employment, housing, and medicine.

—John Borrows[7]

From the very beginning of cross-cultural contact in the early seventeenth century, Native peoples participated economically as well as politically with European and British settlers. Indigenous nations were at first powerful enough to influence these political relationships. Yet from the end of the eighteenth century until Confederation in 1867, colonial (later, Canadian) officials largely ignored Indigenous concerns. As Canada's nation-building project took root, Indigenous peoples were viewed as little more than barriers to westward expansion. Many found that the main obstacle in their struggle to maintain political continuity and to preserve existing political relationships was colonial society's paternalism, which in the 1850s was the fundamental value guiding how federal Indian policy was developed. This led colonial leaders to abandon Indigenous concerns for more pressing national issues. Also, it was assumed that Indigenous peoples were destined for cultural absorption and/or physical disappearance; thus, it was seen as a waste of valuable political resources to deal with these issues.

In 1870, Native leaders in Ontario and Quebec responded by holding a council at the Six Nations Mohawk community near Brantford, Ontario. There, more than 70 representatives from 21 Ojibwa and Mohawk communities met to discuss the rapid settler immigration, which was negatively influencing local economic activities.[8] During that meeting, the Grand General Indian Council of Ontario and Quebec (GIC) was formed to try and stem the loss of political influence attributable to federal Indian legislation and policies. In particular, the GIC was formed to challenge the *Gradual Enfranchisement Act,* a law passed in 1869 to dismantle customary Indigenous governance, which colonial and later Canadian administrators considered an obstacle to assimilation. Under the act, all internal decisions pertaining to band matters were now "subject to confirmation by the Governor in Council." Native leaders across Canada contested these and similar initiatives. The delegates to the Brantford Conference had arrived intending to discuss recent political developments affecting their political autonomy; during the talks, they proposed that their two nations (Ojibwa and Mohawk) form an alliance to challenge the Canadian government's failure to improve social conditions. The attending leaders accepted this proposal, and a week of ceremonies followed. But before the ceremonies ended, the delegates argued over the organization's structure.[9]

Very quickly, the unique political approaches of the two nations undermined attempts to form a collective political organization. After a majority of Ojibwa delegates were elected to the GIC's leadership, this group determined that the best strategy was to integrate the GIC into the federal political system by seeking federal support for an organizational initiative. Mohawk delegates chafed at this approach, and many withdrew their support for the GIC. Much of their consternation had to do with the decision to evaluate the *Gradual Enfranchisement Act,* which had recently been passed. Delegates of the GIC member nations expressed their discomfort with Canada's assimilation policy and its recent attempts to compel Native people to adopt municipal-style elected band councils. The Ojibwa believed they could influence the policy process by suggesting alterations to the act, whereas the Mohawks wanted to demand that the legislation be repealed. Internal discord over this seemingly minor issue emerged.[10]

Compounding Native fears was the withdrawal of Canadian officials from direct talks with Native leaders. Indian Affairs officials were relying instead on legislation and policy to define their relationship with Native peoples. Long gone were the councils and regular discussions characteristic of political contemporaries. Dismayed at this failure to renew relationships, Native leaders seized on an alternative organizing model, one that they believed would bring about the desired meetings. Part of the problem was that Canadian officials saw Native people as still committed to antiquated organizing models and political philosophies. In response, the GIC leaders altered their traditional or customary organizational formats in an attempt to influence federal Indian laws and policies. Interestingly, this involved significant changes. Women began playing a less vital role, and English began to replace Native languages. As younger, school-educated Native men began ascending to leadership positions, they linked up with Native men across Canada who seemed to be of like mind and education. In not too long, most organizations adopted elective models that embraced regular structured meetings during which minutes were kept. This model would become the norm in Native political organizing and is seen to this day in associations such as the AFN and FSIN.

While the GIC was contributing to the creation of the *Indian Act* of 1876 (see Chapter 5), bureaucrats found themselves confronted with Native leaders' reluctance to adopt the band-council model. In British Columbia in 1979, Native leaders tried to reassert their peoples' political agency by compelling federal recognition of tribal land ownership and by demanding treaties with the provincial government. More than 1,200 Coast and Interior Salish from the Fraser and Thompson Rivers, the Nicola Valley, and the Similkameen area met that year at Lytton. The council took one year to plan—a feat that led one provincial official to nod approval of the Thompson Indians' (Nlha7kapmx) self-governing abilities. The council christened itself the Confederation of Tribes of the Mainland and acclaimed 13 councillors for three-year terms. These councillors decided that hereditary tribal chiefs would hold office until death, at which time they would not be replaced. This council also empowered itself to formulate rules and regulations concerning a variety of issues, including education and schools, health, hunting and fishing, and personal conduct. A committee of the council of at least three councillors was selected to act as a judiciary responsible for arbitrating any perceived violations.[11]

To forge an alliance with the Queen, it was decided that several important traditions would be abandoned. No distinction would be made between new and old. Instead, the tribes would represent a unique fusion of "Victorian propriety, Canadian paternalism, and Indigenous tradition."[12] In particular, the younger delegates resolved to abolish the potlatch, something they thought would impress Canadian officials but that the older leaders resisted. This controversy led to group's collapse. As had happened with the GIC, the failure of delegates to agree on a common mandate led to operational difficulties, foreshadowing an issue that still confronts contemporary First Nations, Inuit, and Métis organizations. Furthermore, whereas the GIC's internal discord had been the result of culturally driven political differences, the Tribes of the Mainland dispute was generational. This highlighted a second major barrier to success: the inability to formalize operational guidelines able to reconcile traditional with modern politics.

The latter barrier was a consequence of constant federal and community-based challenges to political legitimacy, as a result of which many government officials came to question each organization's capacity to represent its members' needs. In the GIC's case, for example, community leaders did not accept the organization's claims that it was the legitimate voice for provincial Native interests. The 24 Native political organizations that emerged between 1870 and 1946 were products of a complex balancing act in the course of which community members scrutinized how closely organizational leaders were working with Canadian officials who were seeking Native peoples' assimilation into Canadian society. As organizations attempted to become legitimate representatives of Native people, they found themselves facing competition for government attention and resources. Leading organizations sometimes responded by undermining the band councils, which were also fighting the government for improved local conditions. This balancing act became increasingly difficult once an organization accepted funding from the Canadian government. The GIC needed federal funding to maintain its operations. Organizational leaders who resisted funding found it difficult to generate and maintain the financial support they needed to maintain their effectiveness.

This first wave of formal Native organizing developed slowly. Not until 1909 was the first modern Native political organization formed in Canada. Established after a Vancouver meeting attended by 20 representatives of coastal tribes, the Indian Rights Association (IRA) chose an intricate organizational structure that owed a good deal to "White" models. It was formed to expose the provincial government's refusal to acknowledge Aboriginal title or to negotiate treaties and to protest the arbitrary placement of reserves near unrecognized Native communities. At the IRA's centre was a small executive whose functions included raising funds, organizing conferences, circulating information to local representatives, and maintaining links with legal counsel who could compel a government to respond to demands.[13] The IRA brought together north and south coast tribal groups while consciously adopting an organizing format that was "intended as something White politicians and the White public could readily understand and would take more seriously than they had been taking traditional chiefs in traditional roles."[14] By the end of the twentieth century's first decade, most Native leaders reluctantly acknowledged that the British Crown had abandoned political negotiations and that the Canadian government would have to somehow be engaged.

Three issues came to drive this second wave of organizing. The first was the B.C. land question, which in the late 1920s was a source of alarm for Native leaders.[15] The second was Native participation in the organized labour movement, which enabled large numbers of Native workers to become expert organizers.[16] Third and last, a pan-Indian consciousness was developing, a result of increased interaction among major players, including Andy Paull (Squamish) from B.C., John Tootoosis (Cree) from Saskatchewan, F.O. Loft (Mohawk) from Ontario, and John Callihoo (Mohawk) from Alberta, as well as Saskatchewan Métis leaders Malcolm Norris and James Brady.[17] Their frequent interactions led to an understanding that Native peoples were being treated poorly everywhere in Canada and that they shared overlapping political concerns.[18]

The Second Wave of Political Organizing: 1918–60

The unseen tears of Indian mothers in many isolated Indian reserves have watered the seeds from which may spring those desires and efforts and aspirations which will enable us to reach the stage when we will take our place side by side with the white people, doing our share of productive work and gladly shouldering the responsibility of citizens in this, our country.

—Fred Ogilvie Loft (Mohawk)[19]

The second wave of Native political organizing was incredibly prolific and led to significant changes in the relationship between Native peoples and Canadian officials. It can be traced to the return of a First World War veteran, Lieutenant F.O. Loft (Mohawk). In December 1918, on landing in Canada, he called a meeting at the Six Nations Mohawk community. His intention was to establish an organization that was politically focused and strong enough to compel Canadian officials to accept political guidance. He would rely on Native dissatisfaction with

Conference of League of Indians of Western Canada held at the Thunderchild Reserve, Saskatchewan (1921). Back row from left: Harry Achinam; unknown; Chief Drever; unknown; unknown; unknown; unknown; Joe Samson, Hobbema, Alberta. Middle row from left: unknown; Joe Taylor, Onion Lake, Alberta; Thunderchild; F.O. Loft, organizer from Six Nations Reserve; unknown; unknown. Front row from left: unknown; unknown; unknown.

federal programs to stimulate support for his League of Indians of Canada. Loft anticipated that his league would cooperate with the government to facilitate a dialogue prior to Native people reclaiming political influence. Support for the league was immediate, especially in Saskatchewan, which led him to conclude that it was the duty of Native people across Canada "to join with the forces to create a permanent national brotherhood."[20] Loft proposed a collective bargaining strategy to engender a productive Native–Canada relationship.

By the early 1920s, word of the league had spread to the Prairie provinces. A series of meetings were held in 1920, and by 1922 meetings were often attended by more than 1,500 delegates. By the time the league was formally established as a national organiza-tion later that year, it boasted a total membership of more than 9,000. Despite this success, the 1920s was a difficult period for Loft. In particular, the Deputy Superintendent-General of Indian Affairs, Duncan Campbell Scott, feared Loft's ability to organize Native people nation-ally; to discourage him, he repeatedly tried to enfranchise him. This pressure contributed to the league's downfall by making it harder for Loft to raise the necessary operating expenses.[21] By decade's end, both Loft and his wife were in poor health, which further undermined his political participation. By the time he died in 1934, the league had fallen dormant. One historian cites Loft's legacy as his ability to "engender an awareness of the possibilities of Indian associations as protest and pressure groups among bands on the Prairies and for this he has justly been called the 'Father of Western Canadian Indian Associations.'"[22]

Unity was Loft's goal. In particular, he emphasized strength in numbers while trying to draw Native peoples nationally to support his organization. Unfortunately, he could not find a central issue or concern capable of galvanizing Native peoples nationally to challenge federal officials. And even though he focused on developing national support, his actions inadvertently led to several startling developments in the opposite direction—specifically, the emergence of multiple, distinctive Native political organizations. This in turn led to an incredibly competitive era of political engagement during which a range of groups lobbied for federal recognition, often to the detriment of rival organizations. As a result of all this competition, organizations began expanding their mandates beyond advocating for interac-tive political councils. New ideas were being seized to promote the desired communication with Ottawa.

Take for example the gathering of the Pasqua, Piapot, and Muscowpetung reserves from southern Saskatchewan during the 1920s. These three communities established the Allied Bands to protect remaining reserve lands from forced surrender to federal officials looking to open up reserve lands to settlers. A succession of meetings followed from 1922 to 1924, during which the Allied Bands remained a regional group whose influence did not extend beyond southern Saskatchewan. In 1928 the Allied Bands dispatched a delegation to Ottawa to protest reserve living conditions and the Indian agent's oppressive behaviour and to lobby federal officials for a Royal Commission to investigate Indian administration—a proactive approach more reliant on a federal response, as opposed to demanding an audience with the appropriate officials. The Allied Bands refined many of their concerns into language that has since become the language of Aboriginal self-government and the burgeoning nationhood movement. In particular, when the Allied Bands in 1933 transformed themselves into the Protective Association for Indians and Their Treaties, they also adjusted their mandate to focus on protecting treaty rights and Native lands and resources and on the enhancement of Native education. This, then, was the first Native organization to specifically articulate these specific realms of nation building.[23]

The Allied Bands were altering the language of organizing—in particular, how Native leaders interpreted and defined key political issues. Around the same time, the failure of the Allied Tribes in B.C. to secure federal recognition of Aboriginal title and formally negotiated treaties transformed how Native people approached organizing. One cause was Campbell Scott's concerns about the nascent organizing movement. Scott was especially affronted that non-Native lawyers were helping community members in their agitation, so in 1927 he had the *Indian Act* revised so that it was now illegal for Indians to hire lawyers with band funds for the purposes of pursuing land-claim activities.[24] The revision would stand until 1951. One of its anticipated benefits: the silencing of outside consultants helping Native organizations or Native leaders pursue land claims against the federal government. In the wake of these events the Allied Tribes disbanded. Within a few years, however, William Benyon (Tsimshian) and Ambrose Reid were again politically active and generating the support they needed to form in 1931 the Native Brotherhood of British Columbia (NBBC). At first styling itself as a labour union (in order to avoid Indian Agent scrutiny), it secretly doubled as a clandestine political organization. After a decade of effective bargaining, the NBBC morphed into a political organization, moving gradually from local to provincial political matters and from there into federal politics. In the 1940s it was formally recognized as the Northwest Coast's representative Native organization.

During the 1930s, Saskatchewan and Alberta Native leaders became especially active political organizers, guided by two influential Métis, James Brady and Malcolm Norris. Alberta's John Callihoo and Saskatchewan Cree leader John Tootoosis formed the Union of Saskatchewan Indians (USI) and the Indian Association of Alberta (IAA).[25] Both organizations sought better education, augmented political authority over reserve matters, improved health care, and a formal investigation into Native veterans' concerns. The USI's experience

The late Harold Cardinal speaks at a First Nations meeting in Calgary (1975). Cardinal gained national notoriety with the 1968 publication of *The Unjust Society,* which portrayed poor reserve living conditions while unveiling to the public one of a rising number of politically astute Native leaders ready to challenge the Canadian government's pitiable treatment of Native people.

is especially relevant in terms of the provincial government's role in its development after Tommy Douglas in 1944 became the premier of Saskatchewan (which made him the first socialist government leader in North America). His Co-operative Commonwealth Federation (CCF) government announced its intention to improve Native living conditions and endorsed the founding of a single Native political organization to serve as a unifying force to promote that improvement.[26] Funding for operations was provided after the USI was formed in early 1946. Led by Tootoosis, the USI lobbied for reserve day schools, Native access to higher education, equivalent old-age pensions, and better treatment for Native war veterans.[27]

The USI promoted its involvement in a national Native organization. Yet it also remained ideologically distant from other Native organizations, deferring to Treaty 6 as the framework for future Native–Canada talks. This approach differed from how the leaders of the Manitoba Indian Association (MIA, est. 1934) operated. At their general meeting in 1946, recently returned war hero Tommy Prince (Ojibwa), the great-great-grandson of Chief Peguis, was selected the MIA's vice president and chairman. MIA founders anticipated that Prince would unite the fledgling organization to fight for treaty rights, improved education, better on-reserve conditions, and a revised agricultural policy. Prince himself observed: "My job is to unite the Indians of Canada so we can be as strong as possible when we go to the House of Commons for better education, sanitation, and other things on reserves."[28] But except when it came to promoting treaty rights, the MIA delegates were unable to establish a mandate. John Tootoosis was on hand at the conference, and he applauded the MIA's efforts. He emphasized the need for every community to join as a unit, and he called for a national Native organization.[29]

None of the aforementioned organizations made much political headway, however. Enter former Allied Tribes leader, Andy Paull, who recruited Tootoosis, as well as the Quebec Huron–Wendat political activist, Jules Sioui, and formed the North American Indian Brotherhood (NAIB) in 1944 to "resist the inclusion of Indians under the Canadian conscription act and government attempts to tax them" while impressing on federal officials the need to protect "aboriginal rights and the principle of self-determination."[30] Soon, however, each man's separate political ideology surfaced, which led to internal fault lines. Tootoosis envisioned treaties as the basis of any Canada–Native relationship, whereas Paull called for all Indians to unite under an umbrella organization.[31] Sioui advocated militant protest activity, which led to his ouster when the organization's mandate came to increasingly reflect Paull's concerns.[32] Tootoosis retreated to Saskatchewan to continue building the USI.

The NAIB under Paull in 1945 was promoted as the leader of "the Indian Nation within the Sovereignty of the British Crown, a nation, by treaty obligation, under a protective agreement."[33] The NAIB sought (1) national recognition from the government of Canada of a united Native Nation as one established body within the Sovereignty powers of the Dominion of Canada, while (2) offering European Canadians a chance to cooperate with the Native people in strengthening the bonds of racial unity. Native voting rights, the elimination of liquor laws (to reduce the number of liquor-related offences), and the implementation of pensions and an appropriate welfare system were also organizational goals. Native political mobilization combined with increasing media exposure led the federal government to establish a Special Joint Parliamentary Committee (SJC) in 1946 to investigate the *Indian Act's* continued validity. The SJC sent out formal invitations to Native leaders representing the NAIB, IAA, USI, NBBC, and MIA to testify. Between 1946 and 1948 it held 128 sessions and heard from 122 witnesses, published 411 written briefs, and generated 2,100 pages of evidence containing more than one million words.[34]

For the first time since Canada's civilization policy was implemented in the 1830s, Native leaders were sitting down collectively with federal officials at a forum where they could present their views and complaints about Indian policy and administration (see box). Thirty-one Native leaders representing 17 organizations and associations testified; six other organizations submitted written briefs. Native leaders considered the SJC a moment of renewal

---

NAIB RESOLUTIONS FORWARDED TO THE SJC, JUNE 1946

1. The joint committee should investigate the violation of Indian treaty rights;
2. Indian band membership should be determined by Indians;
3. Treaties guarantee Indian people exemption from federal and provincial taxation;
4. Treaty rights to hunt, fish, and trap are paramount to provincial legislation and regulations;
5. The policy of compulsory Indian enfranchisement should be abolished;
6. Denominational schools on reserves should be abolished; Indian education should be directed by regional boards controlled by Indians;
7. Indians should elect their own members of Parliament;
8. IAB administration should be decentralized and provincial regional boards established, reporting directly to a federal agency or to Parliament;
9. IAB should hire qualified Indians;
10. Local Indian councils should have full authority to manage their local affairs;
11. Indians should ride for half-fair on railroads;
12. Indians should be able to police their own reserves;
13. Reserve centralization schemes should not be implemented without band consent.

Source: Belanger, "Seeking a Seat at the Table," p. 296.

---

necessary to re-establish a political relationship with federal officials (see box).[35] But unbeknownst to Native leaders, the government was perpetuating a trend dating back to the 1870s of relying on a handful of Native organizations to represent national Indian interests. The final recommendations resulted in little change, which led one commentator to conclude that the SJC "in essence . . . approved the goal of Canada's previous Indian policy—assimilation— but disapproved some of the earlier methods to achieve it."[36]

The Native leaders' reaction to the recommendations ranged from complete disgust with the outcome to optimism that federal officials had at least consulted them. Tommy Prince abandoned the MIA in 1951 to re-enlist for the Korean War. Malcolm Norris retired from politics and moved north to become a full-time prospector. John Callihoo continued on as the IAA president. John Tootoosis remained politically active for the rest of his life, though he limited his concerns to Saskatchewan issues. And Andy Paull, whose efforts at forming a national Native organization were hindered by a lack of support, continued to guide the NAIB until his death in 1959. He remained to the end a vocal proponent of Native rights while promoting the need for a united Canadian Native political organization. Over the next ten years, Native leaders would be forced to regroup from the failed SJC process.

INDIAN CONVENTION, BROADCAST MAY 29, 1948 (FROM CBC RADIO ARCHIVES)

Introduction: Canada's Indian's met recently at a National Convention in Ottawa. The gathering had special significance this year, because the *Indian Act* is now up for revision. Tonight Douglas Sanderson of Montreal talks with Edward Beauvais, a member of the Iroquois Tribe at Caughnawaga, Quebec, about some of the problems the Indians discussed.

Mr. Sanderson: Well then, Mr. Beauvais, the Canadian Indians seem to be in the news quite frequently during the past week or so, particularly with regard to the North American Indian Brotherhood (NAIB) Convention that has just been held in Ottawa. I suppose you attended the convention Mr. Beauvais?

Mr. Beauvais: Oh, yes. This was the fifth annual convention and I've been to every one of them. This year, I was one of the executives.

Mr. Sanderson: Oh, good. It seems I've picked the right man to give me some information. Now tell me, Mr. Beauvais, what is the main purpose for holding these conventions?

Mr. Beauvais: I would say that the main purpose is to make it possible for the Indians from all parts of Canada to meet and to get to know each other better. Canada is a big place and even though there are nearly 130,000 Indians in the country, they are so widely scattered that they're inclined to lose touch with each other. The conventions are held so that they are presented [inaudible] and can exchange news and points of view.

Mr. Sanderson: But I suppose you discuss some of the issues affecting the Indians at the moment, things like Old Age Pensions, health schemes, relief, and so on?

cont'd

CHAPTER 8   Political Organizing in Canada

Mr. Beauvais: Well, this year, the main topic of our conversation was the forthcoming revision of the *Indian Act*, but we discussed other subjects besides. For instance I personally brought up the question of health schemes.

Mr. Sanderson: You mean with reference to large sums of money that are going to be spent on improving the health of the Indians?

Mr. Beauvais: That's right. As far as I can see, most of the money will be spent trying to cure the Indians of TB. There is a lot of TB amongst Canadian Indians. Well, the idea is all right up to a point, but I think it would be a better idea if more money was spent on the prevention of TB.

Mr. Sanderson: And how do you suggest that that should be done?

Mr. Beauvais: By improving the conditions in which some of the Indians live. I've travelled quite a lot, especially around the province of Quebec, and the housing conditions of some of the Indians are pitiful. There are houses without floors, others with mud roofs, and in some of these, the lighting is poor and sanitation. That sort of thing breeds TB.

Mr. Sanderson: I see. And you think that some of the money from the health project should be spent on housing for these people?

Mr. Beauvais: That's right. We should aim at preventing TB in the next generation instead of concentrating entirely on curing it in this generation. I think the best method would be to make low-interest loans available to the Indians, so that they can build new roof houses. They could pay back the loans in the form of rent over a period of years.

Mr. Sanderson: And you think that the scheme would work?

Mr. Beauvais: It does work. It has been proven by the fact that TB is almost wiped out on the reservations where the housing conditions are good. And anyway, it's certainly a better idea than spending millions of the taxpayer's money on prolonged health schemes. This they never get back.

Mr. Sanderson: You mentioned just now, that the main topic of conversations at the convention was the revision of the *Indian Act*. For the benefit of listeners who are unacquainted with it, perhaps I should explain that the *Indian Act* is the collection of laws that govern the life of every Canadian Indian. The Canadian government and most certainly the Canadian Indians, consider the various clauses in the Act are now somewhat outdated. So, for the past two years a joint committee made up of repre-sentatives of the Senate and the House of Commons have been in session for the purpose of revising the *Indian Act*. Meantime the entire Indian population of Canada awaits the verdict with bated breath. It will probably be made public towards the end of July. Now, Mr. Beauvais, would you like to tell some of the aspects of the *Indian Act* that you hope will be considered and revised by the joint committee?

Mr. Beauvais: Well, for one, there's the question of taxation. We believe the Indians of Canada are being unfairly and unlawfully taxed, and we have some of the best legal judgments in the country to back us up. And there's the rights of hunting, shooting and fishing that have been taken away from the Indians. There is also the question of Old Age Pension for Indians, which has been promised but never received. And the question of educating the Indians. The matter of compensation for the expropriation of Indian lands. All of these are very big issues, and there are many others like them.

Mr. Sanderson: Well Mr. Beauvais, you were at the convention, did the members of the convention get any indication as to whether these matters were being considered by committee? Did you get any information as to what you could expect from the new Act?

Mr. Beauvais: There were of course a certain amount of rumours, but there was no actual information. We were told by members of the joint committee that nothing could be made public until the revisions have been concluded. To me, that sounds like a sensible point of view.

Mr. Sanderson: Ah, so you actually met some members of the joint committee. How did they impress you, what did they have to say?

Mr. Beauvais: I think what impressed us was their sincerity. They told us that it was a long and hard job that they were doing, but they would do their utmost to make a new law that would be acceptable to all the Indians in Canada. And would be believed they will. The joint committee is made up of different political factions in Ottawa, but when they talk to the Indians they forget their political differences.

Mr. Sanderson: Good heavens, it sounds almost uncanny. By the way, I believe you also met Mr. Mackenzie King.

Mr. Beauvais: We certainly did. It was one of the big events of the convention. At previous conventions we had always met one of his representatives, but this was the first time we had the honour and privilege of meeting Mr. Mackenzie King himself. He invited us up to the House of Commons for the special purpose and we met him in I believe the railroads room.

Mr. Sanderson: Well, tell me about it. How did you find Mr. King?

Mr. Beauvais: We all thought him an extremely fine man; he shook hands with each one of us and told us he was going to see us. And in recognition of the occasion we presented him with a Indian war bonnet.

Mr. Sanderson: Oh yes, I saw pictures of Mr. King wearing that bonnet. I thought it looked very becoming. But what did he say when you gave it to him?

Mr. Beauvais: Well, we put it on his head and then he said, "Well I don't know what I look like but I really feel very happy." After that he asked us to meet his Cabinet, but unfortunately we were scheduled to hear some other speakers so we couldn't go. Before we went, we asked him if it would be possible for five Indian delegates to be allowed to see the new act before it was made law. And he said that it would be.

Mr. Sanderson: I suppose you elected these five delegates during the convention?

Mr. Beauvais: Yes, and I was lucky enough to be elected as one of them. One of the motions made later on at the convention was that the government be requested to allow the five delegates to sit with the Indian Act Committee during their last final weeks of the revision. And a further request that the expenses of the delegates should be paid by the Government.

Mr. Sanderson: You mean that you want five Indians to be allowed to sit with the Joint committee from now until the time the session closes in July? But in what capacity would you expect these delegates to sit?

Mr. Beauvais: We want them to be allowed to hold watching briefs, to give the Indians a chance to study the structure of the new act, and suggest through a member any changes which in their opinion would be necessary for the welfare of our race. Also we feel that in some small way at least, these five men could aid the joint committee in their tremendous task, and in their desire to give the Indians of Canada a better deal. It is our hope that the government are considering our request and will give us their approval in the very near future.

Source: Courtesy CBC.

The Third Wave of Political Organizing: 1960 to 1995

For many, the brotherhood represents the final attempt by Indians to try to solve their problems within the context of the political system of our country. If it fails, and particularly if it is destroyed by the federal government, then the future holds very little hope for the Indian unless he attempts to solve his problems by taking the dangerous and explosive path traveled by the black militants of the United States.

—Harold Cardinal[37]

The influence of the Native leaders who took part in the SJC process set the stage for the next chapter in Native organizing in Canada. That influence would bring Prime Minister John Diefenbaker to grant Native peoples the right to vote in federal elections without compromising their status or making participation contingent on "complete assimilation into Canadian society."[38] Until then, Indians had been barred from voting for a number of reasons: a perceived lack of civilized status, their access to privileges such as treaty rights that were inaccessible to mainstream Canadians, lack of fee simple landholdings (i.e., they did not own private property), and assertions of nationhood that many non-Native politicians found disconcerting.[39] Diefenbaker, however, had established relationships with USI members as far back as the 1940s, and his awareness of Native issues prompted this change.[40] Native voting turnout remains low; even so, since 1867, 14 First Nations, Métis, or Inuit individuals have been appointed to the Senate and 26 have been elected as MPs (see Tables 8-1 and 8-2).[41] This suggests that multiple arenas of participation will be required before Native people's political voices are heard.

This in part is what drove Andy Paull's political vision—the need to create a national organization acknowledged as a third order of government representing the needs of all Indians, thereby making Native people part of Canada's established political process. This model was adopted by his protégé, George Manuel (Shuswap).[42] Drawn into regional politics in the 1950s, Manuel would go on to become, arguably, the most influential and effective leader of the National Indian Brotherhood (NIB), formed in 1968, the precursor to the Assembly of First Nations (AFN), formed in 1982.[43] While Manuel fought for a national organization, provincial and regional groups maintained a high profile. The Union of Ontario Indians (UOI), formed in 1946, maintained a political presence while ensuring Native representation in Parliament. Annual meetings were held throughout Ontario, during which concerns about the *Indian Act*, hunting and fishing rights, medical services, education, and land were addressed. Ontario's sheer size and cultural and regional diversity forced the UOI to reorganize to reflect this diversity. After it was incorporated as a provincial

Table 8-1 First Nations, Inuit, and Métis Senators

Name	Political Affiliation	Province/Territory	Date Appointed (yyyy.mm.dd)	Native Origin
Hardisty, Richard Charles	Conservative	Northwest Territories	1888.02.23	Métis
Boucher, William Albert	Liberal Party of Canada	Saskatchewan	1957.01.03	Métis
Gladstone, James	Independent Conservative	Alberta	1958.01.31	First Nations
Williams, Guy R.	Liberal Party of Canada	British Columbia	1971.12.09	First Nations
Adams, Willie	Liberal Party of Canada	Northwest Territories	1977.04.05	Inuit
Watt, Charlie	Liberal Party of Canada	Quebec	1984.01.16	Inuit
Marchand, Leonard Stephen	Liberal Party of Canada	British Columbia	1984.06.29	First Nations
Twinn, Walter Patrick	Progressive Conservative Party	Alberta	1990.09.27	First Nations
St. Germain, Gerry	Progressive Conservative Party	British Columbia	1993.06.23	Métis
Chalifoux, Thelma J.	Liberal Party of Canada	Alberta	1997.11.26	Métis
Gill, Aurélien	Liberal Party of Canada	Quebec	1998.09.17	First Nations
Sibbeston, Nick G.	Liberal Party of Canada	Northwest Territories	1999.09.02	First Nations
Dyck, Lillian Eva	New Democratic Party	Saskatchewan	2005.03.24	First Nations
Lovelace Nicholas, Sandra M.	Liberal Party of Canada	New Brunswick	2005.09.21	First Nations

Source: Library of Parliament / Bibliothèque du Parlement; please visit the Library of Parliament website (www2.parl.gc.ca/parlinfo) for current listings. Reprinted with permission.

Table 8-2 First Nations, Inuit, and Métis Members of Parliament

Name	Political Affiliation	Constituency	Date Elected (yyyy.mm.dd)	Native Origin
McKay, Angus	Conservative	Marquette, Manitoba	1871.03.02	Métis
Delorme, Pierre	Conservative	Provencher, Manitoba	1871.03.03	Métis
Riel, Louis	Independent	Provencher, Manitoba	1873.10.13	Métis
Boucher, William Albert	Liberal Party of Canada	Rosthern, Saskatchewan	1948.10.25	Métis
Rhéaume, Eugène (Gene)	Progressive Conservative Party	Northwest Territories, Northwest Territories	1963.04.08	Métis
Marchand, Leonard Stephen	Liberal Party of Canada	Kamloops—Cariboo, British Columbia	1968.06.25	First Nations
Firth, Walter (Wally)	New Democratic Party	Northwest Territories, Northwest Territories	1972.10.30	Métis
Ittinuar, Peter	New Democratic Party	Nunatsiaq, Northwest Territories	1979.05.22	Inuit
Keeper, Cyril	New Democratic Party	Winnipeg—St. James, Manitoba	1980.02.18	Métis
St. Germain, Gerry	Progressive Conservative Party	Mission—Port Moody, British Columbia	1983.08.29	Métis
Suluk, Thomas	Progressive Conservative Party	Nunatsiaq, Northwest Territories	1984.09.04	Inuit
Anawak, Jack Iyerak	Liberal Party of Canada	Nunatsiaq, Northwest Territories	1988.11.21	Inuit
Blondin-Andrew, Ethel Dorothy	Liberal Party of Canada	Western Arctic, Northwest Territories	1988.11.21	First Nations

Name	Party	Riding	Date	Group
Littlechild, Wilton (Willie)	Progressive Conservative Party	Wetaskiwin, Alberta	1988.11.21	First Nations
DeVillers, Paul	Liberal Party of Canada	Simcoe North, Ontario	1993.10.25	Métis
Harper, Elijah	Liberal Party of Canada	Churchill, Manitoba	1993.10.25	First Nations
O'Brien, Lawrence D.	Liberal Party of Canada	Labrador, Newfoundland and Labrador	1996.03.25	Métis
Karetak-Lindell, Nancy	Liberal Party of Canada	Nunavut, Northwest Territories	1997.06.02	Inuit
Laliberte, Rick	New Democratic Party	Churchill River, Saskatchewan	1997.06.02	Métis
Cleary, Bernard	Bloc Québécois	Louis-Saint-Laurent, Quebec	2004.06.28	First Nations
Smith, David	Liberal Party of Canada	Pontiac, Quebec	2004.06.28	Métis
Russell, Todd Norman	Liberal Party of Canada	Labrador, Newfoundland and Labrador	2005.05.24	Métis
Bruinooge, Rod	Conservative Party of Canada (2003)	Winnipeg South, Manitoba	2006.01.23	Métis
Keeper, Tina	Liberal Party of Canada	Churchill, Manitoba	2006.01.23	First Nations
Merasty, Gary	Liberal Party of Canada	Desnethé–Missinippi–Churchill River, Saskatchewan	2006.01.23	First Nations
Clarke, Rob	Conservative Party of Canada (2003)	Desnethé–Missinippi–Churchill River, Saskatchewan	2008.03.17	First Nations

Source: Library of Parliament / Bibliothèque du Parlement; please visit the Library of Parliament website (www2.parl.gc.ca/parlinfo) for current listings. Reprinted with permission.

nonprofit corporation, the issues associated with geographic diversity led to its fragmentation into four Native organizations, which together comprise the Chiefs of Ontario, a coordinating secretariat.[44]

The MIA struggled after Tommy Prince's departure. Not until the early 1970s would it resurge under the banner Manitoba Indian Brotherhood (MIB). Soon after that it became one of Canada's more powerful Native organizations. Perhaps best known for its 1971 release of the report *Whabung: Our Tomorrows*, the MIB helped set the stage for Native community-development policy, which resonates with Native leaders to this day. It also brought public attention to the dismal state of health care in Manitoba's Native communities. The report provided Canadians with the policy directions that Native people would pursue in the coming years to achieve a stronger, more self-reliant economic base.[45] But a number of tumultuous years followed, and in 1981 the MIB disbanded, leaving behind a provincial leadership gap until the Assembly of Manitoba Chiefs (AMC) formed in 1988.

The USI still exists. Its initial goal had been to strengthen the collective Native voice in Saskatchewan while defending the sanctity of the treaties. In 1958 it renamed itself the Federation of Saskatchewan Indians (then the FSIN in 1982), at which point its leaders began asserting their rights as distinct nations all the while arguing for the recognition and protection of treaty rights. Similarly, the IAA lingered for a decade following the SJC, returning to national prominence in the late 1960s under Harold Cardinal's (Cree) leadership, only to dissolve one decade later.[46] Farther west, the NBBC altered its approach to organizing in the decades following the SJC. The Union of British Columbia Indian Chiefs (UBCIC) emerged in 1969 as B.C.'s Native organization, absorbing several offshoot groups, including the Indian Homemakers Association of B.C., the Southern Vancouver Tribal Federation, and remnants of the NAIB.[47]

In the decade following the SJC's recommendations, federal officials paid little attention to Native organizing. A second SJC (1959–61) highlighted once again the expanding political base of Native groups nationally. In an attempt to consolidate these interests into a representative political organization, the National Indian Council (NIC) was created in 1961, to reflect the needs of three of Canada's four groups of Native people: treaty and Status Indians, Non-Status Indians, and the Métis (the Inuit were not involved).[48] Led by prairie Native leaders, the NIC emphasized unity but was faced with the difficult task of reconciling the diverse interests of Native peoples nationally. The NIC met with limited success even if its lobbying efforts generated awareness of the federal government's benign neglect of Native peoples. Its presence helped keep the Hawthorn–Tremblay Report, commissioned in 1963 to provide recommendations to improve Native social and economic living conditions, in the public eye. This was vital, since the report offered several innovative suggestions, which included rejecting Native assimilation. Native people should be considered "citizens plus," the report's authors argued. In other words, Native people had a unique status as treaty signatories who should simultaneously benefit from Canadian citizenship.[49]

Increasingly "troubled by tensions between treaty Indians, principally from the prairie provinces, and Métis and non-status Indians over the strategy to be followed," the NIC in 1968 split into two organizations: the National Indian Brotherhood (NIB) and the Canadian Métis Society (CMS). This occurred the same year that a new Liberal government led by Pierre Trudeau expressed its formal opposition to the Hawthorn–Tremblay Report's direction. In 1969, Trudeau and his Minister of Indian Affairs, Jean Chrétien, tabled a policy proposal in the House of Commons titled "A Statement of the Government of Canada on Aboriginal Policy." The legislation that statement proposed would, supposedly, "enable Indian people to be free to develop Indian cultures in an environment of legal, social and economic equality with other Canadians." Native leaders responded that the federal government was more inclined to offload its federal responsibilities for Native peoples by transferring bureaucratic control over social programs to the provinces.[50]

Native resistance to the White Paper proposal was strong, in particular because the policy aimed to dismantle the unique legal relationship that already existed between Indians and the federal government. Representing the Indian Chiefs of Alberta, the late Harold Cardinal penned *Citizens Plus,* the first written response from a Native organization to the White Paper proposal. In what became popularly known as the Red Paper, Cardinal censured the Trudeau government for its lack of political and cultural sensitivity. He further chastised the government for its weak political vision and for embracing the Hawthorn-Tremblay Report's recommendations to repudiate Native concerns.[51] *Citizens Plus* presented a Native political vision for a new Native–Canada relationship.

Ironically, by tabling the White Paper in an effort to undermine Native political agitation, Trudeau provided Native people with an important issue they could all rally against: Indian termination. For many decades, Native organizations had competed with one another for federal attention; now, Trudeau's attempts at legislative termination of Native people became the focus of general Native animosity. The NIB, to this point little more than a paper organization, seized the opportunity and quickly became Canada's national Native political organization.[52] New organizations quickly formed, and several provincial groups reaped the protest's benefits. The protracted resistance that followed led Trudeau to call a meeting with Native leaders, where he declared *Citizens Plus* to be the official response to Canada's treatment of Native people. This was followed by the Liberal government's formal withdrawal of the White Paper proposal in 1971.

Under the scrutiny of several Native political organizations producing innovative reports and policy papers, the federal government struggled throughout the 1970s to establish a cogent Indian policy. Many Native leaders started to believe that their resistance to the White Paper had done little to break Ottawa from its intention to systematically ignore Aboriginal rights and the newly coined idea of Aboriginal self-government. Native organization did have an impact, however. In particular, the federal government in 1972 initiated a transfer of responsibility for Native education to community councils in response to the NIB's demand for Indian control of Indian education. This was followed by a long line of devolved programs in the coming years. Then, in 1973, the Supreme Court of Canada in *Calder v. The Attorney General of British Columbia* recognized the existence of Aboriginal rights, which resolved for many the Indian land question challenged by the IRA between 1916 and 1927. As an acknowledgment of *Calder*'s impact and the Aboriginal right to land, the Indian Claims Commission was established in 1973; this was followed in 1975 by the first modern-day treaty, which Canada signed with the James Bay Cree.

A tumultuous decade to be sure. By the close of the 1970s, Native peoples had begun their transition from "wards of the state" reliant on federal programs to political players focused on educating the public and federal politicians about Canada's treaty obligations.[53] The influence of Native organizations was also attributable to federal programming that resulted in Native concerns becoming more visible, thereby attracting Parliament's attention.[54] This was evident during the constitutional discussions of the late 1970s, which led to the entrenchment of existing Aboriginal and treaty rights in Section 35 of the *Constitution Act* (1982). Native activists were now politically aware and effective, and this led to greater political influence. In 1978 the NIB, the Aboriginal Council of Canada (ACC), and the Inuit Committee on National Issues (ICNI) were invited to participate in the constitutional discussions. Not satisfied to watch from the periphery, 11 other Native organizations launched an influential lobbying effort.[55] It was during this period that Native groups such as the FSIN began to formally articulate the foundational ideas that would eventually become known as Aboriginal self-government.[56]

Assembly of First Nations

To demonstrate the strengths and weaknesses of Native organizations, the Assembly of First Nations is examined next. The AFN was formed in 1982 and is open to the chiefs representing all Status Indian bands in Canada. It is not an organization of regional delegates. The most recognizable of the estimated 4,000 national Native political organizations, the AFN is traceable to the NIC's dissolution and the NIB's formation in 1968. Initially influential, by the end of the 1970s factionalism had begun to take its toll as delegate complaints surfaced that the NIB lacked accountability to the nation's chiefs. This led to a fractious debate over whether NIB members should continue to be appointed, or whether an elected council would be more appropriate. Uncertain whether the NIB could represent their interests effectively, 300 Status Indians and First Nations chiefs arrived in London, England, in 1979 to try to stop Prime Minister Trudeau from repatriating the constitution. This caused even greater dissention among First Nations leaders. First Nations' confidence in the NIB failed after a number of questionable moves by its founder, Del Riley, which were followed by calls for organizational reform. Restructuring debates focused largely on the need to create an organization that was representative and accountable to First Nations community leaders. At this point the NIB began its transition, and in 1982 the AFN was born.

In response to First Nations lobbying efforts, Canada revised its constitution in 1982 to formally acknowledge the existence of Aboriginal rights. The constitution also recognized

At a ceremony in the House of Commons in Ottawa, Canadian prime minister Stephen Harper and other MPs watch as AFN Chief Phil Fontaine (right, wearing headdress) responds to the government's apology for more than a century of abuse and cultural loss involving Indian residential schools (June 11, 2008).

Aboriginal people as the Métis, Inuit, Status Indians, and Non-Status Indians of Canada, while affirming "existing aboriginal and treaty rights." From 1983 to 1987 the AFN met with the provincial premiers at four First Ministers' Conferences in an attempt to define Aboriginal self-government. However, this series of conferences failed to define the pith and substance of Aboriginal rights or explain what Aboriginal self-government represented. It seems that politicians preferred to rely on the courts for such decisions rather than engage with Native leaders for their interpretations.

The AFN began working closely with other prominent lobby groups and organizations such as the United Nations in an attempt to convince Canada to uphold the spirit and intent of the treaties it had signed. By the mid-1980s, the AFN had become an influential lobby group and contributor to the ongoing constitutional debates, as well as a critic of the U.S.–Canada Free Trade Agreement and other proposed legislative changes affecting First Nations. AFN resistance and Elijah Harper's (Cree) "no" vote undermining the unanimity needed to propel the Meech Lake Accord into law scuttled that accord in 1990; that accord proposed constitutional amendments that would have recognized Quebec's distinct-society status while ignoring distinctive First Nations cultures. The federal government would consult openly with First Nations leaders before drafting the Charlottetown Accord in 1992. Aboriginal self-government would have been realized had that second accord succeeded, thereby augmenting First Nations political influence. But Canadians rejected that second attempt at an accord in a national referendum in 1992. A final note: AFN lobbying in part led to the Inherent Rights Policy of 1995, which formally recognized Aboriginal self-government and the expansion of Aboriginal rights.

The Fourth Wave of Political Organizing: 1995 to the Present

Native organizations have been strikingly silent since the post-1995 recognition of the inherent right to Aboriginal self-government. Yet an estimated 4,000 Native political organizations are currently operating nationally. The fact that this number grows daily suggests that they are perceived as useful. This was evident in April 2001, when the Canadian

government tabled proposed changes to legislation known as the First Nations Governance Initiative (see Chapter 5). Speaking before an assembly at the Kainai High School on the Blood Reserve in Alberta, Indian Affairs Minister Robert Nault told the audience that he was instituting new legislation entitled the *First Nations Governance Act* (FNGA). This was followed by two years of loud opposition from an assortment of Native organizations angered with the government's proposed changes, which many considered analogous to the Trudeau White Paper's termination policy. Two further bills were nevertheless tabled and subsequently passed: Bill C–6, the *Specific Claims Resolution Act,* and Bill C–19, the *First Nations Fiscal and Statistical Management Act.* However, Native resistance to the FNGA proved too strong, and in 2003 the Liberal government rescinded its unpopular initiative.

Whereas Native organizing developed in the 1870s to safeguard local economies and landholdings, by the 1940s a national Native organization was being promoted as a potential third tier of governance.[57] By the 2000s, Native peoples and Canadian officials largely viewed Native organizing as a collection of special-interest groups lacking political teeth. Competition for federal funding dilutes political potency as organizations aggressively compete with one another for a set amount of money. The jobs associated with these organizations are also significant—that is, funding competition often becomes heated if employees are to be retained. Existing funding arrangements have the potential to hamper Native organizations, since the government can withhold funding to organizations it deems too aggressive. For example, the federal government in 2002 slashed AFN funding from $19 million to $11 million following Grand Chief Matthew Coon Come's (Cree) negative comments about the failed FNGA process. The AFN had to lay off 70 people just while delegates were considering their leadership choice.[58]

This demonstrates the complexity of Native issues nationally; it also highlights the differences between today's political environment and the atmosphere guiding the first attempts at post-contact Native organizing. Whereas Indigenous communities in the seventeenth century held the upper hand economically and therefore politically, forcing Europeans to adapt to North American diplomacy, Canada today is the guiding political force. As such, Native organizations have been forced to alter their operations to better reflect accepted Canadian organizational practices. This has undermined historic approaches that even so continue to inform modern-day operations. Take for instance the number of men running organizations to the exclusion of women. This issue became front-page news during the 1992 Charlottetown Accord dialogues, when the Native Women's Association of Canada (NWAC, est. 1974) successfully sued for the right to participate in constitutional discussions. The NWAC's formation suggests that the lack of women in Native organizations was deemed a problem: prior to the 1970s few women claimed high-profile leadership positions. The reasons for this were historically rooted: most early leaders reasoned that in order to be heard, it was essential to emulate Canada's Parliamentary tradition, which emphasized men's participation to the detriment of women's. This was a logical decision, considering that Canadian male politicians were unlikely to engage Native female leaders.

It also went against tradition in most Indigenous communities. Women were responsible for rearing the community's children, and in that sense they educated the next generation of male and female leaders. In the process, women became revered leaders, hunters, warriors, and religious and political leaders.[59] And while women usually did not sit at official councils, their presence was felt in how they advised the men dealing with broader community issues. Women's opinions, which had once been heard during council debates, were largely silenced in 1876.[60] Furthermore, the *Indian Act* made it illegal for women to hold band-council positions. Finally, many of the leaders of early organizations were enfranchised individuals, and in the GIC's case, for instance, the key delegates were ministers and doctors, most of whom had married non-Native women. The women in their lives had no stake in politics outside the fact that their husbands were directly involved.[61]

Alternative Organizing Models

While national and provincial political organizations generate the most media coverage, often forgotten alternative organizing models have emerged to press for federal and provincial acknowledgment of Native claims. Tribal councils, as an example, have become important voices representing many Native peoples nationally. Defined as "a grouping of bands with common interests who voluntarily join together to provide advisory and/or program services to member bands," tribal councils are flexible political bodies that do not confine themselves to advocating on one or a small number of issues. Rather, they embrace a wide variety of concerns. Recent statistics indicate that 78 tribal councils are providing advisory and program services to around 475 First Nations. An additional 135 First Nations are not affiliated with a tribal council, though 16 of these receive funding for advisory services. About four-fifths of Canadian Native people living on reserves are touched either by a tribal council or by an unaffiliated First Nation that provides advisory services. Tribal councils have taken over the tasks of service delivery as these have been devolved from Indian and Northern Affairs Canada (INAC) (see box). They are required to provide to their members all five advisory services: (1) economic development, (2) financial management, (3) community planning, (4) technical services, and (5) band governance.[62]

Tribal councils may enter into agreements with other federal departments such as Health Canada and Human Resources Development Canada to deliver programs and services. Funding for tribal councils is administered by the Tribal Council Program (TCP), which is one aspect of the First Nation Indian Government Support Funding Program. Introduced in 1984, the TCP is funded through annual parliamentary appropriations, which tribal councils then utilize to provide the necessary advisory services while promoting program and service delivery. Each tribal council receives an annual disbursement based on a formula that takes into account the services delivered, the number of First Nations forming the tribal council, the on-reserve population, and the geographic location of the Tribal Council Office.

CASE STUDY: MANITOBA KEEWATINOOK ININEW OKIMOWIN (MKIO)

The Manitoba Keewatinook Ininew Okimowin (MKIO) was established in 1981 to promote, advance, and protect the interests of its 30 member First Nations, which represent 53,000 people. Acknowledging the need for a political territorial organization to lobby provincial and federal officials for recognition of Aboriginal rights, the MKIO believes "that the member First Nations of the MKIO set direction and approve all positions undertaken." Each year the MKIO Chiefs Annual General Assembly results in seven chiefs being elected to sit on the Executive Council, on which they assume one or more of the following portfolios:

- Finance and Administration
- Child Welfare, Women, and Youth
- Social Development, Education, and Recreation
- Self-Government and Treaties
- Bill C–31 and Housing
- Justice, Land Claims, and Treaty Land Entitlement
- Health
- Roads and Transportation

Recently the MKIO adopted a new constitution and restructured its operations, discarding the tribal-council designation and choosing to describe the organization as a Legislative Governance House. This new house is developing a regional process for passing laws that are consistent with the inherent rights of self-government and the sovereignty of First Nations in northern Manitoba, the implementation of which is ongoing.

Conclusion

The solemn objective and aim of the North American Indian Brotherhood is to give leadership to the Indian nation within the sovereignty of the British Crown, a nation—by treaty obligation— under a protective government. It aims to salvage material from the ashes of the past, and thereby awaken the Indian race in the dormant nobility which is, by heritage, rightfully theirs, preserved for them and guaranteed to them by the proclamation of King George III, 1763.

—Andy Paull[63]

The complexity of the matrix of Native organizations makes it very difficult to present in depth the associated political and operational dynamics. This chapter has instead provided an overview of Indigenous political activities dating back to 1870. Through their political organizations, Native people in Canada continue to agitate against the Canadian government for political reform. From the SJC of the 1940s to the resistance to the White Paper of

1969 to the recent opposition to the proposed FNGA, Native political organizations have become prominent voices in Canadian politics. The early organizations were more than a manifestation of political activism, however. They represent a considered effort by Native leaders to compel federal officials to listen to Native concerns; they also set out to impress on federal representatives the importance of incorporating the concerns of what John Ralston Saul has described loosely as the third tier of Confederation (Native along with francophone and anglophone).[64] Despite long and hard efforts by Native political organizations and their leaders' hard-won skill at Canadian politics, the federal government refuses to abandon the *Indian Act*, which delegates political authority to municipal-style councils that are in many ways impotent to effect positive change in reserve communities. This in turn has frozen out Native political organizations. The same system that resulted in the imposition of the band-government model and the corresponding rise of Native political organizations remains largely in place in the year 2009. The question of what the future holds for Native organizations, as yet unanswered, is inviting to consider.

FURTHER READING

Barron, F. Laurie. *Walking in Indian Moccasins: The Aboriginal Policies of Tommy Douglas and the CCF.* Vancouver: UBC Press, 1997.

Belanger, Yale D. "'An All 'Round Indian Affair': The Aboriginal Gatherings at MacLeod, 1924 and 1925." *Alberta History* 53, no. 4 (2005): 13–23.

Cardinal, Harold. *The Unjust Society: The Tragedy of Canada's Indians.* Edmonton: Hurtig, 1969.

Dobbin, Murray. *The One-and-a-Half Men: The Story of James Brady and Malcolm Norris.* Vancouver: New Star, 1981.

Galois, R.M. "The Indian Rights Association, Aboriginal Protest Activity, and the 'Land Question' in British Columbia, 1903–1916." *Native Studies Review* 8, no. 2 (1992): 1–34.

Harris, Douglas. "The Nlha7kapmx Meeting at Lytton, 1879, and the Rule of Law." *B.C. Studies* 108 (Winter 1995–96): 5–25.

Kulchyski, Peter. "'A Considerable Unrest': F.O. Loft and the League of Indians." *Native Studies Review* 4, nos. 1 and 2 (1988): 95–117.

Manuel, George, and Michael Posluns. *The Fourth World: An Indian Reality.* Toronto: Collier Macmillan Canada, 1974.

McFarlane, Peter. *Brotherhood to Nationhood: George Manuel and the Making of the Modern Indian Movement.* Toronto: Between the Lines, 1993.

Meijer-Drees, Laurie. *The Indian Association of Alberta: A History of Political Action.* Vancouver: UBC Press, 2002.

Patterson, E. Palmer. "Andrew Paull and the Early History of British Columbia Indian Organizations." In *"One Century Later": Western Canadian Reserve Indians Since Treaty 7*, ed. Ian A.L. Getty and Donald B. Smith. Vancouver: UBC Press, 1978, pp. 43–54.

Pitsula, James. "The CCF Government and the Formation of the Union of Saskatchewan Indians." *Prairie Forum* 19 (1994): 131–51.

Sawchuk, Joe. *The Dynamics of Aboriginal Politics: The Alberta Métis Experience.* Saskatoon: Purich, 1998.

Shewell, Hugh. "Jules Sioui and Indian Political Radicalism in Canada, 1943–1944." *Journal of Canadian Studies 34*, no. 3 (1999): 211–42.

NOTES

1. Quoted in Yale D. Belanger, "Seeking a Seat at the Table: A Brief History of Indian Political Organizing in Canada, 1870–1951" (Ph.D. diss., Trent University, 2006), p. 345.

2. For an excellent description of the purpose of and diplomacy associated with what the author described as international conferences, see Gilles Havard, *The Great Peace of Montreal of 1701: French-Native Diplomacy in the Seventeenth Century,* trans. Phyllis Aronoff and Howard Scott (Kingston and Montreal: McGill–Queen's University Press, 2001), pp. 20–26.

3. William N. Fenton, *The Great Law of the Longhouse: A Political History of the Iroquois Confederacy* (Norman: University of Oklahoma Press, 1998).

4. See Jose Brandao, *Your Fyre Shall Burn No More: Iroquois Policy Toward New France and Its Native Allies to 1701* (Lincoln: University of Nebraska Press, 1997).

5. John Borrows, *Recovering Canada: The Resurgence of Indigenous Law* (Toronto: University of Toronto Press, 2002), p. 147.

6. Mark Walters, "'According to the Customs of Our Nation': Aboriginal Self-Government on the Credit River Mississauga Reserve, 1826–1847," *Ottawa Law Review* 30 (1998–99): 1–45.

7. Borrows, *Recovering Canada.*

8. Norman D. Shields, "Anishinabek Political Alliance in the Post-Confederation Period" (M.A. thesis, Queen's University, 2001).

9. Ibid.

10. Ibid.

11. Douglas Harris, "The Nlha7kapmx Meeting at Lytton, 1879, and the Rule of Law," *B.C. Studies* 108 (Winter 1995–96): 5–25.

12. Ibid., 9.

13. R.M. Galois, "The Indian Rights Association, Native Protest Activity, and the 'Land Question' in British Columbia, 1903–1916," *Native Studies Review* 8, no. 2 (1992): 34.

14. Paul Tennant, *Aboriginal Peoples and Politics: The Indian Land Question in British Columbia* (Vancouver: UBC Press, 1990), p. 86.

15. Ibid.

16. Rolf Knight, *Indians at Work: An Informal History of Native Indian Labour in British Columbia, 1858–1930* (Vancouver: New Star, 1978); see also Belanger, "Seeking a Seat at the Table."

17. Tennant, *Aboriginal Peoples and Politics.*

18. See, generally, Belanger, "Seeking a Seat at the Table."

19. Quoted in Belanger, "Seeking a Seat at the Table," p. 157.

20. Ibid., p. 159.

21. E. Brian Titley, *A Narrow Vision: Duncan Campbell Scott and the Administration of Indian Affairs* (Vancouver: UBC Press, 1986).

22. Quoted in Richard R.H. Lueger, "A History of Indian Associations in Canada" (M.A. thesis, Carleton University, 1977), p. 145.

23. See Belanger, "Seeking a Seat at the Table."

24. The amendment resulted in Section 141 of the *Indian Act.* One of the anticipated benefits of the legislation was that outside consultants assisting Indian organizations or Indian leaders wishing to pursue land claims against the federal government would forever be silenced.

25. Murray Dobbin, *The One-and-a-Half Men: The Story of James Brady and Malcolm Norris* (Vancouver: New Star, 1981); Laurie Meijer-Drees, *The Indian Association of Alberta: A History of Political Action* (Vancouver: UBC Press, 2002); and Joseph F. Dion, *My Tribe the Crees* (Calgary: Glenbow Museum, 1979).

26. F. Laurie Barron, *Walking in Indian Moccasins: The Native Policies of Tommy Douglas and the CCF* (Vancouver: UBC Press, 1997).

27. Jean Goodwill and Norma Sluman, *John Tootoosis* (Winnipeg: Pemmican, 1984).

28. See Bruce Larsen, "Indian War Hero Heads New Battle," *Winnipeg Tribune,* December 4, 1946, 1, 5; see also "Indians Find Champion In Indian World War Hero," *Winnipeg Tribune,* December 7, 1946, 17; and "New Champion of the Indian" (editorial), *Winnipeg Tribune,* December 7, 1946), 6.

29. Parliament of Canada, "Special Joint Parliamentary Committee of the Senate and the House of Commons appointed to examine and consider the *Indian Act,*" Minutes of Proceedings and Evidence, No. 30 (June 5, 1947), p. 1580 (hereinafter referred to as the *SJC*).

30. Hugh Shewell, "Jules Sioui and Indian Political Radicalism in Canada, 1943–1944," *Journal of Canadian Studies* 34, no. 3 (1999): 221.

31. Belanger, "Seeking a Seat at the Table," Chapter 8, "The North American Indian Brotherhood: An Attempt at Creating National Indian Political Organizations, 1943–1946," pp. 259–98.

32. Shewell, "Jules Sioui and Indian Political Radicalism."

33. *SJC,* Minutes of Proceedings and Evidence, No. 18 (May 5–6), p. 853.

34. Belanger, "Seeking a Seat at the Table," Chapter 8.

35. Ibid.

36. John Goikas, "The *Indian Act*: Evolution, Overview, and Options for the Amendment and Transition," in *For Seven Generations: An Information Legacy of the Royal Commission on Aboriginal Peoples* [CD-ROM] (Ottawa: Canada Communications Group, 1996).

37. Harold Cardinal, *The Unjust Society: The Tragedy of Canada's Indians* (Edmonton: Hurtig, 1969).

38. J. Rick Ponting, "Historical Overview and Background, Part II: 1970-96," in *First Nations in Canada: Perspectives on Opportunity, Empowerment, and Self-Determination,* ed. J. Rick Ponting (Toronto: McGraw-Hill Ryerson, 1997), p. 29.

39. See Committee for Aboriginal Electoral Reform, "The Path to Electoral Equality," in *Report of the Royal Commission on Electoral Reform and Party Financing,* Vol. 4 (Ottawa: Supply and Services Canada, 1991), p. 235.

40. I am currently researching a book on Diefenbaker's Indian Policy. This conclusion is the result of primary archival research conducted to date.

41. Parliament of Canada [online], http://www2.parl.gc.ca/Parlinfo/Compilations/Parliament/Aboriginal.aspx?Menu=HOC-Bio&Role=Senators&Current=False&NativeOrigin= and http://www2.parl.gc.ca/Parlinfo/Compilations/Parliament/Aboriginal.aspx?Menu=HOC-Bio&Role=MP. Last accessed August 26, 2008.

42. See, generally, George Manuel and Michael Posluns, *The Fourth World: An Indian Reality* (Toronto: Collier Macmillan Canada, 1974).

43. Peter McFarlane, *Brotherhood to Nationhood: George Manuel and the Making of the Modern Indian Movement* (Toronto: Between the Lines, 1993).

44. Belanger, "Seeking a Seat at the Table," pp. 361–62.

45. Manitoba Indian Brotherhood, *Whabung: Our Tomorrows* (Winnipeg: 1971).

46. Meijer-Drees, *The Indian Association of Alberta.*

47. Tennant, *Aboriginal Peoples and Politics.*

48. J.R. Miller, *Skyscrapers Hide the Heavens: A History of Indian–White Relations in Canada,* 3rd ed. (Toronto: University of Toronto Press, 2000), Chapter 13: "The Beginnings of Political Organizing," pp. 311–35.

49. Harry H. Hawthorn, *A Survey of the Contemporary Indians of Canada,* Vols. 1 and 2 (Ottawa: Indian Affairs Branch, 1966–67); see also Alan Cairns, *Citizens Plus: Aboriginal Peoples and the Canadian State* (Vancouver: UBC Press, 2000).

50. Sally Weaver, *Making Canadian Indian Policy: The Hidden Agenda, 1968–1970* (Toronto: University of Toronto Press, 1981).

51. McFarlane, *Brotherhood to Nationhood.*

52. Ibid.

53. Yale D. Belanger and David R. Newhouse, "Emerging from the Shadows: The Pursuit of Aboriginal Self-Government to Promote Aboriginal Well-Being," *Canadian Journal of Native Studies* 24, no. 1 (2004): 129–222.

54. Yale D. Belanger, Kevin Fitzmaurice, and David R. Newhouse, "Creating a Seat at the Table: A Retrospective Study of Aboriginal Programming at Canadian Heritage," *Canadian Journal of Native Studies* 28, no. 1 (2008): 33–70.

55. D.E. Sanders, "The Indian Lobby," in *And No One Cheered: Federalism, Democracy, and the Constitution Act,* ed. Keith G. Banting and Richard Simeon (Toronto: Methuen, 1983).

56. Yale D. Belanger and David R. Newhouse, "Reconciling Solitudes: A Critical Analysis of the Self-Government Ideal," in *Aboriginal Self-Government in Canada: Current Trends and Issues,* 3rd ed., ed. Yale D. Belanger (Saskatoon: Purich, 2008), pp. 1–19.

57. Belanger, "Seeking a Seat at the Table."

58. Paul Barnsley, "MP Wants Liberals to Question Budget Cuts," *Windspeaker,* May 1, 2002.

59. Having women in leadership positions was (and in many communities today remains) a common trend throughout Canada. Politics in this case can be broken down into a more holistic way of governance in which individuals with specific skills rise to leadership positions as the situation demands. As an example, among the Blackfoot the Sundance is an important period of renewal that involves renewing political alliances and relationships. The women are responsible for calling the Sundance and making sure it operates properly. During this time women are important political leaders.

60. For this overview, see Ruth Landes, *The Ojibwa Woman: Male and Female Life Cycles Among the Ojibwa Indians of Western Ontario* (New York: Norton, 1971); Christopher Vecsey, *Traditional Ojibwa Religion and Its Historical Changes* (Philadelphia: American Philosophical Society, 1983); and William Warren, *History of the Ojibway People* (St. Paul: Minnesota Historical Society Press, 1984).

61. An overview of the available evidence and government correspondence indicates that key GIC officers were members of the clergy and considered by federal officials to therefore be civilized and able to guide the GIC.

62. Indian and Northern Affairs Canada (INAC), "Tribal Council Funding Program Policy." [online] http://www.ainc-inac.gc.ca/ap/gov/igsp/tcf/tcfp-eng.pdf. Last accessed December 8, 2008.

63. Quoted in Belanger, "Seeking a Seat at the Table," p. 268.

64. John Ralston Saul, *Reflections of a Siamese Twin: Canada at the End of the Twentieth Century* (Toronto: Penguin, 1997), in particular Chapter 5, "A Triangular Reality," pp. 81–100. See also his *A Fair Country: Telling Truths About Canada* (Toronto: Viking Canada, 2008).

9 Native People and the Canadian Justice System

When authorities of the Government of Canada, represented by the Royal Canadian Mounted Police, became the chief arbiters of justice among Inuit, traditional methods and customs of dispensing justice were immediately and completely displaced by the new order. The King's (or Queen's) authority, represented by the police and courts, became the only system of justice. There was no place for Inuit traditions, and neither was there any regard for how things were done before. An utterly foreign system of justice was imposed upon the Inuit, and the role of the Elders and leaders rendered useless. The new representatives of British justice totally ignored the values, traditions, and customs of the Inuit in their determination to have their laws abided by. Crown law, vaguely and not understood at all by Inuit (Wishes of the Great White Monarch for His Subjects), became supreme.

—Zebedee Nungak (Inuit)[1]

Indigenous peoples and the law have long been strange bedfellows. Prior to first contact, Indigenous law regimes were common in North America. After several centuries of chipping away, in 1867 the Canadian government started replacing customary legal systems by adopting oversight for justice for Native people. At first, the system operated with seemingly few difficulties, but by the 1970s the first signs appeared that the Canadian justice system was centring out Native people for incarceration. Officials responded by claiming that poor economic conditions resulted in increased levels of violence, that poor self-esteem resulting from unemployment led to drinking and substance abuse, and that Native people were simply more prone to getting into trouble. In other words, the issue was cast as a Native people's problem. Or at least that is how it was portrayed. However, a handful of studies beginning in the late 1960s hinted that the problem was rooted in the justice system, not in Native populations.

Specifically, the *Indian Act* (1876) and subsequent laws and policies had made several aspects of Native culture illegal—a process that over time was internalized by law enforcement officers and Canadians in general, leading to an attitude that equated Native people with criminal behaviour. This systemic discrimination, as it has been identified, manifests itself to this day, most strongly in the overrepresentation of Native people in the criminal justice system.

Since the 1960s, more and more studies have highlighted the issues Native people face when confronted by Canadian justice; but only in the past decade have those issues received any significant attention. Perhaps this is understandable, considering how little change there has been in the historic ideas guiding Canadians' collective understanding of justice and punishment.[2] Those old ideas, combined with the entrenched policy to "civilize" Native peoples, led officials to conclude that Native people were committing more crimes than other Canadians because of their slow "rise" from tribal cultures into the Canadian mainstream. What was missing from this dialogue was a discussion of how customary law continued to guide personal interactions in Native communities, and how Native legal systems had reflected the beliefs of Native communities since before first contact.

We are just beginning to grasp that the Canadian criminal justice system has operated mainly to contain and control Native people. Furthermore, the higher incarceration rates for Native people are mainly the result of dominant social, economic, and legal-political structures that employ ideologies that are foreign to Native people (see Table 9-1). This chapter will place these issues in context.

Customary/Traditional Law

The emphasis [in European-based justice systems] is on the punishment of the deviant as a means of making that person conform, or as a means of protecting other members of society. The purpose of a justice system in an Aboriginal society is to restore the peace and equilibrium within the community, and to reconcile the accused with his or her own conscience and with the individual or family who has been wronged.

—Justice Murray Sinclair (Ojibwa) and Justice A.C. Hamilton[3]

North American Indigenous cultures always had their own systems for maintaining law and order. Today referred to as customary or traditional law, those systems embraced the values and foundational beliefs of the people who lived according to them. Those beliefs and values in turn guided day-to-day community interactions. Typically those systems were not written down; instead, Indigenous laws and related methods for keeping the peace were passed on orally to each generation, along with an account of their origins. Thus they were integral to Indigenous society. For various reasons ranging from distinctive ecological contexts to community size and unique cultural characteristics, Indigenous law and order regimes varied considerably across Canada. But there were also a number of consistencies across communities, which makes it possible to discuss Native customary law as a whole and in a variety of contexts. For example, many communities pursuing self-government embrace customary law both as a guide and as yet another means for maintaining community values.

Law and order as framed by customary law is about instructing the community's youth in community-sanctioned behaviour. Proactive approaches curtail inappropriate behaviours of the sort that could lead to a loss of balance within a community and among its people. Proper behaviour is rewarded; poor behaviour is scorned and ridiculed. All of this is tied directly to establishing and maintaining ongoing relationships with family and neighbours. Referring back to Chapter 1, Native people's understanding of kinship requires them to make constant efforts to maintain balance, for only a balanced community can be healthy. Because societies are integrated, poor behaviour may damage the community, assigning to each relationship its own responsibilities and obligations. This is the main lesson inculcated in children from an early age. Shaming and teasing in particular are utilized to discourage inappropriate behaviour. The goal is impress on young people the need to model their behaviour according to accepted localized codes based on tried-and-true community values. To summarize, teaching about law and order is an informal process that is meant to gradually introduce the young to the role they are expected to play in the community.[4] Usually, children grow into adulthood with a clear understanding of proper behaviour.

It would be foolish to suggest that all Indigenous communities operated harmoniously before European judicial systems were introduced. All communities, however, had in place mechanisms for meting out justice. Policing authorities were common in Indigenous communities, appointed for specific purposes such as ensuring an orderly hunt. Operated by experienced members of the community, these authorities were fluid in nature—that is, they were organized for specific purposes and might not be seen or heard from for extended periods. Someone in the community who acted inappropriately would be identified and his or her actions reviewed. Unlike the Europeans, who applied militaristic means to maintain law and order, Indigenous societies promoted the participation of community members, who would examine an individual's actions and determine an appropriate penalty. Because lawbreakers were viewed as serious threats to community stability, conflict resolution was everyone's responsibility, though the older people and community leaders were especially influential.

The goal of customary law was to maintain strong relationships. Those charged with specific indiscretions remained in the community to work on their interpersonal skills, thereby to ease their reintegration into the kinship network(s) that their transgressions had destabilized. Methods of punishment varied from teasing and ridicule to forms of corporal punishment and to banishment. The latter was often considered the ultimate penalty: individuals raised in a communal environment emphasizing kinship ties were often emotionally devastated on being forced to leave the community. Thus, banishment was a last resort reserved for the most serious offenders. A period of shaming was often effective; typically, this gave way to a period of rehabilitation, followed by an evaluation by community elders and the offended family members. Having been "approved," the offender would be expected to participate in a reintegration ceremony during which all could heal.

Table 9-1 JUSTICE SYSTEMS IN COMPARATIVE FORMAT

	Western Justice	Traditional Native Justice
Justice System	Adversarial	Nonconfrontational
Guilt	Guilty or not guilty	No concept of guilty/not guilty
Pleading Guilty	The right to avoid self-incrimination means that it is not seen as dishonest to plead not guilty even when a person has committed a crime.	It is dishonest to plead not guilty if you have committed a crime.
Testifying	Witnesses testify in front of the accused.	Testifying before the accused is seen to be a confrontational act.
Truth	Expectation to tell the whole truth.	It is impossible to know the whole truth about any situation.
Witnesses	Only certain people are called to testify in relation to certain subjects.	Everyone is free to provide their opinion. Also, witnesses seeking to provide answers to please counsel often alter or change their testimony.
Eye Contact	Maintaining eye contact is a sign that the individual is being truthful.	In some Native cultures maintaining eye contact with a person in authority is a sign of disrespect.
Verdict	Accused is expected to show remorse for his/her acts while demonstrating a desire to be rehabilitated.	Accused must accept the decision without showing emotion.
Incarceration/ Probation	Means of punishment and rehabilitation.	Completely absolves Native offender of responsibility of restitution to victim.
Function of Justice	Ensure conformity, punish deviant behaviour, and protect society.	Heal the offender. Restore peace and harmony within the community. Reconcile the offender with the victim or the victim's family. Punishment is not the overarching objective.

Source: "Aboriginal People and the Justice System." *Aboriginal Peoples and the Criminal Justice System.* 1998. Canadian Criminal Justice Association. 4 March 2009. <http://www.ccja-acjp.ca/en/aborit.html>. Reproduced and Copyright by permission of the Canadian Criminal Justice Association.

The North-West Mounted Police/Royal Canadian Mounted Police

I thank you very much for coming here to let the poor Indians know of the Queen's love towards them and I hope that they will be thankful for it as I have, and the papers at law that I got from you at Fort Pelly I have got yet and I intend to keep them as long as I live. I cannot give them up for any Indian talk or law for I think a great deal of your law and will do nothing against them.

—Chief Gabriel Cote (Ojibwa)

The North-West Mounted Police (NWMP) was founded in 1873. Its officers were dispatched to the West in response to reports that several American hunters and trappers had killed 30 Assiniboine (the Cypress Hills Massacre), and to contain a whisky trade that was causing havoc among Indigenous populations. Increasing requests from Native leaders for assistance convinced government officials of the need to establish a police presence in the West. A centralized, paramilitary police force was deemed the best approach for maintaining peace until settlement of the West was complete. Based on the testimony of a number of Native leaders who feared that the liquor trade would destroy their people, this early relationship-building period was successful.[5] Praising the NWMP, Medicine Calf (Blood) stated: "Before the arrival of the police, when I laid my head down at night, every sound frightened me; my sleep was broken; now I can sleep sound and not afraid."[6] Siksika chief Crowfoot (Blackfoot) later declared that the "police have protected us as feathers of the bird protect it from the frosts of winter."[7] Quite quickly, the Mounties established their authority from the United States border to Fort MacLeod and east to the Cypress Hills. Satellite detachments helped the divisional posts patrol the extensive frontier while maintaining a visible presence, much to the relief of Indigenous populations.

Behind this hopeful veneer, there were ominous signs. The NWMP had been mandated to ensure justice for Indians. In practical terms, though, this meant enforcing European moral codes, including European justice and punishment. In 1873, Parliament passed "An Act respecting the Administration of Justice and for the Establishment of a Police Force on the North-West Territories," which made it illegal for Native groups to oppose or deny territorial access to any and all government officials. The NWMP, through their presence, helped Canada gain social control in the West; as a result, Indian Agents and missionaries were able to enter Indian lands freely and to compel Indigenous people's adherence to mainstream beliefs. The *Indian Act* (1876) offered Europeans even more leverage: they could now force Native populations to remain on reserves; moreover, bureaucratic power was now concentrated in the Department of the Interior, with the NWMP on the ground in the West to ensure compliance with its strictures. This is how the NWMP were able to remove the Blackfoot from Cree territory, for example, and to establish a pass system to restrict the territorial movement of chiefs and their extended families.[8] The Queen's Law was thereby established. Notwithstanding provisions in the Numbered Treaties acknowledging that traditional policing and justice systems would be maintained, the NWMP came to be acknowledged as an oppressive colonization agent.

For instance, while protesting the extension of the Canadian Pacific Railway across his people's territory, Cree chief Piapot had his lodge kicked over by Officer Sam Steele, who then forced him and his followers to leave the vicinity.[9] Later the Mounties compelled the conversion of Indigenous individuals to Canadian ways by threatening jail time to those refusing to pledge allegiance to the Queen. Blue tickets were used to identify malcontents, who saw any and all charges against them dropped, but only if they agreed to leave the region. The NWMP was utilized in 1882 to break up the interregional tribal councils of Cree (Nehiyaw) chiefs, who were meeting to discuss political strategies for forcing Canada to adhere to Treaty 6. It was now clear to Native leaders that the once revered NWMP had broken its promises to maintain the peace as equals; instead, the force was breeding discontent and fostering distrust. The NWMP's role in defeating the Métis in 1885 confirmed to Native leaders that it was an agent of assimilation.

Little had changed by 1923, when the NWMP was reconfigured as the Royal Canadian Mounted Police (RCMP). One of its first actions was to raid the Six Nations reserve nearby Brantford, Ontario. The raid lasted three days; its ostensible purpose was to search for alcohol. Tensions rose, and the police fired shots, though no one was injured. The Department of Indian Affairs later proposed establishing an RCMP detachment at Six Nations, a move that angered the governing hereditary council, who accused federal officials of trying to dismantle the hereditary system of government. One year later an RCMP occupation force was established on the Six Nations reserve. The Hereditary Council House was secured and declared off limits to further political activity. The authorities removed the wampum belts cataloguing Six Nations history.[10]

For the next four decades, the RCMP, as the national police force, was responsible for the day-to-day policing of reserve communities, which, of course, were isolated pockets of Crown land contained within provincial/territorial boundaries. Provincial police were forbidden to enter reserves on policing matters. Almost no studies have been done about the RCMP's impact on Native communities, but it appears that until the 1940s all considered the just described arrangement satisfactory. The 1940s was a decade of growing Native populations and heightened Native activism. As a result, more resources were needed to properly police reserve communities. Perhaps more important, political activists began floating the term "self-government," and various media began to call for strengthened powers at the reserve level. These calls often included demands for Indigenous control of local policing.

Until the 1960s, community-based policing was the RCMP's primary model for policing Native communities. It is still employed in many regions, and as a result, the police have found themselves entangled in a number of large-scale confrontations, including the Oldman River Dam standoff (1991) and the Burnt Church protests (2000).[11] Most notably, it was the RCMP who ended the occupation at Gustafson Lake in 1995; their success there owed more to aggressive military tactics and superior firepower than to negotiating skills.[12] Well-worn images of the heroic Mounties entering the West to ensure justice for Indians are being challenged today—and have reason to be challenged. The Native–RCMP relationship has often been adversarial and remains so to this day.

Native Overrepresentation in the Criminal Justice System

He isn't a man. He was a boy. He was only 17. He never—he never had a chance to become a man. They never gave him that chance to become a man and have a family of his own, to give me the grandchildren that I would have loved like my other children.

—Mrs. Stella Bignell, Neil Stonechild's mother[13]

In February 2000, within the span of one week, two Native men were found frozen to death in an industrial area in southwest Saskatoon. The day following the second discovery, Darrell Night came forward with allegations of police brutality: after being picked up by the police several weeks earlier, the police had driven him to the outskirts of Saskatoon and kicked him out of the cruiser in –22°C weather wearing only a jean jacket and summer shoes. Within days the two officers responsible were suspended. The RCMP was asked to take over the investigation. Concerns lingered, the key one being the uncanny similarities of these recent deaths to that of 17-year-old Neil Stonechild in November 1990. Stonechild's partly clothed body had been found in a vacant field outside Saskatoon. He had last been seen in the rear of a police car frantically calling for help to a friend. Saskatoon police concluded that Stonechild died trying to walk from a convenience store to a provincial correctional centre in –28°C weather to surrender himself after escaping from a group home where he had been serving a sentence for breaking and entering. Things began to spin quickly out of control for local authorities after the RCMP announced that the Stonechild investigation would not be reopened owing to time constraints (i.e., they were too busy). It is interesting that after the two police officers responsible for dropping off Night had been convicted of unlawful confinement, the RCMP task force received 25 complaints alleging police brutality. This was only three days after the Federation of Saskatchewan Indian Nations hired a private investigator to pursue the allegations. Finally, three years after the

A native ceremony outside the B.C. Supreme Court in New Westminster, B.C.

Night case made headlines and 13 years after his death, an inquest into the death of Neil Stonechild was convened.[14]

The inquiry uncovered some disturbing facts. It found evidence that Stonechild had received injuries believed to be caused by handcuffs, and it concluded that the principal investigator assigned to the case had carried out a superficial and inadequate investigation. For example, a witness had informed him that he had seen Stonechild in police custody. He had been the last person to see Stonechild alive, yet the investigator had not recorded this in his notebook. Nor had he considered important information voluntarily provided by two members of the Saskatoon Police Service who were willing to discuss Stonechild's disappearance and death. Finally, the report concluded that "chiefs and deputy chiefs of police . . . rejected or ignored reports from the Stonechild family members and investigative reporters that cast serious doubts on the investigation. The self-protective and defensive attitudes exhibited by the senior levels of the police service continued. These same attitudes were manifested by certain members of the Saskatoon Police Service during the Inquiry."[15] The report made eight recommendations. Two of these: provide better training in race relations and anger management for police officers, and make it easier to file complaints against police officers.

Had this been the first inquiry into allegations of mistreatment of Native people by the police and justice-system employees, this story would perhaps be shocking. Unfortunately, it was only one among many inquiries into this very issue produced since 1967. One of the most extensive was the Manitoba Justice Inquiry established in 1988 to investigate the deaths of Helen Betty Osborne and J.J. Harper (see below). What is disturbing is that the Manitoba inquiry reached the same conclusions as had been made in the bulk of reports investigating how to improve relations between police and the criminal justice system and Native populations. In no particular order, that inquiry found that Native people in Canada:

- are more likely to be denied bail;
- spend more time in pretrial detention;
- are more likely to be charged with multiple offences, and often for crimes against the system;
- are more likely not to have legal representation at court proceedings;
- spend less time with their lawyers, especially if they are from northern communities, where the court party flies in the day of the hearings;
- have limited time with judges, who visit Native communities intermittently;

- are more than twice as likely to be incarcerated as non-Native offenders; and
- often plead guilty because they are intimidated by the court and want to get the proceedings over with.[16]

A final point made by the inquiry: Native elders are not given the same status as prison priests and chaplains.

It is also not a coincidence that the increasing rates of Native participation in the Canadian justice system correspond to the growing numbers of Native people moving to urban centres. The phenomenon is not strictly an urban one, however; it extends to rural communities, where many crimes are traceable to the dearth of activities available for the young and to frustration experienced by adults facing limited employment opportunities.

Overrepresentation of Native people in Canadian jails was first identified in the 1970s. The situation continues to deteriorate. For example, in 1976 it was estimated that the chances of a Status Indian male being jailed by age 25 were about 70 percent. The corresponding figure for male Non-Status Indians and Métis was 34 percent. For non-Native males, it was only 8 percent. By 1991, even though Native people were less than 3 percent of the Canadian population, they were 11 percent of the inmates in federal correctional institutions and 15 percent of the provincial prison population. This phenomenon was most pronounced in the Prairie provinces, where Native-inmate admissions to the provincial prison system were as follows: 55 percent in Manitoba, 66 percent in Saskatchewan, 60 percent in Yukon, and 88 percent in the Northwest Territories. The rates were even more striking for Native women; they were 15 percent of the federal prison population.[17] Recent data demonstrate frightening trends. In 2003–04, Native adults represented 21 percent of admissions to provincial and territorial sentenced custody and 18 percent of admissions to federal facilities. In Saskatchewan, Native people make up 80 percent of those admitted to provincial custody while representing only 10 percent of the provincial adult population. In Manitoba, Native people represent 68 percent of admissions to provincial custody though they are 11 percent of the provincial adult population. And in Alberta, 39 percent of admissions to provincial facilities are Native people even though they are only 4 percent of the provincial population.[18]

Incarcerated Native adults are on average three years younger than non-Native adults. Native people are less likely to be employed at the time of admission to a correctional facility. These data of course do not take into account the social costs of crime. In that regard, Native people are more likely to witness or be a victim of crime (see Figure 9-1). In 2004, Criminal Code crime rates on reserves across Canada were higher than for Canada as a whole. Research into these issues has led to the following conclusions. Native people:

- are more likely to fall victim to someone they know;
- suffer high levels of spousal abuse;
- are more likely than non-Native people to be victims or accused in incidents of homicide; and
- are highly represented in the criminal justice system.[19]

Figure 9-1 IMPACT OF SELECTED CRIMES ON NATIVE PEOPLES

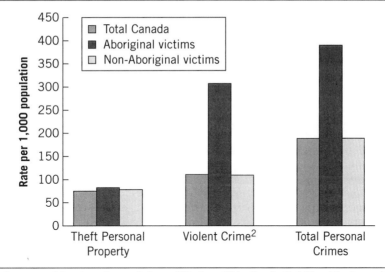

Source: *Basic Departmental Data* 2001. Ottawa: Indian and Northern Affairs Canada: find this publication on the INAC website, http://www.ainc-inac.gc.ca/. Reproduced with the permission of the Minister of Public Works and Government Services Canada, 2008.

The following four incidents encapsulate the central issues confronting Native people in Canada who seek justice.

Helen Betty Osborne. Born in Norway House, Manitoba, Helen Betty Osborne was a 19-year-old nursing student pursuing her education in The Pas, Manitoba. One night in 1971 while walking home she was abducted by four men and murdered in what has become an infamous national event. At first the police suspected Osborne's boyfriend, who was quickly cleared during the course of an investigation that turned up little evidence and that eventually went cold. Yet the day following the murder, one of the conspirators informed various townsfolk of his exploits: friends, acquaintances, people in stores, fellow workers, and individuals he had just met. Several years later another conspirator boasted of the murder, going so far as to ask people if they knew what it felt like to murder another person. No one stepped forward to inform the police of this evidence, and it was later discovered that some friends of the murderers in fact helped shield the perpetrators from the law. In 1985, while examining old files, a newly arrived RCMP officer picked up the Osborne case. After several failed efforts to entice witnesses, he placed an ad in a number of daily newspapers on the Prairies requesting assistance. A witness eventually came forward with vital information that led to the arrests of the four men. A trial led to one conviction, one acquittal, and a plea agreement involving no jail time for a third; the fourth man was never charged. The Aboriginal Justice Inquiry reported in 1991 that the most significant factor prolonging the case was inadequate police work, which was hampered by a community that tolerated racism against Native people.[20]

Inmates at the Aboriginal Healing Range at the Stony Mountain Institution participate in a drum circle. They have committed themselves to a lifestyle behind bars that follows traditional teachings; they also participate in mainstream correctional programs. Visits with elders, cultural and spiritual ceremonies, sharing circles, stints in a sweat lodge, drumming, and arts and crafts are all part of the path to healing.

Donald Marshall, Jr. In 1971, 16-year-old Donald Marshall was charged with non-capital murder in the stabbing death of a young African-Canadian man. Despite limited physical evidence and no motive for the crime, Marshall was arrested on the Membertou Reserve on July 4, 1971. His preliminary inquiry was held July 5. Within four months, Marshall, now 17 years old, was in court. His three-day trial, from November 2 to 5, resulted in a conviction. He was sentenced to life in prison for murder. Two people testified for the Crown even though they had not witnessed the murder, only to quickly recant their testimony on being led from the witness stand.

In addition, the prosecution refused to admit evidence that would have exonerated Marshall. Perhaps most important, Marshall's jury of peers was composed of 12 non-Native men, who quickly convicted him. Years of appeals and requests for a new trial by Marshall's lawyers finally resulted in the Nova Scotia Court of Appeals reviewing the case in 1982. At first the system refused to release Marshall, but intense public pressure led to his exoneration and the overturning of his sentence. Various reasons have been offered for this wrongful conviction, including police and prosecutorial misconduct, incompetent defence counsel, perjured testimony, jury bias, and judicial error. A Royal Commission investigating the case concluded that "the criminal justice system failed Donald Marshall, Jr. at virtually every turn, from his arrest and wrongful conviction in 1971 up to—and even beyond—his acquittal by the Court of Appeal in 1983."[21]

J.J. Harper. On March 9, 1988, a Winnipeg police officer in pursuit of two suspected car thieves stopped J.J. Harper, executive director of the Island Lake Tribal Council, as he was walking home. Within minutes Harper was dead. The police claimed that he had been shot when he attempted to grab the officer's service revolver. At the time of the confrontation with Harper, a broadcast had already been relayed that the car thieves had been apprehended. As well, the suspects were listed as young, white males, and Harper was a 36-year-old Native man. Within 36 hours of the shooting, the police announced that the officer involved had followed procedure. This was after a half-hearted investigation during which the investigating team missed Harper's smashed glasses a few metres from the scene of the shooting. Outraged Native leaders in Winnipeg protested what they portrayed to be the aggressive actions of a racist police force. Municipal and provincial leaders were unable to quell the outcry. In September 1988 the Aboriginal Justice Implementation Commission was established to investigate both the Harper shooting and the 1971 Osborne murder (see above). In referring to the

Harper incident, the Justice Commission concluded: "What started as an unnecessary, racially motivated approach to an Aboriginal citizen on a city street has had profoundly disturbing results." In the end, the Winnipeg Police settled with the Harper family for $450,000.[22]

Pamela George. Like Helen Betty Osborne, the case of Pamela George acquired regional notoriety even if it has gone largely unnoticed by the Canadian public. Originally from the Sakimay First Nation and a 28-year-old mother of two, George was working in Regina as a prostitute when she was picked up on April 17, 1995, by 20-year-old Steven Kummerfield and 19-year-old Alexander Ternowetsky, who was hiding in the vehicle's trunk. The two men claimed that after driving George to a gravel road near the airport, they had oral sex with her. After this, they beat her to death. Her body was discovered the next day. When asked by a friend about the previous evening, Kummerfield replied, "We drove around, got drunk, and killed this chick." He also admitted that he had threatened George's life if she refused his advances. The same individual testified that Ternowetsky glibly informed him, "She deserved it. She was an Indian." Before discharging the jury for deliberations, Justice Ted Malone instructed the panel to remember that George was "indeed a prostitute" and that the issue of consent was central in determining a sentence of manslaughter or first degree murder. The two men were found guilty of manslaughter and sentenced to 6 to 12 years each. Kummerfield was paroled in November 2000 after serving less than four years in a New Brunswick prison. Officials had feared for his safety were he to be incarcerated among the large Native prison population in Saskatchewan. Both men are free today, having served their sentences.[23]

These four case studies suggest that Native people are regularly and aggressively confronted by individuals working within the criminal justice system, people who have arguably been conditioned to view Native people as inherently criminal. They also suggest that the justice system often lacks interest in pursuing the perpetrators of crimes against Native people. In the Osborne case, the failure of the criminal justice system and racist undercurrents in The Pas point strongly toward systemic discrimination. Native women bear the brunt of Canadian society's contempt for Native people, which through racism and violence has exacted a significant toll. Warren Goulding, in *Just Another Indian,* which profiles the life of serial killer John Martin Crawford, who preyed on Native prostitutes, reported that between 1990 and 1994 more than 500 Native women were reported missing in western Canada, with no one seeming to notice.[24] Goulding's book eventually compelled the Alberta RCMP in 2003 to announce the formation of a task force to investigate 83 cases of murdered and missing women, many of them Native, dating back to 1982.[25] Little to date has resulted from this announcement.

Goulding was critical of the Crawford case—in particular, he excoriated the media's failure to report these women's suspicious deaths and the police's late or flawed investigations: "In Canada, only Clifford Olson has taken more lives than John Martin Crawford. Crawford's victims ranged in age from 16 to 35, and forensic evidence suggests that some of them were brutally assaulted and raped as well as murdered. His name should be as notorious as those of Olson or Charles Ng, but since his 1996 conviction, he has been serving his concurrent murder sentences in comfortable obscurity.[26]"

Then there is Vancouver's Robert Pickton, who is probably Canada's most prolific serial killer. Pickton was convicted of six counts of second degree murder in connection with the deaths of 15 missing prostitutes, many of them Native.[27] Indeed, Pickton has admitted to killing 49 women, many of whom are still missing.[28]

More recently, the B.C. RCMP have concluded that since 1969, 18 Native women hitchhiking along a 720-kilometre stretch of the Yellowhead Highway, between Prince George and Prince Rupert, have been abducted and murdered. That stretch of road has since been nicknamed the Highway of Tears. On September 17, 2005, several ceremonies titled "Take Back the Highway" were held in a number of communities along that road; the events included marches, moments of silence, speeches, and prayers, all to promote awareness of the violence against these women. Only recently has this case been examined, despite a four-decade window of events.[29] In many cases the police were informed of a woman's disappearance but failed to conduct any significant investigation. This may be because, as Goulding concludes, the woman who had gone missing was viewed as "just another Indian" (see box).

NATIVE LANGUAGES IN CANADIAN COURTS

Integrating Native languages into the court system through translators is a seemingly simple way to improve the existing situation. But often this is not done, leading to increased Native incarceration rates. Unquestionably the language the justice system uses is confusing and takes time to master.

Now imagine what it is like to be a Native individual from a remote community. Following your arrest you are placed in detention. If you do not understand English you will not realize that you have the right to make a phone call and to contact your family or a lawyer. On entering a courtroom that lacks translators, you are unable to understand the proceedings. Yet according to the Charter of Rights and Freedoms, all Canadians have the fundamental right to have their own language used during proceedings.

With the issue of translation come two additional problems. First, some English words simply do not translate into Native languages. The second problem arises when you attempt to translate complex legal concepts into Native languages; this can lead to cultural misunderstandings. For example, in the Anishinaabe language, truth and knowledge are always relative, which sparks problems in court, since many of the situations dealt with during proceedings are relative to the speaker. One individual could see breaking up a fight as ending a physical conflict and simultaneously initiating reconciliation. Involve the police, however, and the event extends to reports being filed, a time line being developed, witnesses being engaged to determine who swung first, and so on. Such an approach is not relevant to how life in the community is to be lived after the event. These differences may sound minor, but when the courts are involved in a serious criminal case, they take on paramount importance.

Native Policing

If we are to put . . . self-government and our own policing and administration . . . in place, we must ensure that all our people will have a means to take their complaints forward. We must ensure that all our administration and self-governing is accountable to ensure that the basic rights and freedoms our grandfathers and our mothers suffered starvation for will be assured.

—Linda Ross, Kingsclear Indian Band, New Brunswick[30]

At the start of the 1960s the RCMP withdrew from policing Native communities in Ontario and Quebec. It did so without consulting community leaders about the transition from federal to provincial police services. That transition was completed in 1971, timed with the abolition of Indian Agents. This change had many provincial and national Native leaders concerned about the diminished police presence in their communities, which often was weak to start with. Significant grassroots consultation followed, at which point several leaders proposed that their own people take over local policing. Officials of the recently created Department of Indian and Northern Affairs (DIAND; est. 1966) had similar worries. That year, funds were set aside to establish and finance a national band-constable program.

Figure 9-2 BADGE FROM BLOOD TRIBE POLICE SERVICE

Source: Courtesy Blood Tribe Police Service.

By 1968 the first band constables had been hired. This was followed by heightened lobbying by several Native communities for greater control over local policing. The band-constable program enabled band councils to influence policing under the aegis of the RCMP and provincial police. By 1971 there were 121 band constables in Canada and community leaders were demanding control over local policing. Buckling under the pressure, DIAND issued Circular 55, which spelled out specific policing principles for Native communities and opened the possibility for alternative policing arrangements. Among the principles identified: the need for community input into policing programs, better policing across the board, and the need to ensure policing techniques that respected Native peoples' unique cultures. Circular 55 led to band-council policing initiatives at the Blood (Kainai) First Nation in Alberta, for the Mohawks (Kanien'kehá:ka) at Kahnawake in Quebec, and for the James Bay Cree.[31]

The band-council program proved popular and was expanded in 1975, with the RCMP and provincial police services promoting the Indian Special Constable Program. These special constables, originally branded 3B officers, were community-based recruits. The RCMP provided them with limited training. They were permitted to carry weapons and made arrests even though they lacked full officer status. This strategy was ineffective for several reasons. The special constables lacked the powers and authority of their RCMP brethren and were thus seen as second-class officers. Also, the program had a cost-cutting component: it was anticipated that the insertion of special constables into Native communities would reduce the need for band-constable programs by encouraging community participation in local policing. In other words, it would save money and bureaucratic effort while keeping control of policing in Native communities firmly anchored with the RCMP (and in Quebec and Ontario, with the provincial police services). Finally, the role of the special constables was never formalized, nor was the role of band councils in directing the special constables.[32]

These difficulties did not block the formation of the Ontario Indian Special Constable Program in Ontario (1975), the Amerindian Police Program in Quebec (1975), or the Dakota–Ojibway Tribal Council Policing Program (1978). Nor did they impede the signing of the James Bay Agreement, which authorized police services among the James Bay Crees and the Naskapis. By 1982, 500 officers were employed in Native communities, including 130 band constables.[33] Canadian officials acknowledge the need to improve training for officers and other individuals working with Native people in the criminal justice system. The benefits of existing programs have so far included these:

- Fewer arrests.
- Reduced tensions when a Native police officer is involved
- The combining of police training with an officer's knowledge of and commitment to the community.[34]

Despite various improvements, many still expressed concerns about the aforementioned issues. This led the federal government to request that DIAND and the Solicitor General of

Canada conduct a formal program review of federal involvement in policing services. The RCMP was asked to conduct a similar assessment.

Released in 1990, the federally requested Task Force Report criticized what it identified as ineffective policing in Native communities. The same report highlighted the lack of cultural sensitivity toward Indigenous groups. Also identified as problems were a lack of community input, inadequate crime-prevention programs, and biased investigations, all of which resulted in Native people's alienation from the criminal justice system.[35] The First Nations Policing Policy (FNPP) was adopted the next year; this was followed in 1992 by the transfer of federal responsibility for policing to the newly established Aboriginal Policing Directorate. At that time, $116 million was earmarked for a new policing policy for reserves, one that would emphasize tripartite agreements.[36] Perhaps most important, the FNPP provided direction for improvements to Native policing standards—somewhat ironically, by emphasizing the Circular 55 approach tabled in 1971. The principles of community input, culturally appropriate policing techniques, and quality policing were reiterated.

In its own review, the Head Report, published in 1989, the RCMP highlighted difficulties in its programs. This report criticized existing policing programs in reserve and Native communities and concluded that changes were needed if the RCMP was to continue policing those communities. The 3B program was portrayed as paternalistic and outdated; so were the related cultural-awareness programs. Significant changes followed, including these: the 3B program was incorporated into mainstream policing, a national Native advisory committee was established, cultural-awareness programs were improved, and new operational and organizational structures were built for police services in Native communities.[37]

Currently there are two policing models operating nationally. The first are the Self-Administered Agreements, under which policing agreements are struck between Canada, the participating province or territory, and the particular First Nations community. Here, the First Nations community manages a police service according to provincial legislation, and oversight for those self-administered services is provided by independent police commissions. These autonomous police services are staffed mainly by Native officers. The second model is the Community Tripartite Agreement (CTA), which involves the following: the federal government (represented by Public Safety Canada), the province or territory in which the First Nations community is located (usually represented by the provincial or territorial Minister of Justice), and the governing body of the First Nations community (represented by the Band Council).[38]

The CTAs provide a community-based body of officers from an existing police service, usually the RCMP, though efforts are being made to staff these police services with Native officers. By 1995, 46 tripartite agreements had been signed and more than 800 Native officers were policing Native communities across the country. By 1998, there were 111 agreements and 850 Native officers. Currently, there are 142 FNPP agreements providing services for 319 Native communities representing a total population of nearly 240,000. In all, the program guides 1,000 police officers, most of whom are Native.

The program also has internal variations. For instance, it includes single-community services, such as the one operating at Six Nations, which has a population of 10,000; and it includes multicommunity agreements such as in Nishnawbe-Aski, which serves 44 communities. The RCMP has strengthened its efforts to integrate Native people into its complement; estimates are that today, 7 percent (1,260) of the country's nearly 18,000 RCMP officers are of Native ancestry.[39]

There have been obvious improvements to policing in Native communities. The FNPP has resulted in decreased numbers of arrests, as well as reduced tensions when a Native officer is involved. In addition, more police can now combine their training with specific knowledge of and commitment to the community. Yet problems persist that have yet to be fully examined. One is the impact of inadequate or variable funding; another, related to the first, is low salaries for band constables. Then there are issues related to police having to serve their own family and friends. Finally, physical plant is often poor, in terms of detachment housing and administrative offices. The RCMP is still involved on multiple levels, for example, by providing personnel, programs, and organizational structure.

Native Justice Strategies

The idea of justice is to adjust the behaviour of people so that they will live in more harmony with one another. If a person makes a mistake in his actions and it hurts somebody then there should be a chance for the victim to be a part of the process of getting satisfaction, and the satisfaction would not be revenge, it would be real satisfaction in that if something is stolen then the equivalent is given back.

—Ernie Benedict (Mohawk)[40]

In response to pressure from several Native organizations and following on various reports' recommendations, the Canadian government established the Aboriginal Justice Initiative in 1991 to foster improvements in the responsiveness, fairness, inclusiveness, and effectiveness of the justice system as it affected Native people. In 1996, its mandate was renewed in the form of the Aboriginal Justice Strategy (AJS). The AJS has undertaken a number of initiatives to reduce Native incarceration rates; for example, it has evaluated 84 operational community-based justice projects (see Table 9-2), promoted Aboriginal–government talks to improve conditions facing Native inmates, and fostered self-sufficiency in Native communities seeking to improve their justice programs.

Table 9-2 R‌ESTORATIVE J‌USTICE

Province/Territory	Community-Based Justice Programs
Alberta (5)	Métis Settlements General Council (MSGC) Justice Program Saddle Lake First Nation Restorative Justice Program Siksika Nation Aiskapimohkiiks Program Tsuu T'ina Nation Peacemaker Court Yellowhead Tribal Community Corrections Society First Nations Custom Advisory Panels
British Columbia (18)	Esketemc Alternative Measures Program Gitxsan Unlocking Aboriginal Justice Program Haida Gwaii Restorative Justice Program Lower Post First Nation Community Justice Program Nicola Valley Aboriginal Community Justice Program Nisga'a Yuuhlamk'askw Justice Program Nuxalk Restorative Justice Program Prince George Urban Aboriginal Justice Society Prince Rupert Urban Aboriginal Justice Program Qwi:qwelstóm–Stó:lo Nation Justice Program Secwepemc Community Justice Program Ska'ls—Beliefs in Justice Program Sliammon Justice Program St'at'imc Restorative Justice Program Stikine Aboriginal Justice Program Tl'azt'en "Healing Circle" Justice Program Tsilhqot'in Community Justice Program Wet'suwet'en Unlocking Aboriginal Justice Program
Manitoba (5)	Awasis Agency of Northern Manitoba Inc. Hollow Water Community Holistic Circle Healing Program Manitoba Keewatinowi Okimakanak Inc. Onashowewin Inc.—"Rekindling the Spirit Within" St. Theresa's Point First Nation Tribal Court System
Newfoundland/Labrador (2)	Community Holistic Justice Program Community Justice Program
New Brunswick (1)	Restorative Justice Initiative Program and Victims' Assistance Program
Northwest Territories (1)	Community Justice Committees (Fort McPherson, Deline, Lutsel K'e, Fort Good Hope, Inuvik, Rae/Edzo)
Nova Scotia (1)	Mi'Kmaq Legal Support Network Customary Law Program
Nunavut (2)	Community-Based Program Community Justice Committees (Cambridge Bay, Arviat, Baker Lake, Coral Harbour, Rankin Inlet, Repulse, Cape Dorset, Clyde River, Pangnirtung, Sanikiluaq, Iqaluit Igloolik, Kimmirut)

cont'd

Table 9-2 RESTORATIVE JUSTICE (CONT.)

Province/Territory	Community-Based Justice Programs
Ontario (6)	Aboriginal Community Council Program Biidaaban–Mnjikaning Community Healing Model Community Council Program Community Justice Program Restorative Justice Program United Chiefs and Councils of Manitoulin Justice Program
Prince Edward Island (2)	Aboriginal Community Justice Program (partnership between Lennox Island and Abegweit First Nations, the Aboriginal Women's Association of Prince Edward Island)
Quebec (10)	Alternative Justice and Court Worker Programs Community-Based Justice Program—Council of the Naskapi Nation of Kawawachikamach Community Justice Panel and Youth Justice Program Community Justice Program—Listuguj Mi'gmaq Government Community Justice Program—Algonquians of Barriere Lake Justice of the People Program—Makivik Corporation Justice Healing Program—Cree First Nation of Whapmagoostu Le Projet de Conseil des Sages d'Opiticiwan Restorative Community Justice Program—Mohawk Council of Kahnawake Youth Justice Initiative—Conseil de la Nation Atikamekw
Saskatchewan (22)	Agency Chiefs Tribal Council Community Justice Initiative Ahtahkakoop Community Justice Program Battlefords Tribal Council Community Justice Initiative Beardy's and Okemasis First Nation Justice Initiative Cowessess First Nation Community Justice Program Extrajudicial Measures Program and Youth Circles Preventative Program File Hills-Qu'Appelle Tribal Council Community Justice Initiative Justice Secreteriat Agreement Recipient: Federation of Saskatchewan Indian Nations (FSIN) LaLoche Alternative Measures Program Meadow Lake Tribal Council Community Justice Program Métis Family & Community Justice Services Community Justice Initiative Mistawasis Community Justice Program Onion Lake Cree Nation Tribal Justice Program Prince Albert School Mediation Program Prince Albert Grand Council Justice Initiative Prince Albert Urban Alternative Measures Program Regina Alternative Measures Program Saskatoon Tribal Council Community Justice Program Thunderchild First Nation Community Justice Program Touchwood Agency Tribal Council Justice Initiative Yorkton Tribal Council Community-Based Justice Initiative

Yukon (9)	Community Group Conferencing—Dawson Community Group Conferencing Society
	Community Social Justice Program—Kwanlin Dun First Nation
	Dena Keh Justice Program
	Haines Junction Community Justice Program
	Southern Lakes Justice Committee
	Old Crow Justice Committee
	Tan Sakwathan Skookum Jim Diversion Program
	Teslin Tlingit Peace Council
	The Dena Gude' Guk'E; Kuk'Uts'Ets Program (The People Talk, Everybody Decides)

Restorative Justice

There are three justice models operating in Canada today. The first is the primary criminal justice system, which uses law to compel individuals by threat of coercive force to act in appropriate ways. The second is the criminal justice system, to which structural changes are being made to integrate restorative-justice processes based on the understanding that Native people are unreasonably represented in federal and provincial prisons and jails. The third model is community-based Native justice systems that apply traditional-justice ideas as the basis of living together. The latter two models rely in many ways on the concept of restorative justice, which recognizes a criminal act as an injury done to another person as opposed to simply an overtly criminal act in need of punishment. This perspective creates obligations on the part of the accused to make reparations or provide compensation to the victim and the community. Restorative justice also emphasizes the need to restore relationships rather than simply assign guilt and ensure that the punishment fits the crime.

There is a strong relationship between current restorative-justice models and Native justice concepts. In both the emphasis is on healing, forgiveness, and community involvement when resolving disputes. While healing relationships is paramount to the process, there is also a need to determine and address the root causes of the accused's inappropriate behaviour. This is a long and at times drawn-out process because of the time required to address all the factors leading to an incident. It has also been found that restorative-justice programs require government *and* community participation if they are to succeed. As in any negotiation framework, each party must concede certain principles so that a unique program can emerge in which all parties can achieve their aims. In other words, all parties must accept responsibility, and the government must accept Native communities as equal partners. The end result is reduced pressure on the criminal justice system and improved outcomes for Native individuals. The following processes are currently operating as alternative programs in federal and provincial justice systems for the purposes of fostering culturally sensitive approaches to justice.

Sentencing Circles

Sentencing circles are employed when an individual in a community has broken the law and has been found guilty of an offence by the mainstream justice system. Usually a circle is established when the accused has admitted guilt and is willing to accept responsibility for his or her actions, while acknowledging the harm done to family and neighbours. The goal of a sentencing circle is to shift the focus from punishment to rehabilitation; it also offers the courts an alternative to incarceration. For example, a sentencing circle:

- approaches the conflict in a culturally appropriate manner;
- contributes to a wide-ranging examination and exploration of ways to change the circumstances of the offender;
- brings together the resources of family, community, and institutions to find a solution; and
- makes recommendations to promote law-abiding behaviour instead of simply punishing the criminal act.[41]

Many Native communities in Canada have adopted sentencing circles, which have also become popular with federal and provincial officials. Sometimes, though, customary law is unable to reconcile itself with sentencing circles. All the same, most Native communities are developing alternatives to incarceration.

Alternative Measures for Youth

Diversion programs. Diversion councils bring together police and the victim along with the parents of a youth charged with a minor offence. At that time, punishment is determined. The youth in question may have to pay a fine, perform community service, or simply apologize for his or her actions. These programs are effective in keeping youth out of the criminal justice system and keeping those in the community affected by the youth's actions involved, permitting them to play a role in the outcome.

Bush camps. Bush camps remove youth affected by crime or engaged in criminal activities to remote camps to instruct them in traditional ways. These camps impress on youth the proper ways to interact in a community; they also foster a sense of belonging, leading to community reintegration. Bush camps have proven their worth since their implementation in the 1980s.

Aboriginal youth-justice committees. Under Section 69 of the *Young Offenders Act,* as an alternative to formal judicial proceedings, youth justice committees (YJCs) may be formed with members of a community and a respected elder to identify the needs of the accused and recommend an appropriate sentence. The YJC has the authority to hand down a number of decisions: it can call for a written or verbal apology to the victim, for community-service work, for a written essay related to the offence, and/or for abiding by curfew restrictions and/or counselling. YJCs have had positive results to date; however, administrative costs often work against them. Also, eligibility restrictions limit the use of committees to nonviolent offenders, which prevents many young people from benefiting.

Federal Corrections

Over the past decade, statistics detailing the level of Native overrepresentation in provincial and federal prisons, and research highlighting the unique philosophical and operational differences that separate customary Native legal systems from those of mainstream Canada, have led the Correction Service of Canada (CSC) to promote Native corrections. In particular, the CSC has developed programs based on the understanding that Native people have unique needs that require special attention. These programs have involved hiring Native liaison officers and making provisions for inmate access to elders' spiritual services.[42] Also, several Native communities have accepted control of correctional facilities and healing lodges. For example, the Okimaw Ochi Healing Lodge for female offenders in Saskatchewan incorporates Native approaches to healing, personal growth, and safe reintegration. The minimum-security Pe Sakastew Centre, which accommodates 60 male federal offenders in Hobbema, Alberta, operates in a similar way.

Other approaches include a National Aboriginal Strategy to ensure the provision of programs and services to meet Native offenders' needs and to improve the reintegration of Native offenders back into their communities. The Framework for the Enhanced Role of Aboriginal Communities has been fashioned to provide guidelines by which some or all aspects of federal corrections can be transferred to Native communities. The Aboriginal Research Forum's role is to maintain a constructive dialogue about Native people; to that end, it has brought together researchers whose expertise is correctional programs and practices. Finally, the CSC and the National Parole Board Advisory Committee have advisory boards with specific policies for addressing the social and cultural differences of Native offenders.

Provincial/Territorial Programs

Some provinces, including Ontario, Alberta, and B.C., have justice branches or directorates that deal specifically with Native issues and policies. Unfortunately, Native-specific policies are largely informed by the general principles informing federal policymakers. Examples of Native-specific programs include the Native Liaison Services, traditional spiritual practices, substance-abuse programs, Native literacy and educational programs, community reintegration, sweat lodge ceremonies, employment training, and anger-management and family-violence programs.

Conclusion

Our experiences are such that, [even] if you make [the current system] more representative, it's still your law that would apply, it would still be your police forces that would enforce the laws, it would still be your courts that would interpret them, and it would still be your corrections system that houses the people that go through the court system. It would not be our language that is used in the system. It would not be our laws. It would not be our traditions, our customs or our values that decide what happens in the system.

—Ovide Mercredi (Cree)[43]

In recent years, millions of dollars have been spent and significant policies implemented with the intention of fixing the problems identified in this chapter. Yet despite the level of attention being paid to the issue of Native overrepresentation in the criminal justice system, and despite attempts to integrate traditional judicial approaches with the Canadian system, available statistics indicate that Native people continue to face inordinate levels of violent crime in communities where such acts were literally unheard of prior to first contact. Native people's rates of violent crime exceed the national rates, and offences such as rape and child abuse have been introduced into these populations. Meanwhile, incarceration rates continue to rise, especially in the Prairie provinces, where Native populations continue to grow. The Europeans' criminalization of Native culture has resulted in a criminal justice system that discriminates against Native people—all in all, a tough legacy to contend with from the Native perspective.

FURTHER READING

Aboriginal Justice Inquiry of Manitoba. "The Justice System and Aboriginal People: The Aboriginal Justice Implementation Commission: Bibliography." [online] http://www.ajic.mb.ca/volumel/ bibliography.html

Bell, Catherine, and David Kahane, eds. *Intercultural Dispute Resolution in Aboriginal Contexts.* Vancouver: UBC Press, 2004.

Chiste, Katherine Beatty. "Getting Tough on Crime the Aboriginal Way: Alternative Justice Initiatives in Canada." In *Hidden in Plain Sight: Contributions of Aboriginal Peoples to Canadian Identity and Culture,* ed. David R. Newhouse, Cora J. Voyageur, and Dan Beavon. Toronto: University of Toronto Press, 2005, pp. 218–32.

Denis, Claude. *We Are Not You: First Nations and Canadian Modernity.* Peterborough: Broadview, 1997.

Fiske, Jo-Anne, and Betty Patrick. *Cis Dideen Kat, When the Plumes Rise: The Way of the Lake Babine Nation.* Vancouver: UBC Press, 2000.

Goulding, Warren. *Just Another Indian: A Serial Killer and Canada's Indifference.* Calgary: Fifth House, 2001.

Green, Ross Gordon. *Justice in Aboriginal Communities: Sentencing Alternatives.* Saskatoon: Purich, 1998.

Miller, Bruce. *The Problem of Justice: Tradition and Law in the Coast Salish World.* Lincoln: University of Nebraska Press, 2000.

Ross, Rupert. *Returning to the Teachings: Exploring Aboriginal Justice.* Toronto: Penguin, 1996.

Waldram, James B. *The Way of the Pipe: Aboriginal Spirituality and Symbolic Healing in Canadian Prisons.* Peterborough: Broadview, 1997.

NOTES

1. Zebedee Nungak, presentation before the Royal Commission on Aboriginal Peoples (RCAP), Ottawa, November 25, 1992.

2. For this discussion, see in particular Michel Foucault, *Discipline and Punish: The Birth of the Prison* (New York: Pantheon, 1977).

3. Manitoba, *Public Inquiry into the Administration of Justice and Aboriginal People: Report of the Aboriginal Justice Inquiry of Manitoba* (Winnipeg: Queen's Printer, 1991).

4. See Rupert Ross, *Dancing with a Ghost: Exploring Indian Reality* (Markham: Reed, 1992).

5. Hugh Dempsey, *Firewater: The Impact of the Whiskey Trade on the Blackfoot Nation* (Calgary: Fifth House, 2002).

6. Treaty 7 Elders and Tribal Council with Walter Hildebrant, Sarah Carter, and Dorothy First Rider, *The True Spirit and Intent of Treaty 7* (Kingston and Montreal: McGill–Queen's University Press, 1996), p. 243.

7. Quoted in Rene Fumoleau, *As Long as This Land Shall Last: A History of Treaty 8 and Treaty 11, 1870–1939* (Toronto: McClelland and Stewart, 1975), p. 5.

8. F. Laurie Barron, "The Indian Pass System in the Canadian West, 1882–1935," *Prairie Forum* 13, no. 1 (1988): 25–42; and Sarah A. Carter, "Controlling Indian Movement: The Pass System," *NeWest Review* (May 1985): 8–9.

9. J.R. Miller, *Skyscrapers Hide the Heavens: A History of Indian–White Relations in Canada,* 3rd ed. (Toronto: University of Toronto Press, 2000), p. 176.

10. E. Brian Titley, *A Narrow Vision: Duncan Campbell Scott and the Administration of Indian Affairs* (Vancouver: UBC Press, 1986); and Yale D. Belanger, "The Six Nations of Grand River Territory's Attempts at Renewing International Political Relationships, 1921–1925," *Canadian Foreign Policy* 13, no. 3 (2007): 29–43.

11. Jack Glenn, *Once Upon an Oldman: Special Interest Politics and the Oldman River Dam* (Vancouver: UBC Press, 1999); and Ken Coates, *The Marshall Decision and Native Rights* (Kingston and Montreal: McGill–Queen's University Press, 2000).

12. Sandra Lambertus, *Wartime Images, Peacetime Wounds: The Media and the Gustafsen Lake Standoff* (Toronto: University of Toronto Press, 2004).

13. Evidence of Stella Bignell, inquiry transcript, Vol. 1 (September 8, 2003), p. 107.

14. Saskatchewan, *Report of the Commission of Inquiry into Matters Relating to the Death of Neil Stonechild* (Regina: October 2004).

15. Ibid., p. 212.

16. Canadian Criminal Justice System, *Aboriginal Peoples and the Criminal Justice System* (Ottawa: Canadian Criminal Justice System, 2000). [online] http://www.ccja-acjp.ca/en/abori5.html. Last accessed September 8, 2008.

17. These data are found in Patricia A. Montue-Angus, "Lessons in Decolonization: Aboriginal Overrepresentation in Canadian Criminal Justice," in *Visions of the Heart: Canadian Aboriginal*

Issues, ed. David Alan Long and Olive Patricia Dickason (Harcourt Brace & Company, Canada, 1996), pp. 335–55.

18. Statistics Canada, "Aboriginal People as Victims and Offenders," *The Daily* (June 6, 2006). [online] http://www.statcan.ca/Daily/English/ 060606/d060606b.htm. Last accessed September 7, 2008.

19. Ibid.

20. Manitoba, *Public Inquiry into the Administration of Justice and Aboriginal People;* see also Lisa Priest, *Conspiracy of Silence* (Toronto: McClelland and Stewart, 1989).

21. Nova Scotia, *Royal Commission on Donald Marshall, Jr., Prosecution* (Nova Scotia: Queen's Printer, 1989).

22. Manitoba, *Public Inquiry into the Administration of Justice and Aboriginal People;* and Gordon Sinclair, *Cowboys and Indians: The Shooting of J.J. Harper* (Toronto: McClelland and Stewart, 1999).

23. Albert Angus, "Saskatchewan Justice on Trial: The Pamela George Case," *Saskatchewan Indian* 27, no. 1 (1997): 5

24. Warren Goulding, *Just Another Indian: A Serial Killer and Canada's Indifference* (Calgary: Fifth House, 2001).

25. Chris Purdy, "Serial Killer Who Roamed Saskatoon Met with Indifference by Police, Media: Journalist-Author Accepts Award for Book About Slain Aboriginal Women," *Edmonton Journal,* November 26, 2003.

26. Daniel Paul, "Racism Keeps Native Women's Killer Anonymous." *Halifax Herald,* May 25, 2001.

27. "Pickton Verdict Evokes 'Elation,' 'Disappointment' from Victim's Friends, Family," *CBCNews.ca,* December 9, 2007. [online] http://www.cbc.ca/canada/british-columbia/story/2007/12/09/bc-picktonfamilies.html. Last accessed July 23, 2008.

28. Philip Stavrou, "Lawyers to Give Closing Arguments in Pickton Case," *CTV.ca News,* November 19, 2007. [online] http://www.ctv.ca/servlet/ArticleNews/story/CTVNews/20071116/ Pickton_arguments_071116/20071119. Last accessed January 17, 2008.

29. "List of Women on 'Highway of Tears' Doubles," *CTV News,* October 12, 2007.

30. Linda Ross, presentation before the Royal Commission on Aboriginal Peoples (RCAP), Kingsclear, May 19, 1992.

31. See Don Clairmont, "Aboriginal Policing in Canada: An Overview of Developments in First Nations," report submitted to the Ipperwash Inquiry established to inquire and report on events surrounding the death of Dudley George. [online] http://www.attorneygeneral.jus.gov. on.ca/inquiries/ipperwash/index.html. Last accessed September 7, 2008.

32. Ibid.

33. Ibid., p. 5.

34. Canadian Criminal Justice System, *Aboriginal Peoples and the Criminal Justice System.*

35. Clairmont, "Aboriginal Policing in Canada," p. 6.

36. Ibid., p. 116.

37. Ibid., p. 38.

38. Public Safety Canada, *Overview of the First Nations Policing Policy.* [online] http://www.publicsafety.gc.ca/pol/le/fnpp_ov-eng.aspx. Last accessed September 7, 2008.

39. Ibid.

40. Peter Kulchyski, Don McCaskill, and David Newhouse, *In The Words of the Elders: Aboriginal Cultures in Transition* (Toronto: University of Toronto Press, 1999), p. 135.

41. Canadian Criminal Justice System, *Aboriginal Peoples and the Criminal Justice System.*

42. See James B. Waldram, *The Way of the Pipe: Aboriginal Spirituality and Symbolic Healing in Canadian Prisons* (Peterborough: Broadview, 1997).

43. Quoted in Law Reform Commission of Canada, *Report on Aboriginal Peoples and Criminal Justice: Equality, Respect, and the Search for Justice* (Ottawa: Law Reform Commission, 1991), p. 13.

CHAPTER

10

Self-Government

Our rights, both aboriginal and treaty, emanate from our sovereignty as a nation of people. Our relationships with the state have their roots in negotiation between two sovereign peoples. ... The Indian people enjoy special status conferred by recognition of our historic title that cannot be impaired, altered or compromised.

—Manitoba Indian Brotherhood[1]

Aboriginal self-government is a seemingly simple concept that has become increasingly complex in recent years. Best described as a set of relationships involving Aboriginal law, politics, administration, financial management, community and economic growth, and natural-resource development and maintenance, as well as both individual and community-based entrepreneurship, a single definition to describe Aboriginal self-government continues to elude us. To date the best definition that is palatable to the major players reads something along these lines: Aboriginal self-governments are governments designed, established, and administered by Native people. They usually take the form of negotiated arrangements that provide First Nations with greater control over local affairs in areas such as health care, child welfare, education, housing, and economic development. The key points of contention relate to Canada's refusal to acknowledge Aboriginal self-government as a third level of government that matters deeply to First Nations' desires to preserve their cultural identities.

Perhaps most important, modern definitions of self-government embraced by government officials ignore the clear fact of Indigenous political independence prior to extended contact—a fact that Native leaders want to see formally acknowledged in federal laws and policies. For instance, from a Native perspective, "self-government is referred to as an 'inherent right,' a pre-existing right rooted in Aboriginal peoples' long occupation and government of the land before European settlement." Ideas such as sovereignty are described as "responsibilities given to them by the Creator and of a spiritual connection to the land." According to this model, "Aboriginal peoples do not seek to be granted self-government by Canadian governments, but rather to have Canadians recognize that Aboriginal governments existed long before the arrival of Europeans and to establish the conditions that would permit the revival of their governments." Adding to this complexity are treaty signatories' conceptions of self-government—specifically, that the "treaties with the Crown [acknowledge] the self-governing status of Indian nations at the time of treaty signing."[2]

Aboriginal self-government as an idea remains ill-defined, and this can lead to passionate exchanges between advocates and opponents. This chapter begins by examining historic self-governing powers, and then reviews some of the more important events in the evolving self-government debate since the 1960s.

The Setting: Historic

We are nations within Canada, and we have not given up our sovereignty. We have shared with Canada and have given all we can give. In order to meet our objectives, Canadians must now share with us.

—Del Riley, Assembly of First Nations[3]

Prior to first contact, a complexity of political, economic, social, and cultural systems were in place in North America. There were hundreds if not thousands of small Indigenous communities spread across Canada that developed culturally specific ideas about land. This resulted in versatile political economies and complex social and cultural institutions, which were maintained through individual and community-based actions overseen and guided by community leaders. Codes of conduct and laws developed and were taught to children; this negated the need for localized military and police forces to manage community conduct. Instead, elders' councils were petitioned to resolve disputes. If that process failed, the individuals and families involved were permitted to take independent action. In sum, each nation had an established history and its own language, and hence a unique culture with specialized traditions that required community leaders who were adept at self-governance.

Striving for balance was an important goal, one that led most people to place the community over self-interest. Leaders were chosen for particular tasks based on their experience; their specific leadership ended when the task was completed. When an individual accepted a leadership role, that person's primary duty was to establish and maintain good relations with other communities so as to preserve regional balance. Even that leadership role ended until the same skills were again required. Individuals were not permitted to make decisions on behalf of the entire community. Rather, consensus was promoted. If consensus could not be reached, the issue was debated further and alternative solutions were developed. Individuals who did not approve of a specific decision were free to leave and establish their own community.[4]

Indigenous leaders extended this approach to the French and British. The Mohawks (Kanien'kehá:ka), for example, in 1618 established a diplomatic network that came to be known as the Silver Covenant Chain. An iron chain (at first it had been a rope) was forged with the Dutch colonists. In 1664 the English accepted a renewed iron chain with the

Iroquois (Haudenosaunee) Confederacy's five nations. Each group associated with the chain remained autonomous; that is, the chain did not necessarily signify the merger of tribal nations with non-Native nations to form a single political unit. Instead, each group's autonomy was preserved in an effort to maintain balance and political harmony. As a result of such interaction, French and Indigenous ways eventually fused to form a unique cultural environment described as the Middle Ground (*pays d'en haut*).[5]

Despite these promising beginnings, Indigenous nations changed as a result of these early cross-cultural encounters. Faced with new economic, social, and political forces, they tried as well as they could to adhere to culturally specific ideas about political and economic order. In a political environment characterized by ongoing social and political interactions, adaptability was arguably the hallmark of self-governing nations. Most Indigenous nations held councils (or similar) for the purpose of renewing relationships; inevitably, these led to individual and collective interactions with peoples from other political assemblies.[6] The Cree (Nehiyaw) and the Blackfoot (Niitsítapi), for example, employed councils to negotiate peace treaties. To the east, the Cree and Ojibwa (Anishinaabe) used councils to establish trade relationships and to demarcate territorial boundaries so as to prevent hostilities. As the late Sioux (Lakota) philosopher Vine Deloria, Jr. pointed out, the world was "not a global village so much as a series of non-homogeneous pockets of identity that must eventually come into conflict because they represent different historical arrangements of emotional energy."[7] Indigenous nations in Canada, too, represented diverse pockets of identity that interacted regularly with one another.

By the end of the seventeenth century the colonial powers in North America included the English, French, Dutch, and Spanish, with the first two emerging as the key competing interests in what is now Canada. Both powers regularly engaged Indigenous leaders in political negotiations. Because Indigenous political and economic ways were viewed as at odds with European norms, colonial officials gave little consideration to "the existence of relatively strong, organized and politically active and astute Aboriginal nations."[8] Escalating cultural and political interaction led European settlers "to recognize in practice, and later in law, the capacity of Indigenous nations not only to govern their own affairs [but also to] possess their own lands."[9] In an effort to maintain peaceful relations, many Indigenous leaders adopted certain colonial practices such as living in permanent settlements and participating in the fur trade. British officials were less open to working with Indigenous leaders, but needed them as trade agents. Even so, the colonists were unmoved by growing complaints about the encroachment of settlers.

The Royal Proclamations of 1761 and 1763

Early British colonial policy acknowledged Indian land title and, more important and somewhat ironically, the need to protect Indians from British settlers and entrepreneurs. To those ends, the Crown attempted to buffer Indigenous nations from increasingly aggressive westward-moving settlers.[10] On receiving word of territorial incursions and the resultant hostilities, King George III issued a Royal Proclamation in 1761 to the governors of Nova Scotia, New Hampshire, New York, North and South Carolina, and Georgia. It declared that it would no longer be permissible to obtain land grants or to interfere with Indigenous populations and that settlers found on Indian land would be removed.[11] Indigenous leaders quickly found, however, that local officials regularly ignored this edict, choosing instead to narrowly interpret this line: "those treaties and compacts which have been heretofore solemnly entered into with the said Indians by our Royal predecessors Kings and Queens of this realm." North American officials suggested that the proclamation applied to previous Crown–Indian agreements and thus did not apply to all Indigenous lands.[12] To counter these inconsistencies, the king made a second Royal Proclamation in 1763, which declared all lands west of the Appalachians to be reserved for the Indians' use and benefit and which prohibited settlement in the Ohio Valley.

The 1763 Proclamation also stated that Indigenous lands could only be sold or otherwise disposed of to the Crown (which in effect launched the treaty-making process beginning in 1850). It read in part: "Where it is just and reasonable, and essential to our Interest, and the security of our Colonies, that the several Nations or Tribes of Indians with Whom we are connected, and who live under our Protection, should not be molested or disturbed in the Possession of such Parts of our dominions and Territories as, not having been ceded to or purchased by Us, are reserved to them, or any of them, as their Hunting Grounds."

Indigenous leaders were reluctant to permit colonial officials to arbitrarily ratify legislation affecting their political autonomy. In response, the Crown invited Indigenous leaders of the Great Lakes and upper Ohio Valley to attend a conference at Niagara in 1764 to debate the key principles governing Indigenous–Crown relations. Indigenous leaders envisioned the council as a forum for setting "the framework by which the parties would relate to one another" (see Chapter 4). In July to August around 2,000 chiefs representing more than 24 nations met to renew political relationships and, more important, to clarify the proclamation's provisions. They believed that their right to self-government had been recognized by the fact that the conference had been called and that the words they spoke while there amounted to key provisions in the resulting treaty: the Treaty of Niagara of 1764.[13]

The 1763 Proclamation has often been cited since then as an "Indigenous Bill of Rights," because of its explicit recognition of Indian title and because it reserved most of western North America to Indigenous nations. This is a somewhat dubious claim, considering that George III's proclamation asserted British sovereignty over all of North America, and that notwithstanding Indigenous claims, these former homelands were now the exclusive domain of the British Crown.[14] Indeed, the proclamation initiated the slow, systematic dispossession of Indigenous peoples and their sequestration on reserves, which greatly undermined local governance.

In 1867, Section 91(24) of the *British North America (BNA) Act* assigned to the federal government responsibility for "Indians and lands reserved for the Indians." This led the Canadian government to pass the *Gradual Enfranchisement Act* (1869), followed by the

Indian Act (1876), both of which enabled Ottawa to impose a band-council model on Native communities. That model holds to this day—an indication of how Canadian officials conceptualize Aboriginal self-government (i.e., as a delegated right). Native leaders have never wavered from their belief that the inherent right of each First Nation community to self-government flows from the Creator.

Band Councils: Yesterday and Today

Hereditary councils and their variations had always guided Indigenous political processes. In 1869 the Canadian government passed the "Act of '69" in an effort to "free Indians from their state of wardship under the Federal Government" and to "effect gradual assimilation only after Indians could manage the 'ordinary affairs of the 'whiteman.'"[15] The legislation took aim at community-based self-government, which federal officials had long viewed as an obstacle to assimilation. The "Act of '69" also empowered officials—and, later, Indian Agents—to interpret and apply its provisions so that, for example, they could remove elected leaders for "dishonesty, intemperance or immorality." The law also restricted the jurisdiction of band councils to matters of municipal government. Finally, all internal decisions concerning band matters would be "subject to confirmation by the Governor in Council," the latter being the Governor General acting on the advice of the federal Cabinet. Band councils were modelled after municipal councils then governing towns and cities. A band council consisted of one chief as well as one councillor for every 100 members of the band, though the number of councillors could not be less than 2 or more than 12. Native communities were soon electing councils that were responsible for all of the reserve's daily political activities; slowly but surely, those councils displaced hereditary councils.[16]

Band-council government still holds, under the *Indian Act*. That overarching piece of federal legislation was written at a time when Native people were viewed as little more than wards of the state. That largely explains why it dictates leadership selection, council authority, and community governance. Besides declaring who an Indian is, the act provides a legal framework for band governments' operations, governs reserve lands, dictates election procedures, and sets the terms of office for chiefs and councillors. *And* it states how federal government monies are to be spent. In 1880, in response to strong Native opposition to the act's local-governance restrictions, Ottawa revised the act, at the same time founding the Department of Indian Affairs (DIA), which was granted the authority to impose band-council elections. The *Indian Advancement Act* (1884) consolidated Ottawa's powers by authorizing the Superintendent-General of Indian Affairs to depose chiefs whom Indian Agents and other Indian Affairs officials considered unfit for duty.[17]

Adding insult to injury were the limited powers assigned to band councils. The federal government could now establish its own community bylaws, whose operations were overseen by Indian Agents, who were stationed on reserves to ensure the transition from customary to European-style government. Bands could still pass bylaws in certain limited

SECTION 81—POWERS OF COUNCIL

The council of a band may make by-laws not inconsistent with this Act or with any regulation made by the Governor in Council or the Minister, for any or all of the following purposes, namely,

(a) to provide for the health of residents on the reserve and to prevent the spreading of contagious and infectious diseases;

(b) the regulation of traffic;

(c) the observance of law and order;

(d) the prevention of disorderly conduct and nuisances;

(e) the protection against and prevention of trespass by cattle and other domestic animals, the establishment of pounds, the appointment of pound-keepers, the regulation of their duties and the provision for fees and charges for their services;

(f) the construction and maintenance of watercourses, roads, bridges, ditches, fences and other local works;

(g) the dividing of the reserve or a portion thereof into zones and the prohibition of the construction or maintenance of any class of buildings or the carrying on of any class of business, trade or calling in any zone;

(h) the regulation of the construction, repair and use of buildings, whether owned by the band or by individual members of the band;

(i) the survey and allotment of reserve lands among the members of the band and the establishment of a register of Certificates of Possession and Certificates of Occupation relating to allotments and the setting apart of reserve lands for common use, if authority therefor has been granted under section 60;

(j) the destruction and control of noxious weeds;

(k) the regulation of bee-keeping and poultry raising;

(l) the construction and regulation of the use of public wells, cisterns, reservoirs and other water supplies;

(m) the control or prohibition of public games, sports, races, athletic contests and other amusements;

(n) the regulation of the conduct and activities of hawkers, peddlers or others who enter the reserve to buy, sell or otherwise deal in wares or merchandise;

(o) the preservation, protection and management of fur-bearing animals, fish and other game on the reserve;

(p) the removal and punishment of persons trespassing on the reserve or frequenting the reserve for prohibited purposes.

Source: The Indian Act. Indian Act (R.S., 1985, c. I-5). Not the official version.

areas, including these: the control or prohibition of public games, sports, races, athletic contests, and other amusements; the construction and regulation of public wells, cisterns, reservoirs, and other water supplies; the destruction and control of noxious weeds; the regulation of beekeeping and poultry raising; and the preservation, protection, and management of furbearing animals, fish, and other game on the reserve.

As an indication of band councils' lack of genuine authority over community affairs, the Indian Affairs Minister may disallow an attempt to pass a bylaw. Native leaders refer to this governance model as "delegated" self-government in the sense that their governing powers are derived exclusively from the federal government. In other words, band councils lack independent administrative authority. Put another way, band councils are a form of self-administration, not true self-governing bodies. The resulting relationship has been one of federal control over Native lands, peoples, and governance.

A band council can pass bylaws related to taxation of reserve land for local purposes. It can also pass bylaws related to the right to occupy, possess, or use reserve land. Again, these powers are limited, for according to the *Indian Act* all bylaws must first be accepted by the Indian Affairs Minister before they can be implemented. It has been estimated that the minister disallows upwards of 60 percent of all bylaws passed in First Nations communities. Clearly, the Canadian government still sees itself as a guardian to its Indian wards, and its purpose as promoting their social advancement. This is in direct contradiction to the Inherent Rights Policy (discussed below) passed in 1995, which acknowledges the inherent right to Aboriginal self-government.

The guidelines established by the Musqueam band in British Columbia are instructive. The Musqueam band elects its council according to Sections 74(1), (2), (3)(a)(i), and (3)(b)(i) of the *Indian Act*. The council's role is to manage the band's affairs as delegated under the *Indian Act,* in accordance with the objectives of the Musqueam community. Section 81 of the *Indian Act* grants council the powers to make bylaws over reserve lands, and the band council is entrusted by the general band membership to represent the band's political views and aspirations at the reserve, district, provincial, and national levels. Band members hold council accountable for the actions of the band administration, and the council is answerable to the general band membership and the Indian Affairs Minister. At the start of each term, the Musqueam councillors swear an oath of service to the Musqueam band for its welfare and advancement. To simplify the council's tasks, the Musqueam band council has adopted relatively simple and hardy policies.[18]

Dakota Tipi[19]

The complexity of the current *Indian Act* has given rise to contentious moments in recent years. In 1999 the Auditor General reported that Indian and Northern Affairs Canada (INAC) had received more than 300 allegations related to 108 First Nation governments over the two-year period leading up to its audit. That same report revealed that INAC had had to intervene in the management of 167 out of 585 band governments. An additional Access to Information request revealed 984 allegations of criminal and noncriminal wrongdoing against Native governments and organizations. As of March 2004, 23 percent of First Nations tribal councils were under some form of management intervention.[20]

Take, for example, the difficulties experienced at Dakota Tipi. In 1997, citing corruption, Dakota Tipi community members Corrine Smoke and Leona Freed came forward declaring that the chief and council were obtaining increased federal transfers by using the band identification numbers of departed residents; they further alleged certain band members' misappropriation of bingo-hall intakes for their personal use. The heart of the debate was Chief

Dennis Pashe's declaration that he had accepted the role of chief in 1978 through hereditary succession, which is permissible under Section 74 of the *Indian Act*. Pashe further contended that according to band custom he was not bound by law to call an election. During his two decades as chief, Pashe's supporters obtained privileges that included access to education money, bus services, jobs, and social assistance. His opponents were openly critical of these policies, which included a workfare program established in 2001 whereby social assistance cheques were withheld by the band administration, forcing people to work for food vouchers.

In December 2001, Chief Pashe's 67-year-old mother, Elsie, his eldest brother, Steven, two of his sisters, the mother of three of his children, the community's holy man, and 30 community members passed a no-confidence motion and elected Pashe's sister, Marjorie Prince, as interim chief. An indignant Pashe refused all demands for an election, arguing that such practices "are against our history." Corrine Smoke argued that these claims were ludicrous in light of the fact that "the whole band custom concept is phony. It's alien to our culture. Plains Indians like the Dakota were always democratic; we chose leaders based on merit and decisions were made by consensus." With community stability fractured, the Dakota Ojibway Police Service spent Christmas break of 2001 investigating at least six shootings on Christmas and New Year's Eve involving Pashe, his ex-wife, and interim Chief Marjorie Prince's nephew.

In April 2002 the Premier's Office was petitioned to investigate Dakota Tipi for the misuse of gaming revenues. The following month the Indian Affairs Minister invoked Section 74 of the Indian Act to impose third-party management on the Dakota Tipi to resolve the conflict and determine how an estimated $10 million a year generated by a gas bar, a bingo palace, VLTs, and government funding was being spent. In an attempt to resolve the budding conflict, the Manitoba Gaming Control Commission (MGCC) initiated contact with the band's chief and council, community representatives, the band's legal counsel, INAC, and other organizations. Further allegations had nevertheless surfaced in mid-July linking gaming revenue to criminal activity on the reserve. After suspending the band's gaming privileges, the MGCC hired the accounting firm Deloitte & Touche LLP in September to assess the allegations. In October the provincial Finance Minister announced that the Auditor General (AG) would conduct a special audit. First reviewing the governance and accountability framework to determine the structure of First Nations gaming management, the AG sought to recommend ways to improve both First Nations gaming agreements and accountability.

The Auditor General's report, released to the Manitoba legislature on April 30, 2003, concluded that corruption had occurred; specifically, the Dakota Tipi First Nation had mismanaged its books and had possibly broken a number of laws. "As a result of an absence of effective governance," the report read, "there was virtually no accountability over the raising and spending of gaming revenues." The report's author, Jon Singleton, went on to suggest that as part of former Chief Pashe's battle to remain in power, bingo and Video Lottery Terminal (VLT) money had possibly been used for criminal activities. Singleton also indicated that VLT proceeds had been used to pay legal and travel expenses for people who were not band members to appear in a Winnipeg court and to influence a band member to swear a false affidavit against Pashe's enemies. Even though a new council had been elected the previous October in what was the community's first open vote in 24 years, the report recommended that the province maintain its suspension of Dakota Tipi gaming activities until a stable band council was elected.

Toward Defining Aboriginal Self-Government

While the exercise of power may have its source in the inherent right to self-government, the exercise of the power transpires in a fashion that is completely new to the people employing it. The exercise is neither adopted nor traditional, but is an amalgamation of the two perspectives.

—John Borrows (Anishinaabe)[21]

Between 1867 and 1985, few substantial changes were made to the *Indian Act,* meaning that the operational aspects of band councils changed little during this period. Developments in the early 1960s, however, suggested a positive start to the decade for Native people. The Canadian Bill of Rights was introduced in 1960, which made it illegal to discriminate on the basis of race, colour, or creed—clearly, that protected Native interests. That same year, Native people were extended the right to vote along with full citizenship rights. Native people could now vote in federal elections without compromising their status. A Special Joint Parliamentary Committee struck in 1959 to study the *Indian Act* recommended in 1961 that a comprehensive study be conducted to determine the living conditions of Canada's Native people. Two academics, sociologist Harry Hawthorn (UBC) and anthropologist Marc-Adélard Tremblay (Laval), were assigned to head this study and to make recommendations. Their two-volume report (1966 and 1967) focused on living conditions on reserves, and on the federal government's economic, political, and administrative programs.[22]

The Hawthorn–Tremblay Report rejected assimilation as a goal, proposing instead the concept of "Citizens Plus." The goal in this would be to enable Native people to benefit from both Canadian citizenship and the rights guaranteed by status and treaty.[23] The recommendations challenged the Canadian government to respond. In 1968 a new Liberal government led by Pierre Trudeau came to power and rejected the direction charted by the Hawthorn–Tremblay Report. In 1969, Trudeau and his Indian Affairs Minister, Jean Chrétien, tabled a White Paper titled "A Statement of the Government of Canada on Indian Policy." It contended that the legal status of Native people was keeping them from participating in Canadian society; it then suggested that Native people should no longer have a special legal status defined by the *Indian Act.* Among other measures, reserves would be dissolved, treaties would be interpreted narrowly, and federal responsibility for "Indians" would be delegated to the provinces.[24]

Resistance to the White Paper was strong (see Chapter 8). The first written response to it came from the Indian Chiefs of Alberta (ICA), who, in what came to be known as the Red Paper, condemned the government for its lack of vision, using the Hawthorn–Tremblay Report as a basis for rejecting the government's proposed changes. Soon after, the Union of British Columbia Indian Chiefs (UBCIC) issued a report (*A Declaration of Indian Rights;* 1970); as did the Association of Iroquois and Allied Indians (AIAI). The Manitoba Indian Brotherhood (MIB) followed with their own report: *Whabung: Our Tomorrows* (1971). But it was the Hawthorn– Tremblay Report that captured the most attention when it came to the future relationship between First Nations and the Government of Canada and the role that self-determination could play. That relationship came to be referred to as "Aboriginal self-government." Native leaders met with Trudeau to propose a new and more open relationship and to declare the Red Paper the official First Nations response to the government's policy statement. The government responded by formally withdrawing the White Paper in 1971. Also contributing to the discussion was the Council of Yukon Indians (CYI). In 1973 it presented *Together Today For Our Children Tomorrow,* which highlighted the desire of Yukon Native people to regain control of their lands and resources. The CYI emphasized the importance of establishing a land base *before* establishing self-government, and of fostering a formal relationship with the federal government. All the while, self-government models were being developed that would be accountable to Native people and rooted in their own traditions.[25]

In 1977 the Federation of Saskatchewan Indians (FSI) became the first Native organization to articulate the principles of Aboriginal self-government. Its position paper was titled *Indian Government.* Arguably, this was the most important document to emerge during this period, for it captured and conveyed a Native perspective on Aboriginal self-government. Its "fundamental and basic principles" were as follows:

- That Indian nations historically are self-governing.
- That Section 91(24) gives the federal government the authority to regulate relations with Indian nations but not regulate their internal affairs.
- That Indian government powers have been suppressed and eroded by legislative and administrative actions of Canada.
- That Indian government is greater than what is recognized or now exercised and cannot be delegated.
- That treaties reserve a complete set of rights, including the right to be self-governing and to control Indian lands and resources without federal interference.
- That treaties take precedence over provincial and federal laws.
- That the trust relationship imposes fiduciary obligations on the trustee, but the federal government has mismanaged this relationship.
- That Indians have inalienable rights, including the "inherent sovereignty of Indian Nations, the right to self-government, jurisdiction over their lands and citizens and the power to enforce the terms of the Treaties."[26]

The FSI defined sovereignty as absolute, and also as an inherent right that had never been surrendered, for Indigenous governments had always exercised the powers of sovereign nations. According to this line of thought, the most fundamental right of a sovereign nation is its ability to govern its people and territory under its own laws and customs.[27] The same report suggested that self-government was not a right that could be granted by Parliament or by any other branch of government, and that self-government was entrenched in the treaties.

Often forgotten when discussing Aboriginal self-government is the instrumental role that Native people played in (1) promoting a unique self-government ideology rooted in traditional governance frameworks and advocating for formal recognition of those frameworks, and (2) developing self-government models to guide future political operations. For instance, it was Native lobbying efforts that compelled the federal government to initiate the Parliamentary Task Force on Indian Self-Government in 1982 (the Penner Report), which formally acknowledged Aboriginal self-government; that brought about the inclusion of Section 37 of the *Constitution Act,* which mandated First Ministers, Conferences between 1983 and 1987 to define Aboriginal self-government; and that led to the Indian Self-Government Community Negotiations policy statement of 1986. Many Native leaders viewed these and similar events as ways to reverse centuries of oppressive government policies and to improve poor socioeconomic conditions. These high-profile events led politicians and citizens alike to a better understanding of the issues at hand. From the 1970s on, Native leaders and their political organizations were increasingly involved in political lobbying at the federal and (to a lesser extent) provincial and municipal levels.

The Penner Report, 1983

The 1983 Parliamentary Task Force on Indian Self-Government was a turning point in the debate over Aboriginal self-government. Chaired by Keith Penner, the committee in its final report called for Native governance in the form of enhanced municipal-style governments within a federal legislative framework. This report offered three key findings:

- It envisaged Aboriginal government as a "distinct order" of government within Canada with a set of negotiated jurisdictions and fiscal arrangements.
- It recommended that the right of Aboriginal self-government be constitutionally entrenched, along with enabling legislation that recognized Indian governments.
- It defined areas of authority for Aboriginal governments as education, child welfare, heath care, membership, social and cultural development, land and resource use, revenue raising, economic and commercial development, justice and law enforcement, and intergovernmental relations.[28]

The Penner Report accepted and reinforced the FSI's argument that Indigenous nations had always been self-governing. The House of Commons agreed, and proceeded to develop

Nunavut premier-elect Paul Okalik holds a replica of the new Nunavut coin in Iqaluit, NWT, the day before Nunavut becomes a territory on April 1, 1999.

a detailed plan to recognize Aboriginal self-government. Many of the report's recommendations have yet to be addressed. This, however, does not take away from the fact that by the mid-1980s both Aboriginal leaders and the Canadian government were embracing the Aboriginal right to self-government.

In 1985, as the idea of Aboriginal self-government gained traction, the federal government announced a "two-track" model that was intended to result in strengthened self-government powers for First Nations. One track was the entrenchment of Aboriginal self-government in the constitution. The other track would entail either engaging First Nations in community-based discussions or entering into tripartite negotiations with Métis and Non-Status Indians and their provincial governments. The negotiations were to be guided by a cabinet minister designated the Interlocutor for Non-Status Indians and Métis. One year later the federal government announced its Policy on Community-Based Self-Government Negotiations. This policy's goal was to augment band control and local decision-making powers—something previously considered unattainable under the *Indian Act*. Several unique self-government models were later negotiated in conjunction with and independent of land claims (see below).

COMPARING THREE SELF-GOVERNMENT MODELS

Each Aboriginal self-government agreement is unique; generally, however, they all provide a framework for negotiations and for interpreting self-governing powers. Owing to the diversity of Native peoples and broad variations in governing ideologies and socioeconomic and sociopolitical aspirations, the Canadian government does not rely on a single self-governing model. Coates and Morrison's summary of three self-government agreements provides a sense of what is negotiated and the powers associated with Aboriginal self-government.[39]

Nisga'a Government. Implemented in 2000, the Nisga'a treaty immediately attained national notoriety due to the sweeping range of authority granted the newly established Nisga'a Lisims government. Comprising four villages as well as urban locals representing the interests of Nisga'a living outside the Nass Valley, this self-government agreement compels the Nisga'a to function under the authority of the Canadian Constitution and the Charter of Rights and Freedoms. This means that the Nisga'a Lisims government must reconcile its jurisdiction and align its lawmaking authority with equivalent federal and provincial laws. It must also simultaneously provide comparable or improved levels of service in areas newly assumed from other levels of government. Nisga'a traditional authority guides governance within the Canadian legal framework. Like many First Nations, the Nisga'a manage their own membership lists according to internally developed membership guidelines.

cont'd

Previous *Indian Act* authority for management of resources, lands, and other assets has been transferred to the Nisga'a Lisims, along with lawmaking and regulatory authority over language and culture, and specific areas such as marriage, emergency protection, health, transportation, child welfare, and education. Unlike earlier self-government agreements, which were proscribed municipal-type governments, the Nisga'a Treaty embraces a wide range of municipal, regional, provincial, and federal responsibilities. Included here is the authority to operate community-based courts and police services.

Champagne-Aishihik First Nation. After an initial agreement was signed in 1973, 22 years later the Champagne-Aishihik First Nation reached a final agreement with the Government of Canada in 1995. Various accords comprise the Council for Yukon First Nations (CYFN) umbrella agreement that will see Indian Affairs authority gradually dissipate, replaced by local First Nations governments. Like the Nisga'a, the Champagne-Aishihik is responsible for a range of services and establishes laws and local policies to regulate community affairs, including managing settlement lands, resources, and local commercial and related operations.

Though the Champagne-Aishihik First Nation has considerable authority on paper, its small population (1,200 people) in relation to the responsibilities that come with assuming authority over a large territory (41,000 square kilometers) pose a significant challenge. This suggests why that First Nation has chosen to cautiously implement its powers of self-government. As Coates and Morrison conclude, whereas "the Nisga'a First Nation demonstrates the legal capacity and political ability of a First Nation to assume effective control of wide-ranging administrative powers," the Champagne-Aishihik arrangements "illustrate a more normative Canadian approach: a fairly open-ended aspirational agreement, followed by careful and step-wise implementation of actual self-government, focusing on cultural, economic, ecological, and business-related matters." In sum, "Under this arrangement, self-government is a long-term work in progress, adjusting to the needs and capacities of the First Nation and the unique political circumstances of the province or territory."[40]

Gwich'in and Inuvialuit Self-Government Arrangements. Two separate Northwest Territories First Nation communities, the Gwich'in and Inuvialuit, decided to work together, reaching an agreement-in-principle (AIP) in 1993 on a regional-government model for the Beaufort Sea–Mackenzie Delta region. Unlike past self-government agreements, most often representing one culture group or community, the Gwich'in and the Inuvialuit dovetailed their political interests into a common agreement with the Government of Canada. The Gwich'in and the Inuvialuit public governments were to take over the mantle of municipal councils; to that end, they negotiated control and management powers similar to those of Champagne-Aishihik and the Nisga'a. And similar to Nunavut, where the Inuit are the majority of the population, the politically dominant Gwich'in and Inuvialuit were forced to make allowance for non-Native regional-minority interests and group-specific issues and responsibilities. Owing to differing political and cultural priorities, combining the two approaches proved difficult. In 2006 negotiations to regional self-government collapsed as the Gwich'in and Inuvialuit chose separate negotiations leading to separate agreements. According to Coates and Morrison, the Gwich'in–Inuvialuit circumstances "illustrate two critical themes in the development of Aboriginal self-government in Canada. First, that experimentation and flexibility remain highly prized and all parties, including federal, provincial/territorial, and Aboriginal governments, are willing to consider a wide variety of models and processes. Second, Aboriginal self-government can be extremely complicated and time-consuming, particularly in areas with overlapping claims and intertwined populations."[41]

Cree-Naskapi Act

Passed in 1984, the *Cree-Naskapi Act* developed out of the self-government provision negotiated as part of the James Bay and Northern Quebec Agreement (JBNQA; 1975) and the North-Eastern Québec Agreement (NEQA; 1978). Described as the first Aboriginal self-government legislation in Canada, the *Cree-Naskapi Act* replaced the *Indian Act.* It is a constitutionally protected treaty. Under the JBNQA, the Cree and the Inuit have withdrawn their land claims in northern Quebec in return for $225 million, special dispensation for Aboriginal hunting and fishing rights over 45,000 square miles of land, and greater prospects for self-government. The NEQA follows a similar format: the Naskapi of Quebec received $9 million and land rights similar to those outlined in the JBNQA. In return, the Cree have surrendered all of their claims, rights, titles, and interest in the land. *The Cree-Naskapi Act* applies to eight Cree bands and the Naskapi Band. It replaces the *Indian Act* while establishing new legal and political regimes in the form of local governments accountable to the Cree and Naskapi people. The Cree and Naskapi are recognized as having differing title and interests, descending degrees of access to and control over resources, and varied powers of self-government. These powers include but are not limited to the administration of band affairs, internal management, public order, and taxation for local purposes. Also, they are responsible for local services, including fire protection.[29]

Sechelt Indian Band Self-Government Act

The next stage in the evolution of Aboriginal self-government occurred in May 1986 with the passing of the Sechelt *Indian Band Self-Government Act* after 15 years of negotiations. This legislation enables the Sechelt Indian Band, located 50 kilometres north of Vancouver, to exercise delegated powers of governance related to contracts and agreements; to sell and dispose of property; and to spend, invest, and borrow money. Now acknowledged as a municipality under provincial legislation, the community has the power to pass laws related to education, social welfare, and health services; to govern access to reserve lands; and to manage and administer reserve lands. The band also has the authority to determine band membership and residence on Sechelt lands. In addition, the community leaders can now negotiate funding agreements, which the band council then administers.[30]

Yukon First Nations Self-Government Act

In May 1993 the Council for Yukon First Nations (CYFN), the Government of Yukon, and the federal government signed an Umbrella Final Agreement (UFA) that established the basis for negotiating land-claim settlements and self-government agreements with the 14 Yukon First Nations. The First Nations acquired land, cash compensation, wildlife harvesting rights, and land and resource comanagement, as well as culture and heritage protection. Four First Nations signed individual land-claim and self-government agreements in 1993 (Vunut Gwitchin, Nacho Nyak Dun, Champagne and Aishihik, and Teslin Tlingit). All four came into effect in 1995. These were followed in July 1997 by land-claim and self-government agreements for the Selkirk First Nation and the Little Salmon/Carmacks First Nation, which came into effect that October. Finally, in July 1998 the Tr'ondëk Hwëch'in First Nation signed land-claim and self-government agreements. Under the *Yukon First Nations Self-Government Act,* the *Indian Act* no longer applies. The First Nations have gained internal community management and law-making authority on settlement lands as it relates to land use, hunting, trapping, and fishing, the licensing and regulation of businesses, and settlement taxation regimes. The First Nations also have the authority to pass laws to ensure the protection of language and culture as well as to control health care, social and welfare services, and education.[31]

Nunavut

See Chapter 6 for a thorough discussion of the founding of Nunavut.[32]

Nisga'a Treaty

In 1996 the Nisga'a Tribal Council and the Canadian and B.C. governments signed an agreement-in-principle to negotiate the province's first modern treaty. On August 4, 1998, these representatives met to initial the Nisga'a Final Agreement, the purpose of which was to resolve the Nisga'a Nation's land claim in the Nass Valley. The final agreement was ratified in 1999; in 2000 the Nisga'a Treaty became law. That same year the B.C. Supreme Court ruled that the Nisga'a Treaty and its enacting legislation were constitutionally valid and that self-government is a constitutionally protected Aboriginal right. The final agreement acknowledges a central government (the Nisga'a Lisims Government) and four village governments. The Nisga'a Nation has lawmaking authority in a variety of matters, including some that are integral to Nisga'a culture, such as language and traditional laws. It also now has lawmaking authority in matters that are internal to the Nisga'a people, such as membership in the Nisga'a Nation; marriage; education; social services; health services; child and family services; the management of Nisga'a lands (including the development and management of a Nisga'a land title system); access to Nisga'a lands and highways; the use, management, planning, zoning, and development of Nisga'a lands; and management of resources on Nisga'a lands, including forests, fisheries, and wildlife.

More recently, the Lheidli T'enneh and federal and provincial negotiators have signed an agreement in principle for a provincial–First Nations treaty. The Lheidli T'enneh Band has 312 members. It entered treaty negotiations in 1993 and was the first to conclude an agreement-in-principal under the B.C. treaty process, in July 2003.[33]

Community-Based Self-Government and the Inherent Rights Policy

[Inherent] does not connote a desire to separate from the Canadian state. Inherent connotes the notion of human right[s] that can be recognized but not granted, rights that may be unlawfully violated but that can never be extinguished.

—Rosemarie Kuptana, Inuit Tapirisat[34]

Complementing the ongoing First Ministers' Constitutional Conferences designed to determine the pith and substance of Aboriginal self-government, the federal government's Community-Based Self-Government (CBSG) policy was meant to provide practical examples of self-government, demonstrating its potential and thereby informing discussions seeking a constitutional definition. Under the CBSG, communities could negotiate self-government agreements to replace outdated *Indian Act* provisions and thereby secure jurisdiction and authority over a range of matters; this would create a new relationship between the Crown and Native peoples. The negotiated agreements would then be implemented through federal legislation.

More than $50 million was spent before the CBSG policy was cancelled in 1993, by which time 44 *Indian Act* bands had been involved at 14 negotiation tables, with one of them on the verge of proceeding to the legislative-draft stage. An additional 29 groups (tribal councils, associations, etc.) were involved in six CBSG negotiations as part of their comprehensive land claims, with four others proceeding to the legislative-draft stage. The policy failed for several reasons, not the least of which was Native leaders' loud conviction that under the CBSG, self-governing authority would be delegated instead of being predicated on inherent rights. Furthermore, the CBSG would have shifted federal responsibilities onto First Nations without any provisions for money to pay for them.

Native leaders continued to pressure Ottawa to recognize the inherent right of self-government. During these years, several events raised the public's awareness of Native issues, setting in motion further events that to this day strongly affect self-government negotiations. The most notable was the 79-day standoff at Oka in 1990 (see Chapter 7), which led in 1991 to the Royal Commission on Aboriginal Peoples (RCAP). As part of its mandate, the commission was to document the history of the Indigenous–Crown relationship. Its report included recommendations for alleviating social problems on reserves and for solving political problems at the provincial and federal levels. From this emerged the nationhood concept, which Native leaders endorsed as they sought formal recognition of the inherent right of self-government.

By the early 1990s, Prime Minister Brian Mulroney's government was more inclined to negotiate land-claims settlements than to negotiate self-government or accept alternative processes. Ottawa's sluggish response, and Canadians' general misgivings about the concept, were cited as key reasons for the slow emergence of Aboriginal self-government. Then, in 1995, the new Liberal government of Jean Chrétien kept a recent election promise by announcing an Inherent Rights Policy (IRP). That policy recognized that in matters "internal to their communities, integral to their unique cultures, identities, traditions, languages and institutions and with respect to their special relationship to their land and their resources," the right to self-government was inherent and contained in Section 35 of the *Constitution Act*.[35]

The Liberal government envisioned self-government negotiations moving forward based on certain key principles:

- The federal government accepts that the Aboriginal peoples have the right to govern themselves, decide on matters that affect their communities, and exercise the responsibility that is required to achieve true self-government.
- The federal government recognizes the inherent right to self-government as an existing Aboriginal right under subsection 35(1) of the *Constitution Act, 1982*.
- The federal government recognizes that all Aboriginal governments will not all be the same—they will naturally possess varying degrees of authority in areas of federal and provincial jurisdiction reflecting the presence of separate negotiations and the impact of differing local circumstances and community objectives.
- The costs of Aboriginal self-government should be shared among federal, provincial, territorial, and Aboriginal governments and institutions.[36]

Arron Turkey, 6, of the Six Nations Reserve takes part in a protest along with elder Gordon Lee of Ermineskin, Alberta, on Parliament Hill to protest the tabling of the Liberal government's *First Nations Governance Act.*

Both the federal government and Native peoples have since taken the position that the inherent right to self-government is an existing Aboriginal right. But federal officials contend that the right has to be conferred on (delegated to) a band before it is legally recognized.

Despite the federally acknowledged inherent right to Aboriginal self-government, federal officials continue to develop policies and draft laws that affect Native peoples without consulting Native leaders, thus undermining the spirit of the nation-to-nation relationship. In April 2001, for example, Indian Affairs Minister Robert Nault told a Kainai High School audience on the Blood Reserve in Alberta that he would be bringing before Parliament the *First Nations Governance Act (FNGA)*. This generated significant opposition from the Assembly of First Nations (AFN) as well as other Aboriginal organizations across Canada. In B.C., Chief Arthur Manuel of the Interior Alliance described the legislative package as a "gross violation of Indigenous peoples' inherent right to self-determination"; he added that it would accelerate the extinguishment of Aboriginal title and rights.[37] First Nations resisted the package, which included provisions that would have enabled them to establish leadership selection codes as well as modern standards for financial accountability. Other provisions would have enabled bands to tailor their governance structures to suit their needs. Still others would have clarified the legal capacity of bands to make laws and improved their capacity to enforce those laws.

Notably absent from the proposed legislation was any clarification of status and band membership. Nor did the proposed act address Aboriginal women's concerns related to land. Nor was there any mention of program or service delivery. Nor was there any broad review of the *Indian Act*. It seems that the government's perception of Aboriginal self-government was not tied to land or the inherent right to self-government; instead it reflected a more rigid conceptualization of Aboriginal self-government as a legislative byproduct. These proposed changes to the *Indian Act* were withdrawn in 2003.

INAC is currently sitting at 72 national self-government negotiating tables, at which are represented about 445 Aboriginal communities (427 First Nations, 18 Inuit communities, and some Métis locals).[38] A handful of final self-government agreements have been reached. For example, 11 Yukon First Nations have finalized a self-government agreement with Canada. To date, the Nisga'a Nation Treaty of 1999, the Tlicho Agreement of 2003, and the Labrador Inuit Agreement of 2005 are the only comprehensive claims agreements that contain detailed clauses

---

FINAL SELF-GOVERNMENT AGREEMENTS

2005. The Carcross/Tagish First Nation Self-Government Agreement

2005. The Kwanlin Dun First Nation Self-Government Agreement

2004. Anishinaabe Government Agreement

2003. Westbank First Nation—Self-Government Agreement

2003. Kluane First Nation—Self-Government Agreement

2003. Tlicho Agreement (signed August 25, 2003)

2002. Ta'an Kwach'an Council Self-Government Agreement

1999. Nisga'a Final Agreement

1998. Tr'ondek Hwech'in Self-Government Agreement

1997. Little Salmon/Carmacks Self-Government Agreement

1997. Selkirk First Nation Self-Government Agreement

1993. Vuntut Gwitchin First Nation Self-Government Agreement (effective 1995)

1993. Champagne and Aishihik First Nations Self-Government Agreement (effective 1995)

1993. Teslin Tlingit Council Self-Government Agreement (effective 1995)

1993. Nacho Nyak Dun First Nation Self-Government Agreement (effective 1995)

AGREEMENTS-IN-PRINCIPLE THAT HAVE BEEN MADE TO DATE

2005. Yekooche First Nation Agreement-in-Principle

2003. Déline Self-Government Agreement-in-Principle for the Sahtu Dene/Métis of Déline

2003. Blood Tribe Governance and Child Welfare Agreement-in-Principle

2003. Sliammon Agreement-in-Principle

2003. Maa-Nulth First Nations Treaty Negotiations—Agreement-in-Principle

2003. Draft Tsawwassen First Nation Agreement-in-Principle

2003. Tsawwassen First Nation Agreement-in-Principle

2003. Lheidli T'enneh Agreement-in-Principle

2003. Sliammon Treaty Negotiations Draft Agreement-in-Principle

2003. Gwich'in and Inuvialuit Self-Government Agreement-in-Principle for the Beaufort-Delta Region

2001. Meadow Lake First Nations Comprehensive Agreement-in-Principle

2001. Meadow Lake First Nations Tripartite Agreement-in-Principle

2001. Sioux Valley Dakota Nation Comprehensive Agreement-in-Principle

2001. Sioux Valley Dakota Nation Tripartite Agreement-in-Principle

2000. Dogrib Agreement-in-Principle

1998. Anishinaabe Government Agreement-in-Principle

about self-government. In 2003 the Westbank First Nation Self-Government Agreement confirmed that First Nation's right to govern its language, land management, culture, and resources; it also extended the 8,000 non-Westbank members living on reserve land the right to deal with the Westbank government regarding issues affecting them. The Anishnaabe Government Agreement of December 2004 was the first self-government agreement concluded in Ontario. It took 20 years to finalize. It acknowledges the Chippewa Nation of Beausoleil, the Mississauga Nations of Curve Lake and Hiawatha, and the Pottawatomi Nation of Moose Deer Point as a government. Though the agreement would have replaced most of the *Indian Act* for the four affected First Nations, the communities have since rejected it.

Conclusion

It is my conviction that if, in working out a settlement of Native claims, we try and force Native social and economic development into moulds that we have cast, the whole process will be a failure.

—The Honourable Thomas Berger[42]

Until the 1960s, Aboriginal self-government as a concept barely existed in the minds of Canadian politicians. For the most part, Aboriginal people and the issues dominating their lives were all but invisible. The Hawthorn–Tremblay Report (1963–66) brought to the public's attention how poor socioeconomic conditions were in Aboriginal communities nationally; the Trudeau White Paper (1969) spurred Native leaders into action. Following the White Paper, Native leaders throughout Canada took it upon themselves to lead their organizations into developing position papers calling for increased decision-making powers at the reserve and community levels. What followed was an examination of various federal policies by the ICA and the MIB. Then, in the 1970s, Native groups began laying what would become the political and philosophical foundations of self-government. The *Constitution Act* of 1982 recognized Aboriginal rights, and this led to the claim that those rights included the right to self-government. It also led to four constitutionally mandated First Ministers' Conferences to discuss the issue of Aboriginal self-government and how to bring it about. Little came from this dialogue, unfortunately. The 1990s was a time of negotiations and academic involvement in further refining the Aboriginal self-government ideology. Several major themes have emerged from the self-government debate of the past three decades:

1. The idea of self-government has broadened considerably over the past three decades. It has grown from an initial conception as local, municipal-style government rooted in the *Indian Act* to a conception as a constitutionally protected inherent right that has found its most recent expression in the idea of "Aboriginal national government" as a distinct order of government within the Canadian federation.

2. The scope of people affected by the discussions has grown considerably. The initial focus of self-government was on Status Indians residing on reserves. This has now broadened to include Métis, Inuit, and urban Native peoples.

3. The basis of self-government has fundamentally changed. We no longer conceive of Aboriginal self-government as rooted in the *Indian Act;* instead, we see it as an inherent right that is rooted in history and treaties.

4. The scope of authority and jurisdiction for self-government has also enlarged considerably. Aboriginal governments are now seen as more than municipalities; they also encompass federal, provincial, and municipal authority as well as some unique Aboriginal authorities.

5. The debate over self-government has changed greatly. It is now about *how* rather than *why*. There are now multiple sites for the debate: among lawyers, Aboriginal leaders, and academics, the literature focuses on broad issues yet still has an element of *why*, while among Native community leaders and politicians and consultants, it is about *how* to govern on a daily basis.[43]

The sheer determination of the leaders of Indigenous nations in Canada to consistently, continually, and clearly advance their self-government agenda is striking. From the historical reality that Indigenous nations were self-governing to the modern fight for recognition of this inherent right, Aboriginal self-government has taken on many different looks. That First Nations have moved the federal government from a policy of termination to a policy of affirmation of the inherent right of self-government has been a remarkable achievement. It has been the work of a "forceful and articulate Indian leadership," to use the words of the 1969 White Paper.

FURTHER READING

Alfred, Gerald R. *Heeding the Voices of our Ancestors: Kahnawake Mohawk Politics and the Rise of Native Nationalism*. Toronto: Oxford University Press, 1995.

Belanger, Yale D., ed. *Aboriginal Self-Government in Canada: Current Trends and Issues*, 3rd ed. Saskatoon: Purich, 2008.

Boldt, Menno. *Surviving as Indians: The Challenge of Self-Government*. Toronto: University of Toronto Press, 1993.

Borrows, John. "A Genealogy of Law: Inherent Sovereignty and First Nations Self-Government." *Osgoode Hall Law Journal* 30, no. 2 (1992): 291–353.

Cassidy, Frank, and Robert L. Bish. *Indian Government: Its Meaning and Practice*. Lantzville: Oolichan, 1989.

Henderson, Ailsa. *Nunavut: Rethinking Political Culture*. Vancouver: UBC Press, 2007.

Kulchyski, Peter. *Like the Sound of a Drum: Aboriginal Cultural Politics in Denedeh and Nunavut*. Manitoba: University of Manitoba Press, 2005.

Long, J. Anthony, Leroy Little Bear, and Menno Boldt. "Indian Government and the Constitution." In *Pathways to Self-Determination: Canadian Indians and the Canadian State*, ed. Leroy Little Bear, Menno Boldt, and J. Anthony Long. Toronto: University of Toronto Press, 1984, pp. 169–80.

Russell, Dan. *A People's Dream: Aboriginal Self-Government in Canada*. Vancouver: UBC Press, 2000.

Slowey, Gabrielle. *Navigating Neoliberalism: Self-Determination and the Mikisew Cree First Nation*. Vancouver: UBC Press, 2008.

Warry, Wayne. *Unfinished Dreams: Community Healing and the Reality of Aboriginal Self-Government*. Toronto: University of Toronto Press, 1998.

NOTES

1. Manitoba Indian Brotherhood, *Whabung: Our Tomorrows* (Winnipeg: 1972).

2. Jill Wherret, *Aboriginal Self-Government* (Ottawa: Library of Parliament, 1999).

3. Del Riley, "What Canada's Indians Want and the Difficulties of Getting It," in *Pathways to Self-Determination: Canadian Indians and the Canadian State*, ed. Leroy Little Bear, Menno Boldt, and J. Anthony Long (Toronto: University of Toronto Press, 1984), p. 163.

4. Russel Lawrence Barsh, "The Nature and Spirit of North American Political Systems," *American Indian Quarterly* (Spring 1986): 181–98; and Menno Boldt and J. Anthony Long, "Tribal Traditions and European–Western Political Ideologies: The Dilemma of Canada's Native Indians," in *The Quest for Justice: Aboriginal Peoples and Aboriginal Rights*, ed. Menno Boldt and J. Anthony Long (Toronto: University of Toronto Press, 1985), pp. 333–46.

5. See John Borrows, "Wampum at Niagara: The Royal Proclamation, Canadian Legal History, and Self-Government," in *Aboriginal and Treaty Rights in Canada: Essays on Law, Equality, and Respect for Difference*, ed. Michael Asch (Vancouver: UBC Press, 1997), pp. 155–72; and

Richard White, *The Middle Ground: Indians, Empires, in the Great Lakes Region, 1650–1815* (Cambridge: Cambridge University Press, 1991).

6. Yale D. Belanger, "Seeking a Seat at the Table: A Brief History of Indian Political Organizing in Canada, 1870–1951" (Ph.D. diss., Trent University, 2006).

7. Vine Deloria, Jr., *God Is Red: A Native View of Religion* (Golden: Fulcrum, 1994), p. 65.

8. See *For Seven Generations: An Information Legacy of the Royal Commission on Aboriginal Peoples,* CD-ROM (Ottawa: Canada Communications Group, 1996).

9. Ibid.

10. Francis Jennings, *The Invasion of America: Indians, Colonialism, and the Cant of Conquest* (New York: Norton, 1975).

11. Richard Bartlett, *Indian Reserves and Aboriginal Lands in Canada: A Homeland* (Saskatoon: University of Saskatchewan, Native Law Centre, 1990).

12. Ibid., p. 9.

13. John Borrows, *Recovering Canada: The Resurgence of Indigenous Law* (Toronto: University of Toronto Press, 2002), p. 125.

14. Yale D. Belanger, David R. Newhouse, and Heather Shpuniarsky, "The Evolution of Native Reserves," in *Handbook of North American Indians: Indians in Contemporary Society,* Vol. 2, ed. Garrick A. Bailey (Washington: Smithsonian Institution, 2008), pp. 197–207.

15. John Leslie and Ron Maguire, *The Historical Development of the Indian Act* (Ottawa: Treaties and Historical Research Centre, DIAND, 1978), p. 54; and Martina L. Hardwick, "Segregating and Reforming the Marginal: The Institution and Everyday Resistance in Mid-Nineteenth-Century Ontario" (Ph.D. diss., Queen's University, 1998).

16. John Leslie, *Commissions of Inquiry into Indian Affairs in the Canadas, 1828–1858: Evolving a Corporate Memory for the Indian Department* (Ottawa: Treaties and Historical Research Centre, DIAND, 1985).

17. See John S. Milloy, "The Early *Indian Acts:* Developmental Strategy and Constitutional Change," in *As Long as the Sun Shines and Water Flows: A Reader in Canadian Native Studies,* ed. Antoine S. Lussier and Ian L. Getty (Vancouver: UBC Press, 1983), pp. 56–64; and John Tobias, "Protection, Civilization, Assimilation: An Outline History of Canada's Indian Policy," in *As Long as the Sun Shines and Water Flows: A Reader in Canadian Native Studies,* ed. Antoine S. Lussier and Ian L. Getty (Vancouver: UBC Press, 1983), pp. 39–55.

18. See *Governance and Administration.* [online] http://www.musqueam.bc.ca/Governance.html. Last accessed September 9, 2008.

19. This section is derived from Yale D. Belanger, *Gambling with the Future: The History of Aboriginal Gaming in Canada* (Saskatoon: Purich, 2006), specifically pp. 143–46.

20. In Don Sandberg, Rebecca Walberg, and Joseph Quesnel, *Aboriginal Governance Index: A 2007 Ranking of Manitoba and Saskatchewan First Nations* (Winnipeg: Frontier Policy for Public Policy, 2007), pp. 5–6.

21. John Borrows, "A Genealogy of Law: Inherent Sovereignty and First Nations Self-Government," *Osgoode Hall Law Journal* 30, no. 2 (1992): 291–353.

22. Harry Hawthorn and Marc-Adélard Tremblay, *A Survey of the Contemporary Indians of Canada,* Vols. 1 and 2 (Ottawa: Indian Affairs Branch, 1966–67).

23. See Alan Cairns, *Citizens Plus: Aboriginal Peoples and the Canadian State* (Vancouver: UBC Press, 2000).

24. Sally Weaver, *Making Canadian Indian Policy: The Hidden Agenda, 1968–79* (Toronto: University of Toronto Press, 1981).

25. Council for Yukon Indians, *Together Today for Our Children Tomorrow: A Statement of Grievances and an Approach to Settlement by the Yukon Indian People,* Whitehorse, 1973.

26. Federation of Saskatchewan Indians, *Indian Government* (Saskatoon: 1977).

27. See also Federation of Saskatchewan Indians, *Indian Treaty Rights: The Spirit and Intent of Treaty* (Saskatoon: 1979).

28. Canada, *Special Committee on Indian Self-Government* (Task Force) (Ottawa: Queen's Printer, 1983); see also Bradford Morse, "Regaining Recognition of the Inherent Right to Aboriginal Governance," in *Aboriginal Self-Government in Canada: Current Trends and Issues,* 3rd ed., ed. Yale D. Belanger (Saskatoon: Purich, 2008).

29. *Cree-Naskapi (of Quebec) Act,* S.C. 1984; also Morse, "Regaining Recognition"; and Yale D. Belanger, *"Cree-Naskapi Act,"* in *Encyclopedia of American Indian History,* Vol. 2, eds. Bruce E. Johansen and Barry M. Pritzker (Santa Barbara, CA.: ABC-CLIO, 2008), pp. 519–520.

30. *Sechelt Indian Band Self-Government Act,* S.C. 1986, c. 27; see also Morse, "Regaining Recognition."

31. *Yukon First Nations Land Claim Settlement Act,* S.C. 1994, c. 34; *Yukon First Nations Self-Government Act,* S.C. 1994, c. 35; see also Morse, "Regaining Recognition."

32. See Ailsa Henderson, *Nunavut: Rethinking Political Culture* (Vancouver: UBC Press, 2007).

33. See, generally, Tom Molloy, *The World Is Our Witness: The Historic Journey of the Nisga'a into Canada* (Calgary: Fifth House, 2000).

34. Quoted in Canada, *Report of the Special Joint Committee on a Renewed Canada* (Ottawa: Minister of Supply and Services, 1992).

35. Canada, *Gathering Strength: Canada's Aboriginal Action Plan* (Ottawa: Queen's Printer, 1998).

36. Ibid.

37. Quoted in Yale D. Belanger and David R. Newhouse, "Emerging from the Shadows: The Pursuit of Aboriginal Self-Government to Promote Aboriginal Well-Being," *Canadian Journal of Native Studies* 24, no. 1 (2004): 129–222.

38. Morse, "Regaining Recognition," p. 57.

39. Ken S. Coates and W.R. Morrison, "From Panacea to Reality: The Practicalities of Canadian Aboriginal Self-Government Agreements," in *Aboriginal Self-Government in Canada: Current Trends and Issues,* 3rd ed., ed. Yale D. Belanger (Saskatoon: Purich, 2008), pp. 109–14.

40. Ibid., p. 112.

41. Ibid., p. 113.

42. Thomas Berger, "Native Rights and Self-Determination," *Canadian Journal of Native Studies* 3, no. 2 (1983): 374.

43. Belanger and Newhouse, "Emerging from the Shadows"; Yale D. Belanger and David R. Newhouse, "Reconciling Solitudes: A Critical Analysis of the Self-Government Ideal," in *Aboriginal Self-Government in Canada: Current Trends and Issues,* 3rd ed., ed. Yale D. Belanger (Saskatoon: Purich, 2008), pp. 1–19.

Economic Development

11

The transition from paternalism to community self-sufficiency may be long and will require significant support from the state, however, we would emphasize that state support should not be such that the government continues to do for us that which we want to do for ourselves.

—Indian Tribes of Manitoba (Manitoba Indian Brotherhood)[1]

Economic development can help improve the well-being of Native communities in Canada. Native leaders realize that economic self-sufficiency is key to successful self-government. Recent attempts to improve economic conditions for both reserve and urban Native people through federal and provincial programs have succeeded in many ways. Yet federal transfer payments and social assistance are still the mains sources of funding for reserves, for everything from schools and social services to business start-ups. In an effort to become economically self-sufficient, Native communities in Canada are seeking greater control over local resources as well as the means to expand comprehensive training and economic-development strategies.

The authors of the Report of the Royal Commission on Aboriginal Peoples (RCAP) in 1996 acknowledged that economic stability is important to Native communities. They expressly warned that in order to promote Aboriginal self-governance, drastic measures were required to rebuild Native economies that had been severely disrupted by federal policies that had done little more than promote a subsistence lifestyle. Without immediate changes, little opportunity existed for progress. Doing their part, many Native people have over the past four decades become entrepreneurs; meanwhile, Native political organizations and bands continue to battle for greater control over economic activities. Native entrepreneurs are entering sectors such as fine arts, business services, retail, trade, manufacturing, natural resources, consulting, and tourism. Federal and provincial officials lament that underdeveloped economies still exist. Why does the situation remain so dire, considering the amount of federal capital available to Native peoples and the growing numbers of Native business owners? This chapter tries to answer that question.

A Historical Overview of Shifting Economies

History reveals that the economies of Aboriginal nations were not always underdeveloped. Many carried on in largely traditional ways well past the time of first contact and trade with Europeans, while others adapted and flourished. Factors largely outside the reach of human intervention, such as periods of drought, played a role. But the principal factor that brought Aboriginal communities to the point of impoverishment over the centuries was the intervention—deliberate or unintended, well-intentioned or self-interested—of non-Aboriginal society.

—Royal Commission on Aboriginal Peoples[2]

With more than 60 distinct nations and more than 1,000 communities, the Native peoples of Canada constitute a unique mix of cultures, languages, histories, organizations, and values. These factors and others—including geography, climate, and available resources—have always influenced how a given community approaches economic development. Traditional economies made localized decisions that reflected ecologically contextual customs and traditions; these in turn encouraged economic, political, and cultural ties with neighbouring communities (see Chapter 2). Each community developed a dynamic and varied economic system from its ecological context. Common features of these systems included links to traditional lands and animals, spirituality, and collectively owned assets. All too often, Europeans have characterized these systems as hunter-gatherer groups who underutilized their labour, ignored available technologies, and misunderstood the value of local natural resources, all the while employing manufactured goods for utilitarian purposes rather than to generate profits. Somewhat paradoxically, some writers contend that these societies had once prospered as a result of abundant natural resources that required little labour to produce the goods people needed.

Contact and Cooperation

As early as the mid-ninth century, Norse explorers reached Iceland, settling nearby and trading with local Indigenous peoples. Within five decades the Norse had settled on the coast of Newfoundland. Local Inuit populations took exception to this invasion of their lands, and an extended period of hostilities followed. Eventually the two sides established an uneasy trade relationship, a tenuous peace that lasted for about one century before the Norse abandoned their settlement.[3] By 1497, eastern Indigenous peoples once again were in contact with Europeans, this time with John Cabot, who had been commissioned by the British Crown to find the Northwest Passage. Over the next two years Cabot and his sons

By the 1880s, buffalo jumps such as the one depicted by artist Alfred J. Miller (1837) had been utilized by Plains peoples for hundreds of years, supplying them with their food and material-cultural needs.

explored the coasts of Newfoundland and northern Nova Scotia, reporting back to their benefactors that they had found large stocks of cod.[4]

News of this find led to the gradual arrival of European fishers, who competed for resources along the East Coast. By the early 1600s this competition had expanded onto the land. At first there was little trade between the Europeans and the Native people, though the historical record (oral and written) describes generally peaceful relations, which were sometimes disrupted by trade wars. The main point: the Europeans introduced Indigenous communities to new economic ideas based on resource consumption and population growth. This process would accelerate when the fur trade began in the early seventeenth century.[5]

Many Indigenous communities began trading with the newcomers, which led to strong economic and political ties. At first, the fur trade was rooted in mutual desires: the Europeans wanted animal pelts, and the Native people wanted new technologies and European products. This fostered economic relationships and regional political stability, which made everyone's lives easier.[6] Over time, Indigenous economies became linked more and more strongly with the expanding settler economies. Eventually, the two economic ideologies fused into a distinctively Canadian economy that embraced Indigenous *and* European beliefs and processes. Indigenous ways of knowing had merged with European economic systems. In part, this was because the settlers realized that militarily and economically, the Native peoples held the stronger hand. By then it was clear that Native people were shrewd traders. Indeed, Europeans came to rely on them as trade agents.[7]

Strong relationships were highly valued. Regional balance depended on integrating non-Native traders with neighbouring Indigenous peoples to form local kinship networks. The goal in this was multifaceted. Expanding local kinship networks to neighbouring regions was an attempt to establish new trade monopolies and thereby ensure peaceful relations. It also provided many communities with the leverage they needed to control the quality of the materials being exchanged. French entrepreneurs, for instance, accepted Indigenous people as economic equals in their efforts to grow the burgeoning fur trade. Though these links began as commercial ones, a matrix of relationships soon developed, which led to discussions of military and political issues.[8]

Then in May 1670, by Royal Charter, the British Crown bestowed on the Hudson's Bay Company (HBC) the exclusive right to govern and extract resources from Rupert's Land. A mercantilist economy slowly developed based on the export of raw materials such as beaver pelts. This led to entire regions being overhunted. Hunters and traders, both

European and Native, inevitably drifted west in search of regions that had not been trapped out. This led to the slow but steady absorption of Indigenous economies as more and more local men took up employment with the HBC. One result was that Native people had less time to maintain their traditional economies. More and more, they found themselves forced to embrace the economic strategies employed by neighbouring groups (Indigenous and non-Native). This generated conflict in Indigenous communities as men and women were increasingly drawn away from their historic pursuits, thus losing their self-reliance.

Displacement and Assimilation

As a result of resource exploitation, Indigenous people gradually lost control over their land and, it follows, their economy. Specialized economies also eroded. By the late seventeenth century the fur trade was both helping and hurting the Native peoples of eastern and central Canada. That trade's impact was not entirely predictable, for Indigenous economies varied. For instance, where the fur-trade economy proved fragile, Indigenous leaders proved adaptable; in other words, the fur trade could continue to expand without compromising local Indigenous economic pursuits. Ironically, it was in the regions where the fur trade's economic influence was initially most beneficial that people found it most difficult to re-engage traditional economic pursuits. After the HBC merged with the North West Company in 1821, for example, many Indigenous men returned home due to a lack of work.[9] Others sought employment as trappers, guides, or carriers of goods and people; or they supplied traders with commodities such as fish, corn, maple sugar, wild rice, canoes, snowshoes, and other necessary items.[10] Some became wage labourers. On the West Coast in the 1880s and 1890s, Native men and women worked in the fishery and in resource-extraction industries such as logging, milling, and canning.[11] On the East Coast, many Mi'kmaq worked as road builders and stevedores, or they cut pit props for the coal mines or produced arts and crafts.[12] On the Plains, the Cree (Nehiyaw) and the member nations of the Blackfoot (Niitsítapi) Confederacy engaged in farming, ranching, and sometimes mining.[13]

The move away from traditional economic practices was the direct result of federal policies as set out in the *Indian Act* (1876), the overarching goal of which was to assimilate Indians into Canadian society. That act contained few provisions related to economic development, and many more whose purpose was to punish Native leaders for refusing to accede to government demands—demands that included access to reserve lands for mineral exploration, rights of way for highways and railways, and the leasing of reserve lands to farmers and ranchers.[14] It was anticipated that Native people would be abandoning their traditional ways and embracing European ones, so policymakers made scant mention of economic development beyond the Indians' limited right to hunt, fish, and trap. Native people were being encouraged to adopt farming and ranching in lieu of traditional pursuits. Their leaders repeatedly pointed out to government officials that the treaties they had signed had promised assistance (food, tools, financial assistance) during this transitional period.

But Canadian officials viewed these promises as little more than temporary measures that would end once the Indians had evolved from hunters and trappers into economically independent individuals.

Yet Canadian policy in many ways worked against the progress for which it called. For instance, Indian Agents were granted strong authority over Native people. Located in or near reserve communities, these officials served as local magistrates and as facilitators for the government's assimilation project. They were empowered to determine rations and distribution cycles, which meant they could withhold food from those who failed to adapt to Canadian ways. Even when Native people succeeded as farmers or ranchers, they needed the Indian Agent's permission to sell their products. Complaints from competing non-Native farmers and ranchers often led to denial of that permission. This made it difficult for Native people to integrate their reserve economies into broader regional and provincial economies; it also perpetuated their dependency on government largesse.

There were some success stories, however. As part of Treaty 7, the Crown provided farming implements and minimal training to aspiring Blackfoot farmers. A flourishing ranching operation took hold, yet between 1896 and 1902 Indian Affairs exerted tremendous pressure on Chief Red Crow to surrender portions of the Blood (Kainai) Reserve. This pressure failed. The Bloods remained economically viable despite federal cutbacks, owing in part to a 1904 grazing-company lease that was worth $5,000 annually. This enabled the tribal council to authorize a $10,000 purchase for, among other implements, a steam-ploughing outfit needed to expand the reserve's farming and ranching operations. By the end of the 1910s this farming and ranching operation was the envy of local non-Native operators, in part because it was located on what "without a doubt [was] the best stock raising land in western Canada."[15] Continued resistance to surrender persisted, and eventually the Indian Agent's frustration manifested itself in increasingly restrictive measures regarding livestock sales and grazing permits. By 1921 the reserve's once flourishing livestock enterprise had collapsed.[16]

By the 1940s most reserve economies were based on either agriculture or treaty-secured trapping and fishing rights; the Indian Affairs Branch (IAB) also offered limited assistance to industrial development on reserves. During the first half of the twentieth century, this lack of economic development was not a particular problem for those fortunate enough to live on reserves with good hunting and fishing and fertile soil.[17] But this was not the norm, and by the mid-1950s, in response to the belief that the traditional Indian hunting economy had been ruined, a long-term federally sponsored Native socioeconomic development program had been established. Its goal was to develop industry in the Canadian North by introducing mining and petroleum exploration; this would help regional populations acquire the skills they needed to participate in the wage economy. Despite these efforts, poverty on reserves persisted into the early 1960s, mainly because the federal government had failed to integrate Native communities into the broader market economy (see box on next page). Another factor was strengthened federal and provincial demands for prairie farmlands and their

IMPORTANCE OF ECONOMIC DEVELOPMENT

Until the 1940s little thought was given to reserve and rural Native economic development. During that decade, an increasingly vocal Native leadership impressed on federal officials the importance of economic development to political, economic, and (most important) social progress in Native communities. Below are several statements drawn from government records detailing the importance of economic development.

The Pas Band (Manitoba): "Our hunting rights should be extended, and trapping grounds more favourable. Indian people complain that too many white men are being put to trap on the muskrat area."

Native Brotherhood of British Columbia: "The need for assistance in the field of agriculture generally is most urgent. Even after centuries of farming life, the white people find it necessary to send their sons and daughters to obtain the most advanced scientific training in farming, fruit growing and gardening. . . . The Indians, who are just beginning this life, need more practical training along these lines."

Waterhen Reserve (Manitoba): "[We] suggest that more farming implements be given us in the future and that a shelter be erected on the Reserve for the protection of same."

Indian Association of Alberta: "[We are] opposed to any further alienation of Indian land for any purpose whatsoever, whether a post-war immigration scheme, land settlement scheme, or any other purpose."

Shoal Lake Reserve (Manitoba): "The horses we have in the reserve are not sufficient power to break land. And it is the wish to ask for a tractor. . . . The Indian Agent sells our production and distributes to us not enough to buy anything to be useful to us."

Chemawawin Reserve (Manitoba): "[If] our licenses are taken away from us when we leave the reserve we will not be able to sell the rats we get from our reserve."[18]

desire to foster natural-resource development.[19] The inferior standard of living faced by Native communities was further aggravated by federal policies encouraging Native people to move from reserves into the cities. Politicians anticipated that after the reserve lands had been abandoned, they could be opened to economic development.

By the early 1960s, poverty on reserves was becoming a national scandal. Native economic development had finally appeared on the public's radar. To counteract this, federal officials launched a community-development program to address issues such as Native poverty, ill health, and social dysfunction. The Department of Indian Affairs followed this up in the 1970s with the Indian Economic Development Fund, which was meant to help reserves develop economic projects. Direct loans, loan guarantees, equity contributions, and advisory services were provided for both individual and community-owned projects.[20] Unfortunately, Native economic development remained a peripheral issue for federal politicians, who still thought that assimilation was inevitable. The impact of that mindset is visible to this day in statistical data showing that Native people lag behind other Canadians in employment and annual earnings. In October 1983, federal officials established the Aboriginal Economic Development Program. Unfortunately, that program was poorly funded, which made it difficult to hire consultants for project planning and therefore impossible to create the projects needed. One academic, writing during this period, described how in one district the DIA's entire economic development budget for 1985–86 amounted to less than $10,000 per band.[21]

Renewal and Negotiation

As could only be expected because of poor federal policy and Indian Agents' shortsightedness, by the 1980s most reserves in Canada were burdened with welfare economies. The combination of easy access to welfare and the displacement of communities from their ecological context proved incredibly damaging. It was during this low point that the Royal Commission on Aboriginal Peoples (RCAP) was established in 1991. Native economies were a key research item. After reviewing 340 reports and consulting with the leaders of more than 100 communities and 140 organizations, RCAP's final report (1996) presented nine important suggestions related to Native economies; seven of these were specific to improving economic conditions for Native people living both on and off reserve:

- Rebuild Aboriginal nations.
- Build institutional capacity.
- Expand lands and resources.
- Build Aboriginal businesses.
- Support traditional economies.
- Overcome barriers to employment.
- Develop new approaches to income support.[22]

At the same time, economic development was presented as more than simply a means of improving socioeconomic conditions on reserves through an infusion of cash. If properly cultivated, the commissioners argued, a combination of financial and social capital could lead to diversified economies, effective institutions of governance, and healthier communities. Native nation building soon emerged as an important concept. Defined as the policy of legitimate self-rule, as exercised by American Indian tribes in the United States, the tenets of nation building inform our general understanding of Aboriginal self-government in Canada. The key characteristics of nation building among American tribes have been presented as these:

The exercise of de facto sovereignty. De facto sovereignty means the power to carry out day-to-day, real-life decisions. Governments now for the most part acknowledge legal sovereignty for Native people, but genuine self-governance requires that the people affected be willing and able to assert their decision-making in practice. The tribes that have accomplished this have been the only ones to break the cycle of dependency and become economically self-standing. As long as outside organizations carry the main responsibility for economic conditions on reserves, "development decisions will reflect the goals of those organizations, not the goals of the tribe." Outsiders do not pay the price of bad decisions, and they have few long-term incentives to improve their decisions. No single case of sustained development has occurred outside a framework of de facto sovereignty.

Strategic direction. This requires a shift from reactive thinking to proactive thinking (not "what can be funded" but rather "what we want to create"). It also requires consideration of what kind of society a First Nations community wants to be 25 years from now, which requires an answer to this question: "How does this option fit our conception of our society?" A broader societal focus is needed to improve a society; stop-gap measures to fix problems will not suffice.

Effective institutions and policies. Through formal constitutions, charters, laws, codes, and procedures, and through informal but established practices and norms, a society establishes relationships among its members and between the society and outsiders; it also distributes rights and powers and sets the rules under which programs, businesses, and even individuals operate. Those who deal with that society, be they members or not, look to those institutions to understand the rules of the game.

Fair and effective dispute-resolution procedures. Governing institutions have to be able to provide consistently fair and nonpoliticized dispute resolution. They have to be able to assure people that their claims and disputes—including disputes with the tribe itself—will be fairly adjudicated.

Separation of politics from business management. On many American reservations and Canadian reserves the government—typically the tribal council or the tribal president/chief—controls tribal businesses. Business decisions are made by the council, administrative and personnel disputes are referred to the council, and the council or president often assumes responsibility for much of the day-to-day running of enterprises. Tribal governments have to be able to separate politics from day-to-day business decisions.

Competent bureaucracy. As Indian nations increasingly take over the management of social programs and natural resources on reservations, as they undertake ambitious development programs, and as their governing tasks become more financially and administratively complex, their bureaucratic capabilities become even more essential to their overall success. Attracting, developing, and retaining skilled personnel; establishing effective civil-service systems that protect employees from politics; putting in place robust personnel grievance systems; establishing regularized bureaucratic practices so that decisions are implemented and recorded effectively and reliably—all of these are crucial to a tribe's ability to govern effectively and thereby to initiate and sustain a successful program of economic development.

Cultural match. Cultural match refers to the match between governing institutions and prevailing ideas in the community about how authority should be organized and exercised. Such prevailing notions are part of the culture of a tribe—indeed, of any cohesive society.[23]

It should be clear from all of this that economic development's importance to effective self-government cannot be ignored. Aboriginal self-government requires independently generated sources of funding. Moreover, federal officials in Ottawa will only acknowledge self-government after a band has achieved a stable reserve economy. The Inherent Rights Policy of 1995 states this clearly:

> All participants in self-government negotiations must recognize that self-government arrangements will have to be affordable and consistent with the overall social and economic policies and priorities of governments, while at the same time taking into account the specific needs of Aboriginal peoples. In this regard, the fiscal and budgetary capacity of the federal, provincial, territorial and Aboriginal governments or institutions will be a primary determinant of the financing of self-government.[24]

Federal officials justify this stance by arguing that reserve-based economic ventures have rarely succeeded and that in many ways those ventures continue to play an insignificant role in terms of securing personal incomes and generating band revenues. As described below, however, this policy demand will be difficult for Native leaders to meet as long as the government continues a myopic approach to defining "proper" economic development in Native communities.

Government Proscribed Economic Development

During this renewal period, government officials remained dedicated to promoting industry and resource extraction on Native lands, often to the detriment of traditional economic endeavours. Many Native leaders opposed a policy-intervention approach, relying instead on Aboriginal and treaty rights to protect traditional economies. Ottawa's present-day Indian policy envisions Native economic development as subject to strict regulation through legislation, Indian policy, and the courts. There are five key components to this.

1. The Aboriginal Workforce Participation Initiative is designed to increase the participation of Aboriginal people in the labour market.
2. The Community Economic Development Program provides core funding to First Nation and Inuit communities or to the organizations they mandate for public services in economic development.
3. The Community Economic Opportunities Program provides opportunity-based funding to First Nation and Inuit communities and organizations, or organizations they mandate, for public services in economic development.
4. The First Nations Forestry Program promotes sustainable forest management, as well as forest-based development opportunities and businesses.
5. The Procurement Strategy for Aboriginal Business encourages opportunities for Aboriginal businesses to do business with the federal government.

In all of this, little thought is given to protecting traditional economies. Instead, local infrastructure projects and partnerships with industry are promoted.[25]

Legislation has had a strong impact on Native economic development (see Figure 11-1). For example, any business established on a reserve is subject to the *Indian Act;* this directly

Figure 11-1 Historic and Modern Treaties and Unsettled Land Claims

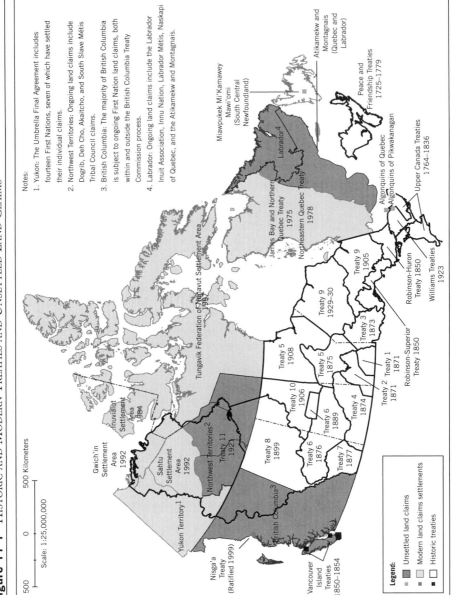

Source: Adapted from Global Forest Watch Canada. "Map 10." *Canada's Forests at a Crossroads.* Washington: World Resources Institute, 2000. Adapted by permission of Global Forest Watch Canada.

influences access to short- and longer-term financing for economic development. According to Section 89 of the act, neither the real nor the personal property of an Indian or a band on a reserve may be used as collateral to secure financing. As a result, private lenders impose higher costs on Native people and reserve residents to offset the risks of loans. Certain incentives do exist, however. Reserves, surrendered lands, and the personal property of an Indian or an Indian band situated on a reserve are not taxable. The courts have also ruled that the income of a Status Indian on reserve is tax exempt; so is investment income, business income, and income from a trust on reserve. There are several reasons for these tax exemptions: they protect reserve lands, they protect Status Indians' use of property on reserve lands, they restrict the government's ability to tax reserve lands, and they prevent creditors from seizing assets of a Status Indian.

An example of legislating Native economic development is found in the Natural Resources Transfer Agreement (NRTA), implemented in Manitoba, Saskatchewan, and Alberta in 1930. The NRTA transferred full administration and control of Crown lands to the provinces while limiting treaty rights to their concise wording (e.g., the right to hunt for food only). Many Native leaders protested the NRTA, contending that the Numbered Treaties secured an obligation of the British Crown to ensure an enriched way of life for the Native beneficiaries and their descendants.[26] Treaty 4, for example, acknowledged the existence of Native economies and Indians' need to "remain self-supporting by hunting, fishing, farming, construction and education [and] to learn something of the cunning of the white man."[27] The commissioners for Treaty 6 informed Native leaders that they were not expected to abandon their "present mode of living"; furthermore, government officials promised to never "interfere with your hunting and fishing . . . through the country as you have heretofore done."[28] Also, governance and economics were viewed as interdependent. With this in mind, Treaty Commissioner Alexander Morris assured the chiefs: "What I have offered does not take away your living, you will have it then [following the treaty] as you have it now, and what I offer now is put on top of it."[29] The NRTA was unilaterally implemented despite all the treaty promises elaborated above.

Several outstanding economic issues require resolution. Take Native forestry as an example. The NRTA protects the continuing right of Indians to hunt, trap, and fish for food in the Prairie provinces, yet it makes no mention of forestry. Indeed, the *Constitution Act* (1938) transferred ownership of forestry resources to the provinces and is viewed as prerogative legislation. This compels Native adherence to provincial guidelines whenever treaty provisions fail to specifically mention forestry. That sector, if properly managed, could be an economic boon to Native people. Currently, 240 of the 2,300 First Nations reserves in Canada have more than 1,000 hectares of forest; all First Nations in total boast more than 1.4 million hectares.[30] Yet there is no national policy framework describing where Aboriginal and treaty rights fit into provincial land-use schemes, which employ tenure systems geared toward industrial forestry.[31] This, along with the lack of community capacity and capital, and along with exploitable forestry reserves that are too small to provide a self-sustainable economic base, makes it difficult for Native people to access forestry-related markets. This may soon change. Comprehensive land-claims resolutions will translate into larger Native landholdings at a time when the forestry industry is moving north into Native communities. But for now, the policy framework remains inadequate.

Finally, the courts are often petitioned to determine the pith and substance of the NRTA—for example, when an Indian has been charged with an offence that challenges treaty-protected rights. This is due to the complexities of interpreting Native economic development through the often contradictory lenses of Aboriginal and treaty rights and government economic-development policies. To date the courts have chosen to narrowly define what is considered legitimate Native economic activity. Three important cases demonstrate the Court's restrictive interpretation of Indigenous economic development. In 1984 in British Columbia, a Musqueam First Nation member named Ronald Sparrow was charged with fishing with an oversized drift net in contradiction of the *B.C. Fisheries Act.* Claiming an Aboriginal right to a livelihood, Sparrow contested his arrest. The case wound its way through the Canadian court system before being heard by the Supreme Court of Canada (SCC) in 1990. The SCC affirmed that where an Aboriginal group has an Aboriginal right to fish for food for social and ceremonial purposes (albeit not for profit), those purposes take priority over conservation measures.[32]

Yet government continues to regulate the exercise of that right. Similarly, the SCC in *Van Der Peet* (1996) determined that the Aboriginal right to a particular kind of trade in fish—specifically, large-scale commercial trade—did not exist.[33] Finally, the court in *Marshall* (1999) (the same Donald Marshall who was exonerated for murder; see Chapter 9) affirmed the Mi'kmaq treaty right to hunt, fish, and gather in pursuit of a moderate livelihood based on local treaties signed in the eighteenth century.[34] In other words, the Court in *Marshall* determined that Mi'kmaq communities fishing under these treaties could sell their catch to ensure a moderate livelihood, albeit without engaging in trade that might generate "wealth which would exceed a sustenance lifestyle." Traditional economic development, then, is often undermined by government and court interpretations regarding how Native economic development should proceed.

Contemporary Native Economies

The real tragedy of . . . the practices of public policy over the past century has been to destroy that element essential to all people for their survival, man's individual initiative and self-reliance. A century of pursuit of [such polices] finds Indian people on the lowest rung of the social ladder, not only suffering deprivation and poverty to a greater extent than other Canadians but also suffering from psychological intimidation brought about by their almost complete dependence upon the state for the necessities of life.

—David Courchene (Ojibwa)[35]

Despite several existing barriers (e.g., restrictive laws and policies, the lack of capital), economic development in Native communities across Canada has improved, even if a number of communities continue to report dire economic circumstances. For instance, over a recent ten-year period (1996–2005), Native self-employment grew by an average of 8 percent per year, or four times the rate of the non-Native population. As of 2001 there were approximately 30,000 Native entrepreneurs in Canada. Statistics Canada recently reported that off-reserve Native employment in western Canada grew by 23 percent between 2001 and 2005, compared to 11 percent for non-Natives. Most of this growth was dominated by the three largest occupational sectors: sales and services (35 percent); business, finance, and administration (19 percent); and trades, transport, and equipment operation (18 percent).[36]

Some of the more sophisticated community economic-development work fuses modern processes with traditional ones (see box on previous page), not unlike how fur-trade era Indigenous leaders integrated aspects of European economic ways into their existing economic

MEMBERTOU FIRST NATION

The Membertou First Nation in Nova Scotia is a good example of economic development with community needs in mind. In 1995, close to 85 percent of all adults were on some form of social assistance. In addition, the band was running a budget deficit, and attempts at economic development had failed. Tired of this poor performance, Chief Terrance Paul hired community member Bernd Christmas, who was working as a lawyer in Toronto, as CEO and general council for the band. Together, Paul and Christmas reorganized the band as a corporation and reinvested its profits in community-building projects. The new economic-development program included one major step: obtaining ISO certification— an international standard for management and internal governance. Two years later the Membertou First Nation was certified; soon after, it entered into business partnerships with Lockheed Martin, to help it with a maritime helicopter project bid; with SNC-Lavalin, which sells engineering services and environmental technologies; with Sodex'ho Canada, which provides onshore and offshore catering services; and with Fujitsu Consulting, which provides health-records management for military personnel. The First Nation also established the Membertou Trade and Commerce Centre and Business Park, Membertou Fisheries, Mi'kmaq Gas Bar and Convenience, and gaming operations on the reserve. The band's revenues from these businesses now exceed $40 million annually, and over the past decade education levels have increased and the Mi'kmaq language has been successfully reanimated.

Membertou is a bright spot in the Cape Breton economy, employing 700 in peak season—close to half of them non-Aboriginals—while contributing more than $133 million to the local economy. Band-generated revenues are pumped into community programs. Certified by the international quality standards auditor ISO for the past seven years, Membertou is now poised for further growth in a variety of ever more sophisticated industries, from offshore oil and gas to aerospace, geomatics, consulting, environmental clean-up, real estate, information technology, and data storage.

Source: Bernd Christmas, "Membertou: Welcoming the World." Powerpoint Presentation, September 18, 2003. [online] www.edo.ca/pages/download/6_450.

ways. Today, Native leaders continue to work toward a collective approach that embraces five key elements: local control, holistic development, comprehensive planning, cooperation, and local capacity development. Many economic strategies emphasise the following:

- The importance of history and culture.
- Governance, culture, and spirituality.
- The nation's unique qualities and values.
- The link between self-government and economic development.
- The role and importance of traditional economies.[37]

These ideas are by no means universal. As an example, the Meadow Lake Tribal Council of Saskatchewan has identified five values to guide economic development. These demonstrate a commitment to tradition, heritage, and culture:

- Communal rather than individual ownership.
- Sharing and group recognition rather than individual rewards.
- Respect for elders and Mother Earth.
- A concern for future generations.
- Consensus decision making.[38]

Native leaders and economic development officers have found, however, that is it difficult to blend traditional teachings and Native culture with the ways of Western business. One academic has reminded Native leaders that it is impossible to remain unchanged by capitalism.[39] He also asks, "What will red capitalism look like?"—an intriguing question that most Native leaders involved in economic development will have to seriously consider.[40] From the perspective of some, Native communities are well situated to develop their economies because they are rooted in local cultures that emphasize ingenuity, initiative, and collective effort, all of these aimed at striking a balance between collective and individual action. To identify barriers to development and the strategies currently being employed by Canada's Native people to combat stagnant economic growth, the following discussion examines events in (1) the territorial North, (2) the provincial North, (3) southern rural Canada, and (4) urban centres with large Native populations.

Territorial North

The North is home to traditional economic activities centred on hunting, fishing, and trapping. While subsistence economies are still prevalent, Inuit, Dene, and Métis populations are being drawn into broader regional, territorial, national and (in certain cases) global economies. The challenge—a big one—is to balance resource and territorial preservation with economic development. Government is one of the North's largest employers. Except perhaps for grocery stores, construction companies, a handful of small businesses, arts and craft providers, and tourism companies, the North has yet to fully diversify its economy. A unique aspect of the northern economy is cooperatives. Co-ops are organized, owned, and operated

Figure 11-2 SUSTAINABLE DEVELOPMENT STRATEGY

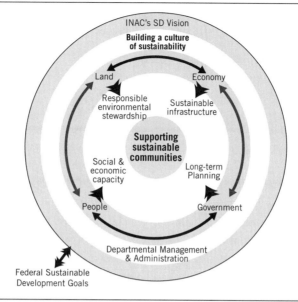

Source: Sustainable Development Strategy 2007–2010. Ottawa: Indian and Northern Affairs Canada, 2006. http://www. ainc-inac.gc.ca/enr/sd//pubs/sd0710/sd0710-eng.pdf. Reproduced with the permission of the Minister of Public Works and Government Services Canada, 2008.

by like-minded groups of individuals who are seeking to provide their communities with required goods and services and employment while fostering community-generated wealth in a fair and equitable way. Since the 1950s the Northwest Territories, Nunavut, and Nunavik have established more than half of all Native co-ops in Canada. Co-ops provide services ranging from housing to craft marketing, food retail, forestry, fishing, and bus transportation. Some co-ops also provide training, development, management, and support. The co-op model has been so popular that there are few communities in the North that do not have one.

Co-ops are not the only economic-development model utilized in the North. With the recent discovery of $24 billion (estimated) worth of diamond deposits in Nunavut and the Northwest Territories, and the south's increasing demand for oil and natural gas, the North has become home to a number of mining and resource-exploration interests. Small communities are entering into joint ventures with companies like De Beers; they are also developing quarrying operations that will provide the materials needed to improve the region's roads.

Yet however great the financial incentives, Inuit leaders and private interests initially faced opposition to various proposed projects. For example, at Lac de Gras (300 kilometres north of Yellowknife), where $12 billion (estimated) of diamonds had been found, Native leaders were concerned whether the mine could be developed without damaging the land

Diavik Diamond Mine

and its wildlife.[41] Related concerns often include these: how increased competition for resources will affect community stability, the impact of non-Native people on the community, whether local health will be compromised by increased pollution resulting from newly introduced industry, and how traditional economies will fare in the changed economic environment. An environmental panel studied the issue at Lac de Gras and endorsed the Ekati Diamond Mine (owned and operated by BHP Billiton of Australia) and the Diavik Diamond Mine (operated by Diavik Diamond Mines Inc. (DDMI), a subsidiary of Rio Tinto plc of London, England).

These two mines are located near a large project operated by Deton'Cho Diamonds Inc. in the Northwest Territories. Located in and operated by the Yellowknife Dene First Nations, Deton'Cho Diamonds is a subsidiary of Deton'Cho Corporation and has cornered the diamond cutting and polishing market. The company's 25 employees work in diamond finishing. Several Dene students are currently being trained in Europe to saw, laser, and polish the stones. The corporation at its summer peak employs 150 workers while maintaining 65 in the winter. Included in its portfolio are Bouwa Whee Catering, which it fully owns; Environmental Venture, a mine-site clean-up and tank-farm firm; Dettah Cable; We le Dai Corporation, which operates the Vital Abel medical boarding home in Ndilo; and Ek'Ati Services, a mining camp and camp caterer.[42]

Provincial North

The northern regions of most provinces offer similar employment and economic opportunities as the territorial North. The main difference is that fewer people are involved in hunting, fishing, gathering, and trapping, even though these still play an important cultural role (and augment both food supplies and incomes). The provincial North is a dynamic environment: there are forest-based activities in the more northern reaches and agricultural opportunities farther south. This region also attracts resource development, including hydroelectric development (i.e., dam construction). Environmental pollution is an issue with these industries. In particular, the hydro sector has compelled many Native communities to relocate.[43]

RCAP in its 1996 report noted that provincial-government approaches to economic development had long made a negative impact on Indigenous lands, resources, and traditional economies. Furthermore, provincial decisions often damaged traplines and other wildlife-management systems. Recently, many Native communities have responded by trying to enter the broader global economy with both traditional and contemporary economic ventures. In 1986, for example, the La Ronge Indian Band in Saskatchewan founded the Kitsaki Development Corporation, which has since grown to include sole and joint ventures in trucking, insurance, mining, lumber, food products, and hospitality. Canada's largest producer of organic wild rice, which is harvested from remote lakes and streams, Kitsaki currently sells its product throughout North America, Germany, the Netherlands, Britain, and Japan. It continues to seek new international markets. Currently, two million pounds of wild rice are harvested each year, generating jobs for locals and an improved regional economy.[44]

Southern Rural

Native communities in this region tend to be closer to non-Native urban centres. This has a direct impact on economic development. Despite that proximity, these communities have found it hard to integrate themselves with regional economies, partly because they lack clear economic and political goals. Most urban centres can boast established infrastructures and services. By contrast, most Native communities are mired in the early stages of development, which makes it difficult for them to establish partnerships with outsiders. These communities often do not offer the diversity of goods and services that outside consumers may find attractive; as a result, they find it difficult to attract capital. At the same time, the proximity of non-Native urban centres alters Native shopping patterns and employment possibilities. As an example, in the early 1990s it was estimated that nearly $30 million annually leaked from the Blood (Kainai) and Peigan (Piikuni) reserves into the Lethbridge economy. By 2006, the Blood economy alone was hemorrhaging $100 million to various surrounding communities.[45] Yet Native employment rates in those surrounding communities were low.

Many communities are turning to tourism and resource extraction (fishing, forestry, mining) to capitalize on local resources. *The First Nations Oil and Gas and Moneys Management Act* (2005) permits First Nations to assume control over the management of their oil and gas resources and the monies arising therefrom. Exporting goods to nearby urban markets—and to international ones—is becoming more common. One way or another, all economic development entails investing in community infrastructure. This means finding capital, planning what to do with it, and passing laws to control it. In this regard, southern rural governments tend to be more advanced than others. In part this is because education is more accessible in the south, which makes for band members with training in health, education, social services, and economic development.

Urban

In the 1950s, nine-tenths of Canada's Native people lived on reserves or in rural communities. By the end of the 1960s, a general lack of economic opportunities combined with pressure to abandon reserve communities led to growing urban migration. By 2001 nearly half of all people who self-identified as Native lived in urban areas. Today more than 71 percent of Canadian Native people do not live on reserve lands. Native people tend to say they move to cities for economic reasons. Urban Native economies are unique in a number of ways:

- Native people are spread out among larger populations of non-Native people.
- Urban Native populations are a mix of different nations or cultural backgrounds, making it more difficult for them to gather collectively.
- Urban areas provide larger markets for Native businesses.
- Conflicts over who leads or speaks for a community or a collection of communities can arise from the mix of different nation and culture groups.
- Jurisdiction for urban Native people is not decided, and Métis have had little recognition in federal programs.
- There is rarely an urban Native land base.

The available evidence suggests that cities lack the capacity to successfully absorb Native people. The debate over who is responsible for urban Native people is ongoing (see Chapter 10). There are three facets to the problem: (1) urban Native people are not provided the same level of services as they would receive on reserves or in their communities; (2) urban Native people find it harder to access provincial programs that are available to other urban Canadians; and (3) culturally appropriate programs are lacking in urban centres (see Chapter 14). Variations in policy, gaps and overlaps in policy, and mismatches between policies and needs have been identified as serious problems for urban Native populations.[46] Ottawa has acknowledged the need for collaboration between different levels of government to help urban Native populations, yet to date little has been done to address jurisdictional issues.[47]

Urban Native leaders acknowledge the need to formulate economic-development strategies to counter prevailing forces. A positive example is Neechi Foods Co-op Limited, a worker-owned co-op that operates Neechi Foods Community Store in Winnipeg's North End. The idea for the co-op evolved out of (1) the Aboriginal Community Economic Development Officer training program, and (2) the need felt by various people and organizations to see Winnipeg's inner-city neighbourhoods revitalized. A single store that sold grocery items such as produce and dry goods opened in 1997 and quickly expanded, developing specialty projects such as the fresh fruit basket for kids. That store also participated in the Christmas Lights campaign and promoted the annual sale of fresh wild blueberries. In August of the same year, it opened a second store in a different neighbourhood, which caters to a middle- and upper-class clientele. Neechi is pursuing a pilot project supported by the Assiniboine Credit Union.[48] Its goals are to:

- develop a system that will enable cooperatives and other community enterprises to assess their own development needs and to build solid management teams;

- develop a business mentorship–apprenticeship system; and
- establish shared technical services.

The cooperative has consistently provided stable employment with decent wages. Most of the Native employees have been introduced to new skills and have acquired valuable work experience.

The "New Buffalo": First Nations Casinos and Economic Development[49]

Even though there is some ethical and moral questions behind gaming, I think that ultimately it is the answer for many First Nations' communities.

—Denise Birdstone[50]

No discussion examining Native economic development would be complete without a brief look at the current state of First Nations gaming. Often described as the "new buffalo," this phenomenon can be traced back to 1984 in Manitoba, when the Opaskwayak Cree Nation (OCN) launched a government-sanctioned community-based lottery. The economic potential of gaming excited First Nations leaders, who were looking for ways to stimulate local economies, which badly needed it. These leaders argued that gaming was more than a means of generating quick money. It was an economic seed that if planted carefully could fuel local economies, from which healthier communities would then spring. The resulting jobs would keep local youth at home; no longer would they have to seek work far away. Reliance on government programs would decrease, and political stability would result. The federal government's long failure to foster economic development on reserves was key to the OCN's decision to pursue gaming—a fact that other First Nation leaders would later emphasize. Encouraged by success stories filtering into Canada from the United States describing how once-destitute tribes became economically viable after they built casinos, Canadian Native groups entered the gaming industry in a big way. By 1996 they were operating five casinos in Saskatchewan and Ontario. By 2008 there were 15 for-profit casinos and two charity casinos operating in Canada, in every province from B.C. to Ontario. Add to those the large video lottery terminal (VLT) casinos in Nova Scotia (see Figure 11-3).

Perhaps the most famous First Nations casino is Casino Rama, on the Mnjikaning (Rama) First Nation in Ontario, 15 kilometres east of Orillia in Ontario's cottage country and 135 kilometres north of Toronto. The community is situated on 951 hectares of land divided into eight separate parcels and has a population of 1,266, of whom 505 live on reserve. In 1992 the Ontario government under Premier Bob Rae announced that it intended to see a reserve casino operated by provincial First Nations. Four years later,

Figure 11-3 FIRST NATIONS CASINOS IN CANADA

1. St. Eugene Mission Resort, Cranbrook
2. Eagle River Casino, Alexis First Nation
3. Stoney Nakoda Resort Casino, Stoney Nakoda First Nation
4. River Cree Resort and Casino, Enoch First Nation
5. Grey Eagle Casino, Tsuu T'ina First Nation
6. Casino Dene, Cold Lake First Nation
7. Living Sky Casino, Swift Current (est. Dec 2008)
8. Gold Eagle Casino, North Battleford
9. Dakota Dunes Casino, Whitecap First Nation
10. Northern Lights Casino, Prince Albert
11. Bear Claw Casino, Carlyle
12. Painted Hand Casino, Yorkton
13. Aseneskak Casino, Opaskwayak Cree Nation
14. South Beach Casino, Brokenhead First Nation
15. Golden Eagle Casino, Kenora
16. Casino Rama, Mnjikaning First Nation
17. Blue Heron Charity Casino, Scugog Island   (Casino locations are approximate.)

Source: Adapted from Belanger, Yale. *Gambling With the Future: The Evolution of Aboriginal Gaming in Canada.* Saskatoon: Purich Publishing, 2006.

Casino Rama prepared to open. Construction was halted when a new premier, Mike Harris, announced that his government would be imposing a "win tax" on what was supposed to have been a tax-free economic initiative. Casino Rama finally opened to the public on July 31, 1996. During its first two months, it attracted 889,200 gamblers through its doors—an average of 14,200 people per day—and generated $66.3 million in gross revenues.

Casino Rama located on the Mnjikaning First Nation just outside Orillia, Ontario

That first year, the annual payroll for the 2,663 employees, 700 of whom were Native, was around $60 million. Unemployment at Mnjikaning dropped from 70 percent to 8 percent, and band staff jumped from 50 to 230. By 2000, close to 25 private and band-owned businesses were operating. The Mnjikaning Kendaaswin Elementary School opened in 1998 to both First Nations children and those from neighbouring non-Native communities. Soon after, the community built its own fire department; established a first-response emergency unit; and founded its own police unit, which works in conjunction with the Ontario Provincial Police (OPP). Water and sewage treatment facilities were constructed for both the local community and nearby businesses.

All other provincial First Nations benefit from Casino Rama's revenues through a revenue-sharing agreement. Thus, 65 percent of net revenues are split among the province's 133 First Nations: of that amount, 50 percent is distributed to First Nations by population, 40 percent is distributed equally among all First Nations, and 10 percent is distributed to those communities designated as remote. The remaining 35 percent of casino revenues remains with the Mnjikaning First Nation so that it can deal with issues such as the impact of increased traffic on reserve infrastructure, as well as fund local programs to deal with problem gaming.[51]

NATIVE ECONOMIC DEVELOPMENT AGENCIES

Aboriginal Business Canada

Aboriginal Resource Guide

Aboriginal Youth Business Council

Alberta Chambers of Commerce

All Nations Development Corporation

Assembly of First Nations

Buffalo Point International Resort

CESO-SACO Canadian Volunteer Advisors to Business

Congress of Aboriginal Peoples

Indian Taxation Advisory Board

JEDI Joint Economic Development Initiative

Native Commercial Credit Corporation

Resistance

Native gaming has over the past decade shown itself to be a moneymaker. Yet resistance to new projects is the norm. Perhaps the best example of resistance was to the proposed Native casino in Saskatoon. In December 2002 the Saskatoon Tribal Council (STC) presented Saskatoon City Council with a 200-page report outlining every aspect of the project. The proposed 105,000-square-foot complex would include a casino, a showroom, and an attached six-storey parkade. It would offer more than 40 table games and 700 slot machines. The STC anticipated that the $65 million downtown complex would generate $100 million in economic activity and roughly $5 million for local charities. Casino employment would exceed 700, including 17 management jobs paying $40,000 to 75,000 per year, 106 supervisory jobs paying $30,000 to 38,000, and 590 operational jobs paying $20,000 to 29,000.

In late November 2002, STC and Saskatchewan Indian Gaming Authority (SIGA) representatives asked the city council for permission to build their complex, which was expected to generate close to $70 million annually in economic activity and create 1,000 new jobs. Six months later, at the May 12, 2003, council meeting, a petition for a referendum was submitted by the Coalition Against Gambling Expansion in Saskatoon (CAGES), after nearly 28,000 signatures (7,000 beyond the minimum needed) had been collected to force a plebiscite. The STC announced that it would be abandoning its casino plans. However, Ed Bellegarde, president and CEO of SIGA, told the mayor and council that he was not officially withdrawing the proposal, nor did he object to the upcoming referendum. At the same time, he presented the 2003 Dakota Dunes Resort Project Proposal, and he described how other Saskatchewan communities had benefited from First Nations gaming. He claimed that both Whitecap Reserve residents and the Rural Municipality of Dundurn were receptive to the proposal, and he asked for council's endorsement. Saskatoon City Council supported the proposal for a casino on the Whitecap Dakota First Nation and held the plebiscite concurrent with the October 22 municipal elections. The results: 44,307 against Resolution 1 and 35,766 for; 41,356 against Resolution 2 and 37,885 for. The City of Saskatoon was obligated to reject both resolutions.

Table 11-1 SIGA REVENUE AND PROFIT—5-YEAR OVERVIEW

YEAR	TOTAL NET REVENUE	TOTAL NET PROFIT
2006–07	$126,095,168	$48,836,918
2005–06	112,858,873	40,157,971
2004–05	100,637,018	33,954,945
2003–04	95,830,473	33,179,599
2002–03	87,334,276	29,199,520
Total	**522, 755, 808**	**$185,328,953**

Source: Adapted from "SIGA Annual Report 2006–2007." *Saskatchewan Indian Gaming Authority.* 4 March 2009. http://www.siga.sk.ca/06SIGA1008_AR_lo.pdf.

Table 11-2 NOVA SCOTIA BAND SHARE OF GAMING REVENUE—5-YEAR OVERVIEW

Year	VLT Revenue	Sydney Casino Profits	Net Revenue
2006–07	$39,936,366.65	$2,725,400.00	$42,661,766.65
2005–06	39,024,043.80	1,715,500.00	40,739,543.80
2004–05	37,098,126.70	283,314.00 (2004)	37,381,440.70
2003–04	32,708,556.76	1,631,872.31 (2003)	34,340,429.07
2002–03	26,744,915.80	2,764,259.96 (2002)	29,509,175.76
Total	$175,512,009.71	$9,120,346.27	$184,632,355.98

Source: "First Nation Gambling." *Nova Scotia Office of Aboriginal Affairs* (NSOAA). 2007. Government of Nova Scotia. 9 March 2009. <http://www.gov.ns.ca/abor/resources/firstnationsgaming>. Reproduced with permission, NSOAA.

Conclusion

Self-government without a significant economic base would be an exercise in illusion and futility. How to achieve a more self-reliant economic base is thus one of the most important questions to be resolved. What measures need to be taken to rebuild Aboriginal economies that have been severely disrupted over time, marginalized, and largely stripped of their land and natural resource base?

—Royal Commission on Aboriginal Peoples[52]

Various committees, commissions, academics, and community leaders see economic development as key to improving the lives of Native people. In response to this generally accepted view, criteria for economic development have been put forward that reflect Indigenous values. One author has argued that Native people's economic development must embrace the spiritual as much as the scientific approach so that it reflects First Nations' unique philosophies and aspirations.[53] This, however, obscures the fact that Native economic development historically has been complex—that is, based on more than hunting, fishing, and trapping. It has always depended on intricate trade relationships rooted in treaties governing compensation for territorial access. At the same time, a number of mechanisms such as the potlatch and gaming were used to distribute wealth throughout the communities.

There is evidence that technology exchange occurred among Native peoples and that leaders of one community often had an in-depth understanding of regional partners' economic needs and of their adversaries' motives. Pre-contact economic activity was undertaken not just for profit or material gain, as we would understand it from a market-economy perspective. Yet despite this long history of economic activity, the Canadian government has

Figure 11-4 THE ABORIGINAL DEVELOPMENT CIRCLE

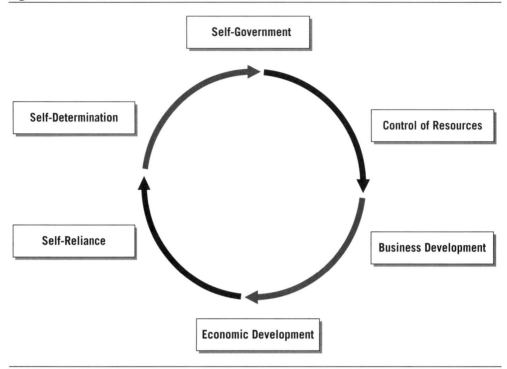

Source: Reprinted with permission from *Economic Development Among the Aboriginal Peoples in Canada: The Hope*, by Robert Brent Anderson (Concord, ON: Captus Press Inc., 1999). Permission to use has been granted by Captus Press Inc. http://www.captus.com.

been slow to respond to grassroots requests for greater jurisdiction over community-based economic initiatives. Things are slowly changing: Native communities are seeking out partners and sole-source financing; and models such as the one presented in Figure 11-4 have been developed to promote a more holistic approach to economic development—one that is supportive of political and social initiatives and that is designed to promote both.

There are various reasons for this lack of government support. In many ways, Native people still tend to be viewed by mainstream society as remnants of the fur trade—that is, as dependent on hunting, trapping, gathering, and fishing. Or, as *nouveau* capitalists, they are depicted as naive entrepreneurs interested in quick returns from gaming revenues and gas and oil royalties. Some critics even argue that successful economic ventures are not so much the product of business acumen and hard work as they are the result of Native leaders exploiting race-based Aboriginal rights—rights, indeed, that are an outgrowth of the federal government's yearning to repair the damage wrought by decades of ill-treatment.[55] There is a common thread running through these two perspectives: that Native people are incapable of participating in regional, national, and global economic networks because of their reliance on traditional economic ways that embrace collective traditions. Put another way, that Native people are mired in poverty because they refuse to compromise their traditional cultures and values and to abandon their languages.

Complicating matters is the political nature of Native economic development. Native business owners often cite the need to challenge the policies, laws, and attitudes that so often have prohibited them from participating as partners in the Canadian economy. At the same time, Native communities must seek ways to promote economic development and foster political self-sufficiency. Native leaders and aspiring business owners will simply have to keep pursuing projects that they believe will benefit their communities and families. That will mean overcoming these restrictive forces.

FURTHER READING

Anderson, Robert M. *Economic Development and Aboriginal Peoples in Canada: The Hope for the Future.* Don Mills: Captus, 1999.

————. and Robert M. Bone. *Natural Resources and Aboriginal People in Canada: Readings, Cases, and Commentary.* Don Mills: Captus, 2003.

Calliou, Brian. "The Business Approach to Self-Government: The Significance of Building Leadership and Community Capacity." In *Aboriginal Self-Government: Current Trends and Issues,* ed. Yale D. Belanger. Saskatoon: Purich, 2008, pp. 332–47.

Harvard Project on American Indian Economic Development. [online] http://www.ksg.harvard.edu/hpaied/docs/CornellKalt%20Sov-NB.pdf

Helin, Calvin. *Dances with Dependency: Indigenous Success Through Self-Reliance.* Vancouver: Orca Spirit, 2006.

Newhouse, David R. "Modern Aboriginal Economies: Capitalism with a Red Face." *Journal of Aboriginal Economic Development 1,* no. 2 (2000): 55–64.

Notzke, Claudia. *The Stranger, the Native, and the Land: Perspectives on Indigenous Tourism.* Don Mills: Captus, 2006.

Wuttunee, Wanda. *Living Rhythms: Lessons in Aboriginal Economic Resilience and Vision.* Kingston and Montreal: McGill–Queen's University Press, 2004.

————. *In Business for Ourselves: Northern Entrepreneurs.* Kingston and Montreal: McGill–Queen's University Press, 1992.

NOTES

1. Manitoba Indian Brotherhood, *Whabung: Our Tomorrows* (Winnipeg: 1971).

2. Canada, "Restructuring the Relationships: Economic Development," in *For Seven Generations: An Information Legacy of the Royal Commission on Aboriginal Peoples,* CD-ROM (Ottawa: Canada Communications Group, 1996).

3. Kaj Birket Smith, *Eskimos* (Copenhagen: Rhodos, 1971).

4. See, generally, Samuel Eliot Morison, *The European Discovery of America: The Northern Voyages* (New York: Oxford University Press, 1971); James Alexander Williamson, *The Cabot Voyages and Bristol Discovery Under Henry VII, with the Cartography of the Voyages by R.A. Skelton* (Cambridge: Cambridge University Press, 1962); and Melvin H. Jackson, "The Labrador Landfall of John Cabot," *Canadian Historical Review* 44, no. 2 (1963): 122–41.

5. See, generally, Arthur J. Ray, *Indians and the Fur Trade: Their Role as Trappers, Hunters, and Middlemen in the Lands Southwest of Hudson Bay, 1660–1870* (Toronto: University of Toronto Press, 2001); Arthur J. Ray, "Periodic Shortages, Native Welfare, and the Hudson's Bay Company, 1670–1930," in *Out of the Background: Readings on Canadian Native History,* ed. Ken Coates and Robin Fisher (Toronto: Copp Clark, 1996); and idem, "Indians as Consumers in the Eighteenth Century," in *Old Trails and New Directions: Papers of the Third North American Fur Trade Conference,* ed. Carol M. Judd and Arthur J. Ray (Toronto: University of Toronto Press, 1978), p. 268.

6. Sarah Carter, *Aboriginal Peoples and Colonizers of Western Canada to 1900* (Toronto: University of Toronto Press, 1999), p. 48.

7. Klaus E. Knorr, *British Colonial Theories, 1570–1850* (Toronto: University of Toronto Press, 1968).

8. Richard White, *The Middle Ground: Indians, Empires, in the Great Lakes Region, 1650–1815* (Cambridge: Cambridge University Press, 1991).

9. Ray, "Periodic Shortages, Native Welfare."

10. For an excellent collection of essays dealing with this and like issues, see Martha C. Knack and Alice Littlefield, "Native American Labor: Retrieving History, Rethinking Theory," in *Native Americans and Wage Labor: Ethnohistorical Perspectives,* ed. Alice Littlefield and Martha C. Knack (Norman: University of Oklahoma Press, 1996).

11. See James K. Burrows, "'A Much Needed Class of Labour': The Economy and Income of the Southern Interior Plateau Indians, 1897–1910," *BC Studies* 71 (Autumn 1986): 27–46; Thomas Dunk, "Indian Participation in the Industrial Economy on the North Shore of Lake Superior, 1869 to 1940," *Thunder Bay Historical Museum Society Papers and Records* 15 (Spring 1987); and John Lutz, "After the Fur Trade: The Aboriginal Labouring Class of British Columbia, 1849–90," *Journal of the Canadian Historical Association* 87 (1992): 69–93.

12. Harald E.L. Prins, "Tribal Network and Migrant Labor: Mi'kmaq Indians as Seasonal Workers in Aroostook's Potato Fields, 1870–1980," in *Native Americans and Wage Labour: Ethnohistorical Perspectives,* ed. Alice Littlefield and Martha C. Knack (Norman: University of Oklahoma Press, 1996), pp. 45–65.

13. Rolf Knight, *Indians at Work: An Informal History of Native Indian Labour in British Columbia, 1858–1930* (Vancouver: New Star, 1978); and Sarah Carter, *Lost Harvests: Prairie Indian Reserve Farmers and Government Policy* (Kingston and Montreal: McGill–Queen's University Press, 1990).

14. Treaty 7 Elders and Tribal Council with Walter Hildebrant, Sarah Carter, and Dorothy First Rider, *The True Spirit and Intent of Treaty 7* (Kingston and Montreal: McGill–Queen's University Press, 1996), p. 217.

15. Robert N. Wilson, *Our Betrayed Wards: A Story of Chicanery, Infidelity, and the Prostitution of Trust* (Ottawa: 1921), p. 4; see also Keith Regular, "Trucking and Trading with Outsiders: Blood

Indian Reserve Integration into the Southern Alberta Economic Environment, 1884–1939—a Case of Shared Neighbourhoods" (Ph.D. diss., Memorial University, 1999).

16. Wilson, *Our Betrayed Wards.*

17. See Cam Mackie, "Some Reflections on Indian Economic Development," in *Arduous Journey: Canadian Indians and Decolonization,* ed. J. Rick Ponting (Toronto: McClelland and Stewart, 1986); and T.R.L. MacInnes, "History of Indian Administration in Canada," *Canadian Journal of Economics and Political Science* 12, no. 3 (1946): 393.

18. Quoted in Yale D. Belanger, "Seeking a Seat at the Table: A Brief History of Indian Political Organizing in Canada, 1870–1951" (Ph.D. diss., Trent University, 2006).

19. For this detailed history, see Canada, *For Seven Generations: An Information Legacy of the Royal Commission on Aboriginal Peoples,* CD-ROM (Ottawa: Canada Communications Group, 1996).

20. Ibid.

21. J. Rick Ponting, "Economic Development Provisions of the New Claims Settlements," in *Arduous Journey: Canadian Indians and Decolonization,* ed. J. Rick Ponting (Toronto: McClelland and Stewart, 1986), p. 90.

22. See Fred Wien, "Economic Development and Aboriginal Self-Government: A Review of the Implementation of the Report of the Royal Commission on Aboriginal Peoples," in *Aboriginal Self-Government in Canada: Current Trends and Issues,* 2nd ed., ed. John H. Hylton (Saskatoon: Purich, 1999).

23. See "Harvard Project Lessons on Self-Government: Improving Aboriginal Self-Government in Canada," *Frontier Centre for Public Policy: Backgrounder.* [online] http://www.fcpp.org/main/publication_detail.php?PubID=517. Last accessed December 16, 2008. See also Stephen Cornell and Joseph P. Kalt, *Two Approaches to Economic Development on American Indian Reservations: One Works, the Other Doesn't* (Cambridge, MA: Harvard Project on American Indian Economic Development and the Native Nations Institute for Leadership, Management, and Policy, on behalf of the Arizona Board of Regents, 2006); Stephen Cornell, Miriam Jorgensen, Joseph P. Kalt, and Katherine A. Spilde, *Seizing the Future: Why Some Native Nations Do and Others Don't* (Cambridge, MA: Harvard Project of American Indian Economic Development, 2005).

24. Canada, *Aboriginal Self-Government: The Government of Canada's Approach to Implementation of the Inherent Right and the Negotiation of Aboriginal Self-Government* (Ottawa: Minister of Public Works and Government Services, 1995); see also Indian and Northern Affairs Canada, *Towards Sustainable, Successful First Nation Communities: Good Governance, the Governance Continuum, and Governance Programming,* Discussion Paper (Ottawa: Self-Government Branch, Indian and Northern Affairs, 2000).

25. Canada, Indian and Northern Affairs Canada (INAC), *Economic Development Programs Guide, 2005* (Ottawa: Minister of Indian Affairs and Northern Development, 2005). [online] http://dsp-psd.pwgsc.gc.ca/Collection/R2-163-2005E.pdf. Last accessed December 13, 2008.

26. James [Sakej] Youngblood Henderson, "The Constitutional Right of an Enriched Livelihood," *Journal of Aboriginal Economic Development* 4, no. 1 (2004): 43–58.

27. Alexander Morris, *The Treaties of Canada with the Indians of Manitoba and the Northwest Territories* (Toronto: Fifth House, 1991), pp. 92–93, 96.

28. Ibid., p. 184.

29. Ibid., p. 211.

30. Canada, "Aboriginal Population and Forested Areas" (Ottawa: Natural Resources Canada, 2004). [online] http://atlas.nrcan.gc.ca/site/english/maps/environment/forest/forestpeople/aborigpop/1. Last accessed September 4, 2008.

31. See Michael Lee Ross, *First Nations Sacred Sites in Canada's Courts* (Vancouver: UBC Press, 2005).

32. *R. v. Sparrow* [1990] *1 S.C.R.* 1075.

33. *R. v. Van Der Peet* [1996] *2 S.C.R.* 507.

34. *R. v. Marshall* [1999] *3 S.C.R.* 456.

35. David Courchene, "Problems and Possible Solutions," in *Indians Without Tipis: A Resource Book by Indians and Métis,* ed. D. Bruce Sealy and Verna J. Kikness (Winnipeg: William Clare, 1973), p. 179.

36. Jacqueline Luffman and Deborah Sussman, "The Aboriginal Labour Force in Western Canada," in *Perspectives on Labour and Income* 8, no. 1 (2007). [online] http://www.statcan.ca/english/freepub/75-001-XIE/10107/high-2.htm. Last accessed September 8, 2008.

37. See, generally, David R. Newhouse, "Modern Aboriginal Economies: Capitalism with a Red Face," *Journal of Aboriginal Economic Development* 1, no. 2 (2000): 55–64.

38. See Robert Brent Anderson, *Economic Development Among the Aboriginal Peoples of Canada: The Hope for the Future* (Concord: Captus, 1999), pp. 192–224.

39. David R. Newhouse, "Resistance Is Futile: Aboriginal Peoples Meet the Borg of Capitalism," in *Ethics and Capitalism,* ed. John D. Bishop (Toronto: University of Toronto Press, 2000), pp. 141–55.

40. Newhouse, "Modern Aboriginal Economies."

41. Tom Fennell, "Northern Gems: Natives Battle a Proposed $12-billion Diamond Mine," *Maclean's,* March 4, 1996, pp. 54–55.

42. Indian and Northern Affairs Canada, "Backgrounder: Diamond Mining in Canada's North" (Ottawa: 2003). [online] http://www.ainc-inac.gc.ca/ai/mr/nr/s-d2005/02736bka-eng.asp. Last accessed December 13, 2008.

43. See James B. Waldram, *As Long as the Rivers Run: Hydroelectric Development and Native Communities in Western Canada* (Winnipeg: University of Manitoba Press, 1988).

44. Raymond Lawrence, "Muskox Makes for Culinary Treat, and More," in *Building Aboriginal Economies* (Ottawa: Indian and Northern Affairs Canada, 2002), p. 4. [online] http://dsp-psd.pwgsc.gc.ca/Collection/R12-10-2002-2E.pdf. Last accessed December 13, 2008.

45. See Helen Buckley, *From Wooden Ploughs to Welfare: Why Indian Policy Failed in the Prairie Provinces* (Kingston and Montreal: McGill–Queen's University Press, 1992), p. 11; and Sarah McGinnis, "Blood Tribe Calls for Urban Reserves: Federal Officials Warn Process is Lengthy," *Calgary Herald,* March 15, 2006, B8.

46. Calvin Hanselmann, *Urban Aboriginal People in Western Canada: Realities and Policies* (Calgary: Canada West Foundation, 2001); idem, *Uncommon Sense: Promising Practices in Urban Aboriginal Policy Making and Programming* (Calgary: Canada West Foundation, 2002); and idem, *Enhanced Aboriginal Programming in Western Canada* (Calgary: Canada West Foundation, 2002).

47. Katherine A.H. Graham & Evelyn Peters, *Aboriginal Communities and Urban Sustainability* (Ottawa: Canadian Policy Research Networks, 2002), p. 18.

48. John Loxley, "Aboriginal Economic Development in Winnipeg," unpublished manuscript; see also Canada, "Neechi Foods Co-operative Limited: Update 2000," in *Aboriginal Co-operatives in Canada: Case Studies* (Ottawa: Minister of Public Works and Government Services Canada, 2001), pp. 97–103. [online] http://www.ainc-inac.gc.ca/ai/rs/pubs/re/abo/abo-eng.pdf Last accessed December 13, 2008.

49. All statistics and findings related to Aboriginal gaming in Canada can be found in Yale D. Belanger, *Gambling with the Future: The Evolution of Aboriginal Gaming in Canada* (Saskatoon: Purich, 2006).

50. Denise Birdstone, speaking to Royal Commission on Aboriginal Peoples commissioners during public consultation phase at Cranbrook, November 3, 1992.

51. Belanger, *Gambling with the Future,* p. 92.

52. Canada, *For Seven Generations,* p. 775.

53. Wanda Wuttunee, *Living Rhythms: Lessons in Aboriginal Economic Resilience and Vision* (Kingston and Montreal: McGill–Queen's University Press, 2003).

54. Anderson, *Economic Development,* p. 12.

55. For this argument see Tom Flanagan, *First Nations? Second Thoughts* (Kingston and Montreal: McGill–Queen's Press, 2000); and Melvin Smith, *Our Home OR Native Land? What Governments' Aboriginal Policy Is Doing to Canada* (Toronto: Stoddart, 1995).

PART 4

CONTEMPORARY ISSUES

12 Health and Well-Being in Canada

We have already paid the price. It's time to accept the many blessings that the creator has in store for us. We must honour our people who sacrificed everything through honouring ourselves and healing ourselves. By healing ourselves, we will also heal the wounds of our ancestors and the unborn generations.

—Eduardo Duran et al.[1]

Tremendous debate rages today in government circles regarding exactly who is responsible for health-care costs for reserve and urban Native people. Deeply concerned about the rising numbers of Native people who have fallen into this legislative bog and about the political infighting associated with determining government responsibility for Native health, the *Canadian Medical Association Journal* published an editorial in August 2007 urging the federal, provincial, and territorial governments to pay the medical bills for First Nations children after their initial treatment—and *then* determine who will pay those bills. The editorial writers concluded that the time was right to highlight this issue and elicit a grassroots response. Specifically, they urged Native leaders to sue the federal government for what they viewed as discriminatory behaviour that contravened the Canadian Charter of Rights and Freedoms. The experience of "Jordan" was the catalyst for this scathing editorial.

Born in 1999, "Jordan" was from the Northern Manitoba community of Norway House. Afflicted with a rare disorder, he was transferred to Winnipeg for treatment. On the advice of physicians, his family decided it would be best to discharge him to a specialized foster-care home near his community. Unfortunately the federal and Manitoba governments began squabbling over everything from who should shoulder the costs of foster care and transportation back to his community to the expense of a specialized showerhead. After two years of this bickering, Jordan died in a Winnipeg hospital. To date, no government official associated with this travesty has accepted responsibility for this preventable death or has apologized to Jordan's family.

The *CMAJ* editorial writers were clear on one issue, however: "Canada's Charter of Rights and Freedoms forbids discrimination. Many of the services Jordan needed would be paid for without question for a white Manitoban, or off-reserve Native resident. It was Jordan's living on-reserve that caused the bureaucracy to choke. That is discrimination pure and simple." Emerging from the tragedy was what the authors termed Jordan's Principle: "Consistent with the Convention on the Rights of the Child, we endorse putting the medical needs of First Nations' children first. . . . If the provincial, territorial and federal governments ignore Jordan's Principle and entangle themselves in financial or jurisdictional battles first, then governments deserve to be sued, in the most winnable test case that First Nations' advocates can manage. Let the courts decide, if the bureaucrats and politicians continue to refuse to find a timely resolution."[2]

The *CMAJ* editorial was addressing an issue that is both long-standing and timely: Native people's health-care needs have always been overlooked. Dating back to the first reliable data on Native health in Canada—specifically, reports from the early twentieth century on the health of children in residential schools—and continuing into the present day, as reflected in statistics gathered by the Native Peoples Survey, the Royal Commission on Aboriginal Peoples (RCAP), Statistics Canada, and Health Canada, it is apparent that Native health in Canada continues to suffer.

The problem is partly political—the costs of health care are constantly rising, and no one is willing to accept full responsibility for Native health. A second issue is rooted in history, in how the Europeans introduced Old World pathogens during the first three centuries of contact—pathogens that unleashed epidemics that devastated a number of Indigenous populations. One can argue that Native people continue to this day to face epidemics: HIV and diabetes, for example. Directly associated with this second issue, the European colonists perceived Indigenous peoples as too "primitive" to have acquired their own medical knowledge, or they dismissed that knowledge as babble about evil spirits or as misguided optimism.

Only in recent years have medical professionals begun to promote a more holistic approach to medicine, one that affirms traditional Indigenous concepts of health and well-being. Though progress has been made, a gap still exists: reserve and urban Native health still lags behind that of non-Native society. Moreover, good health is still largely regarded as a strictly medical issue rather than as inseparable from land claims and reserve economic development.[3]

Pre-Contact Indigenous Health

But it's not the healers doing that healing. They're the vessel. We all have a Spirit of that and some people can use it better than others who haven't learned how to use that gift because you have to have balance in your life to be able to use that. If you abuse it, it will disappear. You can see what is wrong with that sick person and you can see what kind of medicine you can use. It's a gift certain people have.

—Liza Mosher (Odawa)[4]

Before first contact in the late sixteenth century, health conditions among Indigenous people were similar to those in European societies. People developed beliefs and processes in response to health problems posed by the surrounding environment. Where the two groups differed was in the prevalence of disease. Europe by the time of first contact with South American Indigenous populations in the late 1400s was a very unhealthy place: smallpox and bubonic plague were virulent, widespread, and deadly. These devastating pathogens were foreign to the New World's Indigenous populations.[5] This is not to suggest that North America was pathogen-free or that diseases were unknown. The point is that Indigenous populations developed their own regionally specific healing systems—for example, they developed their own ways to mend broken limbs, alleviate joint pain, and cure cataracts.[6] In matters of health, they accepted that humans are an integral part of the environment and that balance must constantly be sought. In their efforts to achieve equilibrium, they developed ideas related to health that focused on more than simple absence of disease. Health, to them, meant more than physical well-being; it also involved promoting mental, emotional, and spiritual well-being through ceremony.

According to Indigenous people, health and well-being depended on a balance of mind, body, emotion, and spirit. Sickness was primarily an imbalance, often the result of an individual's failure to respect local moral codes. Thus it was thought that angry spirits could cause sickness. In all Native groups there were people specially trained in the medicinal properties of plants and animals; there were also people who had been trained to maintain the balance that was necessary to restore equilibrium and general health. For our purposes, Native health and well-being had 12 unique principles.[7]

Life Is a Spiritual Journey

Health, like life in general, was viewed by Native people as an important part of an ongoing journey in which the destination mattered less than the process itself. Those who neglected the process invariably found themselves victims of "dis-ease." Conversely, those who acknowledged the flux in life understood that everything was always changing and that well-being could only be achieved by anticipating change. From many Native perspectives, health is an ongoing, natural process that is both mental and physical and that requires constant attention. Unlike in Western medicine, there is an important spiritual aspect to Native health that is directly related to the network of relationships described in Chapter 1. Allowing relationships to deteriorate can compromise an individual's balance as well as that of the community. Thus, a person can fall ill by angering the spirits; furthermore, individuals who are skilled in bad medicine (i.e., witchcraft) can inflict illness and suffering on others. Clearly, a proactive approach to one's health is required, in order to keep the community and its individuals healthy and in balance.

Holism: An Integrated Approach

The holistic aspect of Native health is perhaps its most identifiable trait. This process-driven approach to health and wellness emphasizes mental, emotional, physical, and spiritual well-being. One area out of balance will mean that the individual is at dis-ease. Thus relationships are vital: the patient's relationships with human and nonhuman entities, but also the healer's relationship with the patient. Healers must constantly be improving their technical skills; on top of that, they must show compassion when dealing with individuals; and they must utilize their intuition when helping a person return to spiritual or physical balance. Health and well-being are in this sense spiritual, not just physical, and they are affected by all aspects of community and ceremonial life.

Balance

The world is always inherently unstable, so each member of the community must do his or her best to counteract that instability through ceremony and good living. Ceremonies are a way to renew relationships so that one can continue to strive for balance in an imperfect world. Balance is never permanent, but an individual who strives for it will be more stable. Those who fail to seek balance may fall ill.

Cause of Disease

Disease and ill health can have a multitude of causes: physical, mental, emotional, spiritual. All are the result of imbalance, which can take various forms; thus, ill health must be carefully diagnosed and the proper treatments developed. Native healers are expected to address a wide variety of health problems, from the physical to the mental to the psychosocial and psychospiritual. As in Western medicine, healers are always learning, and when faced with a problem they often seek advice from others with more expertise. Some healers have special areas of expertise; that said, the holistic approach to health requires they become as educated and knowledgeable as possible about as many health issues as possible. This suggests why it takes so long to train healers and why they have such high status in Native communities.

Healing as Opposed to Curing

There is a popular adage that it is possible to be healed but not cured. Western health models focus strongly on developing cures, whereas the Native health model promotes healing. For Native healers, cures are important but the greater goal is to bring a person back into balance from a state of imbalance. Note well that health, for Native people, is not specifically about the absence of problems, for an individual may demonstrate no outward signs of sickness and still not be feeling well. The idea of constant flux and the emphasis on relationships mean that imbalance can have multiple causes; thus, for healers, the goal is to determine just where balance has been challenged so that what is wrong can be righted. The patient is told about his or her role in maintaining wellness; this often involves being instructed in how to direct more energy toward improving their general state of mental, emotional, physical, and spiritual well-being.

Spiritual Medicine

Native medicine is multifaceted, so it is very difficult to generalize about it, except to say that we can talk about two broad categories of approaches: (1) nature-based and (2) ceremonial. Nature-based approaches use herbal medicines to heal both minor ailments and more serious ones. Each medicine has a spiritual value and its own purpose and promotes healing in a distinctive way. Ceremonial approaches are more difficult to explain. We can say, though, that all ceremonies have their specific purposes in the general project of helping individuals to maintain balance in all their relationships. "Sweats" are often resorted to in purification ceremonies and to help an individual on a vision quest. The holistic approach means that ceremonies and plant medicines are often used in concert.

Mystery

Many things in life are not understood, and some changes that happen to people have no discernable cause. Creation often manifests itself in this way—the spirit world crosses over to the realm of human experience. The well-being of humans depends on the will of the spirit beings, and healers can help this along with their ceremonial knowledge. Ultimately, though things happen for a reason and sometimes it is difficult if not impossible to know why something happened the way it did. All that can be said at those times is that the universe unfolds as it will, and that destabilization sometimes happens in ways that cannot be answered. This reminds humans that no matter how knowledgeable they may consider themselves to be, no situation can ever really be controlled.

Respect for Individuality and Diversity

The generally held view is that Indigenous people live communal lives and that an individual's existence invariably reflects the community's needs. But that is not an accurate view—respect for individuality has always been important to Native people. Indeed, individuality is vital to balance. The Native perspective is subjective at its base—in other words, the reality of each and every observer is unique to that individual's experience. How does this relate to health and well-being? We can say that healing and spirituality are also individual. Put another way, each person is free to have his or her own personal relationship with all relations, including those with the spirit world. It follows that each person must be treated in terms of his or her own unique life experiences and relationships with the spirits. So there may be similarity of experience but there can be no single "textbook" diagnosis. Adding further complexity is the unique background of each healer; each has had a unique training, and this, too, influences a patient's diagnosis and treatment.

The Healing Power of Relationships

Failing to understand the spirit world's impact on an individual can lead to dis-ease, which in turn invariably damages the community. That everything is interconnected makes the healer's task difficult, for it requires a jack-of-all-trades approach to medicine. When attempting to heal an individual, it is impossible to change one part of the universe in isolation. Every action produces an equal and opposite reaction unless properly acknowledged. This is why, for example, tobacco is offered when applying a seneca-root cure—the root's spirit must be properly acknowledged, lest it become angry and refuse to do its work. The spirits of medicines must be respected if balance is to be maintained and health returned to the individual.

Natural Process

There are patterns that observers can learn to read that enable them to see the gifts of the secular *and* spirit worlds. These patterns are in constant flux. The most obvious example is that different medicines are available during different seasons. Spending time in natural settings and developing relationships with medicinal spirits is central to the healer's craft. Witnessing and participating in this cyclical world leads to accumulated wisdom and a general understanding of what the ecological context has to offer and how to access this knowledge. Healing emerges from such observation. The earth itself is a healer.

Spiritual Interface

The importance of renewing relationships with the spirits is often viewed as integral to health and well-being. But how are those relationships to be promoted? Visions and dreams are often mentioned as effective means of accessing the spirit world to renew relationships. These moments of interaction between spiritual beings and the individual or group can be transformative for the dreamer, for those moments are when knowledge is passed on or when advice about healing is provided that can be used once awake. These visions may in fact be what does the healing.

The Patient as Healer

Finally, and perhaps most significant, is the role the patient plays in remaining healthy. The patient needs to be less a passive recipient of health care than an active participant in his or her own health. An individual's own capacity to heal is a prominent aspect of Native approaches to health and well-being. This requires work on the individual's part. People must choose healthier lifestyles and make informed choices about diet and exercise. Also, health's holistic nature demands that Native individuals not only improve their physical health but also work at improving their mental, emotional, and spiritual being. In this regard, seven important healing attitudes have been identified by Ellerby:

- Working toward healthier lifestyles places people in a position of being co-creator (guiding their own destiny).
- Investment/sacrifice is required.
- Faith is needed, especially when dealing with the mystery of health and well-being.
- Gratitude for what you have in life and for what you may receive is basic to the Native perspective.
- Forgiveness is essential to mental and emotional health.
- Humility and respect enable individuals to better understand and engage within their ecological context.
- One must have joy and humour in one's life.[8]

Introduction of European Diseases

Epidemics just about killed all our people. . . . Smallpox was real bad.

—Sally Provost (North Piikuni)[9]

First contact was in many ways uneventful. The Europeans knew very little about the local environment, and the Indigenous groups were far stronger. Indeed, the newcomers needed the goodwill of local populations in order to survive. The history books note that the French navigator Jacques Cartier's first winter along the St. Lawrence in 1534 would have been a catastrophe had the local Native people not shown him how to treat scurvy with a tonic made from bark, cedar needles, and water.[10] What the Europeans did bring to North America (albeit unknowingly) was various debilitating diseases, which in the near future would tip the scales in the settlers' favour.

On their arrival in the New World, the first European explorers and missionaries unwittingly launched what has been described as the Columbian Exchange. That term refers to the global exchange of plants, animals, and human populations, which in turn led to the introduction of destructive diseases to Indigenous populations. In North America, for example, by the 1630s European diseases—smallpox, measles, influenza, diphtheria, tuberculosis (TB), and cholera—were infiltrating Indigenous communities and causing havoc. Many native communities suffered 90 percent mortality rates.[11] The loss of life affected Indigenous peoples in a variety of ways. Shrinking populations resulted in reduced military

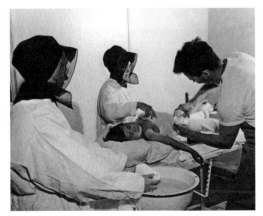

Sisters J. Marchand and M. Lachambie assist Doctor Mulvihill place a cast at St. Joseph's Hospital, Fort Resolution, NWT (ca. 1949).

strength, which allowed settlers to invade traditional territories. This in turn accelerated the fur trade, for less resistance meant quicker and deeper westward movement and increased contact with Indigenous people, which further accelerated the spread of diseases. All of this, in turn, undermined Indigenous understandings of health and well-being (review the 12 principles, outlined earlier).

Traditional practices were unable to counter the new diseases. Alternative approaches to health and well-being needed to be developed rapidly.

Perhaps most catastrophic was the incalculable loss of knowledge resulting from the recurrent outbreaks of disease. The old and young in particular lacked the strength to resist smallpox—significant epidemics occurred in 1781, 1838, and 1869. The loss of the elderly, who held each community's corpus of knowledge and whose responsibility it was to pass on those teachings, was especially devastating. With each elderly individual's premature death, a tremendous amount of knowledge was lost. The elderly died before they could instruct the young in the ecological context; as a result, a middle-aged cohort developed with a deficient body of knowledge. This diminished knowledge base was then disseminated to the young. All of this meant that a continually waning corpus of knowledge was passed on to each succeeding generation.

The loss of the very young had a different though equally severe impact. Fewer individuals were available to learn the remaining teachings; in addition, there were fewer young people born with the gifts older people looked for when choosing apprentices to instruct in the ceremonies and medicines. To summarize, the elders died without having passed on their knowledge; the result was a less informed middle-aged group with less knowledge to pass on to fewer and fewer young people. The cumulative effect was felt within a few generations and arguably influenced how Indigenous leaders interacted politically and economically with settler society.

Diseases spread quickly among Indigenous populations as a result of trade, in particular the fur trade. Most epidemics began in port settlements.[12] Over time, improvements in transportation resulted in more and more ships carrying settlers and their diseases to Canada. As the frontier opened, infected individuals began migrating west into Indigenous territories, which worsened an already terrible situation. In the more remote regions, non-Native traders were often the carriers of disease, which penetrated Indigenous nations along pre-established trade routes.

Indigenous traders often unwittingly infected their friends and neighbours when they returned home. Epidemics left some regions uninhabited. Settlers then filled these lands. Decimated Indigenous communities sometimes merged to form larger communities. In a perverse turn, the spread of diseases was often aided by traditional curative measures such as the sweat lodge, during which several men, both infected and not, gathered in a closed, humid space for a ceremony. Adding to all of this, many communities became too weak to feed themselves because too many hunters had died. Poor nutrition further weakened people and made them more susceptible to diseases.

Post-Confederation Native Health

The decline in Indigenous health continued well into the twentieth century. Poor health leading to falling populations led many government officials to declare that the Indians were a dying race. Native leaders at the community level noticed the same trends and acknowledged the need for outside help to end the suffering. Health issues and the influx of non-Native settlers into traditional lands compelled Native leaders to request treaties with the British Crown and, later, the fledgling Canadian government. The goal of these Native leaders was straightforward: to protect their peoples' lands and resources and thereby ensure cultural survival. In return for granting access to their lands, Native leaders agreed to relocate onto reserves with the understanding that the Crown would ensure their peoples' well-being.[13] Health and its related issues are not mentioned in many of the treaties, though oral histories indicate that Native leaders were concerned about their communities' well-being and realized as well that pathogen-induced poor health was being exacerbated by the loss of hunting grounds and the associated foods.

For one example, Treaty 6 specifically mentioned the Crown's responsibility for Indian health. The Plains Cree (Nehiyaw) leaders in 1876 insisted that each Indian Agent assigned to a Treaty 6 reserve be provided a medicine chest for times of pestilence and famine. This was the "medicine chest clause." Treaty Commissioner Alexander Morris highlighted the substance of this request in his notes: "The Indians were apprehensive of their future. They saw the food supply, the buffalo, passing away, and they were anxious and distressed. . . . Smallpox had destroyed them by hundreds a few years before, and they dreaded pestilence and famine."[14] Following this trend, Treaty 8 negotiators promised health care to the Dene signatories.

Besides this, federal responsibility for Indian health was spelled out in the *Indian Act* (1876), which empowered the minister to establish regulations to "prevent, mitigate and control the spread of diseases on reserves; to provide medical treatment for infectious diseases . . . and to provide for sanitary conditions . . . on reserves." But at the same time, the policies for regulating societal advancement took aim at traditional healing practices. In western Canada, for example, the Sundance and associated healing ceremonies were banned in 1895; the ban would stay in place until 1951. Health care was, however, never an important concern among government officials. After Treaty 7 was signed in 1877, Native health continued to deteriorate as once mobile bands were forced onto reserves, where they relied more and more heavily on Indian Agents for rations such as bacon and flour. This resulted in the "colonization of the body"—that is, a forced transition from country foods such as moose, elk, deer, buffalo, and fish to a diet high in sugar and fat.[15]

The residential schools (see Figure 12-1) did much to increase the damage by taking children from their families and introducing them to a more sedentary lifestyle, one that was reliant on farmed foods. It is estimated that in the early 1900s, close to one-quarter of all students entering the schools died of tuberculosis. Even Duncan Campbell Scott, Deputy Superintendent-General of Indian Affairs and a staunch assimilationist, felt compelled to state that "it is quite within the mark to say that fifty percent of the children who passed through these schools did not live to benefit from the education which they had received therein."[16] The trauma suffered in residential schools would lead to what has been described as residential school syndrome, a combination of posttraumatic stress disorder (PTSD) and historical trauma.[17] Residential school syndrome continues to work its way through contemporary Canadian society. Its symptoms include the following:

- Acute self-conflict
- Reduced self-esteem
- Emotional numbing (inability to trust or form lasting bonds)
- Somatic disorder
- Chronic depression and anxiety
- Insomnia and nightmares
- Disassociation
- Paranoia
- Sexual dysfunction
- Heightened irritability, tendency to fly into rages
- Strong tendencies toward alcoholism/drug addiction
- Suicidality.[18]

Aggravating the dreadful state of Native health was the substandard food doled out by Indian Agents. Another factor was poorly heated and ventilated homes and schools.

Except as reflected in the *Indian Act* provisions, bureaucrats paid little attention to the health and welfare of Native people as the decades passed. TB sanatoriums were founded to house the stricken, but little health infrastructure was built on reserves. Responsibility for Native health was sometimes assigned to Indian Agents or to officers of the NWMP or the Canadian military, who from time to time implemented relief measures to improve Native health. In 1922 a mobile nurse-visitor program resulted in the placement of nurses in various communities to supplement existing health services.[19] It eventually became apparent that, despite limited action and notwithstanding federal pronouncements, the Native population was not dying off. This conclusion was supported by the 1941 census, which showed that the Native population was in fact rising again. Yet even at that point, federal and

Figure 12-1 Residential Schools in Canada

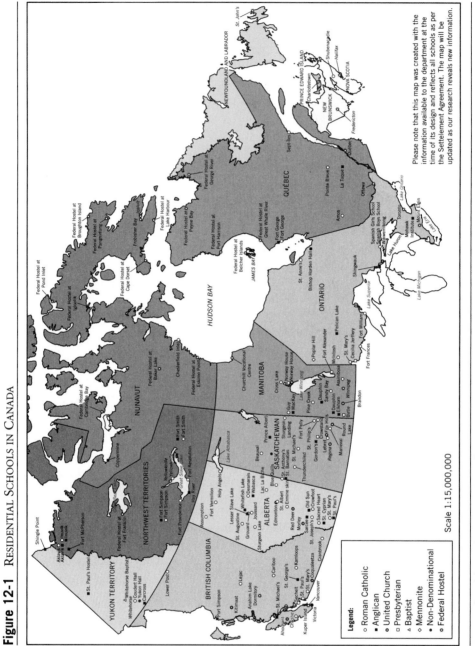

Scale 1:15,000,000

Legend:
- ○ Roman Catholic
- ■ Anglican
- ◎ United Church
- □ Presbyterian
- ▲ Baptist
- ◆ Mennonite
- ■ Non-Denominational
- ◇ Federal Hostel

Please note that this map was created with the information available to the department at the time of its design and reflects all schools as per the Settlement Agreement. The map will be updated as our research reveals new information.

Source: Adapted from Indian and Northern Affairs Canada. *Indian Residential Schools of Canada, version 2007-2.* Ottawa: Indian Residential Schools Resolution Canada, 2007.

provincial policies did little to address the growing populations, relying instead on policies designed to expedite assimilation.

Indian Agents and their superiors did their best to discredit Native healers. This forced culturally specific medicine underground and often halted it entirely. Yet federal officials failed to provide reserve residents with the required medical assistance, which left to their own devices Native groups with waning connections to tradition. Then in 1927, Colonel E.L. Stone was appointed Medical Superintendent for the Department of Indian Affairs; this coincided with the creation of that department's Medical Branch. To that point, Indian Agents had been responsible for cataloguing Native health issues and for treating illnesses, often without the aid of medical training. Appalled by what he saw, Stone called for a halt to Indian Affairs health cutbacks while declaring that every Native person in Canada deserved appropriate health care. This was easier said than done. In 1935 the Medical Branch employed 11 full-time medical officers and counted eight Indian Agents with medical training. An additional 250 physicians were employed part-time or as needed. Eleven full-time field nurses, supplemented by missionary and provincial organizations, rounded out the Department of Indian Affairs Medical Corps. This handful of medical practitioners was responsible for 112,500 Native people in 800 communities.[20]

During the 1930s, in an attempt to meet Native health needs, primary-care clinics and regional hospitals were constructed, and a public-health program was launched. Unfortunately, these institutions were often in urban centres far from reserve communities, which meant that Native people often had to travel a considerable distance to obtain health care. Also, the doctors and nurses at these centres viewed traditional medicine as little more that superstition. As a result, Native social and cultural institutions were replaced by an impersonal medical system characterized by busy and often emotionally distant doctors doing their best to interact with people who in many cases did not speak English or fully comprehend the medical concepts being described. If this were not enough, the 1950s saw a more concerted effort by federal officials, citing spiralling costs and jurisdictional authority, to persuade provincial premiers to accept responsibility for Native health.

Now the federal government began scaling back its local health programs, the goal being to compel the provinces to assume responsibility for Native health care. Animosities simmered until 1964, when, at the Dominion-Provincial Conference on Indian Affairs, the federal government infuriated the premiers by proposing to devolve Native health care and its costs to the provinces.[21] Many premiers viewed this as an overt attempt to offload federal responsibility for Native health care. So began the debate over responsibility for Native health care as recently articulated in the Jordan Principle. The provinces to this day cling to the belief that the federal government has responsibility for "Indians, and lands reserved for the Indians" under Section 91(24) of the *Indian Act*, including responsibility for their health care. This, even though the provinces are responsible under Section 92(7) of the *British North America Act* for "the Establishment, Maintenance, and Management of Hospitals, Asylums, Charities, and Eleemosynary Institutions in and for the Province." In this regard, the Supreme Court of

Canada has ruled that Section 92(16) translates into largely local authority over public health. A recent court ruling suggesting that the Treaty 6 medicine chest clause "may well require a full range of contemporary medical services" has yet to be fully articulated in federal policy.[22]

Contemporary Native Health

Native people in Canada are not as healthy as non-Native people. This has been confirmed many times in reports by various health agencies. Furthermore, Native people suffer from what most commentators contend is an unacceptable level of physical and emotional illness. Even so, researchers must recognize that Native people's health is not homogeneous: each community is unique, and variations exist between communities and among First Nations, Métis, and Inuit. Reports such as the First Nations and Inuit Regional Health Survey and the First Nations Regional Longitudinal Health Survey, and data collected by the Aboriginal Peoples Survey (designed by Statistics Canada, the Congress of Aboriginal Peoples, the Inuit Tapiriit Kanatami, the Métis National Council, the National Association of Friendship Centres, and the Native Women's Association of Canada) provide us with essential data that have been interpreted within specific frameworks designed to offer a Native perspective on Native health and related issues. This innovative approach has generated new information that speaks volumes about the current state of Native health in Canada. Overall, the study of Native health since Confederation, while quite top-heavy with late-twentieth-century analyses, indicates that Native health in Canada has long suffered from official neglect.

Alana Hill, acting director of the new White Pines Wellness Centre, a band-run clinic offering programs such as early childhood development, mental-health services, and nutritional programs.

Perhaps the most famous report is the one made by Dr. Peter H. Bryce, Chief Medical Officer for the Departments of the Interior and Indian Affairs. Following his appointment in 1904, he released a report that excoriated the recordkeeping of his medical officials. He began demanding monthly reports from them. In 1906 this statistical foundation led him to conclude that Native deaths from tuberculosis were 20 times higher than among the non-Native population. He released another report the following year after conducting a study of Native children attending residential schools. In it he condemned the Canadian government for its pitiable treatment of the schoolchildren, which he blamed on the absence of a coherent federal health policy and on the federal government's failure to commit the needed resources required for proper maintenance and adequate food.[23]

Bryce concluded that the 24 percent residential-school mortality rate from tuberculosis was directly attributable to poor sanitary conditions, lack of medical knowledge among school officials, and the ill-defined relationship between the churches contracted to operate the schools and the federal government, which was responsible for managing them. Federal officials responded immediately with a variety of measures, unveiled in 1911. These imposed construction standards for new schools and required proper maintenance of existing ones. Though Indian Agents generally agreed with Bryce's conclusions, his charges of neglect offended religious leaders.[24] Two years later, in 1913, the DIA established the position of Medical Inspector for Indian Agencies and Residential Indian Schools and procured additional funding to improve health conditions. Even so, Bryce had maligned a number of high-ranking church and government officials and was effectively shut out of policy development. Sealing his fate was the 1922 publication *The Story of a National Crime: An Appeal for Justice to the Indians of Canada,* which made public his concerns.[25]

It is striking that many of the issues Bryce raised in the early twentieth century are still issues today. In particular, his criticisms about incoherent health policy and limited funding are still relevant. For example, he was concerned about the lack of infrastructure and its debilitating effects. To this day, First Nations, Métis, and Inuit communities lag behind mainstream communities in terms of general infrastructure. On August 31, 2008, Health Canada reported that 102 First Nations communities across Canada were under boil-water advisories.[26] Also, 29 percent of water-treatment facilities on reserves posed a high risk to human health.[27] And more than half of the more than 88,000 houses on reserves were contaminated with mould and about 5,500 were without sewage mains. In all, one-quarter of First Nations adults were living in overcrowded homes. The current housing shortage is between 20,000 and 35,000 units.[28]

As in Bryce's day, Native health continues to lag behind Canadian norms. The following statistical overview will be useful (see also Figures 12-2 and 12-3):

- In 2000, life expectancy at birth for the Registered Indian population was estimated at 68.9 years for men and 76.6 years for women. This was 8.1 years and 5.5 years lower, respectively, than for the 2001 Canadian population as a whole.
- First Nations cancer mortality rates are lower than those for the overall Canadian population.
- Acute myocardial infarction (AMI) rates among First Nations are about 20 percent higher than the Canadian rate.
- Stroke rates among First Nations are almost twice as high as the comparable Canadian figures.
- In 2000, tuberculosis rates among First Nations populations were 6 to 11 times higher than for the Canadian population.

Figure 12-2 LIFE EXPECTANCY, REGISTERED INDIANS

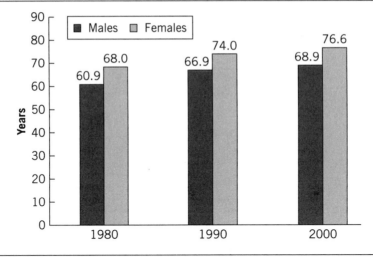

Source: *Basic Departmental Data* 2001. Ottawa: Indian and Northern Affairs Canada: find this on the INAC website, http://www.ainc-inac.gc.ca. Reproduced with the permission of the Minister of Public Works and Government Services Canada, 2008.

Figure 12-3 SELECTED MORTALITY RATES, FIRST NATIONS ON-RESERVE (2000) AND CANADA (2001)

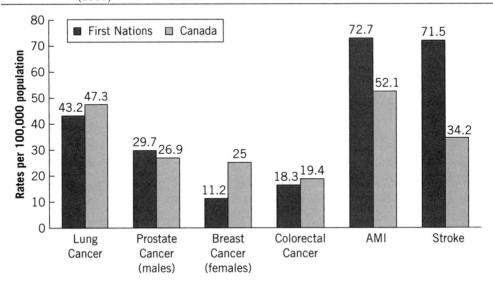

Source: First Nations Comparable Health Indicators, Health Canada, January 2005, Reproduced with the permission of the Minister of Public Works and Government Services Canada, 2008.

- The proportion of AIDS cases among Native people had climbed from 1.7 percent of all cases in Canada in 1992 to 7.2 percent in 2001.
- The 2000 reported rate of genital chlamydia was very high in the First Nations population—about six times higher than the Canadian rate (178.9 per 100,000 population in 2001).[29]

The data also suggest that reserve residents are not that different from off-reserve individuals when it comes to health status. For example, more on-reserve Native people report diabetes (8 percent versus 6 percent), though fewer report respiratory diseases (16 percent versus 18 percent). Also, more off-reserve individuals report seeing a physician (75 percent versus 62 percent). Yet more folks on reserve report seeing a registered nurse (37 percent versus 24 percent), a community counsellor (16 percent versus 6 percent), and/or a traditional healer (7 percent versus 5 percent). Fewer on-reserve individuals report cardio-vascular disease (6 percent versus 7 percent), and hypertension (12.7 percent versus 13.1 percent). On-reserve Native people generally have worse health and utilize health care less often that off-reserve Native people.

Regional variances also exist. Take, for example, Inuit health in Canada's Far North. In a region where patients with serious illnesses often must wait 8 to 12 hours for a flight in order to see a southern physician, it is estimated that less than 40 percent of Inuit living in the Arctic get to see a doctor throughout the year. Compare this with the 70 percent listed for other Canadians. Food costs more than 2.5 times more in the North than in the south, and regional suicide rates for the Inuit are six times higher than the national average.[30]

Separating data into the above-mentioned categories is required if we are to better understand First Nations, Métis, and Inuit health issues. But then these categories often obscure the fact that diseases adversely affect *all* Native communities. Take diabetes. Before 1940 there was no evidence of diabetes among Native people in Canada. By the mid-1980s, a staggering increase was evident among the Native population. Besides being a life-altering disease that can lead to limb amputation, blindness, and even death, the costs associated with diabetes are extremely high and expected to rise significantly. The Native community is currently on the verge of—and by some accounts already beset by—a full-blown diabetes epidemic. A number of recent studies have concluded that diabetes among Native people is between 3.6 and 5 times more prevalent than among non-Native men and women.[31]

Additional research reflects this prevalence, especially among the Cree–Ojibwa, Mohawk (Kanien'kehá:ka), Oneida (Onyota'a:ka), Algonquian and James Bay Cree. Some groups, such as the Inuit, seem to be at lower risk. Despite this promising trend—which suggests that so far diabetes has not gravely affected all Native populations—a recent study from Manitoba observes a trend toward the earlier onset of Type II diabetes during the young teen years.[32] This suggests that the threat of diabetes will be a recurrent theme for some time to come among Native people in Canada. The age of onset is younger among Native people—the youngest Native person to develop Type II diabetes mellitus to date was only six, and complications such as renal and cardiovascular disease are more frequent and develop more quickly among Native people than among non-Native people. Furthermore, a study of mortality on First Nations reserves conducted between 1977 and 1982 in seven provinces found that the risk of death from diabetes was 2.2 and 4.1 times higher among Native men and women respectively than in the national population.[33]

In December 1992 the executive director of the Sioux Lookout First Nation Health authority, Nellie Beardy, in her presentation to the RCAP commissioners, outlined how prevalent diabetes had become in the Native community. Describing how non–insulin-dependent diabetes mellitus had come to be regarded as a major disease among North American Native communities in the 1980s, she showed that in the Sioux Lookout region about 1,095 people in the population 25 years and over and 2,040 people in the population 55 years and over were known to be diabetic. Close to 50 percent of the cases had been diagnosed within five to ten years of Beardy's RCAP presentation.[34] To the northeast, the Cree community of Moose Factory on the western shore of James Bay had recently been introduced to a more sedentary lifestyle—to fast-food vendors, restaurants, department stores, and the like. She cited this new access to Western dietary choices as increasing the prevalence of diabetes in the community, where among people 15 years of age and older, diabetes was now close to two times more common than in the Canadian population as a whole.[35]

The reality could be far worse than Beardy suggested. Researchers from Mount Sinai Hospital in Toronto conducted a study at Sandy Lake, a community of 1,600 Oji-Cree about 2,000 kilometres northwest of Toronto. Their final report, released in 1997, concluded that in Sandy Lake the overall prevalence of Type II diabetes was five times the national average. Young women in the community had high rates of obesity, low levels of physical fitness, and impaired glucose tolerance, which is a pre-diabetes condition. Some ten-year-olds were already diabetic. The study highlighted how students gravitated toward the popular local deli counter to purchase pizza, nachos, hamburgers, cereal, fried chicken, and chips. At home these students regularly ate hamburgers, french fries, wieners, soup, and french toast. The more sedentary, consumer-based approach to eating had resulted in a 26 percent diabetes rate at Sandy Lake—four to five times the national average and the third highest rate in the world.[36]

HOUSING[37]

The World Health Organization (WHO) has concluded that housing is a key social determinant of health. The United Nations (UN) has declared that adequate housing is a distinct human right. Poor housing can result in poor health, family violence, suicide, substance abuse, and other social problems; it can also damage economic well-being. A causal relationship has been identified between children's poor health and substandard housing; the drivers in this include increased stress related to parents' financial and psychosocial struggles. Those who experience overcrowded housing conditions before 11 years of age are more likely to catch infectious disease, for example. For adults, overcrowding is linked to greater likelihood of respiratory disease. Other studies have linked inadequate heating and dampness to poor health, in particular among children and the elderly.

Table 12-1 NATIVE LIVING CONDITIONS, LETHBRIDGE, AB

	North Lethbridge	South Lethbridge	West Lethbridge
No power supply	6%	3.2%	2.2%
No kitchen facilities	8%	3.2%	2.2%
No refrigerator	9%	3.2%	2.2%
No sewage connection	8%	3.2%	4.5%
No bathroom facilities	12%	10%	4.5%
No hot water system	8%	10%	18.2%
No washing machine	20%	19.4%	18.2%
No dry food storage	26%	20%	18.2%

A 2006 study examined Native housing in Lethbridge, Alberta. The findings were startling (see Table 12-1). The Native population is younger and growing more rapidly than the non-Native population in Lethbridge—owing, in part, to high birth rates and fertility rates and urban migration from surrounding reserves. The demand for rental housing is severe: Lethbridge's rental vacancy rate is falling, resulting in rent competition. It is expected that the town's Native population will be forced out of contention for rental units as landlords choose to rent to non-Native families.

Reconciling Native Health and Federal Policies

When it comes to Métis health, traditional knowledge and healing practices have always been passed from generation to generation through storytelling, observation and direct experience. Using and understanding traditional medicines and the importance of our connection to the land is founded within Métis culture, language and traditions. Our Elders are respected as our teachers and guides.

—National Aboriginal Health Organization, Métis Centre[38]

Native health in Canada is increasingly compromised by the provincial and federal governments' refusal to accept responsibility for First Nations, Métis, and Inuit well-being. Citing Canada's responsibility for Indians under Section 91(24) of the *British North America Act* (1867), provincial officials contend that Native health is a federal responsibility, even though Section 92 states clearly that health is a provincial responsibility. Federal officials respond that the *Canada Health Act* clearly assigns the provinces the burden of health-service delivery to all provincial citizens, Native people included. Interjurisdictional disputes like these leave many people waiting for health services. This issue is especially serious for those individuals who are unable to register under the *Indian Act.* The federal government has identified this population as ineligible for health benefits; in addition to that, the provinces have rejected any liability for Native people, suggesting that the federal government is responsible for their health care. This conflict will deepen as urban Native populations continue to grow. Often lost in the mix are those First Nations, Métis, and Inuit communities managing their own health facilities—as reserve and rural Native populations continue to grow, so too will their need to expand health services. Generally speaking, there is a moral imperative to care for community members, notwithstanding their membership status. Without a corresponding increase in funding, and without better structured health policies that outline federal and provincial governments' responsibilities, Native people will continue to suffer poor health.

Improving health care for Native people is absolutely vital and arguably will require the federal government to expand its role in public-health and nursing services in northern Canada. As happened in the 1930s with nursing stations, nurses provide primary health care in most remote and northern Native communities (see chart below). Where it is cost-effective, doctors are flown in. However, as in Jordan's case, northern and remote Native patients are often expected to travel to southern medical institutions. This leads to disputes over who is responsible for paying expenses such as food, lodging, and travel. Unfortunately for Native people, the federal government's definition of "health service" is narrowly defined as including primary-prevention services. The inevitable downsizing requires cost-cutting measures, which are tied to provincial funding formulas. During the 1980s, cost cutting occurred as health-care costs increased; the result was fewer services and a revamped provincial health-service structure, brought about by transferring substantial responsibilities to regional health boards. In some cases this offered an opportunity for Native communities to engage nearby health boards, to be heard and to have their concerns dealt with. This is a fairly new process, and to date not all of the myriad concerns related to Native health care have been reconciled.

CHART (TIMELINE)

1945. The Department of National Health and Welfare is formed, and includes within it an Indian Health Program. Infrastructure to support a health system for the on-reserve First Nations population is developed; this includes establishing health centres, nursing stations, and hospitals.

1952. The federal government agrees, as a matter of policy, to provide health services to the entire populations of Yukon and the Northwest Territories. Thus, the Inuit come under federal responsibility for the provision of health services.

Early 1950s. The administration of First Nations and Inuit health services is decentralized from Ottawa to regional offices.

1962. The Medical Services Branch is formed, comprising all federally mandated health services, including the following:

- Indian health
- Occupational health for federal public servants other than the RCMP and the military
- Civil-aviation medicine
- Quarantine services
- Medical support for the Department of Immigration in screening immigrants coming to Canada, and for Canadian embassy personnel overseas
- Emergency health services, including the stockpiling of emergency supplies nationwide.

1988. Responsibility for the provision of health services for the entire Northwest Territorial population, including First Nations and Inuit, is transferred to the Northwest Territories.

1997. Responsibility for the provision of health services for the entire Yukon population, including First Nations and Inuit, is transferred to Yukon.

2000. All federal health responsibilities, other than First Nations and Inuit health services, are transferred from the Medical Services Branch back to the respective federal departments. The First Nations and Inuit Health Branch (FNIHB) of Health Canada is formed.

These jurisdictional issues—in particular, provincial efforts to avoid responsibility for Indian health care—are beginning to negatively affect Métis and Non-Status Indians living off-reserve.

Conclusion

There is still some medicine around that we use. When I go into the woods, I see medicines that my grandmother used to use. There is a certain kind of medicine made of tree gum, it is used for pain, sore throat, that kind of thing. They would put in on your chest and they would use a paper from a prayer book to stick it on, it could not just be any paper, it had to be like a sacred paper.

—Elizabeth Penashue (Innu)[39]

Native people maintain that to improve health in both rural and urban centres, communities will have to administer their own, culturally relevant heath programs and associated services. Only then will community healing begin. This is as much about strengthening self-government capacity as it is about establishing healthy communities and improving social environments. It was recently reported that only 100 of Canada's 58,000 physicians were of Native heritage. Worsening an already difficult situation is that little is being done to revise outdated policies or to bridge the jurisdictional gap that has left many Native people without adequate health care. Some provincial governments have initiated research, but the issue is one of relationship—that is, the ongoing struggle between the provincial and federal governments regarding who should look after the health care of an already impoverished group of Canadians. It should be no surprise that Native leaders believe that with a transfer of authority, they and their communities would be better suited to improve Native health nationally.

FURTHER READING

Duran, Eduardo, and Bonnie Duran. *Native American Post Colonial Psychology.* New York: SUNY Press, 1995.

Hackett, Paul. *A Very Remarkable Sickness: Epidemics of the Petit Nord, 1670 to 1846.* Winnipeg: University of Manitoba Press, 2002.

Kelm, Mary-Ellen. *Colonizing Bodies: Aboriginal Health and Healing in British Columbia, 1900–1950.* Vancouver: UBC Press, 1998.

Waldram, James B. *Revenge of the Windigo: The Construction of the Mind and Mental Health of North American Aboriginal Peoples.* Toronto: University of Toronto Press, 2004.

———, D. Ann Herring, and T. Kue Young. *Aboriginal Health in Canada: Historical, Cultural, and Epidemiological Perspectives.* Toronto: University of Toronto Press, 2006.

Young, T. Kue. *Health Care and Cultural Change: The Indian Experience in the Central Subarctic.* Toronto: University of Toronto Press, 1988.

NOTES

1. Eduardo Duran, Bonnie Duran, Maria Yellow Horse Brave Heart, and Susan Yellow Horse-Davis, "Healing the American Indian Soul Wound," in *International Handbook of Multigenerational Legacies of Trauma,* ed. Yael Danieli (New York: Plenum, 1998), pp. 341–54.

2. Noni MacDonald and Amir Attaran, "Jordan's Principle, Government's Paralysis," *Canadian Medical Association Journal* 177, no. 4 (2007): 321.

3. Russel Lawrence Barsh, "Ecocide, Nutrition, and the 'Vanishing Indian,'" in *State Violence and Ethnicity,* ed. Pierre van den Berghe (Colorado: University Press of Colorado, 1991), p. 245.

4. Peter Kulchyski, Don McCaskill, and David Newhouse, *In the Words of the Elders: Aboriginal Cultures in Transition* (Toronto: University of Toronto Press, 1999), pp. 161–62.

5. Paul Hackett, *A Very Remarkable Sickness: Epidemics in the Petit Nord, 1670 to 1846* (Winnipeg: University of Manitoba Press, 2002).

6. James Waldram, D. Ann Herring, and T. Kue Young, *Aboriginal Health in Canada: Historical, Cultural, and Epidemiological Perspectives* (Toronto: University of Toronto Press, 1995), pp. 97–121.

7. The twelve principles discussed can be found in Jonathan H. Ellerby, "Spirituality, Holism, and Healing Among the Lakota Sioux: Towards an Understanding of Indigenous Medicine" (M.A. thesis, University of Manitoba, 2001), pp. 96–158.

8. Ibid., pp. 141–45.

9. In Treaty 7 Elders and Tribal Council with Walter Hildebrant, Sarah Carter, and Dorothy First Rider, *The True Spirit and Original Intent of Treaty 7* (Kingston and Montreal: McGill–Queen's University Press, 1996), p. 102.

10. J.R. Miller, *Skyscrapers Hide the Heavens: A History of Indian-White Relations in Canada,* 3rd ed. (Toronto: University of Toronto Press, 2000), pp. 30–31.

11. For a brief but excellent overview, see Russell Thornton, "Health, Disease, and Demography," in *A Compilation of American Indian History,* ed. Philip J. Deloria and Neal Salisbury (Malden: Blackwell, 2004), pp. 68–84; and Waldram, Herring, and Young, *Aboriginal Health in Canada,* pp. 3–47. For the effects of smallpox on the Prairie populations, see C. Stuart Houston, "The First Smallpox Epidemic on the Canadian Plains: In the Fur-Traders' Words," *Canadian Journal of Infectious Diseases* 11, no. 2 (2000): 112–15.

12. Hackett, *A Very Remarkable Sickness,* pp. 21–36.

13. James [Sakej] Youngblood Henderson, "The Constitutional Right of an Enriched Livelihood," *Journal of Aboriginal Economic Development* 4, no. 1 (2004): 43–58.

14. Alexander Morris, *The Treaties of Canada with the Indians of Manitoba and the Northwest Territories* (Toronto: Fifth House, 1991), p. 177.

15. Mary Ellen Kelm, *Colonizing Bodies: Aboriginal Health and Healing in British Columbia, 1900–1950* (Vancouver: UBC Press, 1998).

16. Quoted in J.R. Miller, *Shingwauk's Vision: A History of Native Residential Schools* (Toronto: University of Toronto Press, 1996), p. 133.

17. Lloyd Hawkeye Robertson, "The Residential School Experience: Syndrome or Historic Tauma," *Pimatisiwin* 4, no. 1 (2006): 1–28.

18. Ward Churchill, *Kill the Indian, Save the Man: The Genocidal Impact of American Indian Residential Schools* (San Francisco: City Lights, 2004), pp. 68–76.

19. Waldram, Herring, and Young, *Aboriginal Health in Canada,* pp. 141–76.

20. Ibid.

21. Canada, *Federal–Provincial Conference on Indian Affairs: Report of Proceedings* (Ottawa: Indian Affairs Branch, Department of Citizenship and Immigration, 1964).

22. *Wuskwi Sipihk Cree Nation v. Canada* (Minister of National Health and Welfare) [1999] F.C.J. No. 82, p. 5.

23. Megan Sproule-Jones, "Crusading for the Forgotten: Dr. Peter Bryce, Public Health, and Prairie Native Residential Schools," *Canadian Bulletin of Medical History* 13 (1996): 199–224.

24. Ibid.

25. Peter H. Bryce, *The Story of a National Crime: An Appeal for Justice to the Indians of Canada* (Ottawa: James Hope and Sons, 1922).

26. Canada, *First Nations, Inuit and Aboriginal Health: Drinking Water Advisories* (Ottawa: Health Canada, 2008). [online] http://www.hc-sc.gc.ca/fniah-spnia/promotion/water-eau/advis-avis_concern-eng.php. Last accessed September 8, 2008.

27. Canada, *Backgrounder: Water Quality and First Nations Communities* (Ottawa: Indian and Northern Affairs Canada, 2003). [online] http://www.ainc-inac.gc.ca/ai/mr/nr/j-a2008/2-3019-bk-eng.asp. Last accessed December 16, 2008.

28. Canada, *Fact Sheet: Aboriginal Housing* (Ottawa: Indian and Northern Affairs, 2006). [online] http://www.ainc-inac.gc.ca/ai/mr/is/res-hsng-eng.asp. Last accessed December 16, 2008.

29. Canada, *First Nations, Inuit, and Aboriginal Health: First Nations Comparable Health Indicators* (Ottawa: Health Canada, 2007). [online] http://www.hc-sc.gc.ca/fniah-spnia/diseases-maladies/2005-01_health-sante_indicat-eng.php. Last accessed September 10, 2008.

30. "Aboriginal Health Care 'Shameful,' Summit Told," *CBCNews.ca,* September 14, 2004. [online] http://www.cbc.ca/canada/story/2004/09/13/health_natives040913.html. Last accessed June 16, 2008.

31. T. Kue Young, Emoke J. Szathmary, S. Evers, and B. Wheatly, "Geographical Distribution of Diabetes Among the Native Population of Canada: A National Survey," *Social Science Medicine* 31, no. 2 (1990): 129–39; and David A.L. Maberly, Will King, and Alan F. Cruess, "The Prevalence of Diabetes in the Cree of Western James Bay," *Chronic Diseases in Canada* 21, no. 3 (2000): 128–33.

32. T. Kue Young, "Diabetes Mellitus Among Native Americans in Canada and the United States: An Epidemiological Review," *American Journal of Human Biology* 5, no. 4 (2005): 399–413.

33. Y. Mao, H. Morrison, R. Semenciw, and D. Wigle, "Mortality on Canadian Indian Reserves, 1977–1982," *Canadian Journal of Public Health* 77 (1986): 263–68.

34. Nellie Beardy, Executive Director, Sioux Lookout Aboriginal Health Authority. Presentation to Royal Commission on Aboriginal Peoples (RCAP), Sioux Lookout, December 1, 1992.

35. Ibid.

36. "Diabetes Researchers Find 'Virtual Epidemic' in Native Community," *Globe and Mail,* November 7, 1997, C6.

37. The information for this box and the following chart can be found in Yale D. Belanger, "Assessing Urban Aboriginal Housing Needs in Southern Alberta," *Saskatchewan Institute on Public Policy,* Public Policy Paper no. 51 (June 2007), p. 34.

38. National Aboriginal Health Organization, Métis Centre. [online] http://www.naho.ca/metiscentre/english/index.php. Last accessed August 27, 2007.

39. Kulchyski, McCaskill, and Newhouse, *In the Words of the Elders,* p. 213.

Communications

Many of the myths and misperceptions that persist among non-Aboriginal people are perpetuated by no communication, poor communication, or one-sided communication. . . . The depth and diversity of the Aboriginal perspectives must be communicated through both First Nations and "mainstream" news media, to as broad a public as possible.

—Bud White Eye, Native News Network[1]

For thousands of years, inter- and intratribal communication systems were prominent features of North American Indigenous societies. As discussed in Chapter 3, stories and songs were utilized both to catalogue social and historical information and to pass that information on to subsequent generations. The late Gail Valaskakis (Chippewa) concluded: "Communication is not just the cultural glue that [held] communities together. Communication is the dynamic ground in which individuals and communities are formed."[2] These systems of communication ranged from simple face-to-face dialogues to more elaborate councils where leaders representing various communities conferred for periods lasting weeks, sometimes even months. Information-exchange methods ranged from neighbouring nations crossing paths during their travels and exchanging quick stories to extended discussions held during large trade conventions. Family members visiting their relations in neighbouring communities revelled in the recent gossip while obtaining up-to-date news about local and regional happenings. Extended war and trade parties returned with stories chronicling recent events.

The extent of communications systems is not known precisely, but we can say they were impressive; as an example, consider that the Blackfoot (Niitsítapi) and Cree (Nehiyaw) on the Plains knew decades in advance that settlers might be moving onto their territories. Canadian officials responded to what they viewed as well-established communications networks by sequestering Native people on reserves. This made it easier for Indian Agents to watch them; it also halted regional movement, thus undermining communications. Federal policies impeded regional communications, compelling Native people to embrace new methods for transmitting information, such as newspapers and newsletters. Eventually Native Canadians developed their own historians, poets, novelists, journalists, and (later) actors in an effort to present a more accurate image of "Indians" to Canadians—and to one another.

Since the 1970s, Native people in Canada have been developing media that are relevant to their communities. They often use the media they control to contest mainstream Canada's largely simplistic perceptions of them, to promote self-determination, to resist outside cultural influences, and for entertainment and cultural expression. All of these are good uses for local media. Native people's efforts to influence the electronic media date back to the 1960s; those early efforts set the stage for the today's proliferation. Television and the Internet are now ubiquitous in Native communities. Native Canadians now operate a national TV network (Aboriginal Peoples Television Network), dozens of radio stations, and several prominent newspapers, yet little has been written about the Native media in Canada. This chapter describes the evolution of Native communications in Canada.

Challenging Stereotypes

[Stereotypes] vary over time, and range from the extremely pejorative to the artificially idealistic, from historic depictions of Indians as uncivilized primal men and winsome women belonging to a savage culture, to present day Indians as mystical environmentalists, or uneducated, alcoholic bingo players confined to reservations. It is little wonder, then, that we have misinformed our teachers in our schools, who pass along their misconceptions to their students.

—Devon A. Mihesuah (Choctaw)[3]

To understand how Native media developed, it is important to understand the harmful impact of stereotypes. For much of Canada's history as a nation, the European-controlled media determined what was newsworthy. (Media, for this chapter's purposes, include journals, travelogues, official correspondence, settler diaries, and academic discourse.) From the moment of first contact, the European media controlled the image of Indigenous peoples.[4] Low literacy rates in Europe encouraged the dissemination of false or sensationalistic images of them to the masses. As literacy rates improved, diaries, travelogues, and government correspondence gave way to academic writing and newspapers; by that point, the stereotypes had been planted. Writers circulated sensationalized accounts of Indigenous people to susceptible readers, posing as "educators" on Native ways, and the public accepted their views without questioning them. The resulting stereotypes came to be accepted as the truth—so much so that by the late nineteenth century, those stereotypical images were being utilized to sell newspapers and manufactured goods. That process continues to this day, with marketers resorting to Native stereotypes to sell cars, ties, chewing tobacco, and alcohol, to name a few of the products.[5]

Stereotypes mask the strong diversity of Native peoples—their different languages and beliefs, their different ways of life. Typically, non-Natives are presented with two well-worn images: (1) the noble, peace-loving savage and (2) the bloodthirsty and inherently warlike savage. The latter image dates back to philosopher John Locke's 1651 description of Indians as "the savage people of America," the former to John Dryden's reference to the innate goodness of man in the state of nature in his 1670 play *The Conquest of Granada*.[6] The noble savage was given additional currency in the mid-eighteenth century by Jean-Jacques Rousseau and other Enlightenment philosophers. Both stereotypes flourished over the next two centuries and well into the modern era. According to the late Paula Gunn Allen, stereotypes, while especially harmful to Indigenous peoples, also undermined Europeans' ability to realize their own folly since they "they haven't any means of noticing or assessing the psychic damage done to themselves because they lack any outside reference."[7] Janice Acoose writes that images of Native women in Canadian literature, for example, "perpetuate unrealistic and derogatory ideas, which consequently foster cultural attitudes that legitimize rape and other kinds of violence."[8]

Native people who express frustration with harmful stereotypes and who demand that such images be combated are often labelled "angry" or "irrational."[9] Take, for example, the debate over sports-team mascots in the United States, which dates back to the 1970s. It has recently taken on new life with the University of North Dakota's (UND) refusal to change its "Fighting Sioux" nickname. Those who support Indian mascots often note that the Irish could conceivably be offended by Notre Dame's Fighting Irish moniker, and that People for the Ethical Treatment of Animals (PETA) might try to force the Illinois Bears to change their name. In other words, they contend that opposing Indian mascots is political correctness run amok and that the nicknames must be defended to halt the Native leaders' senseless posturing.

Yet in 2008 the National Collegiate Athletic Association (NCAA) announced that UND had three years to gain Sioux approval to use the tribe's name for the mascot. Soon after, National Basketball Association coach and UND alumnus Phil Jackson challenged his alma mater to change the name.[10] The American Anthropological Association has followed suit, voting to cease all meetings in Illinois until the administration and trustees of the University of Illinois replace their "Chief Illiniwek" symbol. In a less publicized incident, Northern Colorado University intramural students decided to protest a local high school's team name, the "Fighting Reds," by anointing their team the "Fightin' Whities." Using humour to make a point, they produced a logo, began selling T-shirts, and established a scholarship fund.

But stereotypes are not always this obvious. It is the subtle yet well-worn clichés that have done the most damage, by objectifying Native people, who as a result have found themselves on the periphery of Canadian society, socially, economically, and politically. This false imagery inspired the First World War veteran F.O. Loft, a former *Brantford Expositor* reporter who understood the power of the written word to connect people. In his attempts to found a Canadian Indian political organization, he often distributed news releases to announce his upcoming appearances. Loft's work was predated by some four decades by the Grand General Indian Council's newspaper, *The Indian*. Both Loft's work and *The Indian* were aimed at establishing what Shannon Avison has described an alternative sphere of influence: a communications realm that can accommodate nontraditional perspectives and that promotes social equality by influencing mainstream discussions about Native people.[11] As we will see, early Native newspapers did establish this alternative arena. Television, radio, and more recently the Internet have in their turn expanded this sphere of influence.

Early Native Print Media

Many scholars contend that the Native Communications Program (NCP), established in 1973, was the crucible for Native print media in Canada. The suggestion is that only in the early 1970s did Native people begin to develop their own media. Actually, the Native media in Canada date back to the 1880s. The Native media have always served two objectives:

- to interpret events from a Native perspective, one that the mainstream media do not provide, and
- to balance mainstream analyses of events with Native analyses.

In the United States, there were Native newspapers by the mid-1800s. The *Cherokee Phoenix* was the first such newspaper. It began regular publication in 1827, after the Cherokee tribal council allocated funding for an office and a printing press. Under the editorship of Elias Boudinot, the paper operated until 1834, when a financial crisis forced it to close doors temporarily. In its early years, the *Phoenix* was published in Cherokee and English to a readership spanning Georgia, Alabama, Tennessee, North Carolina, Arkansas, Oklahoma, and Texas. Besides printing political and human-interest stories, it published notices of meetings and of new federal and state laws that might affect the Cherokee. The paper helped the geographically dispersed Cherokee populations remain politically united. The *Phoenix* eventually resumed publication and is still published today.[12]

The *Phoenix* was published in Cherokee. But English was the language of North America's print media, which meant that to participate in print, Native people would have to work in that language. A number of Native journalists wrote in English; and a number of those journalists branched out, writing histories and literary stories to express a Native perspective. In 1772, Samson Occum (Mohegan) published an anti-alcohol sermon in English; and in the mid-1800s in Canada, the Reverends George Copway and Peter Jones (both Ojibwa) penned popular autobiographies as well as detailed histories of the Ojibwa people (see Chapter 3). English slowly flourished in Native communities, and apprentice publishers seized the chance to distribute their works to larger audiences. The loss of language is lamentable, but Indian newspapers had to be printed in English, for most Native languages had no alphabet. Also, the myriad languages and dialects spoken across Canada made translation of news stories a serious challenge. So English became the language of Native politics.

In 1885 the first Native-controlled newspaper in Canada, *The Indian,* began publishing under the editorship of Dr. Peter E. Jones (Ojibwa), a medical doctor and one-time Indian Agent who was also the son of the Methodist missionary and author Peter Jones. Jones the Younger was also the secretary-treasurer of the Grand General Indian Council of Ontario. He worried that the federal government would dissolve all reserves in order to enforce assimilation. So he founded *The Indian* as an organ for providing news from "all of the principle reserves in North America and especially Canada." *The Indian* dealt with local elections, provided forums to discuss proposed legislation affecting Indians, and reported on band conditions. It also offered explanations of "game laws and treaty rights . . . whenever applicable."[13] Though initially successful—circulation tripled in the nine months after the first issue—by the end of 1886 *The Indian* had ceased publication.

Native leaders during this period began turning to mainstream newspapers for insights into Canadian culture. While the Cree leader Big Bear was in exile in the United States following the Riel Resistance in 1885, he asked English-speaking colleagues to translate the *Saskatchewan Herald* so that he could stay apprised of political events—for example, of which bands had accepted treaty adhesions and reserve placements. Three years earlier, in an attempt to offset the bad press generated by government officials, Big Bear had published a statement in the *Herald* countering their assertions.[14]

The next six decades saw various failed attempts to establish Native newspapers. By then, more and more Native people were learning English. One impediment to communications among Native people was the diversity of languages. Another was high operating costs, which made it difficult to maintain a regular publishing schedule. In the 1930s, Ben Christmas (Mi'kmaq) founded the short-lived *Micmac News*. The Native Brotherhood of British Columbia (NBBC), a political and labour organization, established *The Native Voice*. Edited by the Reverend Peter Kelly (Haida), a political activist, *The Native Voice* was inspired by the Alaska Native Brotherhood's *The Native Fisherman*.

In the beginning, *The Native Voice* was owned and operated by a non-Native woman named Maisie Hurley, though the editor, assistant editor, and directors were all Native. Free subscriptions were offered to help keep NBBC members informed. The paper's stated purpose was to instill "a closer relationship between ourselves and our good white friends who we appeal to at this time for the support in our advancement."[15] Following the NBBC's lead, long-time political activist, organizer, and former journalist Andy Paull (Squamish) established *The Thunderbird* (1949–53). This was followed by a second publication, *The Totem Speaks*, which was published for one year (1953). Both these papers received financial backing from the Roman Catholic Church and were geared toward compelling the Canadian government to call a Royal Commission to investigate the administration of the Indian Affairs Department.

Clearly, Native newspapers during those years had set out to challenge mainstream media discourses so that a more balanced understanding of events could emerge. Between 1946 and 1948 a Special Joint Committee (SJC) was struck to investigate the *Indian Act*, and Indian political leaders from across Canada were invited to Ottawa to participate. The issues dealt with were complex, generating dynamic presentations from Native leaders, who critiqued Canada's Indian policy from legal, economic, political, and cultural perspectives. Yet the mainstream press distilled two years' worth of hearings and one million words of testimony and submissions from Indian organizations into simple conclusions. Headlines such as "Survey of Indian Problems Asked," "Indian Debate Brings Out M.P. in 'Warpaint'—He's an Ojibway," "Indians Indignant," "B.C. Indians Stalk MP's in Their Lair," "Indians Give Up 2 Million Acres in Last 67 Years," "Assimilation of All Indians Recommended," and "Our Forgotten One Per Cent" graced the pages of regional and national newspapers, framing the issues quite rigidly.

These headlines in themselves conveyed to readers that an Indian problem existed and that indignant Indians were intent on remedying the situation, if necessary by stalking government officials. No doubt, their strategies would involve the repatriation of lands lost through Indian Affairs mismanagement as well as improvements to on-reserve living conditions.[16]

In contrast, the Native press as represented by *The Native Voice* and *The Thunderbird* offered insights about Native rights, citizenship, and enfranchisement, as well as the costs the federal government might incur in implementing the committee recommendations. The mainstream media had condensed the SJC findings into simple calls for liberalized drinking laws for Indians and for the right to vote in Canadian elections; the Native media were more diligent, calling for an increased Old Age Pension for Native people, the removal and/or abolition of outdated sections of the *Indian Act* restricting access to funding for on-reserve economic development, and the right to vote in Dominion elections without submitting to forced enfranchisement. *The Thunderbird* argued that the revised *Indian Act* contravened the UN's "Universal Declaration of Human Rights" and noted that Native leaders from across Canada were generally dissatisfied with the outcome of the SJC. Clearly, the issues at hand were far more complex than was suggested in the mainstream media. Each side considered its perspective uniquely valid.

With the help of a $10,000 provincial grant, the Federation of Saskatchewan Indians (FSI) between 1960 and 1963 published the *Indian Outlook*, which was more a newsletter than a newspaper. Except for that, there was little Native publishing between 1953 and 1968. This cannot be blamed on the government: in 1964, Native groups were provided nearly $150,000 for similar projects, but the money found few takers, and few regular publications emerged.[17] Native publishers faced a variety of barriers, not the least of which was a lack of operating funds. In the pre-Internet age, long-distance telephone service and postage rates could be crippling. Also, the delivery of newspapers to far-flung reserve communities was costly.

Native Communications in the 1970s

Some of the Aboriginal communications initiatives over the years were just temporary, and others have somehow died along the way, but they all gave birth to a rather vibrant network of professionals who have become a unique element of the Canadian public communication landscape, albeit poorly paid and in some cases unemployed.

—Roy Fox, National Aboriginal Communications Society[18]

Toward the end of the 1960s, a rise in Native political activism and an infusion of federal funding combined to assist the development of Native cultural organizations. This prepared the ground for a national Native newspaper industry. The 1969 White Paper had left Native leaders openly hostile to the federal government, which was proposing to eradicate

"Indians" through legislation. The circulation of position papers by various political organizations kept Native people apprised of their colleagues' objections to the White Paper. This in turn encouraged many organizations to publish monthly newsletters to keep their members informed. Many Native leaders noted how quickly the information in these newsletters circulated, helping Native people mobilize nationally against the White Paper recommendations. This led to the next bold step: the founding of Native newspapers and magazines. Long-time activist Ben Christmas (Mi'kmaq) revived the *Micmac News* in 1969; the same year, the late Dr. Howard Adams (Métis), educator and political activist, founded the Métis paper *The New Breed.*

There is a direct correlation between the emergence of Native political organizing and the expansion of the Native newspaper industry. The initial purpose of Native newspapers was to spread the word about policy developments and to provide constructive (and, when called for, critical) commentary. These informed critiques surprised many Canadian politicians, many of whom called for the Secretary of the State to fund Native organizations, including Native newspapers. So it happened. A number of Native newspapers were soon in print. They ranged from the *Saskatchewan Indian* (1973), which reached a peak publication of 10,000 in the early 1980s, to the *Cree Ajemoon* (1973), which focused on the James Bay hydroelectric developments and the negotiations that led to the James Bay and Northeastern Quebec Agreement of 1975. The Inuit Tapirisat of Canada (ITC), representing 30,000 Inuit and six regional organizations, founded *Kinatuinamot Ilenjajuk* (1973), an English–Inuvialuit newsletter, as well as *Inuvialuit* magazine (1978). The *Ontario Native Examiner* published for a brief period (1972–73), and *Native Voice*, founded in 1946, re-emerged in 1970 following a two-year suspension.[19]

The funding was welcome, and permitted Native communications to flourish nationally. This kept Native and other politicians abreast of recent events; it also allowed community-based subscribers to follow the political dialogue. But costs were still prohibitive. The Alberta Native Communications Society (ANCS; est. 1968) launched the monthly newspaper *Native People* after procuring donated office space from the Department of Indian Affairs and an additional $139,012 from the Department of the Secretary of State (DSOS). Soon afterwards, the *Kainai News,* based on the Blood Reserve in southern Alberta, also began publication. The ANCS became a popular model for a number of Native communications societies that emerged across Canada in the 1970s.[20] Communications societies were established in response to several impediments to strengthening communications infrastructure. They had four key characteristics:

- They were based in the community and/or region.
- They were controlled completely by Native people.
- They were independent corporations, unaffiliated with political organizations and local councils.
- They shared a common mandate with other Native broadcasters and journalists.[21]

These societies are still active. Their purpose is to enhance Native content in both non-Native and Native-controlled media. In 1983 in Edmonton, the Aboriginal Multi-Media Society of Alberta (AMMSA) was founded. It operates radio studios in Lac La Biche that serve 54 northern Alberta Native communities with several hours of weekly radio broadcasts in Cree. It also publishes the weekly *Windspeaker*, which boasts a circulation of 25,000 and readership in excess of 140,000, in addition to *Alberta Sweetgrass* and *Saskatchewan Sage* (both circ. 7,100), *Raven's Eye* (circ. 6,000), and *Ontario Birchbark* (circ. 5,000). The Wataway Native Communications Society, based in Sioux Lookout, Ontario, operates local television and radio production centres that broadcast 39 hours a week of Native-language radio programs and an additional two hours of Native-language TV to 30 communities. It also publishes the *Wataway News* in Oji-Cree and English, with a readership of 2,400.

Mainstream Media and Native People: A Case Study

The Aboriginal peoples of Canada were the First to frame our multicultural identity. The diversity of our languages and cultures has personified what our country is and can become. It is through the preservation of your traditions that you ensure that Canada's heritage can meet its promise for the future.

—Gerry Weiner, Secretary of State[22]

It would be wrong to suggest that all non-Native media sources misrepresent Native peoples' interests or misportray their cultures. In his 27-year career beginning in the late 1960s, *Globe and Mail* Native Affairs reporter Rudy Platiel was praised for his work examining national Native issues. Non-Native news organizations have made significant strides over the past decade in portraying Native issues in a more balanced manner. But from time to time, questionable coverage of an event undermines years of goodwill and places the Canadian media under intense scrutiny. A recent example is the conflict that erupted in Burnt Church, New Brunswick, in the summer of 2000. After the Supreme Court of Canada in *Marshall* upheld Native fishing rights flowing from treaties signed between the Mi'kmaq and the British Crown in 1760–61, non-Native fishers quickly condemned the Court's decision while Native people cheered their victory. Minor altercations led to larger confrontations during which Native fishers were shot at under the watchful gaze of Herb Dhaliwal, Minister of Fisheries and Oceans. In an insightful article, one author concluded that the mainstream media focused on non-Native fishers' use of violence to protect themselves against Native people.[23]

An image of the Mi'kmaq as hyperaggressive soon developed. The concern here lay with the "manner in which the complexity of the Marshall Decision was dramatically simplified in a one-sided way for popular consumption" and how Native people were, despite the Supreme Court's vindication, depicted as criminals owing to their insistence on fishing out of season.[24] Burnt Church is but one example of how the Canadian media sometimes take a complex historical and legal event and distill it into brief soundbytes for the reading public. Interaction between Native leaders and Canadian officials will only increase in the future; it is likely that more events similar to Oka, Ipperwash, Gustafson Lake, and Burnt Church will spark the interest of the Native and non-Native media. More studies are needed regarding how the Native and non-Native media construct events and the impact these clashing perspectives have on readers.

The media—especially editorial-page writers, who enjoy greater flexibility—are there to help the reader fashion an informed opinion by offering insight into the facts and figures that appear in what are supposed to be nonpartisan news articles. In 2002 the *Calgary Herald* published an op-ed piece by staff writer Ric Dolphin in which he depicted Native people to 800,000 readers as conquered and destitute, as placed on reserves by Crown officials who instituted artificial economies based on imposed government aid that fostered a culture of dependency. He concluded that Native people lack political will owing to their continued reliance on federal funding. And he portrayed them as uncivilized and as unwilling to shake the social pathologies that, in his view, had proliferated in all reserve communities. According to Dolphin, this was because Native people had prospered from the welfare monies they had received, monies that provided the foundation of these communities' local economies. It seems that fact is easy to mix with fiction.[25] Eight themes pervade Dolphin's work, all of which are examined in detail below.

Treaty Indians Receive Free Education

This has become a common belief in recent years. In fact, educational aid is available *only* to registered Indian children living on-reserve; funding for postsecondary education is available through "administering authorities such as First Nation councils."[26] First Nations and registered Indians represent only a portion of all Aboriginal people in Canada; even the proportion of those who are subsidized is quite low. A treaty Indian living off-reserve may not be eligible for the "free education" that according to Dolphin all are privy to.

Unemployment in the Native Population Hovers Between 60 and 80 Percent

Unemployment has long been recognized as an issue for urban and rural Native communities. Notwithstanding Dolphin's statistics, the unemployment rate for Registered Indians in 1996 was "26%, compared to 19% among others with Aboriginal identity and 9% among other Canadians."[27] Furthermore, "the unemployment rate for Aboriginal Canadians is twice the rate for non-Aboriginal Canadians. On reserves, the unemployment rate is about 29 percent, nearly three times the Canadian rate."[28] These data suggest that Dolphin's estimates for "the native population everywhere" are indeed three times the actual case.

Fetal Alcohol Syndrome (FAS) Predisposes Native Children to Unemployment and Criminal Behaviour

Simply put, Dolphin's hypothesis is that Native FAS children are predisposed to criminality and poor employability. FAS children demonstrate growth retardation, facial structure abnormalities, and central nervous system disorders—something to which all FAS children are susceptible. Why, then, does he single out Native children as potentially dangerous future criminals?

Treaty Indians Pay No Taxes

First off, all Native people in Canada must pay the federal goods and services tax (GST). Second, Native people in Canada are required to pay taxes on the same basis as non-Native Canadians, except where the limited exemption under Section 87 of the *Indian Act* applies.[29] This means that Registered Indians do not pay federal or provincial sales tax on their personal or real property that is on a reserve.[30] Both employment income and business income are exempt from income tax if the income is situated on a reserve.[31] In other words, a Treaty Indian working off-reserve must pay taxes.

Treaty Indians Are Accorded Special Treatment by the Courts, Schools, and Employers

This is an unsubstantiated comment. Canada's Criminal Code applies to Native people, and there are no laws in place compelling employers and educational institutions to uniquely treat Native people.

Treaty Indians Can Hunt and Fish Whenever They Want

Treaty rights include the right to hunt and fish, but with unique and detailed provisions.[32] In the Prairie provinces, hunting and fishing is confined to personal use—in other words, it cannot be extended to commercial hunting and fishing.[33] The Supreme Court of Canada further eroded treaty rights when it declared that Native people have the right "to pursue their usual vocations of hunting, trapping and fishing . . . subject to such regulations that may from time to time be made by the Government of the country." The provincial governments and the federal government (more so) regulate constitutionally protected treaty rights, and they have used that authority to restrict Treaty Indians' hunting seasons and to limit hunting, fishing, and trapping quotas.

Rates of Addiction to Alcohol, Cocaine, Gambling, and Glue Are Eight to Ten Times Canadian Rates

Native people in Canada do suffer from higher rates of alcohol abuse, which is different from alcoholism. A Health Canada publication has documented that Native people consume less alcohol than Canadians generally, both daily and weekly.[34] Yet in Dolphin's piece, the image of the drunken Indian comes through loud and clear. Indians are, in fact, heavier gamblers; statistics suggest that rates of pathological gambling are 14.5 percent among Indians, compared to 3.5 percent in the general population.[35] A recent survey of online Health Canada statistics offers no available data for cocaine addiction and glue sniffing.

Native Inmates Account for 50 Percent of the Prison Population

A number of studies have found that Native people are far more likely to be arrested, charged, and convicted under the Criminal Code than Canadians in general, and that they serve more time in prison.[36] In 1991–92, for instance, "Native offenders accounted for 11% of total admissions to federal penitentiaries and 24% of admissions to provincial penitentiaries nationally, while the Native population only represented perhaps 2.3% of the total Canadian population."[37] These numbers have changed little over the past 15 years. For instance, "in Manitoba (1991–1992), Native people accounted for 38% of federal and 50% of provincial inmate admissions, while representing approximately 9% of the total provincial population; in Saskatchewan, they accounted for 55% of federal and 66% of provincial inmate admissions, while also representing approximately 9% of the total provincial population; and in Alberta, they accounted for 22% of federal and 33% of provincial inmate admissions, while representing about 4% of the total provincial population."[38]

NATIVE MEDIA STRATEGIES

The Canadian media influence the public policymakers who devise and implement Indian policies. Newspapers and their editorial teams are staffed by Canada's middle class, who from an early age have been bombarded by stereotypical images of Indians. Marshall McLuhan noted in 1967 that "it is impossible to understand social and cultural changes without a knowledge of the workings of media."[39] Native people have in recent years learned how to use the media for their own purposes—specifically, by learning how to pull the heartstrings of Canadian journalists. This in turn has led to some startling policy developments. Take the Oka Crisis of 1990. Canadian newspapers framed Oka as a law-and-order issue rather than as a Native rights issue.[40] This unorthodox interpretation of events was not challenged by the Oka warriors. Rather, they argued persuasively that the Quebec government's actions were illegal. There was much public support for the men, women, and children involved in the standoff (fewer than 100 in all); politicians gathered from this that the deployment of the Canadian Forces was perceived as overkill. Also, the warriors allowed journalists inside their compound. Most notable among these was the respected *Globe and Mail* reporter Geoffrey York, who filed most of his stories while surrounded by as many as 5,000 members of the Canadian Forces. After Oka, the national media regularly reported Native leaders' intimations that this was the beginning of a full-fledged activist assault. In response, Prime Minister Brian Mulroney established the Royal Commission on Aboriginal Peoples (RCAP) in 1991.

Native Communications Program

The depth and diversity of the Aboriginal perspective must be communicated, through both First Nations and mainstream news media, to as broad a public as possible. Current efforts to remedy inaccuracies in mainstream news coverage of Aboriginal issues are an important beginning, but they are far from enough. [The] stories that are coming out that are not from a Native perspective, coming from the mainstream media, are still causing us harm.

—Bud White Eye (AMMSA)[41]

There is no question that in the early 1970s, Native newspapers and magazines were popular. In 1972, Native communications projects in Alberta, B.C., and the Northwest Territories were funded to the tune of $581,000. The following year this was boosted to $691,109.[42] In 1972, Cabinet approved two programs that would strongly influence Native communications in Canada. The first was the CBC's Accelerated Access Plan to provide radio and television technology nationally to small communities (i.e., those with fewer than 500 residents). This was followed by the Native Communications Program (NCP) in 1973 and by the federal government's CBC Northern TV service. The NCP was meant "to enable Native people to develop and control modern communication networks."[43] Because it made possible a communications infrastructure—mainly, Native newspapers—this period has been described an "Indigenous cultural renaissance in North America. . . . Aboriginal journalism thrived in a climate that supported a wide range of creative writing, from poetry and fiction to history and children's literature."[44] Most publishers initially welcomed the NCP, even if it had been developed to fund nonpolitical societies. The idea was that if publications could be freed from political constraints, Native publishers would be able to adopt the "free press" model utilized by the mainstream media.

One result was that many Native newspapers—many of which described themselves as official organs for political organizations—were forced to sever their political ties and become economically independent. Native publishers contended that NCP funding—which never exceeded $3.4 million in any one year—was insufficient to support all Native newspapers. By the end of the 1980s the generally low levels of disposable income among Native people were making it difficult for publishers to succeed; advertising revenues were steadily dropping. At the same time, the small Native print-media industry that had developed depended heavily on government subsidies and found itself unable to expand.

The NCP provided operational funding for the dozen Native communications societies that emerged between 1973 and 1990. But the program was unable to meet the demand from those communities interested in establishing new communications societies. Squabbling within societies and an economic recession in the late 1980s combined to bring about the NCP's demise in 1990. This gutted the Native print media nationally and forced

Windspeaker Business Quarterly is one of several Native-run newspapers operating nationally. Many of them have attracted non-Native readers. The publication of Native newspapers in Canada dates back to the 1870s.

considerable changes in the industry. Even so, the NCP had offered Native writers the chance to learn the business and skills of journalism. As a result, many properly staffed Native newspapers were able to carry on despite the cutbacks. And newer, more self-reliant papers emerged from the ashes that relied on subscriptions and advertising rather than on government subsidies.

Today the Native newspaper choices seem endless. The National Library of Canada currently subscribes to 15 Native newspapers, which range geographically from the NWT to Nova Scotia to B.C. Among the more popular ones: *Alberta Sweetgrass, Saskatchewan Sage, Windspeaker, Raven's Eye, First Perspective,* and *The Drum.* All of these papers are national or provincial. Then there are the community newspapers, such as the *Nunatsiaq News* (Inuktitut), the *Wawatay News* (Sioux Lookout and Moose Factory), and the *Eastern Door* (Kahnawake). All of these papers offer dynamic writing about complex issues. Most important, they have created an alternative public sphere that is empowering Native people and communities alike, all the while demonstrating that the Canadian mainstream media do not hold a monopoly on writing about Native events.[45]

Radio and Television

The NCP influenced the development of Native television and radio programming in Canada. However, the latter was already being utilized by northern populations in the 1950s. Radio came to northern Canada in the 1920s, though reception during the early years was poor. In the 1930s the RCMP helped establish a strong chain of small radio networks, which they needed in order to communicate with southern officials. Religious missions and trading posts soon began to house high-frequency radios, and the north and south were connected. Over the next 25 years, the northern radio network expanded, owing in part to Canadian and American efforts to secure northern sovereignty while improving northern service delivery. In 1958 the CBC established the Northern Service, acquiring jurisdiction over the series of shortwave transmitters established by the CF and the Transport Ministry.

A scene from the TV series *Mocassin Flats*, featuring actors Candace Fox and Landon Montour.

Radio still had little impact on Inuit communities, mainly because of a lack of useful programming. The first Inuktituk program was broadcast only in 1960. By 1972, almost one-fifth of CBC shortwave programming was in Inuktituk and Native radio programming was becoming more influential, providing relevant and up-to-date information in both English and Native languages. That same year the federal government launched a communications satellite system that made northern broadcasts of southern programs that much easier. In 1974 the NCP began subsidizing Native media, radio included. By 1988, 128 Native communities had access to local Native radio services. Television during this period became increasingly common and could be found in most Native communities, though it was restricted to Canadian and American programs and lacked specialty Native programming.

A 1980 report by the Canadian Radio-television and Telecommunications Commission (CRTC) indicated that the Canadian government had a responsibility to ensure broadcasting in support of Native languages and cultures. In January 1981 the first Native broadcasting network, the Inuit Broadcasting Corporation, began transmitting Inuktituk programming across the central Artic, Labrador, Northern Quebec, and Baffin Island. In 1983 the Northern Native Broadcast Access Program was founded with $13.4 million in annual funds to produce local and regional Native television and radio programs through 13 of the 21 Native communication societies now operating in Canada.

Aboriginal Peoples Television Network

History would have been told differently if our reporters had been there.

—Aboriginal Peoples Television Network[46]

During the early 1990s, significant cutbacks to federal funding nearly crippled the Native print media. A number of publications survived, but it was clear that newspaper readership was declining and that television viewership was continuing to expand. Native leaders began lobbying for a national Native television network.

A small northern Native television network, Television Northern Canada (TVNC), had been broadcasting northern and Native programming from Yukon to northern Labrador

The Aboriginal Peoples Television Network (APTN) website.

since 1991. TVNC was the catalyst for the national debate over a Native TV network. A federal survey in 1998 found that two-thirds of Canadians supported the idea of such a network, even if it meant displacing available services. Further research found that Canadians were willing to pay an additional 15 percent for their monthly cable in order to receive a Native television network. Canadian public support combined with strong lobbying by Native communities, producers, and a variety of organizations led the CRTC to announce in February 1999 that the Aboriginal Peoples Television Network (APTN) would receive a national broadcast licence.

APTN, Canada's first national Native television network, was launched September 1, 1999. APTN was developed to provide Native producers, directors, actors, writers, and media professionals with opportunities to create innovative and relevant programs for national viewers—programs that would reflect Canada's diverse Native cultures from both contemporary and historic perspectives. APTN today offers a window onto these worlds through a variety of programs ranging from dramas and entertainment specials to documentaries, newsmagazines, children's series, cooking shows, and education programs.

As APTN has grown, so has its audience. What began as an upstart network with a limited market has over the past decade evolved into an important entertainment, news, and educational choice delivered to more than 9 million households. About 70 percent of APTN programming originates in Canada; more than 50 percent is broadcast in English, 15 percent in French, and 25 percent in a variety of Native languages including Inuktitut, Cree, Inuinaqtuun, Ojibway, Inuvialuktun, Mohawk, Dene, Gwich'in, Mi'kmaq, Slavey, Dogrib, Chipweyan, and Tlingit. Nearly half its programming is APTN-specific and cannot be seen on other networks. APTN airs 70 percent Canadian content; the remaining 30 percent is devoted to Native programming from Australia, New Zealand, Central and South America, and the United States. Perhaps most notably, most APTN programming originates with independent Native producers, both nationally and internationally, except for news and live events. Network revenues are derived mainly from subscriber fees and advertising. Three-quarters of APTN staff are of Native descent.

APTN has become more important than most people ever expected. Recent statistics indicate that the network is tapping 500 Native producers and broadcasters operating from a limited pool of money and that they require an injection of $10 million. Without this funding, most of them could be off the air in less than a year. With research showing that APTN viewing numbers have grown from 900,000 a week in 1999 to more than 1,750,000 a week in 2003, APTN could become the main source of Native news and entertainment in Canada in the near future.

The Internet

In the late 1990s, Internet use in Native communities was severely limited. Internet use was first advocated by Native leaders, who saw the Web as a means to enhance economic development and provide education to First Nations communities. The Royal Commission on Aboriginal Peoples (RCAP) reported in 1996 that the "Information Highway is an invaluable resource to counteract isolation which Native communities continue to experience."[47] Most Native communities, however, lacked sufficient infrastructure to capitalize on this new technology—they could handle only slow-speed analogue transmissions.

The federal government launched two separate programs to improve Native Internet access: the Community Access Program (CAP) and SchoolNet. Launched in February 1995, CAP was intended to provide all Canadians with Internet access and to provide northern educators with a useful tool for distance education. The goal was to have all Canadians connected by March 2001; this would mean establishing close to 10,000 public-access sites in communities of fewer than 50,000 people. These sites were to be located in schools, libraries, government offices, and hospitality areas. Developed in concert with CAP was SchoolNet, which was intended to provide provincial students with Internet access.

Even after these two programs were in place, difficulties at first persisted. Take the experience of Native leaders in Manitoba, for example. In 1996, as part of SchoolNet, Industry Canada offered every First Nations school Pentium PCs, DirecPC equipment (satellite uplink equipment), and about one year of free satellite time. Almost all schools applied for and received this equipment; however, few school administrators could quickly claim an acceptable level of functionality. In some communities the equipment was still in its original packaging some four years later. Several officials declared their frustration with improperly aligned satellites. The satellite systems installed in the First Nations communities of Pukatawagan, Split Lake, Shamattawa, and Tadoule Lake would initially only accept dial-up support, which was insufficient to ensure effective Internet connectivity. The northeastern communities faced similar problems; in their case, however, the problem was that each community had access to only one telephone line as the Internet connection—a system that proved unstable and unreliable and that resulted in constant disconnections. Yet Native leaders never veered in their support of the Internet's potential in their communities (see box below).[48]

K-NET

The Keewaytinook Okimakanak Tribal Council in Sioux Lookout, Ontario, adopted a proactive approach to ensure that the Internet would be utilized regionally. Their efforts provide a model for Native leaders nationally. Established in 1994, K-Net is a First Nations computer conferencing system developed and managed by the Keewaytinook Okimakanak Tribal Council. Northern Ontario at the time had limited telephone connections, even fewer in more remote communities. The Internet and its accompanying service providers were at this time unknown in the region. A number of local community leaders voiced displeasure that they were unable to use this new technology despite repeated guarantees from Industry Canada officials that they were on the cusp of regional connectivity. So they banded together to enhance Internet communications in an effort to provide free e-mail services to community members. Instead of antagonizing federal officials, local leaders established a working relationship with Industry Canada. This led to K-Net, which provided support for schools in the development, installation, and maintenance of satellite service. Local students and their teachers now had an Internet link. By 2004 more than 20 regional First Nations schools were connected, and residents were regularly sending e-mails to friends and family in other remote communities and in urban centres. Postsecondary training and employment programs are now being delivered through K-Net.[49]

Conclusion

I wonder about our existence in the future and what communication skills will be required to survive. . . . Can we live off our creativity to communicate?

—Gary Farmer (Cayuga)[50]

One could argue that Native print media and the Canadian print media represent two sides of the same coin; it is just that journalists from each group tend to report the same events in different ways. Preconceptions and attitudes specific to Native and non-Native writing styles result from variables as diverse as socioeconomic conditions, collective history, and the reporter's education. All of these influence how stories are framed. The mainstream media habitually portray Native culture as combative and as at odds with Canadian norms.[51] At the same time, Native publishers have always believed that Canadians deserve a Native perspective on events. The Native media enable Native people to tell their side of the story; the mainstream media then present their own; and somewhere in the middle of these two interpretations we are sure to locate a narrative that reflects the truth as Canadians deserve to hear it.

FURTHER READING

Alia, Valerie. *Un/Covering the North: News, Media, and Aboriginal People.* Vancouver: UBC Press, 1999.

Belanger, Yale. "Journalistic Opinion as Free Speech or Promoting Racial Unrest? The Case of Ric Dolphin and the *Calgary Herald's* Editorial Presentation of Native Culture." *American Indian Quarterly* 26, no. 3 (2002): 393–417.

Buddle, Kathleen, "Shooting the Messenger: Historical Impediments to the Mediation of Modern Aboriginality in Ontario." *Canadian Journal of Native Studies* 22, no. 1 (2002): 97–160.

Coward, John. *The Newspaper Indian: Native American Identity in the Press, 1820–90.* Urbana: University of Illinois Press, 1999.

Demay, Joel. "Clarifying Ambiguities: The Rapidly Changing Life of the Canadian Aboriginal Print Media." *Canadian Journal of Native Studies* 11, no. 1 (1991): 95–112.

Fitzgerald, Paul. "Fishing for Stories at Burnt Church: The Media, The Marshall Decision, and Aboriginal Representation." *Canadian Dimension* 36, no. 4 (2002): 29–32.

Francis, Daniel. *The Imaginary Indian: The Image of the Indian in Canadian Culture.* Vancouver: Arsenal Pulp, 1992.

Furniss, Elizabeth. "Aboriginal Justice, the Media, and the Symbolic Management of Aboriginal/Euro-Canadian Relations." *American Indian Culture and Research Journal* 25, no. 2 (2001): 1–36.

Henry, Frances, and Carol Tator. *Discourses of Domination: Racial Bias in the Canadian English-Language Press.* Toronto: University of Toronto Press, 2001.

Rosenstein, Jay. *In Whose Honor? American Indian Mascots in Sports.* New Day Films, 1997. 47m.

Skea, Warren. "The Canadian Newspaper Industry's Portrayal of the Oka Crisis." *Native Studies Review* 9, no. 1 (1994): 15–31.

NOTES

1. Canada, "Gathering Strength," in *For Seven Generations: An Information Legacy of the Royal Commission on Aboriginal Peoples,* CD-ROM (Ottawa: Libraxus, 1996).

2. Gail Guthrie Valaskakis, "Telling Our Own Stories: The Role, Development, and Future of Aboriginal Communications," in *Aboriginal Education: Fulfilling the Promise,* ed. Marlene Brant Castellano, Lynne Davis, and Louis Lahache (Vancouver: UBC Press, 2001), p. 76.

3. Devon A. Mihesuah, *American Indians: Stereotypes and Realities* (Regina: Clarity International, 1996).

4. Robert Berkhofer, *The White Man's Indian: Images of the American Indian From Columbus to the Present* (New York: Vintage, 1979).

5. Daniel Francis, *The Imaginary Indian: The Image of the Indian in Canadian Culture* (Vancouver: Arsenal Pulp, 1992).

6. Ibid., pp. 6–7.

7. Paula Gunn Allen, *Off the Reservation: Reflections on Boundary-Busting, Border-Crossing Loose Canons* (Boston: Beacon, 1998), p. 100.

8. Janice Acoose, *Iskwewak-Kah' Ki Yaw Ni Wahkomakanak: Neither Indian Princess nor Easy Squaws* (Toronto: Women's Press, 1995), p. 71.

9. Emma LaRocque, "Preface, or Here Are Our Voices—Who Will Hear?" in *Writing the Circle,* ed. Jeanne Perreault and Sylvia Vance (Edmonton: NeWest, 1990), p. xvii.

10. "Phil Jackson Challenges North Dakota on Sioux Nickname," *USA Today,* August 26, 2008.

11. Shannon Avison, "Aboriginal Newspapers: The Contribution to the Emergence of an Alternative Public Sphere" (M.A. thesis, Concordia University, 1997); see also Shannon Avison and Michael Meadows, "Speaking and Hearing: Aboriginal Newspapers and the Public Sphere in Canada and Australia," *Canadian Journal of Communication* 25, no. 3 (2000).

12. For an overview of the *Cherokee Phoenix*'s evolution, see Theda Perdue, ed., *Cherokee Editor: The Writings of Elias Boudinot* (Athens: University of Georgia Press, 1996); and Sam G. Riley, "The *Cherokee Phoenix:* The Short, Unhappy Life of the First American Indian Newspaper," *Journalism Quarterly* 53 (1976).

13. Kathleen Buddle, "Shooting the Messenger: Historical Impediments to the Mediation of Modern Aboriginality in Ontario," *Canadian Journal of Native Studies* 22, no. 1 (2002): 113.

14. Hugh Dempsey, *Big Bear: The End of Freedom* (Vancouver: Greystone, 1984), p. 100.

15. Yale D. Belanger, "Seeking a Seat at the Table: A Brief History of Indian Political Organizing in Canada, 1870–1951" (Ph.D. diss., Trent University, 2006).

16. Ibid.

17. Avison, "Aboriginal Newspapers," p. 112.

18. Canada, *Gathering Strength.*

19. See Valaskakis, "Telling Our Own Stories"; and Yale D. Belanger, "Presenting the 'Other' Side of the Story: The Aboriginal Media in Canada," in *Hidden in Plain Sight: Contributions of Aboriginal Peoples to Canadian Identity and Culture,* Vol. 2, ed. David Newhouse, Cora Voyageur, and Dan Beavon (Toronto: University of Toronto Press, forthcoming 2009).

20. Joel Demay, "Clarifying Ambiguities: The Rapidly Changing Life of the Canadian Aboriginal Print Media," *Canadian Journal of Native Studies* 11, no. 1 (1991): 95–112.

21. Valaskakis, "Telling Our Own Stories."

22. Valerie Alia, *Un/Covering the North: News Media and Aboriginal People* (Vancouver: UBC Press, 1999), p. 77.

23. Paul Fitzgerald, "Fishing for Stories at Burnt Church: The Media, the Marshall Decision, and Aboriginal Representation," *Canadian Dimension* 36, no. 4 (2002): 29–32.

24. Ibid.

25. Cited in Yale D. Belanger, "Journalistic Opinion as Free Speech or Promoting Racial Unrest? The Case of Ric Dolphin and the *Calgary Herald*'s Editorial Presentation of Native Culture," *American Indian Quarterly* 26, no. 3 (2002): 393–95.

26. Indian and Northern Affairs Canada (INAC), *You Wanted to Know: Federal Programs and Services for Registered Indians* (Canada: 2002). [online] http://www.ainc-inac.gc.ca/ai/pubs/ywtk/ywtk-eng.pdf. Last accessed December 16, 2008.

27. Indian and Northern Affairs Canada (INAC), *Aboriginal Post-Secondary Education and Labour Market Outcomes Canada, 1996* (Ottawa: Research and Analysis Directorate, 1996), p. v. [online] http://www.ainc-inac.gc.ca/pr/pub/ra/pse_e.pdf. Last accessed December 6, 2002.

28. Indian and Northern Affairs Canada (INAC), *Some Fast Facts on the Funding of Aboriginal Programs* (Canada: 2002). [online] http://www.ainc-inac.gc.ca/bg/som_e.html. Last accessed December 6, 2002.

29. INAC, *You Wanted To Know,* p. 3.

30. Indian and Northern Affairs Canada (INAC). *Information: Frequently Asked Questions About Aboriginal Peoples* (Canada: 2002), p. 5. [online] http://www.ainc-inac.gc.ca/ai/mr/is/info125-eng.pdf. Last accessed December 16, 2008.

31. Canada Revenue Agency, *Information for Status Indians.* [online] http://www.cra-arc.gc.ca/brgnls/stts-eng.html. Last accessed December 16, 2008.

32. INAC, *You Wanted To Know.*

33. INAC, *Some Fast Facts,* p. 4.

34. Health Canada, *Evaluating Strategies in Aboriginal Substance Abuse Programs: A Discussion* (Ottawa: 2002), p. 3. [online] http://www.hc-sc.gc.ca/fniah-spnia/alt_formats/fnihb-dgspni/pdf/pubs/ads/literary_examen_review-eng.pdf. Last accessed December 16, 2008.

35. Rachel A. Volberg, *Establishing Treatment Services for Pathological Gamblers in Manitoba: Report* (Winnipeg: Manitoba Lotteries Foundation, 1993).

36. A number of studies have examined the issue of Native overrepresentation in the Canadian justice system, including A.C. Hamilton and Murray Sinclair, *Report of the Aboriginal Justice Inquiry of Manitoba: The Justice System and Aboriginal People,* Vol. 1 (Winnipeg: Queen's Printer, 1991); Carol LaPrairie, "The Role of Sentencing in the Over-Representation of Aboriginal People in Correctional Institutions," *Canadian Journal of Criminology* 32, no. 3 (1990): 429–40; and Patricia Monture-Angus, "Lessons in Decolonization: Aboriginal Overrepresentation in Canadian Criminal Justice," *in Visions of the Heart: Canadian Aboriginal Issues,* ed. Olive Dickason and David Long (Toronto: Harcourt Brace and Company Canada, 1996), pp. 335–54.

37. Xavier Cattaranich, "Alternative Perspectives on the Overrepresentation Of Native Peoples," in *Canadian Journal of Native Studies* 16, no. 1 (1996): 16.

38. Ibid., p. 16.

39. Marshall McLuhan and Quentin Fiore, *The Medium Is the Massage: An Inventory of Effects?* (New York: Touchstone, 1967), p. 8.

40. Warren Skea, "The Canadian Newspaper Industry's Portrayal of the Oka Crisis," *Native Studies Review* 9, no. 1 (1994): 15–31.

41. Canada, *Gathering Strength.*

42. Demay, "Clarifying Ambiguities," p. 98.

43. Lougheed and Associates, *Report on the Native Communications Program and the Northern Native Broadcast Access Program* (Ottawa: Program Evaluation Directorate of the Secretary of State, 1986), pp. 1–3.

44. Alia, *Un/Covering the North,* p. 76.

45. Avison, "Aboriginal Newspapers."

46. See, generally, Yale D. Belanger, "Aboriginal Peoples Television Network," in *Encyclopedia of American Indian History*, Vol. 3, ed. Bruce E. Johansen and Barry M. Pritzker (Santa Barbara: ABC-CLIO, 2008), pp. 631–32; and Doris Baltruschat, "Television and Canada's Aboriginal Communities: Seeking Opportunities Through Traditional Storytelling and Digital Technologies," *Canadian Journal of Communications* 29 (2004): 47–59.

47. Quoted in Yale D. Belanger, "Northern Disconnect," *Native Studies Review* 14, no. 1 (2001): 46.

48. Ibid.

49. Belanger, "Presenting the 'Other' Side of the Story."

50. Gary Farmer, "Letter from the Editor: Time in a Computer Chip," *Aboriginal Voices* 6 (July–August, 1998).

51. See, for example, Frances Henry and Carol Tator, *Discourses of Domination: Racial Bias in the Canadian English-Language Press* (Toronto: University of Toronto Press, 2001); Skea, "The Canadian Newspaper Industry's Portrayal of the Oka Crisis," pp. 15–31; and Elizabeth Furniss, "Aboriginal Justice, the Media, and the Symbolic Management of Aboriginal/Euro-Canadian Relations," *American Indian Culture and Research Journal* 25, no. 2 (2001): 1–36.

14 | Urban Issues

A great number of Indians are moving to the cities and towns to get jobs, and they often need help in getting re-established. The Government has conducted upgrading classes, paid for vocational training courses, and hired placement officers to help Indians find work.

—Senator James Gladstone (Kainai)[1]

S peaking before the Canadian Senate in 1967, Canada's first Native Senator, James Gladstone of the Blood (Kainai) First Nation in Alberta, highlighted the fact that Native urbanization was occurring nationally. Larger centres such as Toronto, Vancouver, and Winnipeg were bearing the brunt of this immigration, but all major cities were about to face the same trend and would have to contend with growing municipal Native populations. By the 1990s it was evident that urban Native populations had grown to the point that many Native people now saw cities as their permanent home. Jumping ahead, Evelyn Peters and David Newhouse in 2003 published *Not Strangers in These Parts,* a compilation of academic essays that examined urban Native growth and that tried to dispel the persistent notion that cities are foreign environments for Native peoples.[2]

Canadians tend strongly to believe that Native urbanization is just beginning; in fact, it has been happening for many decades. Two generations of Native people now call Canada's cities home, and more are continuing to migrate to urban centres, yet the belief persists that Native people live exclusively on remote reserves. This notion is constantly reinforced by news stories that focus sharply on First Nations political issues (i.e., reserve issues) and that ignore what is happening among the growing urban Native populations. In 1951 the Canadian census found that 6.7 percent of Canadian Native people were living in cities. By 2001 that number had grown to 51 percent, with half those people living in ten of the country's largest cities: Winnipeg, Edmonton, Vancouver, Calgary, Toronto, Saskatoon, Regina, Hull–Ottawa, Montreal, and Victoria (see Figure 14-1). Statistics that same year also showed that 20 percent of Native people were living in rural areas off-reserve with 29 percent living on-reserve.

Clearly, urban Native people are here to stay; their numbers already eclipse those of rural and reserve populations. Unfortunately, the belief that Native people are predominantly rural dwellers runs deep, and so do the ramifications of that belief: federal policymakers have

Figure 14-1

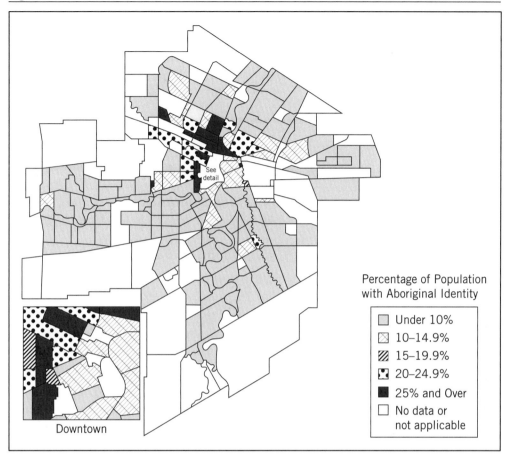

Figure 14-1 Native Identity, Winnipeg Inner City

Percentage of Population with Aboriginal Identity

- Under 10%
- 10–14.9%
- 15–19.9%
- 20–24.9%
- 25% and Over
- No data or not applicable

Downtown

Source: Adapted from "Aboriginal Identity." *Selected Census Topics.* 2001. City of Winnipeg. 4 March 2009. <http://www.winnipeg.ca/Census/2001/Selected%20Topics/Thematic%20Maps/Population/Aboriginal%20Identity.pdf>.

largely forgotten urban Native populations. From this, some interesting and contradictory trends have emerged. For instance, urban Native populations tend to be less educated, and their unemployment rate is higher. Yet when asked why they moved to the city, most will reply that better educational and employment opportunities drew them there. How, then, are we to explain the poor living conditions faced by these people, many of whom are third- or even fourth-generation urban residents? This chapter examines those questions.

Who Are Urban Native Peoples?

Aboriginal people live in cities. This simple declarative statement hides a complex reality. Life in small towns and large cities is part of Aboriginal reality as is life on reserves and in northern and Métis communities. Relationships with urban landlords, searching for employment in urban economies, making space for Aboriginal cultures and building urban Aboriginal programs and institutions is as much a part of Aboriginal realities as are land claims, conflicts over logging, hunting, and treaty rights, and rural economic development. City life is now an integral component of Aboriginal peoples' lives in Canada. This face generates new mental images, research frameworks, and policy challenges.

—David R. Newhouse (Onondaga) and Evelyn J. Peters[3]

At first contact, Indigenous populations in Canada and their settlements were distributed in ways that reflected the ecological context. Specifically, in regions of great resource wealth, large, semipermanent communities of more than 1,000 people could efficiently operate. In regions where resources were limited, smaller and more mobile communities came to dominate. With the arrival of French and British settlers came new and innovative ideas about community. In the early years, farmers dominated socially and economically, establishing ranches and farms on Indigenous lands. Permanent villages and towns soon followed. These social models secured the protection of populations fearing Indigenous threats; they also fostered the development of mercantilist and then capitalist economies.

Citing the demand for Indigenous lands needed to draw settlers, and believing that towns and villages were important centres of civilization, colonial officials aggressively encouraged Native people to abandon their territories. The Europeans contended that Indigenous peoples were underutilizing their lands and that villages and towns, with their schools and churches, were an important tool of assimilation. These ideas were eventually codified in various pieces of legislation designed to dispossess Indigenous populations of their land. As a point of reference, reserves and the *Indian Act* (1876) itself were both seen as temporary measures. Federal laws and policies were expected to become unnecessary once the last Indians had left the reserves.

The gradual urbanization of Native people in Winnipeg offers a good example of all this. That western city at the confluence of the Red and Assiniboine Rivers is home to various Native groups, including the Cree (Niheyaw), Sioux (Dakota), Saulteaux, and Ojibwa (Anishinaabe)—and, since the end of the eighteenth century, the Métis. Over the centuries, the region's Indigenous groups had established economies based on seasonal hunting for moose, elk, deer, and other large animals, as well as fishing. The river junction also served as a meeting place where Indigenous peoples gathered regularly to trade and renew political and military alliances. By the late seventeenth century, the region had also become a stopping point for French and British explorers on their way to and from northern Manitoba and Hudson Bay. The first permanent Hudson's Bay Company (HBC) trading post was established at York Factory on Hudson Bay in 1684; slowly after that, European explorers and company men followed the rivers south, introducing many Native people to the fur trade. Settlers eventually arrived and displaced Indigenous populations from the Red River region.[4]

Table 14-1 Off-Reserve Registered Indian Population by Region, 1980 to 2000

					Region						
Year		**Atlantic**	**Quebec**	**Ontario**	**Manitoba**	**Sask.**	**Alberta**	**B.C.**	**Yukon**	**N.W.T.**	**Canada**
1980	No.	3,050	5,980	22,511	12,689	15,977	9,457	22,170	864	382	93,080
1985	No.	4,066	5,221	25,587	14,460	19,507	11,410	22,868	940	486	104,545
1990	No.	6,345	13,807	52,053	24,290	34,926	20,291	39,539	3,356	2,367	196,974
1991	No.	6,302	14,775	55,270	25,776	36,194	21,604	41,042	3,510	2,559	207,032
1992	No.	6,645	15,347	58,445	27,606	38,271	22,811	42,360	3,508	2,805	217,798
1993	No.	7,048	15,970	60,956	28,403	40,361	23,658	43,916	3,433	3,127	226,872
1994	No.	7,463	16,450	63,928	29,795	42,259	24,560	45,983	3,272	3,304	237,014
1995	No.	7,897	16,641	66,335	30,709	44,272	24,665	47,648	3,376	3,588	245,131
1996	No.	8,227	17,153	68,084	34,419	45,777	25,601	50,029	3,457	3,758	256,505
1997	No.	8,514	18,178	69,825	34,158	47,329	26,380	49,818	3,555	3,872	261,629
1998	No.	8,719	18,091	71,323	34,446	48,890	27,013	50,562	3,634	4,009	266,687
1999	No.	9,089	18,417	73,940	35,363	50,535	27,911	52,010	3,693	4,154	275,112
2000	No.	9,322	19,041	75,600	37,052	52,018	28,828	53,728	3,761	4,156	283,506

Source: *Basic Departmental Data* 2001. Ottawa: Indian and Northern Affairs Canada: find this on the INAC website, http://www.ainc-inac.gc.ca. Reproduced with the permission of the Minister of Public Works and Government Services Canada, 2008.

Jump ahead to the 1950s: a steady migration of Native people into Winnipeg had begun by then. Many were trying to return to their original homeland; others were seeking jobs. By 1981, Winnipeg's Native population had grown to 16,575; by 2002, that figure had increased to 55,755. As of this writing, Winnipeg's population of 661,730 is 8.4 percent Native, and its Native population is growing six times faster than the non-Native population. It is expected that by 2020, Winnipeg's Native population will be more than 100,000. In other words, more than 40 percent of the province's Native people will be living in Winnipeg, and only 23 percent on reserves.[5]

Similar trends are observable in most cities in Canada as more and more Native people migrate from reserve communities (see Table 14-1). We are also witnessing in some parts of Canada a third generation of urban Native residents, which suggests that rising Native birth rates are contributing to growing urban Native populations just as much as migration from reserves. As will be discussed below, urbanization was originally tied directly to Canada's assimilation policy. Native people were encouraged to abandon the reserves for the cities, which led to rising urban Native populations by the early 1960s. Federal and municipal officials were caught off guard by this, which is strange, considering that their policies had been promoting what was now happening. By the 1980s, urban Native communities were exploding in size. Today, these communities differ sharply from reserve communities in a number of ways:

- They are much more heterogeneous.
- They generally have no land base.
- They have variable and complex identities—Métis, Non-Status Indians, and so on—evident in the major changes in Aboriginal identity statistics from census to census.
- Their communities and organizations have limited capacity.
- Their members are highly mobile—put another way, these communities experience considerable "churn" (i.e., urban Native people tend to move from reserves to cities and back again).
- Their leadership is in flux (i.e., there is no certainty regarding who speaks for them).[6]

Much as they do on reserves, urban Native people must contend with poor education, high unemployment, poor health, and overcrowding. A recent study of urban Native populations in the Prairie provinces and the territories made these findings[7]:

- The urban Native population is younger than the non-Native population. By proportion, almost twice as many Native people are under 20 (over 44 percent, compared to about 26 percent).
- The urban Native population is also almost twice as mobile as the non-Native population.
- The urban Native population is less educated—for example, 44 percent of urban Native people in larger centres do not have a high school diploma, compared to 28 percent of the non-Native population.
- The urban Native population faces higher unemployment than the non-Native population—almost 15 percent, compared to 5 percent. This results in household incomes $15,000 to $20,000 less than average.
- The urban Native population is overrepresented in terms of homelessness—26 percent of urban homeless people are Native, though they are less than 5 percent of the total population (in the few centres for which data are available).
- The urban Native population is much more likely to be lone-parent—30 percent, compared to 13 percent for non-Native. Native people are also more than twice as likely to be multi-family (4 percent versus 2.2 percent).

Friendship Centres

The movement of Native people from reserves and rural communities into urban centres dates back to the 1940s. Most cities experienced a steady influx of Native people seeking improved employment opportunities; this early migration was most visible in larger centres such as Winnipeg, Regina, and Vancouver. The federal government actually encouraged this migration through its assimilation policies. Yet it also failed to develop policies or mechanisms to ease the transition for Native people. In the United States, urban migration was fuelled by the forced relocation of Indians from reservations to cities like Minneapolis and San Francisco in the 1950s and 1960s. Later, U.S. government programs terminated various tribes, which drove those populations into urban centres. Canada lacked official policies of this sort.[8]

It was Native people themselves who acknowledged the need to help their neighbours as they arrived in the cities—specifically, to find shelter and employment. The first agency to open for this purpose was the North American Indian Club in Toronto. Staffed largely by volunteers, who planned and organized social events and cultural activities, the Indian Club from the beginning provided limited social services to Toronto's Native community. The Indian Club's initial success led to the founding of the Coqualeetza Fellowship Club in Vancouver in 1952, whose mandate was to ensure that new arrivals to the city had access to appropriate information and services to help their transition. Native leaders in many communities soon found themselves establishing centres and at the same time lobbying federal officials for financial aid. In 1958, after a conference in Winnipeg titled "Indians in the City," sponsored by the Indian and Eskimo Association (IEA), several of the city's residents travelled west to visit Coqualeetza's Vancouver office—an experience they reflected on when they decided to establish the Indian and Métis Friendship Centre, Canada's first friendship center.[9]

Friendship centres proved to be a popular model (see box below). By 1968, 26 of them were operating nationally, and an annual conference of friendship centre representatives—again, sponsored by the IEA and the University of Saskatchewan—was established to promote information sharing on best practices. The need to develop a national association of friendship centres soon took root, and a steering committee was established in 1969 to examine the feasibility of a national body to represent the growing number of centres. This committee included Xavier Michon of Thunder Bay and Andrew Bear Robe of Calgary. Momentum soon

---

EVOLUTION OF FRIENDSHIP CENTRES IN CANADA

1951. North American Indian Club (Toronto).

1952. Coqualeetza Fellowship Club (Vancouver).

1959. Indian and Métis Friendship Centre (Winnipeg).

1968. 26 friendship centres across Canada.

1972. National Association of Friendship Centres incorporated.

1972. 43 friendship centres across Canada.

1983. 80 "core funded" friendship centres across Canada.

1996. 113 friendship centres across Canada.

1996. Administrative transfer of AFCP from Department of Canadian Heritage to the NAFC.

1997. 114 friendship centres and 7 provincial–territorial associations across Canada.

2007. 117 friendship centres and 7 provincial–territorial associations across Canada.

began to build. Members of the newly named Canadian Indian Centre in Toronto were instrumental in founding the Ontario Federation of Indian Friendship Centres. This was followed in 1971 by the National Association of Friendship Centres. To this point, friendship centres relied on volunteer labour and limited operating funds cobbled together through private donations and small government grants. As the influx of reserve residents pushed urban Native population numbers higher, friendship-centre operators found themselves evolving into service delivery agents. By 1972 there were 43 friendship centres in Canada, at which point the federal government decided to launch the Migrating Native Peoples Program (MNPP). Soon these formerly independent centres were evolving into provincial and territorial organizations under the auspices of a national organizing body.[10]

In 1976 a federally sponsored evaluation of the MNPP revealed the friendship centres' true value and the role they played in the urban Native community—especially in the cities. These centres remained underfunded. The shortage of money did not necessarily impair operations, but it did necessitate the creative use of funds. Federal officials monitored the growth of centres nationally. In 1983 the Secretary of State and the National Association of Friendship Centres expanded the MNPP, creating the Native Friendship Centre Program (NFCP). This program acknowledged for the first time that the centres were "legitimate urban institutions responding to the needs of the Native people."[11] The NFCP was a success, which led to the founding of the Aboriginal Friendship Centres Program in 1988, complete with permanent funding secured by the Secretary of State. Friendship centres continue to serve urban Native populations, even though funding cutbacks in recent years have limited program development and service delivery.

The NAFC concluded in 1997 that it was "ideally placed to assume the mantle of political leadership for a large portion of the urban Aboriginal constituency." The NAFC's executive director, Peter Dinsdale, has indicated recently that his organization does not intend to become a political voice for Native people—it will retain its charitable status by continuing to represent the interests and concerns of Canada's 117 friendship centres. This will entail:

- acting as a unifying body for the Friendship Centre Movement;
- promoting and advocating the concerns of Aboriginal peoples; and
- representing the needs of local friendship centres in Canada to both the federal government and the public in general.[12]

The Aboriginal Friendship Centre Program currently serves 757,000 people nationally. Also, 52 percent of friendship-centre directors are women, and 14 percent of members are youth. The NAFC has shown itself to be self-sustaining, with $9 raised for every $1 in core funding. Also a success is the Urban Multipurpose Aboriginal Youth Centre Program, which in 2003–04 provided $10.4 million to friendship centres to operate 111 projects. Finally, Youth Canada Works has a budget of $1.5 million to employ 289 students, who organize cultural, sports, and recreational projects in friendship centres.[13]

Urban Native Growth

The Heritage programming was established at a time when no Indian programming existed. The goal was to address a void in modern Indian leadership by developing programs to help strengthen those leaders while also educating the non-Aboriginal public and helping them to better understand the issues. This has been fostered over time to the point that there is in place solid leadership and the public has an improved grasp of Aboriginal issues in Canada.

—Bill Shead[14]

Concurrent with the friendship centres becoming increasingly important sites of empowerment and cultural development, the federal government in 1969 tabled its White Paper, which called for the dismantling of the unique legal relationship between Indians and the federal government. Around this time, Canada was also attempting to accommodate Quebec's demands for greater autonomy and the country's increasing cultural diversity. Native leaders responded with anger to both developments, arguing that Native peoples were distinct cultures that enjoyed what the Supreme Court of Canada later characterized as a sui generis relationship with the Crown—that is, a unique bond symbolized and codified by treaties as well as by centuries of social and political interaction.[15] But instead of acknowledging Native peoples' claims to nationhood, politicians countered that Indians were an ethnic group—in other words, they lacked complex, European-style political organizations that would enable the federal government to deal with them as nations.[16]

In 1971, Canada adopted multiculturalism as an official policy for fostering a national identity. Native leaders viewed this as a setback in their efforts to promote Aboriginal nationhood within Canada, for multiculturalism was intended to create ethnicities whose contributions to the country could be managed. The Native response to the White Paper, combined with the growing numbers of reserve émigrés in the cities, convinced officials that core funding for Native organizations was warranted as a means to "develop program and project proposals according to the agenda and the degree of interest of the Native people themselves." Concerned about Native people's lack of assimilation, in 1971 the government assigned the Secretary of State the task of developing the Aboriginal Representative Organizational Program (AROP)—Canada's initial attempt to provide core funding to Native political organizations. At the same time, the government began promoting the "development of stable and effective organizational structures capable of interacting with all levels of government and society, and to participate in and effect positive changes to their political, social, cultural, educational and economic lives."[17] This mandate would inform programs and initiatives intended to provide a representative voice, connect communities, and support community services in urban and rural communities in improving Native peoples' quality of life.

These early programs offered urban Native populations access to services that had been unavailable. They also offered Native people input into policy formulation and implementation. It was expected that urban migration would continue to grow in direct relation to weak economic-development opportunities on reserves—weaknesses made worse by limited government programs, the remoteness of reserves from urban centres, a workforce with limited skills, and a lack of local resources. In the early 1970s, reserve populations were beginning to grow steadily; one result was that many reserve residents found themselves getting "squeezed out." Between 1941 and 1979, the Native population in Canada had grown from 122,000 to 309,000.[18] By 1981 this figure had swollen to 335,475.[19] As urban industrial growth slackened in the early 1970s, however, "and as Indians encountered the barriers of discrimination in employment, housing, and social life, data suggest that a movement back to the reserves occurred, along with a diminution of the out-migration from reserves."[20] The 1971 Regina census reported that the city's First Nations population was around 2,900; yet an academic study eight years later, in 1979, reported that it was more than 20,000.[21]

By the late 1980s it was clear that urban Native populations were here to stay. The combination of perceived job opportunities, new programs aimed at improving quality of life, and permanent populations to join on arriving in the city led more and more Native people to abandon reserves. Nevertheless, federal policy was doing little to address these populations' needs. Federal and provincial officials began bickering over who was truly responsible for Native people residing off-reserve. Take health, for example. Federal responsibility for First Nations health is spelled out in Section 66(3)(b) of the *Indian Act,* which empowers the minister in charge of Indian Affairs to establish regulations to "prevent, mitigate and control the spread of diseases on reserves; to provide medical treatment for infectious diseases ... and to provide for sanitary conditions ... on reserves." With First Nations health care deteriorating well into the 1950s, federal officials attempted to offload onto the provinces the responsibility for First Nations health; at the same time, they scaled back health programs for Native people (see Chapter 12).

Provincial resistance was the norm. In 1964, at the Federal–Provincial Conference on Indian Affairs, federal officials again proposed the slow devolution of the Native health-care program and its associated costs to the provinces.[22] The provinces once again balked, responding that the federal responsibility for "Indians, and lands reserved for the Indians" under Section 91(24) included First Nations health care. This interjurisdictional dispute continued its slow burn. In 1974 a ministerial policy statement described the federal responsibility for First Nations health issues as strictly voluntary— clearly, Ottawa had not changed its position.[23] With regard to urban centres, provincial officials maintain that even though Section 92 spells out that the provinces are responsible for providing their citizens with health care, nevertheless Native peoples are a federal responsibility.

URBAN NATIVE MULTICULTURALISM

The multicultural nature of the urban Native community is often ignored, but is evident in most cities that are home to large Native populations. Take Vancouver's Native community as an example. Before first contact there were more than 52 languages and multiple First Nations in what is now British Columbia. The site of present-day Vancouver was once part of Coast Salish territory; today, on any given day in that city, you are likely to encounter any of the province's multitude of First Nations (e.g., Squamish, Nisga'a, Tsimshian, and so on). Vancouver has also become an important political and economic centre for band councils, which maintain offices there. Each of these groups, from its own perspective, is a unique cultural entity that tries hard to keep its members united. Proximity to Vancouver has allowed residents of nearby nations to adjust to the city more quickly than those living in or visiting from the province's northern reaches. Not all nations get along: there is evidence that urban Native peoples tend to remain near folks from their home communities, owing to the cultural differences noted above.

Urban Aboriginal Self-Government

Wrangling over jurisdiction has impeded urban Aboriginal people's access to services. Intergovernmental disputes, federal and provincial offloading, lack of program coordination, exclusion of municipal governments and urban groups from discussions and negotiations on policy and jurisdictional issues, and confusion regarding the political representation of Aboriginal people in cities have all contributed to a situation that has had serious adverse effects on the ability of Aboriginal people to gain access to appropriate services in urban centres.

—RCAP, "Perspectives and Realities"[24]

The movement of Native peoples into urban centres over the past 20 years has caught the attention of those studying self-government—specifically, how to implement urban Aboriginal self-government. Most Canadians still associate Native people with reserves. They view urban Native people as temporary visitors rather than permanent residents—this, despite urban Native people's demands for more input and improved jurisdiction over various aspects of their lives. Urban self-government would mean allowing them some control over their own social services and cultural institutions. Reserve and municipal-government officials see this as a problem. Some suggest that urban Native self-government could result in uncertainty on reserves and encourage significant numbers of discontented Native individuals to move to urban centres. Also, most municipal governments consider urban Aboriginal self-government irrelevant, which places the onus on those populations to devise their own responses, plans, and decisions.

Further complicating this issue is the fact that urban Native people represent a variety of cultural backgrounds and legal statuses. These differences are not normally an issue in reserve governance. Cultural differences and variations in municipal circumstances strongly suggest that urban Aboriginal self-government will have to be very flexible (relative to systems on reserves). The federal government seems to understand this, judging from its official response to the Royal Commission on Aboriginal Peoples (RCAP; 1996), titled *Gathering Strength*. One of its conclusions was that any approach to urban Aboriginal governance must be multidimensional and developed around "communities of interest." The same response added that non-Aboriginal governments should consider providing resources that facilitate consultation, consensus, and community building, besides developing financial strategies to promote urban Aboriginal self-government initiatives.[25]

In the 1990s the Urban Aboriginal Working Group developed three possible approaches to improving governance for urban Native people: (1) establishing self-governing Native institutions in urban areas, which would be responsible for key services; (2) promoting a Native authority that would enter into agreements with a public government; and (3) reforming municipal governments and other local public authorities to make them more representative of Native residents. This multipronged approach is still on paper; the unique and often debilitating circumstances confronting urban Native people have yet to be addressed. Some First Nations governments support extending the jurisdiction of land-based reserve governments to urban Native people, arguing that their purview doesn't end at reserve boundaries. Discussions have centred on establishing urban reserves (see below); these would provide a government centre and commercial development as well as (eventually) some housing. To summarize, the urban Native landscape has become a site of competing claims for representation and service delivery.

Variability in policy formulation, overlaps and gaps in policy areas across cities, and a mismatch between policies and actual community needs have been identified as critical deficiencies in federal Native policies. As policy analyst Calvin Hanselmann has observed, most of today's programs were developed in the *absence* of policy—that is, they were makeshift. He adds that "this has resulted in urban Native programming that is largely disjointed and at times incoherent."[26] The federal government acknowledges the desperate need for coordination and collaboration between different levels of government to mitigate the difficulties faced by urban Native populations, yet "there is no sign that basic issues of jurisdiction and responsibility are being addressed."[27]

Things may be changing in this regard. In 2002 the Federal Court in *Canada v. Misquadis* ruled that Human Resources and Skills Development Canada (HRSDC) had discriminated against the urban Native community. The court defined off-reserve Native people as a group of self-organized, self-determining, and distinct communities, analogous to a reserve community. *Misquadis* further reinforced the political connection between on- and off-reserve Native people articulated in the Supreme Court of Canada's *Corbière* decision (1999), which compelled First Nation bands to permit off-reserve members to vote in *Indian Act*–sanctioned elections and referendums. In other words, living outside the reserve community did not necessarily silence an individual's voice in reserve politics. *Corbière* also ruled that band members must be provided with equal access to programs and services, regardless of residence. This in effect eliminated the political lines between reserve and urban residence. Following *Corbière,* the court in *Misquadis* determined that Native political organizations can represent urban Native interests and that the HRSDC must provide funding for the infrastructure required to deliver services and establish representative governance.[28] It is not yet known what impact this decision will have. It does appear, though, that urban Aboriginal self-government, in the form self-governing urban reserves, is one step closer to fruition.

Urban Native Cultural Identity

If any one theme can be traced back throughout the history of Canada's Amerindians, it is the persistence of their identity.

—Olive Patricia Dickason (Métis)[29]

Native people on reserves have access to traditional beliefs, values, and behaviours. Native people in cities must adapt some of those beliefs, values, and behaviours. Some find themselves trapped between two worlds and suffer an identity crisis. In recent years it has become clear that Native people are adapting to cities and developing a unique identity there. Some commentators reject the notion that Native people can maintain their identity when separated from their traditional territories. Others counter that a city is simply a traditional territory covered in concrete—that it retains its power, that Native people can still hope to connect with it, notwithstanding Western progress. No question, however—urban Native people's identity is thriving despite the difficulties they face.

Returning to the Winnipeg example, recent research has made some telling findings regarding how Native youth in the city develop and maintain a sense of identity.[30] The Native population in Winnipeg is much younger than the non-Native population, and federal and municipal officials are showing new interest in providing programs to help them develop their identity. This is a complex task. For instance, urban youth told the researchers that it was frustrating to have no one to speak to who had already experienced urban acculturation. It may be that remaining in close contact with one or more grandparents is vital if these youth are to learn cultural teachings closely associated with identity. The researchers also found that peers are an important influence on Native youth and that more and more of them do not claim close friendships with non-Native individuals. Finally, urban Native youth view reserves as a negative influence—as places where alcoholism is rampant and violence the norm. The study's main conclusions:

- Reserves are not in fact a place where Native people can connect with their identity.
- Local political infighting is damaging reserve communities.
- People are slowly determining their role in the community.

Most of the participants in the study suggested that the reserve was *not* a repository of culture; yet at the same time, they allowed that elders on reserves were the most appropriate cultural teachers.

The youth in this study saw the lack of programs to strengthen identity as an important political issue. Most of them said they would not bother to vote in formal elections on or off reserve; they perceived a lack of qualified candidates, and they felt that the current political leaders were unable to understand their needs. Most of the respondents rarely left the city to participate in cultural events, though most could have afforded to do so. The resources they utilized to develop their identity were quite varied, and included the Internet, academic and nonfiction books, magazines and newspapers, movies, television, and radio. The Internet was a key resource; they regularly went online to gather information about Native culture and history. Chat lines were also quite popular.

Poster promoting the Canadian Aboriginal festival, Canada's largest Native gathering held annually at the Rogers Centre (Skydome), Toronto.

They did not view mainstream movies, television, and radio as useful for identity development. They thought more highly of books (fiction and nonfiction), newspapers (both mainstream and Native), and movies with significant Native content; they regularly accessed all of these to educate themselves about contemporary and historical issues. Native youth in Winnipeg were clearly adept at culling out information that could strengthen their identity. They well understood that the media consistently portray Native culture in a negative light.

Generally speaking, Native youth in Winnipeg believed it was possible for their identity to flourish in an urban environment. Nine out of ten participants saw racism as an impediment to positive identity development. It is telling that more than half the participants in the study had witnessed an overtly racist act. Yet the lack of programs to improve self-esteem was identified as more debilitating than overt acts of racism. They equated Native culture with traditional pursuits (smudging, dancing, attending powwows); many of them associated culture retention and identity development with a university education and involvement in programs to help urban Native youth. They also believed that they were in the best position to help non-Native people understand urban Native people.

Urban and Satellite Reserves[31]

The creation and operation of each urban reserve serves as an affirmation of certain Aboriginal and treaty rights not only for their own members but possibly for members of other First Nations.

—Noel Starblanket, Star Blanket First Nation[32]

First Nations governments and communities seeking to improve capacity building employ a variety of strategies, including the creation of satellite reserves in urban centres. First Nations in Saskatchewan have taken the lead in this regard: 45 separate First Nations communities have created 32 provincial urban reserves since 1982—24 in the south of the province and 8 in the north. Some reserves are adjacent to urban centres, and over the years municipal boundaries have slowly extended until they abut reserve boundaries. Urban or satellite reserves, as extensions of rural reserves or as separate entities, are a recent phenomenon. There are currently 35 urban reserves in western Canada. Lethbridge is considering the idea, and so is Winnipeg. Urban reserves are considered an effective means to help alleviate the social and economic problems confronting urban Native populations. Urban reserve development addresses three broad concerns:

- Urban Native people do not enjoy the same level of services available on-reserve.
- Many urban Native people are finding it increasingly difficult to access provincial programs available to other urban residents.
- There is a shortage of culturally appropriate programs in urban centres.[33]

Satellite reserves have several key characteristics. They are parcels of land near original First Nations reserves that have been established on surplus Crown or privately owned lands. A satellite reserve is subject to the same regulations as any other reserve in terms of land ownership, land use, and financial management, and it is assigned a different legal status—which has important implications for business development and taxation. Depending on where the reserve is, it may be subject to regulatory provisions related to land use that do not impact the home reserve community (as in the case of the Muskeg Lake First Nation's McKnight Industrial Park in Saskatoon; see below). In B.C., for example, Native lands located within a municipality are exempt from municipal taxation; instead, grants and fees are paid to the municipality to cover the costs of services usually covered by taxes. In Saskatchewan and Manitoba, until Native lands are conferred reserve status the municipality may enforce its municipal taxation regime on those properties. After that, reserve lands are exempt from municipal taxation. The process of converting urban lands to satellite reserve status is complex and by no means routine. The time and costs involved must be considered; in many cases, those have led First Nations to decide against pursuing conversion.[34]

Satellite reserves are established for five main reasons. First, Native leaders pursuing land claims in Manitoba and Saskatchewan have found that provincial politicians are willing to honour past claims and negotiate agreements. These land claims are enabling First Nations communities to expand their land holdings and consider future acquisitions. This is an increasingly important issue, for the Native population is growing (through high birth rates) as well as becoming more urban (through increased migration from reserves). Second, there are attractions to building new subdivisions and schools on satellite reserves. Third, in the wake of recent court decisions that the leaders of reserve communities are responsible for off-reserve residents, the transfer of authority over social programming to band councils has led to various comanagement agreements; this suggests that satellite reserves will be important sites for the provision of urban services. This leads to the fourth reason, which is that satellite reserves will enable Native people to capitalize on economic-development opportunities and thereby achieve their economic, social, cultural, and political objectives. Satellite reserves are viewed as a means for diversifying Native economies, thus encouraging economic development. Fifth and finally, satellite reserves are seen as important sites for advancing Aboriginal self-government—specifically, they can be used to expand the inherent right of self-government beyond the reserves themselves.

Joe Garcea has expressed surprise at how readily Native leaders are gravitating toward the concept of urban reserves:

Given the negative legacy of reserves in this country, the creation of new satellite reserves is an unexpected trend. Most surprising of all is that, unlike the reserves of earlier times, which were created largely at the behest of federal government officials, the new reserves are being created at the insistence of First Nations leaders. Moreover, the reasons for creating them are quite different. Whereas the federal government favoured the creation of reserves as a means to circumscribing the land holdings and mobility of Indians, First Nations leaders are now creating them as a means to further their economic, social, cultural and political development objectives. Never before has the creation of reserves had such strong support among First Nations leaders.[35]

Satellite reserves are gaining popularity among Native *and* municipal leaders. Their success in Saskatchewan—in particular, the success of the McKnight satellite reserve—has

Economic development in Native communities is an increasingly important aspect of self-government. Many communities are expanding their business operations into larger urban markets. An example is the Piapot First Nation's Cree Land Mini-Mart in Regina. (Roy Antal/Regina Leader-Post)

generated important support from municipal leaders in Winnipeg, who are seeking to establish a similar model. Prince Albert, Saskatoon, Yorkton, and North Battleford have all benefited from satellite reserves once they have been developed. Native leaders are pleased with the economic impact of satellite reserves. Some of these reserves have succeeded better than others; overall, though, the revenues generated would not have been possible in reserve communities. The revenues associated with urban land ownership and the related economic development translate into improved housing and education in reserve communities; they also provide First Nations leaders with seed money to promote economic development. Satellite reserves will continue to be founded.

Muskeg Lake Satellite Reserve[36]

The Muskeg Lake Cree Nation's decision to select land in an urban area and have it designated as a reserve was driven by the overarching goals of its treaty land entitlement program, namely economic self-sufficiency and political autonomy. The First Nation placed a high priority on urban land selection to achieve economic diversification.

—Lester Lafond, Muskeg Lake Cree Nation[37]

The relationship struck between the Muskeg Lake Cree Nation and the City of Saskatoon is unique. This reserve is about 100 kilometres north of Saskatoon. Community leaders sought to establish a reserve in Saskatoon for economic and commercial development to benefit the 1,200 people living on-reserve as well as band members living off-reserve. Community leaders decided to use part of the reserve's treaty land entitlement (TLE) settlement to purchase municipal land. TLE claims are intended to settle the land debt owed to those First Nations that did not receive all the land they were entitled to under historic treaties signed with the Crown. After the Numbered Treaties were signed in the 1870s, land surveys were commissioned to establish the guaranteed reserves according to this formula: 640 acres for each family of five, or an average of 128 acres per person. This process was challenging due to fluctuating band memberships, folks refusing to allow their land to be surveyed, and government surveyors' refusal in some cases to provide the required land. The provinces of

Manitoba, Alberta, and Saskatchewan, on entering Confederation, promised to provide provincial lands to expand existing reserves.

In 1983, Muskeg Lake was recognized as having an outstanding TLE of about 19,684 hectares. Community leaders selected provincial Crown lands to make up the shortfall; these lands included a 14-hectare parcel on the eastern edge of Saskatoon. The land had been purchased by the federal government to build a prison; then another site was chosen for the prison and the land was listed as surplus and available for selection by First Nations with land claims. A 1984 study suggested that the site had solid economic prospects. Negotiations began that year and continued until 1988, when an agreement was reached to establish the reserve. The goals of the negotiations were to promote economic stability and growth through diversification, to establish long-term revenue sources to support self-sufficiency and autonomy, to create new business and employment opportunities, and to provide management expertise in support of self-government initiatives. There were five major elements to the 1988 agreement:

- The federal government would transfer the parcel to reserve status in partial fulfillment of Muskeg Lake's TLE.
- Muskeg Lake would lease the land to a development company (owned entirely by the Muskeg Lake Cree First Nation) to build a development similar to an industrial park.
- First Nation members would, in accordance with the *Indian Act,* agree by way of vote to any subleasing of the land.
- The city would install services, and the reserve would be connected to the city's infrastructure.
- Development on the reserve would at all times be in accordance with the laws of Saskatchewan and the bylaws of Saskatoon.

Both sides recognized the importance of the negotiations to forging better relations with each other. However, the band's negotiators surmised that they would need to develop a more flexible strategy in order to secure municipal services such as water and sewage lines, snow removal, and garbage pickup.

A municipal service agreement was negotiated, and the city agreed to provide various services, including fire protection. Muskeg Lake officials agreed to collect property taxes to pay the municipal-service fee, which amounted to what the city would have received in taxes had the land remained under their jurisdiction. In April 1991 the Muskeg Lake Cree Nation obtained the authority to collect property tax under Section 83 of the *Indian Act.* The final agreement was signed in 1993. Economic development was the main driver, and the land has been efficiently designed. The centrepiece of the reserve is the McKnight Commercial Centre (*Asimaknieseekan Askiy*), a 4,680-square-metre building housing Peace Hills Trust, the Saskatchewan Indian Equity Foundation, and the Federation of Saskatchewan Indian Nations (FSIN). The Saskatoon Tribal Council has leased land for 35 years and built its own reserve office complex. The site is now home to 37 businesses and 350 employees. Some of the largest on-reserve employers are First Nations governance and gaming offices, including the head offices of the FSIN, the Saskatoon Tribal Council, and the Saskatchewan Indian Gaming Authority. The FSIN is the largest employer on the reserve, providing jobs for more than 100 people.[38]

Debates

Despite the proven success of satellite reserves, resistance to these innovative economic-development zones continues. Recent research indicates that most Canadians do not understand what an urban reserve is, though this has not halted opposition. For instance, a 2007 survey found that 51 percent of respondents in Sydney, Fredericton, Quebec City, Sarnia, Winnipeg, Saskatoon, Calgary, and Kamloops were opposed to the federal government creating new reserves in urban centres; only 42 percent supported the idea. The same survey found that 46 percent of non-Native respondents thought that urban reserves would have a negative impact on the surrounding region; only 41 percent thought the impact would be positive.[39] Two recent examples of urban reserves being attempted are instructive: Winnipeg, Manitoba; and, Lethbridge, Alberta. In both places, the fears expressed in most letters to the editor printed in each city's main newspaper hinged on the belief that Native businesses on urban reserves would not have to pay taxes, leaving other local businesses at a disadvantage.

Lethbridge

In 2006, Kainai First Nation chief Charles Weaselhead announced that his community intended to establish a business park in Lethbridge. According to a recently resolved TLE claim, the Kainai were entitled to choose 180 hectares of provincial land; this prepared the legal ground to extend reserve rights to new land. Weaselhead contended that Kainai community members spent more than $100 million every year in Lethbridge and that many of those people owned homes and had families in the city. He also noted that the nature of economic development meant that the Kainai could not succeed 75 kilometres from Lethbridge. He maintained that his proposal ought to be considered an economic-development opportunity like any other the city might embark on.[40]

The community's response as reflected in letters to editor was immediate. One person wrote: "If we go by the impression left by existing reservations, their separate enclosure is likely to become a slum where houses are not maintained and refuse is not regularly removed. One does not change ingrained habits by moving 30 kilometres."[41] Tanis Fiss of the Canadian Taxpayers Federation utilized scare tactics: "Native bands are not subject to local property tax. However, native bands negotiate an agreement with municipalities to pay fees for services—such as sidewalk and road maintenance—in lieu of the regular property taxes. Yet, due to the provisions granted under the *Indian Act* there is little the City of Lethbridge can do if the native band decides not to fulfill the service agreement." She concluded forcefully: "City taxpayers will be on the hook."[42] Response was so pronounced that the Kainai satellite reserve was put on hold indefinitely.

Winnipeg

Resistance was less pronounced in Winnipeg. In September 2003, after strong lobbying by several First Nations, Winnipeg City Council voted to accept a proposal for an urban reserve. This would be the fourth one in the province, following behind the Long Plain First Nation zone in Portage la Prairie and the Opaskwayak Cree Nation and Nisichawayasihk Cree Nation zones in Thompson. Led in particular by the Roseau River First Nation, community officials made it known that they intended to purchase 12 hectares once held by Canada Packers for $2 million. The community then launched a court action to compel the federal government to convert the site to reserve status. Around the same time, reserve officials petitioned the courts to prevent the Buffalo Point First Nation from converting land near City Hall into an urban reserve.

Negotiations led to a meeting of minds regarding what the urban reserve would house. Led by Long Plain First Nation, which had purchased municipal land from Manitoba Hydro for $1.9 million (part of a $16 million it won in a 1994 TLE claim), a number of First Nations indicated their willingness to invest some of their TLE claims in a $70 million urban-reserve complex. The ten-storey building would include an attached, 10,000-square-foot government house/assembly hall for Manitoba's 64 First Nations. It would also house a library, museum, restaurant, and daycare, as well as a five-storey office complex for social services, various agencies, and band offices. Upwards of 1,000 people would be employed at the complex.[43] Once again, letters to the editor condemned the project. One writer declared that the urban reserve would be money wasted: "The problems facing the native people in Winnipeg cannot be solved from the top down. More office space is not the answer. It will only produce more paper pushers and bureaucrats and does not address the problems at street level."[44] Nevertheless, in June 2007 it was announced that project development would be completed by 2010.

Economic Development[45]

Urban reserves are seen as key to successfully promoting Native gaming, though once again, resistance has been strong owing to the fears associated with casino development. Efforts to develop a Native gaming industry in Manitoba started with the approval in principle of three proposals: Nelson House (Nisichawayasihk) proposed a casino in Thompson, the Sioux Valley First Nation proposed one in either Sifton or Brandon, and the Swan Lake First Nation set its sights on Headingley, a community of 1,600 just west of Winnipeg. Swan Lake is a community of 1,145 about 115 kilometres southwest of Winnipeg. In 1995 it was awarded a $10.4 million TLE payment to purchase a minimum of 196 hectares, which would be added to its land base.

The community established Swan Lake First Nation Enterprises and launched an economic-development project. It intended to purchase the Alpine Motel in Headingley. That 10-hectare parcel was earmarked for casino development. The land would have to be designated an urban reserve by the federal government; except for that, the casino's advocates believed that few roadblocks existed. It was anticipated that the provincial government would soon issue a request for proposals (RFP) for casino projects. Swan Lake was poised to expedite matters and develop a $100 million complex, which was to include a hotel, a 7,000-seat arena, and a conference centre. The proposal seemed destined for quick acceptance and immediate construction.

By March 2000 a significant number of Headingley residents were protesting against a casino in their community. After weeks of racially charged lobbying, the people of Headingley voted down the proposal by a substantial margin: 85 percent against. Soon after, Headingley's town council withdrew its support. After the plebiscite, Swan Lake's leaders lobbied Headingley's town council for the opportunity to educate community members about the casino's benefits. On December 6 a second plebiscite was held and the people of Headingley again voted down the proposal. This time, 69 percent of eligible voters participated in the plebiscite, with 53.9 percent voting against the casino. This was far less than the original 85 percent opposition. Nevertheless, as the Premier's Office indicated in June, the results of the April plebiscite were binding, and the Swan Lake proposal was dead. On December 7, 2001, the Swan Lake First Nation formally withdrew its casino proposal after the Manitoba government declared that the project would not be proceeding.

Conclusion

On one hand, I say there is a need for my people to progress and take responsible places in society. On the other hand, I say to the government: Stop pushing us! What I say is true: My people must progress in order to survive, but we must do this gradually at our own speed. You cannot force this upon us overnight.

—Senator James Gladstone (Kainai)[46]

The governance of reserves and the management of Native lands are still by and large determined by the 133-year-old *Indian Act*. That act, which is based on the premises of protection and civilization, is inconsistent with the emerging needs of Indian communities both on and off reserve. Band councils have agitated for changes to land-management regimes to facilitate the use of land in economic-development projects; some have succeeded. For example, the *Sechelt Indian Band Self Government Act* (1986) transferred, in fee simple, all Sechelt Indian Reserve land to Sechelt Indian Band jurisdiction. The same legislation created the Sechelt Indian Government District as a B.C. municipality. The previous year, the federal government had passed Bill C–31 (An Act to Amend the *Indian Act*), which expunged the *Indian Act's* gender-discriminatory aspects while extending bands the right to establish their own rules for determining membership and residency. The *First Nations Land Management Act* (1999) further enabled bands to develop and implement land-management codes; this provided for increased local control and decision making over reserve land by removing the requirement that Indian Affairs approve land transactions. Despite these changes, reserves are still little more than pockets of Crown land set aside for the "use and benefit of Indians." Reserves have evolved into homelands for many Native people, reflecting a conceptualization far different from the original idea of reserves as centres where Native people could be protected and/or civilized.

Despite the success of Saskatchewan's urban reserves, provincial governments have refused to implement urban-reserve policies. Indeed, many municipal politicians cringe at the thought of incorporating these economic-development zones within their boundaries. It is evident that urban reserves that house Native agencies have helped urban populations improve their living conditions. They have not, however, led to significant movement in terms of further defining what urban Aboriginal self-government will look like or how it will operate. Also, issues raised in this chapter tend to fly under the radar of politicians and social agencies. Does racism significantly affect the development of Native identity? If so, what programs could be established to counter this? Why are urban Native people not considered provincial citizens? And is it discriminatory to refuse social services to individuals based on their cultural background? These and other questions will continue to fuel political and academic debate for years to come.

FURTHER READING

Barron, F. Laurie, and Joseph Garcea, eds. *Urban Indian Reserves: Forging New Relationships in Saskatchewan.* Saskatoon: Purich, 1999.

Belanger, Yale D. "Assessing Urban Aboriginal Housing Needs in Southern Alberta." *Saskatchewan Institute on Public Policy,* Public Policy Paper no. 51 (June 2007).

Garcea, Joseph. "First Nations Satellite Reserves: Capacity Building and Self-Government in Saskatchewan." In *Aboriginal Self-Government in Canada: Current Trends and Issues,* ed. Yale D. Belanger. Saskatoon: Purich, 2008.

Hanselmann, Calvin. *Uncommon Sense: Promising Practices in Urban Aboriginal Policy Making and Programming.* Calgary: Canada West Foundation, 2002.

Lawrence, Bonita. *Real Indians and Others: Mixed-Blood Urban Native Peoples and Indigenous Nationhood.* Vancouver: UBC Press, 2004.

Newhouse, David R., and Evelyn Peters, eds. *Not Strangers in These Parts: Urban Aboriginal Peoples.* Ottawa: Policy Research Initiatives, 2003.

Peters, Evelyn J. "Conceptually Unclad? Feminist Geography and Aboriginal Peoples." *Canadian Geographer* 48, no. 3 (2004): 1–15.

———. "'Our City Indians': Negotiating the Meaning of First Nations Urbanization in Canada, 1945–1975." *Journal of Historical Geography* 30 (2002): 75–92.

———. "Developing Federal Policy for First Nations People in Urban Areas: 1945–1975." *Canadian Journal of Native Studies* 21, no. 1 (2002): 57–96.

Silver, Jim, and colleagues. *In Their Own Voices: Building Urban Aboriginal Communities.* Halifax: Fernwood, 2006.

Walker, Ryan C. "Social Cohesion? A Critical Review of the Urban Aboriginal Strategy and Its Application to Address Homelessness in Winnipeg." *Canadian Journal of Native Studies* 25, no. 2 (2005): 395–416.

NOTES

1. Canada, *Senate Proceedings and Debates,* March 10, 1967, p. 1068.

2. David Newhouse and Evelyn Peters, eds., *Not Strangers in These Parts: Urban Aboriginal Peoples* (Ottawa: Policy Research Initiative, 2003).

3. Ibid., p. 5.

4. For a general overview of this history and the economic repercussions of non-Native settlement on Aboriginal interests, see Paul Thistle, *Indian–European Trade Relations in the Lower Saskatchewan River Region to 1840* (Winnipeg: University of Manitoba Press, 1986); Raoul McKay, "Fighting for Survival: The Swampy Cree of Treaty No. 5 in an Era of Transition, 1875–1930" (Ph.D. diss., University of Toronto, 1991); and David Meyer and Paul C. Thistle, "Saskatchewan River Rendezvous Centres and Trading Posts: Continuity in a Cree Social Geography," *Ethnohistory* 42, no. 3 (Summer 1995): 403–44.

5. See Statistics Canada, *Aboriginal Peoples of Canada: A Demographic Profile,* 2001 Census: Analysis Series, Vol. 96F0030XIE2001007 (Ottawa: Minister of Industry, 2003), p. 23; Winnipeg, *First Steps: Municipal Aboriginal Pathways* (Winnipeg: 2003), p. 1; and Manitoba Bureau of Statistics, *Manitoba Aboriginal Persons: A Statistical Profile 1996* (Winnipeg: 1998).

6. Institute on Governance, *Roundtable on Urban Aboriginal Governance* (Ottawa: Institute On Governance, 2005), p. 4. [online] http://www.iog.ca/publications/2005_tanaga5summary.pdf. Last accessed 27 July, 2008.

7. Canada, *Depository Services Program.* [online] http://dsp-psd.pwgsc.gc.ca/Collection/ NH18-23-106-024E.pdf. Last accessed December 17, 2008.

8. See Donald L. Fixico, *The Urban Indian Experience in America* (Albuquerque: University of New Mexico Press, 2000); and James B. LaGrand, *Indian Metropolis: Native Americans in Chicago, 1945–1975* (Champaign: University of Illinois Press, 2005).

9. *National Association of Friendship Centres,* "Our History." [online] http://www.nafc-aboriginal.com/history.htm. Last accessed September 8, 2008.

10. Ibid.

11. Ibid.

12. Institute On Governance, *Roundtable on Urban Aboriginal Governance,* p. 7.

13. Ibid., p. 8.

14. Quoted in Yale D. Belanger, Kevin Fitzmaurice, and David R. Newhouse, "Creating a Seat at the Table: A Retrospective Study of Aboriginal Programming at Canadian Heritage," *Canadian Journal of Native Studies* 28, no. 1 (2008): 39–40.

15. *R. v. Sparrow* [1990] *1 S.C.R.* 1075.

16. Tom Flanagan, *First Nations? Second Thoughts* (Kingston and Montreal: McGill–Queen's University Press, 2000).

17. In Belanger, Fitzmaurice, and Newhouse, "Creating a Seat at the Table," p. 38.

18. J. Rick Ponting and Roger Gibbins, *Out of Irrelevance* (Toronto: Butterworths, 1980), p. 32.

19. Andrew J. Siggner, "The Socio-Demographic Conditions of Registered Indians," in *Arduous Journey: Canadian Indians and Decolonization,* ed. J. Rick Ponting (Toronto: McClelland and Stewart, 1986), p. 58.

20. Ibid., p. 34.

21. J. Rick Ponting, "Historical Overview and Background, Part II: 1970–96," in *First Nations in Canada: Perspectives on Opportunity, Empowerment, and Self-Determination,* ed. J. Rick Ponting (Toronto: McGraw-Hill Ryerson, 1997), p. 43.

22. Canada, *Federal–Provincial Conference on Indian Affairs: Report of Proceedings* (Ottawa: Indian Affairs Branch, Department of Citizenship and Immigration, 1964).

23. Roy Romanow, *Building on Values: The Future of Health Care in Canada* (Canada: Commission on the Future of Health Care in Canada., 2002), p. 212.

24. Canada, "Perspectives and Realities," in *For Seven Generations: An Information Legacy of the Royal Commission on Aboriginal Peoples,* CD-ROM (Ottawa: Canada Communications Group, 1996), p. 542.

25. Canada, *Gathering Strength: Canada's Aboriginal Action Plan* (Ottawa: Queen's Printer, 1998).

26. Calvin Hanselmann, *Uncommon Sense: Promising Practices in Urban Aboriginal Policy-Making and Programming* (Calgary: Canada West Foundation, 2002), p. 11.

27. Katherine A.H. Graham and Evelyn Peters, *Aboriginal Communities and Urban Sustainability* (Ottawa: Canadian Policy Research Networks, 2002), p. 18.

28. *Canada (Attorney General) v. Misquadis* [2003] *FCA* 473.

29. Olive Patricia Dickason, *Canada's First Nations: A History of Founding People from Earliest Times* (Toronto: McClelland and Stewart, 1992), p. 419.

30. The information found in this section was derived from Yale D. Belanger, Liz Barron, Melanie Mills, and Charlene McKay-Turnbull, *Urban Aboriginal Youth in Winnipeg: Culture and Identity Formation in Cities* (Winnipeg: Department of Culture and Heritage Canada [DOCH], March 17, 2003), p. 50.

31. The information for this section was largely derived from Joseph Garcea, "First Nations Satellite Reserves: Capacity-Building and Self-Government in Saskatchewan," in *Aboriginal Self-Government in Canada: Current Trends and Issues,* 3rd ed., ed. Yale D. Belanger (Saskatoon: Purich, 2008), pp. 287–308.

32. Noel Starblanket, "An Aboriginal Perspective on the Creation of the Star Blanket First Nation's Reserves," in *Urban Indian Reserves: Forging New Relationships in Saskatchewan,* ed. F. Laurie Barron and Joseph Garcea (Saskatoon: Purich, 1999), p. 242.

33. Canada, "Perspectives and Realities."

34. Garcea, "First Nations Satellite Reserves," p. 288; see also Canada, *Urban Reserves in Saskatchewan: Saskatoon* (Ottawa: Western Economic Diversification Canada, 2008).

35. Garcea, "First Nations Satellite Reserves," pp. 292–94.

36. The data for this section's overview were unless otherwise noted drawn from Lester Lafond, "Creation, Governance, and Management of the McKnight Commercial Centre in Saskatoon," in *Urban Indian Reserves: Forging New Relationships in Saskatchewan,* ed. F. Laurie Barron and Joseph Garcea (Saskatoon: Purich, 1999).

37. Lafond, "Creation, Governance, and Management," p. 188.

38. Canada, *Urban Reserves in Saskatchewan: Saskatoon.*

39. "Urban Reserves Can Be a Win–Win," *Calgary Herald,* January 3, 2007, A10.

40. Sarah McGinnis, "Blood Tribe Calls for Urban Reserve: Federal Officials Warn Process Is Lengthy," *Calgary Herald,* March 15, 2006, B8.

41. Letter to the Editor, "Urban Reserve Plan Akin to Apartheid," *Lethbridge Herald,* April 12, 2006.

42. Tanis Fiss, *Lethbridge Urban Reserve* (Canadian Taxpayers Federation, 2006). [online] http://taxpayer.ca/main/news.php?news_id=2242. Last accessed September 6, 2008.

43. Murray McNeill, "Signature Building to Be a 'One-Stop Shopping Place for First Nations,'" *Winnipeg Free Press,* July 23, 2007, B6.

44. Letter to the Editor, "Invest in Youth," *Winnipeg Free Press,* November 17, 2005, A13.

45. This section is derived from Yale D. Belanger, *Gambling with the Future: The Evolution of Aboriginal Gaming in Canada* (Saskatoon: Purich, 2006), specifically Chapter 8, "Social and Political Responses to First Nations Gaming," pp. 138–50.

46. Canada, *Senate Proceedings and Debates,* March 10, 1967, p. 1608.

Copyright Acknowledgments

Text Credits

Chapter 3. 58: "The Song My Paddle Sings by Pauline Johnson." *Canadian Poetry Archive*. 2002. Library and Archives Canada. 4 March 2009. http://www.collectionscanada.gc.ca/canvers/index-e. html.

Chapter 4. 84: "The Treaty—Page 7." *The Making of Treaty 8 in Canada's Northwest*. 2002. Virtual Museum of Canada. 4 March 2009. <http://www.albertasource.ca/treaty8/eng/The_Treaty/treaty_ text_7.htm>. **85:** Zlotnick, Norman. "Interpretation of the Prairie Treaties." *Beyond the Nass Valley: National Implications of the Supreme Court's Delgamuukw Decision*. Ed. Owen Lippert. Vancouver: The Fraser Institute, 2000. Reprinted with permission. **86–87:** *R. v. Marshall*, [1999] 3 Supreme Court of Canada 456. Not the official version. **91:** *Resolving Aboriginal Claims: A Practical Guide to Canadian Experience*. Ottawa: Indian and Northern Affairs Canada, 2003. http://www. aincinac.gc.ca/al/ldc/ccl/pubs/rul/rul1-eng.pdf. Reproduced with the permission of the Minister of Public Works and Government Services Canada, 2008. **96:** *Fact Sheet: The Nisga'a Treaty*. Ottawa: Indian and Northern Affairs, 2008. www.ainc-inac.gc.ca/ai/mr/is/nit-eng.asp. Reproduced with the permission of the Minister of Public Works and Government Services Canada, 2008.

Chapter 5. 111–112, 113: Parliament of Canada. "Official apology." In Ottawa. House of Commons. *House of Commons Debates Official Report* (Hansard). 39th Parliament, 2nd Session. Online: <http://www2.parl.gc.ca/content/hoc/House/392/Debates/110/HAN110-E.PDF> 4 March 2009. **121:** "Aboriginal Women and Bill C-31: An Issue Paper." *Native Women's Association of Canada*. 2007. 4 March 2009. <http://www.nwac-hq.org/en/documents/nwac.billc-31.jun2007.pdf>. **123:** CBC.CA. **124:** "Specific Claims." *Lands & Resources*. Federation of Saskatchewan Indian Nations. 4 March 2009. <http://www.fsin.com/landsandresources/specificclaims.html>.

Chapter 9. 236: "Changes Within the Present System." *Aboriginal Peoples and the Criminal Justice System*. 1998. Canadian Criminal Justice Association. 4 March 2009. <http://www.ccja-acjp.ca/ en/abori5.html>. Reproduced and Copyright by permission of the Canadian Criminal Justice Association.

Chapter 10. 251: Federation of Saskatchewan Indian Nations. *Indian Government*. Saskatoon: FSIN, 1977.

Chapter 11. 271–272: Adapted with permission, Harvard Project of American Indian Economic Development. **273:** *Economic development programs guide*, 2005. Ottawa: Indian and Northern Affairs Canada. Find this guide on the INAC website, www.aincinac.gc.ca. Reproduced with the permission of the Minister of Public Works and Government Services Canada, 2009. **282–283:** *Aboriginal Co-operatives in Canada: Case Studies*. Ottawa: Research & Analysis Directorate, Indian and Northern Affairs Canada, 2001. http://www.ainc-inac.gc.ca/ai/rs/pubs/re/abo/abo-eng.pdf. Reproduced with the permission of the Minister of Public Works and Government Services Canada, 2009.

Chapter 12. 309, 311: Adapted from *Basic Departmental Data* 2001. Ottawa: Indian and Northern Affairs Canada: find this on the INAC website, http://www.ainc-inac.gc.ca. Reproduced with the permission of the Minister of Public Works and Government Services Canada, 2008.

Chapter 14. 344: Hanselmann, Calvin, Peter Dinsdale, and Patrick Brazeau. *Roundtable on Urban Aboriginal Governance.* 2004–05 Institute On Governance Roundtable Series: "Towards a New Aboriginal Governance Agenda." Ottawa, January 20, 2005. <http://www.iog.ca/publications/2005_tanaga5summary.pdf>. Reprinted with permission of the Institute On Governance.

Photo Credits

Chapter 3. 57: Cochran/Library and Archives Canada/C-085125. **61:** Sault Star/The Canadian Press. **63:** Alanis Obomsawin © National Film Board of Canada. All rights reserved. **67:** (top) Norval Morrisseau (1931–2007) *Artist's Wife and Daughter* 1975 acrylic on hardboard 101.6 x 81.3 cm Purchase 1975 McMichael Canadian Art Collection 1981.87.1; (bottom) Photo © Valerie Jacobs.

Chapter 4. 86: Archives of Manitoba N13598. **93:** The Canadian Press (Nick Procaylo).

Chapter 5. 113: The Canadian Press (Tom Hanson).

Chapter 6. 135: Library and Archives Canada C-81787. **137:** Glenbow Archives NA-2839-4. **138:** Library and Archives Canada PA-012854. **141:** Glenbow Archives PA-2218-109. **142:** (bottom) Saint John Telegraph-Journal/The Canadian Press (Chenier Noel).

Chapter 7. 169: The Canadian Press (Tom Hanson). **171:** The Canadian Press (Jeff McIntosh). **172:** Christopher J. Woods / Canada. Dept. of National Defence / Library and Archives Canada / PA-142289.

Chapter 8. 185: Library and Archives Canada C-033643. **193:** Glenbow Archives NA-928-1. **195:** Glenbow Archives NA-2864-27196. **207:** The Canadian Press (Tom Hanson).

Chapter 9. 223: The Canadian Press (Chuck Stoody). **226:** Winnipeg Free Press/The Canadian Press (Ken Gigliotti).

Chapter 10. 253: The Canadian Press (Kevin Frayer). 258: The Canadian Press (Fred Chartrand).

Chapter 11. 267: Library and Archives Canada (Acc. 1946-110-1). Gift of Mrs. J.B. Jardine. **280:** The Canadian Press (Adrian Wyld). **285:** Maclean's/Canadian Press (Rick Chard).

Chapter 12. 303: © Library and Archives Canada e002414883. **308:** The Canadian Press (Dave Chidley).

Chapter 13. 331: Courtesy of Aboriginal Multi-Media Society. **332:** Copyright © 2003 Big Soul Productions. **333:** Courtesy APTN.

Chapter 14. 352: Courtesy Canadian Aboriginal Festival. **355:** Roy Antal/Regina Leader-Post

Index

Note: Page numbers followed by "f" indicate figures or photographs and those followed by "t" indicate tables.

Battle at Beaver Dams (1813), 161
Battle of Fallen Timbers (1794), 187
Battle of Seven Oaks (1816), 134
B.C. Fisheries Act, 276
Beach, Adam, 62
Beardy, Nellie, 312
Bear Robe, Andrew, 345
Beauvais, Edward, 197–199
Bellegarde, Ed, 286
Belmore, Rebecca, 51
Benedict, Ernie, 20, 232
Benyon, William, 194
Beothuk, 37
Berger, Thomas, 260
BHP Billiton, 280
Big Bear, 165, 323
Bignell, Stella, 222
Bill C–6, 123–124, 208
Bill C–7, 123–124, 208, 258–259
Bill C–19, 123–124, 208
Bill C–23, 124
Bill C–31, 118, 121–122, 360
Blackfoot, 11, 12, 14, 18, 34, 38, 40, 54–56, 109,
   111, 157, 160, 162, 164, 186, 221, 244, 269, 319
Blackfoot Confederacy, 157, 162–163, 186, 268
Blood (tribe), 40, 157, 163, 166, 186, 230, 269,
   281, 325
Blood Tribe Police Service badge, 229f
Bohm, David, 4
Bold Eagle Initiative, 172
Borrows, John, 20, 188, 189, 250
Boudinot, Elias, 322
Boulanger, Tom, 59
Bourassa, Robert, 174
Bouwa Whee Catering, 280
Brady, James, 137–138, 140, 141f, 192, 194
Brant, Beth, 59
Brant, Clare, 17–20
Brant, Joseph, 161
Britain, 79–80, 84, 105–106
British Columbia, 74, 89, 94–96, 192, 256,
   349, 353–354
British Columbia Court of Appeal, 96
British Columbia Treaty Commission (BCTC),
   89, 94–95
British North America Act (1867), 83, 108, 116,
   245, 307, 313
Bryce, Peter H., 308–309
Buffalo, 39f
Buffalo jumps, 267f
Bullchild, Percy, 54–55

Bureaucracy, 272
Burnt Church protests (2000), 222, 326–327
Bush camps, 236

C

Cabot, John, 266
Cajete, Gregory, 6, 7
Calder v. The Attorney General of British Columbia
   (1973), 91, 96, 146, 206
Calgary Herald (newspaper), 327
Callihoo, Felix, 141f
Callihoo, John, 192, 194, 197
Campbell, Maria, 59
Campbell Scott, Duncan, 167, 193–194, 305
Canada Health Act, 313
Canada v. Misquadis (2002), 350–351
Canadian Aboriginal Festival, 62, 352f
Canadian Bill of Rights, 250
Canadian Charter of Rights and Freedoms,
   228, 296–297
Canadian Forces, 169
Canadian Handicrafts Guild, 67
Canadian Indian Centre, 346
Canadian Medical Association Journal, 296–297
Canadian Métis Society (CMS), 205
Canadian Pacific Railway, 221
Canadian Radio-television and Telecommuni-
   cations Commission (CRTC), 332
Canadian Rangers, 170–171
Cape Breton, 277
Capitalism, 278
Cardinal, Harold, 20, 59, 195f, 200,
   204, 205
Carlisle Indian Industrial School, 112
Cartier, Jacques, 132, 302
Casino Rama, 283–285, 285f
Casinos, 283–286, 284f, 286t, 287t, 358–359
Category I lands, 90
Category II lands, 90
Category III lands, 90
Catholic Church, 77, 323
Cayuga, 43, 186–187
CBC (Canadian Broadcasting Corporation),
   51, 61, 330–332
Ceremonies, 16, 300
Ceremony (Silko), 53
Champagne and Aishihik, 93, 254, 256
Charlottetown Accord, 144–145, 207, 208
Charter of Rights and Freedoms. *See* Canadian
   Charter of Rights and Freedoms
Chartrand, Paul, 130, 134

James Bay and Northern Quebec Agreement
    (1975), 87–92, 230, 255, 325
James Bay Cree, 206, 230, 311
James Bay Development Corporation, 89
Jamieson, Roberta, 123
Johnson, Pauline, 57–58, 57f
Johnson, William, 105
Johnston, Basil, 20
Jones, Peter, 19, 57, 110, 188, 322
Jones, Peter Edmund, 110, 322
Jones, Roger A., 9
Jordan Principle, 297, 307
Journalism. *See* Newspapers
Jungen, Brian, 68
Justice, concept of, 217, 219t
Justice system, 216–238
    comparison, 219t
    crime impact, 225f
    customary/traditional law, 217–219
    federal corrections, 237
    language, 228
    Native experiences with, 222–228
    Native policing, 229–232
    Native representation in, 224, 330
    Native strategies, 232–237
    North-West Mounted Police, 220–221
    provincial/territorial programs, 237
    Royal Canadian Mounted Police, 221–222

K

Kahnawake, 173
Kahnesatake (film), 63f
Kainai, 176–177, 357–358
Kainai News (newspaper), 325
Kanesatake, 174
Kaskaskia, 187
Keewaytinook Okimakanak Tribal
    Council, 335
Kelly, Peter, 20, 323
Kickapoo, 187
Kidwell, Clara Sue, 21
Kinatuinamot Ilenjajuk (newsletter), 325
King, Thomas, 50, 52–53, 63
Kirkness, Verna, 20
Kitsaki Development Corporation, 281
Kluskap, 11
K-Net, 335
Kootenai, 163
Kummerfield, Steven, 227
Kunuk, Zacharias, 62–63
Kuptana, Rosemarie, 257

L

Labrador, 132
Labrador Inuit Agreement (2005), 259
Lachambie, M., 303f
Lacombe, Father, 140
Ladner, Kiera, 20, 109
Lafond, Lester, 355
LaForme, Harry, 114
Laing, Arthur, 115
Laird, David, 110
Land
    art and, 66
    economics and, 28
    importance of, 45
    language and, 29
    Native science and, 10–11
    philosophy and, 7–9
    politics and, 28
    warfare and, 162
    See also Nature
Land claims, 88–93, 117, 146, 150, 192, 274f,
    354–356
Language
    in court system, 228
    heritage languages, 20
    journalism and, 322
    land and, 29
    of Métis, 134
    Mi'kmaq, 277
    necessary for understanding Indigenous
        cultures, 5
    power of, 53
    radio, 332
    television, 333
    varieties of Indigenous, 28–29
Larocque, Emma, 20
La Ronge Indian Band, 280–281
Last Post Fund, 167
Law of the Prairie, 135
Leach, George, 61
Leadership, 32–33
League of Indians of Canada, 193
Lethbridge satellite reserve, 357–358
Lheidli T'enneh, 94, 256
Life expectancy, 309, 310f
Literature, 52–60
    non-written, 53–57
    written, 57–60
    See also Stories
Little Bear, Leroy, 4, 10, 12, 13, 15–16, 20, 45
Little Salmon/Carmacks, 256

Loans, 275
Locke, John, 320
Lockheed Martin, 277
Loft, Fred Ogilvie, 167, 177, 192–193, 193f, 321
Lonefighters Society, 175–176
Long Plain tribe, 358
Lovelace, Sandra, 120
Lubicon Cree, 81

M

Maa-nulth, 94
MacDonnell, Miles, 134
MacEwan Committee, 142
The Making of Oldman River, 53–55
Makivik Corporation, 90
Maliseet, 120, 133, 187
Maliseet-Passamaquoddy, 37
Malone, Ted, 227
Manitoba, 136, 138–139, 163–164, 275, 283, 354, 356, 358–359
Manitoba Act (1870), 136–137
Manitoba Gaming Control Commission (MGCC), 249
Manitoba Indian Association (MIA), 195–197, 204
Manitoba Indian Brotherhood (MIB), 204, 242, 251, 261, 265
Manitoba Justice Inquiry, 223
Manitoba Keewatinook Ininew Okimowin (MKIO), 210
Manuel, Arthur, 258–259
Manuel, George, 20, 59, 200
Maracle, Lee, 59
Marchand, J., 303f
Marshall, Donald, Jr., 226, 276
Marshall decision (1999), 276, 326–327
Materialism, 18, 32
McKay, Eva, 158
McKnight, Bill, 97
McLeod, Dave, 63
McLuhan, Marshall, 329
Meadow Lake Tribal Council, 278
Media
    case study, 326–329
    early Native print, 322–324
    and language, 322
    Native portrayals in, 320–321, 326–329
    Native use of, 320, 329
Medical Inspector for Indian Agencies and Residential Indian Schools, 309
Medicine, 300, 301
Medicine Calf, 220

Meech Lake Accord, 207
Meighen, Arthur, 167
Membertou, 77, 277
Mercredi, Ovide, 103, 237
Messamouet, 77
The Metaphysics of Modern Existence (Deloria), 4
Métis, 36, 37, 132–145, 152, 279, 325, 342
    Association of Alberta, 140–141
    Bill of Rights, 139
    birth of nation, 134–137
    camp, 135f
    defined, 141–142
    flag, 142f
    by geographic region, 132–134
    modern politics, 141–143
    origins of, 132
    overview, 130
    population distribution, 131f
    resistance by, 138–139, 164–165
    self-government, 137–139, 144–145
Métis Accord, 143, 144–145
Métis Archival Project (MAP), 144
Métis Association of Alberta, 140–141, 141f
Métis Betterment Act (1938), 141–143
Métis National Council (MNC), 142–144
Métis Settlements General Council, 143
MIA. *See* Manitoba Indian Association (MIA)
Miami (tribe), 187
MIB. *See* Manitoba Indian Brotherhood (MIB)
Michif, 134
Michon, Xavier, 345
Micmac News (newspaper), 323, 325
Migrating Native Peoples Program (MNPP), 346
Mi'kmaq, 11, 25, 29, 37, 77–78, 133, 161, 187, 268, 276, 277, 326
Mi'kmaq Concordat, 77–78
Military Act (1917), 163
Military and warfare, 157–178
    dismantling, 163–165
    enlistment deliberations, 176–177
    Indigenous service in Canadian Forces, 166–170
    post-1951 military relations, 170–177
    post-contact, 160–163
    pre-contact, 158–160
    roles and functions, 158–159, 176
    World Wars One and Two, 166–168
Miller, Alfred J., 267f
Miller, Jim, 79, 158, 165
Mississauga, 86, 260
MNC. *See* Métis National Council
Mnjikaning, 283–285

Mohawk, 43, 161, 174–175, 186–190, 230, 243–244, 311

Mohawk Warriors Society, 173

Momaday, N. Scott, 58

Monture, Patricia A., 120

Morris, Alexander, 85, 275, 304

Morrison, W. R., 253–254

Morrisseau, Norval, 66–67, 67f

Mortality rates, 310f

Moses, Daniel David, 59

Moses, Ted, 87

Mosher, Liza, 298

Mountain Horse, Mike, 59, 163

Mulroney, Brian, 257, 329

Multiculturalism, 347, 349

Mulvihill (doctor), 303f

Munro, John, 148

Muscowpetung, 194

Music, 60–61

Muskeg Lake satellite reserve, 355–357

Musqueam, 248

Mystery, 300

N

Na-cho Ny'a'k Dun, 93, 256

NAIB. *See* North American Indian Brotherhood (NAIB)

Napi, 11, 12, 54–55

Naskapi, 92, 230, 255

National Aboriginal Health Organization, 313

National Aboriginal Strategy, 237

National Association of Friendship Centres, 346

National Basketball Association (NBA), 321

National College Athletic Association (NCAA), 321

National Indian Brotherhood (NIB), 116, 200, 205–206

National Indian Council (NIC), 204–206

National Parole Board Advisory Committee, 237

Nation building, 271–272

Native Brotherhood of British Columbia (NBBC), 173, 194, 196, 204, 270, 323

Native Communications Program (NCP), 322, 330–331

The Native Fisherman (newspaper), 323

Native Friendship Centre Program (NFCP), 346

Native People (newspaper), 325

Native peoples. *See* Indigenous peoples

Native philosophy
  academic study of, 2–5
  overview, 6–9
  See also Ways of knowing

Native science, 10–17
  academic study of, 9
  animate nature/spirit, 13
  constant motion/flux, 11–12
  relationships and, 13–17
  renewal, 15–17
  space/land, 10–11
  See also Ways of knowing

Native Studies, 2–6
  non-Native perspectives challenged by, 26
  origins of, 3–4

The Native Voice (newspaper), 323–325

Native Women's Association of Canada (NWAC), 121, 208

Natural Resource Transfer Act (NRTA), 86, 97, 140, 275

Nature
  European perspective on, 28
  medicine and healing, 302
  See also Land

Nault, Robert, 123, 208, 258

NBBC. *See* Native Brotherhood of British Columbia (NBBC)

Neechi Foods Co-op Limited, 282–283

Negotiations, 75–76

Nelson House, 358

The New Breed (newspaper), 325

Newfoundland, 266, 267

Newhouse, David, 2, 51–52, 340, 342

Newspapers, 58, 320–325, 330–331

Ng, Charles, 228

NIB. *See* National Indian Brotherhood (NIB)

Night, Darrell, 222

Nisga'a, 34, 91, 117, 253–254, 256

Nisga'a Final Agreement (1999), 93

Nisga'a Treaty (2000), 96, 256, 259

Nisga'a Tribal Council (NTC), 96

Noble savage, stereotype of, 320–321

Noey, Mary, 20

Noninterference, 18

Non-Status Indians, 108–109, 120–122

Norris, Malcolm, 140–141, 141f, 192, 194, 197

Norse, 266

North, 278–281

North American Indian Brotherhood (NAIB), 195–196, 204, 210

North American Indian Club, 345

Northeast, 37–38

North-Eastern Québec Agreement (1978), 92, 255

Northern Colorado University, 321

Platiel, Rudy, 326
Poitras, Jane Ash, 50, 67
Police brutality, 222–223
Policing
    community-based, 222
    Native, 229–232
    Native mistreatment, 222–223
    North-West Mounted Police, 220–221
    Royal Canadian Mounted Police, 221–222
Policy on Community-Based Self-Government
    Negotiations, 253
Political economy
    defined, 25–26
    Indigenous, 26
    Iroquois, 42–45
Political organizing, 184–211
    alternative models, 209
    first wave (1870–1918), 189–192
    fourth wave (1995–present), 207–209
    pre-contact, 185–189
    second wave (1918–60), 192–199
    third wave (1960–95), 200–207
    See also Protest and resistance
Politics
    band-council model, 32, 190, 246–250
    business management separated
        from, 272
    economic development and, 289
    geographical regions, 35–42
    governance initiative, 123–125
    Indigenous, 30–33
    journalism and, 330
    land and, 28
    and language, 322
    leadership, 32–33
    methods, 31–32
    Métis, 141–143
    newspapers and, 325
    relationships and, 31–32
Potlatch, 33, 110–111, 117, 118, 191
Pottawatomi, 186, 260
Poundmaker, 165
Poverty, 269
Powley, Roddy, 145
Powley, Steve, 145
Powwows, 62
Pre-contact period
    economic development, 266
    health and well-being, 297–302
    military and warfare, 158–160
    political organizing, 185–189

Prentice, Jim, 97
Prince, Marjorie, 249
Prince, Morris, 172f
Prince, Thomas George (Tommy), 172, 172f, 195,
    197, 204
Prisons, Native representation in, 224, 329
Procurement Strategy for Aboriginal Business, 273
Protective Association for Indians and Their
    Treaties, 194
Protest and resistance
    Burnt Church protests (2000), 222, 326–327
    Gustafson Lake occupation (1995), 222
    Métis, 138–139, 164–165
    Oka Crisis (1990), 173–175, 257, 329
    Oldman River Dam standoff (1991), 222
    sites, 175f
    warrior societies, 174
    See also Political organizing
Provost, Sally, 302
Public Safety Canada, 231

Q

Quebec, 89, 133, 347
Quebec Association of Indians, 89
Quebec Boundaries Extension Act, 89–91
Queen's Law, 221

R

Radio, 331–332
Rae, Bob, 283
Ranching, 268, 269
Raven's Eye (newspaper), 326, 331
RCAP. See Royal Commission on Aboriginal
    Peoples (RCAP)
RCMP. See Royal Canadian Mounted Police
    (RCMP)
Reciprocity, 45
Redbird, Duke, 58
Red Crow, 164, 269
Red Paper, 205, 251
Redskins, Tricksters, and Puppy Dog Stew (film), 63
Reform Party, 96
Reid, Ambrose, 194
Reid, Bill, 67
Relationships
    animal-human, 14–15, 19, 31
    health and, 301
    Native science and, 13–17
    politics and, 31–32
Report of the Royal Commission on Aboriginal
    Peoples (RCAP), 265, 271, 280